Security Operations Center

Joseph Muniz

Gary McIntyre

Nadhem AlFardan

Cisco Press

800 East 96th Street

Indianapolis, Indiana 46240 USA

Security Operations Center

Joseph Muniz, Gary McIntyre, Nadhem AlFardan

Published by:
Cisco Press
800 East 96th Street
Indianapolis, IN 46240 USA

Printed in the United States of America

First Printing November 2015

Library of Congress Control Number: 2015950793

ISBN-13: 978-0-13-405201-4

ISBN-10: 0-13-405201-3

Warning and Disclaimer

This book is designed to provide information about building and running a security operations center (SOC). Every effort has been made to make this book as complete and as accurate as possible, but no warranty or fitness is implied.

The information is provided on an "as is" basis. The authors, Cisco Press, and Cisco Systems, Inc. shall have neither liability nor responsibility to any person or entity with respect to any loss or damages arising from the information contained in this book or from the use of the discs or programs that may accompany it.

The opinions expressed in this book belong to the author and are not necessarily those of Cisco Systems, Inc.

Trademark Acknowledgments

All terms mentioned in this book that are known to be trademarks or service marks have been appropriately capitalized. Cisco Press or Cisco Systems, Inc., cannot attest to the accuracy of this information. Use of a term in this book should not be regarded as affecting the validity of any trademark or service mark.

Special Sales

For information about buying this title in bulk quantities, or for special sales opportunities (which may include electronic versions; custom cover designs; and content particular to your business, training goals, marketing focus, or branding interests), please contact our corporate sales department at corpsales@pearsoned.com or (800) 382-3419.

For government sales inquiries, please contact governmentsales@pearsoned.com.

For questions about sales outside the U.S., please contact international@pearsoned.com.

Feedback Information

At Cisco Press, our goal is to create in-depth technical books of the highest quality and value. Each book is crafted with care and precision, undergoing rigorous development that involves the unique expertise of members from the professional technical community.

Readers' feedback is a natural continuation of this process. If you have any comments regarding how we could improve the quality of this book, or otherwise alter it to better suit your needs, you can contact us through email at feedback@ciscopress.com. Please make sure to include the book title and ISBN in your message.

We greatly appreciate your assistance.

Publisher: Paul Boger

Associate Publisher: Dave Dusthimer

Business Operation Manager, Cisco Press: Jan Cornelssen

Acquisitions Editor: Denise Lincoln

Managing Editor: Sandra Schroeder

Senior Development Editor: Christopher Cleveland

Senior Project Editor: Tonya Simpson

Copy Editor: Keith Cline

Technical Editors: Dr. Fred Mpala, Matthew Waters

Editorial Assistant: Vanessa Evans

Cover Designer: Mark Shirar

Composition: codeMantra

Indexer: WordWise Publishing Services

Proofreader: Sarah Kearns

About the Authors

Joseph Muniz is a consultant at Cisco Systems and security researcher. Joseph started his career in software development and later managed networks as a contracted technical resource. Joseph moved into consulting and found a passion for security while meeting with a variety of customers. He has been involved with the design and implementation of multiple projects, ranging from Fortune 500 corporations to large federal networks. Joseph is the author of and contributor to several books and is a speaker for popular security conferences. Check out his blog, http://www.thesecurityblogger.com, which showcases the latest security events, research, and technologies.

Gary McIntyre is a seasoned information security professional focusing on the development and operation of large-scale information security programs. As an architect, manager, and consultant, he has worked with a wide range of public and private sector organizations around the world to design, build, and maintain small to large security operations teams. He currently holds a Masters degree from the University of Toronto and has also been a long-time $(ISC)^2$ instructor.

Dr. Nadhem AlFardan has more than 15 years of experience in the area of information security and holds a Ph.D. in Information Security from Royal Holloway, University of London. Nadhem is a senior security solution architect working for Cisco Systems. Before joining Cisco, he worked for Schlumbeger and HSBC. Nadhem is CISSP certified and is an ISO 27001 lead auditor. He is also CCIE Security certified. In his Ph.D. research, Nadhem published a number of papers in prestige conferences, such as IEEE S&P and USENIX Security, mainly around cryptoanalysis topics. His work involved him working with organizations such as Google, Microsoft, Cisco, Mozilla, OpenSSL, and many others, mainly to help them assess and fix major findings in the Transport Layer Security/Secure Sockets Layer (TLS/SSL) protocol. His work is referenced in a number of IETF standards.

About the Technical Reviewers

Dr. Fred Mpala is a security professional with broad experience in security and risk management.

Matthew Waters is a seasoned security professional and chief information security officer within the financial sector, specializing in large-scale transformation programs.

Dedications

Joseph Muniz: I would like to give a huge "thank you" to my friends and family for supporting me for this and my other crazy projects. This book goes out to Irene Muniz, Ray Muniz, Alex Muniz, Raylin Muniz, Ning Xu, my friends at Cisco, and the many other great people in my life.

Gary McIntyre: For Candice and Winston, who paid the highest price to see this through.

Acknowledgments

Joseph Muniz: I will start by thanking Gary McIntyre and Nadhem AlFardan for including me on this project. I really enjoyed collaborating on the material and hope that they do not mind my input. If they do, it is probably too late by now anyway.

I had help with validating my content and would like to recognize Jeff Williams and Aamir Lakhani. Jeff is the NetFlow ninja and assisted with reviewing my Lancope contributions. Aamir is my good friend and co-authored two books with me prior to this project. I let Aamir beat up all my drafts and appreciate both his and Jeff's time on this project.

I also want to thank Jamey Heary for helping me line up this opportunity. Jamey is a brilliant engineer and the author of *Cisco ISE for BYOD and Secure Unified Access* (Cisco Press, 2013). I would not have been involved with this project without him.

Finally, I would like to thank Denise Lincoln and the rest of the Cisco Press team for their support while we determined and then polished the final content for this book. They are a very professional group and a pleasure to work with.

Gary McIntyre: As with any book like this, it's hard to acknowledge everyone who might deserve it. Thankfully, a book about security encourages a bit of obfuscation, silence, and mystery.

To Dean T., who first taught me about correlations using Cheap Trick and Queen. For Bev T., for never being boring. For Leslie C., for teaching me not to bore others. For Beth, who could not stay to see this. For my parents, who likely still don't understand what I do for a living and love me anyway. Finally, for all the customers, colleagues, and students I've had over my career: your fingerprints are all over this thing. Thank you.

Contents at a Glance

Contents

Command Syntax Conventions

The conventions used to present command syntax in this book are the same conventions used in the IOS Command Reference. The Command Reference describes these conventions as follows:

- **Boldface** indicates commands and keywords that are entered literally as shown. In actual configuration examples and output (not general command syntax), boldface indicates commands that are manually input by the user (such as a **show** command).
- *Italic* indicates arguments for which you supply actual values.
- Vertical bars (|) separate alternative, mutually exclusive elements.
- Square brackets ([ ]) indicate an optional element.
- Braces ({ }) indicate a required choice.
- Braces within brackets ([{ }]) indicate a required choice within an optional element.

Introduction

Many security books are available, but they focus on either products or on very high-level security best practices. We could not find a book about developing a security operations center. This lack of coverage meant that people interested in this topic would have to take the literature available from security books and interview existing SOC leaders to learn how it should be done. We identified this gap and decided to write this book.

In this book, we use a blend of industry experience and best practices of many of our customers to create a guide for those interested in how a SOC should be developed and managed. This book presents the collective view of its three authors (each a consultant at Cisco Systems). We have worked with hundreds of customers, ranging from Fortune 500 companies to large military organizations, giving us a broad and deep understanding about how SOCs are developed and run in the real world. We hope that our research and experience assists you with your existing SOC or with future security operations projects.

Who Should Read This Book?

This book is written for anybody interested in learning how to develop, manage, or improve a SOC. This book, which is based on a blend of our industry experience and best practices, can serve as a guide for those interested in creating and managing a SOC. A background in network security, network management, and network operations would be helpful, but it is not required to benefit from this book.

How This Book Is Organized

Chapter 1, "Introduction to Security Operations and the SOC": This first chapter provides an introduction to security operations. First, we examine challenges that organizations face that justify the investment in a SOC. This chapter also covers high-level SOC topics such as vulnerability management, threat intelligence, digital investigation, and data collection and analysis, thus setting the stage for the rest of the book.

Chapter 2, "Overview of SOC Technologies": This chapter explains how to deploy and customize SOC technologies. The goal is to gain a basic understanding of technology and services found in most modern SOC environments. Topics include data collection, data processing, vulnerability management, and case management.

Chapter 3, "Assessing Security Operations Capabilities": This chapter describes a methodology for developing SOC requirements and assessing security operations capabilities against those requirements. The purpose is to help define a SOC strategy and create a supporting roadmap.

Chapter 4, "SOC Strategy": This chapter explains how to develop a strategy and roadmap for SOC capabilities using results from tactics learned in Chapter 3. These can be used as a benchmark to validate progress and justify future investment in the SOC.

Chapter 5, "The SOC Infrastructure": This chapter covers design considerations for a SOC infrastructure. Topics include the SOC facility, analyst environment, and various technology considerations.

Chapter 6, "Security Event Generation and Collection": Most SOC environments focus heavily on collecting and analyzing data. This chapter describes common tools found in a SOC environment that are used to produce and collect such data.

Chapter 7, "Vulnerability Management": This chapter explains how a SOC can create and deliver a vulnerability management practice. Topics covered include identifying and managing vulnerabilities, calculating risk, and ranking threats to properly prioritize which vulnerabilities to address first.

Chapter 8, "People and Processes": This chapter focuses on developing an appropriate governance and staffing model based on the range of services the SOC will provide. The goal is to not only recruit the right team but also to retain those valuable resources. The chapter also explains how to leverage outsourcing or managed service providers when the situation calls for such resources.

Chapter 9, "The Technology": SOC technologies were briefly discussed in earlier chapters, but this chapter covers how common technologies found in the SOC fit into a SOC architecture. The focus is on design considerations for SOC network, security, collaboration, and storage technologies.

Chapter 10, "Preparing to Operate": This chapter walks you through common steps required to transition a SOC to a fully operational state. Topics include challenges faced before going live, transition plan development, and the impact of proper project management.

Chapter 11, "Reacting to Events and Incidents": In this chapter, you learn how the people, processes, and technology parts of an effective SOC come together to react to events and incidents. This chapter includes a storyline that walks you through how an effective SOC would react to an identified security incident.

Chapter 12, "Maintain, Review, and Improve": The final chapter of this book wraps things up by explaining how to review and maintain the SOC and its services. This chapter also covers how to continuously improve the SOC services to guide its evolution. Improvement topics include how to identify issues with the SOC so that they can be remediated to improve SOC service.

Chapter 1

Introduction to Security Operations and the SOC

"It's better to light a candle than curse the darkness."

This book focuses on the best practices to develop and operate a security operations center (SOC). The journey begins with a review of important concepts relevant to information security and security operations. This chapter opens with a discussion about the continuously evolving security landscape and how new cybersecurity challenges impact how we perceive security operations. The discussion then turns to information assurance and its link to both risk management and security operations. This chapter does not cover information assurance and risk management in depth, but instead provides you with sufficient background information on these topics while relating them to security operations. The chapter then covers incident response and how it is used by security operations. The chapter concludes by introducing a number of concepts associated with the core topics of the book: planning, designing, building, and operating a SOC.

Cybersecurity Challenges

Security attacks are becoming increasingly complex and exhibiting increasingly sophisticated capabilities. So, addressing the complexity and sophistication of such attacks must include not only investing in preventive measures but also the development of intelligent and integrated monitoring capabilities incorporated into an incident response program.

Arguably, getting compromised at some point is inevitable. As the previous CEO of Cisco Systems, John Chambers, said, "There are two types of companies: those who have been hacked and those who don't yet know they have been hacked." So, be warned: A security breach is not an *if* but a *when*. The good news is that a breach does not necessarily mean that the business will immediately experience negative impact, because attackers usually need time to accomplish their objectives beyond gaining unauthorized access to the network. Discovering and preventing this type of behavior is just one of the many reasons organizations develop a SOC.

One exercise to help people understand the inevitability of cyberthreats is to ask this question: If you knew you were going to be breached, would you perform security differently within your organization? This leads to a series of questions that you should ask leadership within your organization about how your business deals with a security compromise. Somebody needs to be responsible for answering these questions; for most organizations, those people run the SOC or have security operations responsibilities.

If you need to justify a SOC budget, here are some questions focused on dealing with a security compromise:

- **How** can you detect a compromise?
- **How** severe is the compromise?
- **What** is the impact of the compromise to your business?
- **Who** is responsible for detecting and reacting to a compromise?
- **Who** should be informed or involved and **when** do you deal with the compromise once detected?
- **How** and **when** should you communicate a compromise internally or externally, and is that needed in the first place?

The OODA Loop[1] is one methodology that addresses some of these questions. The concept was first developed by military strategist and USAF Colonel John Boyd.[2] Colonel Boyd created a four-step approach designed to determine the appropriate response to a problem. An OODA Loop, as shown in Figure 1-1, consists of the following steps: observe, orient, decide, and act. In the context of cybersecurity, the four steps are as follows:

- **Observe:** Monitor, collect, and store data from various points in your network as the first step in the OODA Loop.
- **Orient:** Analyze collected data in search of suspicious activities. This usually involves the use of tools to process and analyze incoming and stored data.
- **Decide:** Determine an action course based on the results of the analysis phase and the experience you have gained from previous loop iterations.
- **Act:** Execute the action course you determined in the preceding step.

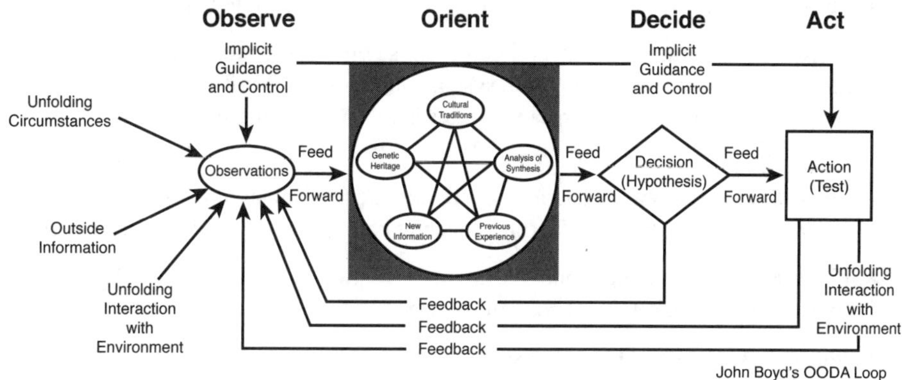

Figure 1-1 *The OODA Loop*

The OODA Loop assumes that continuous improvement is an integrated part of the process, allowing you to learn from your previous experiences, feeding lessons learned into the loop activities to achieve better performance every time you complete the four steps. Continuous monitoring and enforcement concepts are an ongoing theme throughout this book.

The OODA Loop may have been designed to deal with military attacks, but the concepts apply to defending any form of attack, including cyberthreats. For our next model, let's switch to the attacker's viewpoint by reviewing the *cyber kill chain*. The cyber kill chain,[3] developed by Lockheed Martin's Computer Incident Response Team and shown in Figure 1-2, describes the progression an attacker follows when planning and executing an attack against a target. This model helps security professionals identify security controls and actions that can be implemented or improved to detect, deny, and contain an attack scenario.

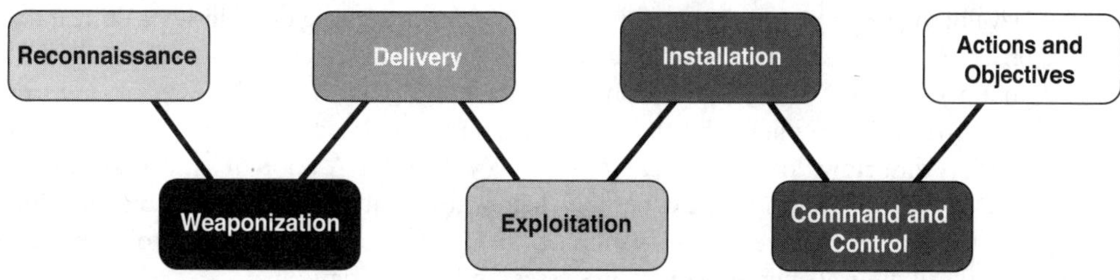

Figure 1-2 *The Cyber Kill Chain*

The various phases of the cyber kill chain are as follows:

- **Phase 1, Reconnaissance:** Research, identification, and selection of targets, often represented as crawling Internet websites such as conference proceedings and mailing lists for e-mail addresses, social relationships, or information on specific technologies.
- **Phase 2, Weaponization:** Coupling a remote-access Trojan with an exploit into a deliverable payload, typically by means of an automated tool also known as a weaponizer.

- **Phase 3, Delivery:** Transmission of the weapon to the targeted environment.
- **Phase 4, Exploitation:** Triggers the intruder's code. Most often, exploitation targets an application or operating system vulnerability, but it could also more simply exploit the users themselves or leverage an operating system feature that auto-executes code.
- **Phase 5, Installation:** Installation of a remote-access Trojan or back door on the victim system enables the adversary to maintain persistence inside the environment.
- **Phase 6, Command and Control:** Beacon outbound to an Internet controller server to establish a command and control channel.
- **Phase 7, Actions and Objectives:** Intruders take actions to achieve their original objectives. Typically, this objective is data exfiltration that involves collecting, encrypting, and extracting information from the victim environment; violations of data integrity or availability are potential objectives as well. Alternatively, the intruders may only desire access to the initial victim box for use as a hop point to compromise additional systems and move laterally inside the network.

These models make up a high-level way to look at cybersecurity attack and defense concepts. According to the cyber kill chain, attackers perform reconnaissance to identify the easiest and most effective way to breach a network. Defense teams using the OODA Loop may catch this behavior during the observing or orientation stage and decide to react by locking down security or raising awareness of a possible threat from an identified source. An attacker may move to Phase 4 of the cyber kill chain by weaponizing and delivering an exploit against a target. The OODA Loop may once again identify the attack during the observe or orientation stage and react through containing the threat and patching the weakness to avoid future attacks. So essentially, the OODA Loop is a defense strategy against every phase of the cyber kill chain.

Developing security operations and security incident response capabilities is critical to breaking or reducing the impact of an attacker executing the cyber kill chain against your organization. The OODA Loop is just one conceptual model that you can use to break the chain or contain the chain of events during an incident. The important question to ask is this: How does your organization apply the OODA Loop or similar concepts against different stages of the cyber kill chain when an attack against your organization occurs? Most SOCs execute a variation of the OODA Loop by using controls associated with these three elements: people, processes, and technology.

Threat Landscape

The Verizon 2015 Data Breach Investigation Report (DBIR)[4] showed that 60 percent of businesses being breached happened within minutes or less. The report also showed that half of these incidents took anywhere from months to even years before being uncovered. So in summary, breaches tend to happen very quickly and on average take a long time to be detected by the targeted organization. These numbers demonstrate the importance of having an effective security operations program in which a mature SOC plays a significant role. Figure 1-3, taken from the DBIR, compares the time spans of when organizations are compromised versus when they are able to discover the breach.

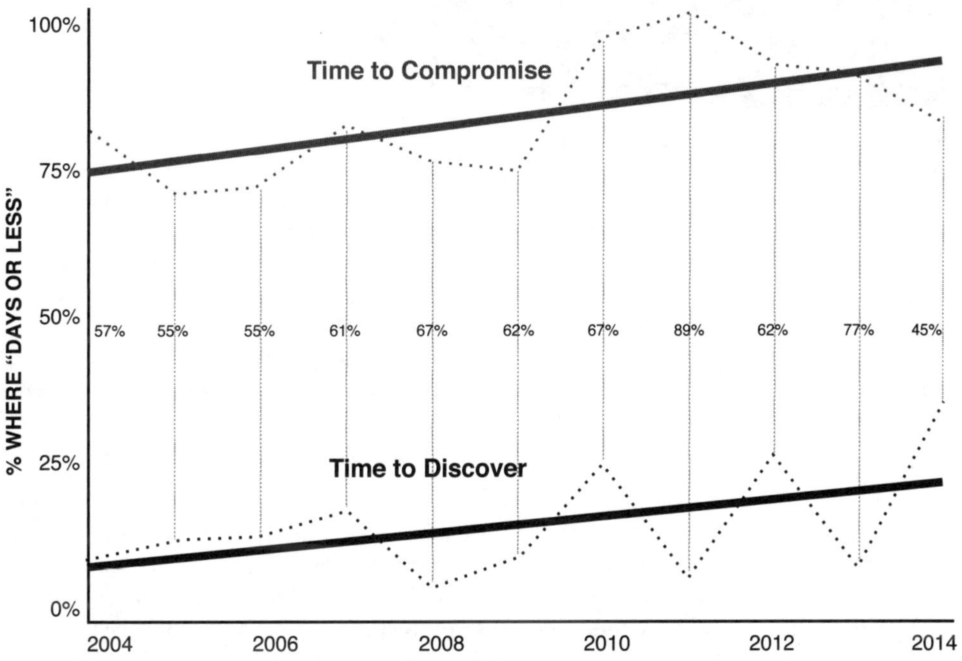

Figure 1-3 *2015 DBIR Comparing Breach and Discovery Time*

As the security landscape continues to evolve, new and automated offensive tools become readily available for a larger audience. Well-organized libraries of offensive tools are now packaged on free-to-download-and-use Linux distributions such as Backtrack[5] and Kali,[6] making it possible for almost anyone to test and develop tools and exploits. Attackers known as Script Kiddies might not understand the details of how the attack works, but packaged offensive tools make launching sophisticated attacks as simple as point-and-click execution. An analogy to this scenario is that the average person cannot build a telephone but can make a phone call as long as the system is prebuilt and ready to use. Many attack tools are developed in a point-and-click fashion, such as shown in Figure 1-4, which showcases a weaponized denial-of-service (DoS) attack application known as Low Orbit Ion Cannon (LOIC).

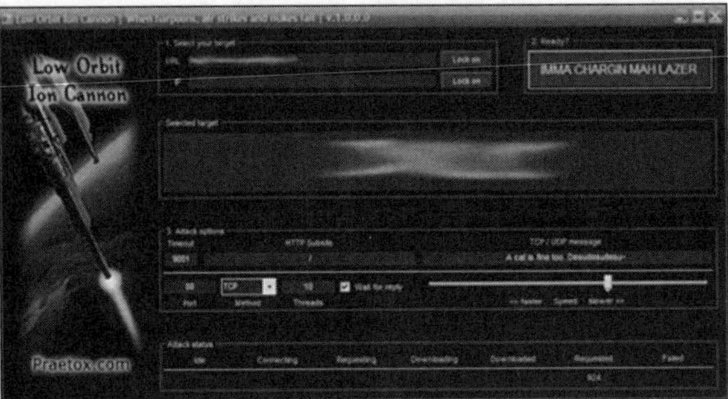

Figure 1-4 *LOIC DoS Attack Application*

Why are security products unable to stop these threats? Aren't governments and big businesses investing significant amounts of money into developing countermeasures to cyberattacks? The answer is yes; however, there is a reason why defense technologies need to continue to evolve. Just like solution providers, attackers have labs for researching products. If a "silver bullet" or single solution hits the market and is effective at preventing cyberattacks, that product will become popular and purchased by many organizations, along with their adversaries. Hackers will test various exploits against the new product until one succeeds, and will then either sell the exploit on underground markets, weaponize it for less-skilled attackers, or use it for some other malicious purpose.

Security researchers saw this pattern when the sandbox concept was introduced to detect malicious software. Administrators put a sandbox security product hosting various vulnerable applications at the edge of their inside network with the intention of making it the first target malware would strike during a breach. Malware would launch inside that monitored sandbox, giving away its identity, and thus the other security products could be made aware of the attack. Attackers learned about this technology and developed techniques such as targeting specific systems versus attacking the most vulnerable system, delaying the attack long enough to bypass the sandbox and so on. Figure 1-5 shows an article[7] from Networkworld.com explaining how hackers are now bypassing sandbox technology. This is why the attack and defense innovations continue to be a cat-and-mouse game, meaning both sides will develop a technique that eventually the other side will adapt to.

Malware-detecting 'sandboxing' technology no silver bullet

University of California researcher says malware authors are aware of sandboxing and are in an 'arms race' to stay ahead of it

By Ellen Messmer | Follow
Network World | Mar 26, 2013 3:37 PM PT

The security technology called "sandboxing" aims at detecting malware code by subjecting it to run in a computer-based system of one type of another to analyze it for behavior and traits indicative of malware. Sandboxing -- one alternative to traditional signature-based malware defense -- is seen as a way to spot zero-day malware and stealthy attacks in particular. While this technique often effective, it's hardly foolproof, warns a security researcher who helped establish the sandboxing technology used by startup Lastline.

RELATED

McAfee acquires ValidEdge sandboxing technology

'Sandboxing' leader FireEye seen moving toward an IPO

12 must-watch security startups for 2013

How to avoid malware on Android devices?

Microsoft Cloud

This cloud stands up to any storm

Figure 1-5 *Networkworld.com Article on Bypassing Sandbox Technology*

Where are these exploits being sold once developed? Many new exploits can be found on underground and notably growing commercial zero-day vulnerability markets operated by private brokers. Examples of boutique exploit vendors that sell *known-unknown* zero-day flaws include the French firm VUPEN Security,[8] Netragard,[9] ReVuln,[10] and Endgame Systems.[11] NSS Labs[12] estimates that on a yearly basis more than 100 *known-unknown* zero-day vulnerabilities are available for sale. To find examples of underground markets selling zero-day exploits, download the Tor browser from https://www.torproject.org/download/download, access the Darknet, and go to the Hidden Wiki at http://wikitjerrta4qgz4.onion/. Figure 1-6 shows a list of websites marketing anything from contract killers to the infamous Silk Road marketplace.

Commercial Services

- Mobile Store - Factory unlocked iphones and other smartphones.
- Rent-A-Hacker - Hacking, DDOS, Social Engeneering, Espionage, Ruining people.
- Onion Identity Services - Selling Passports and ID-Cards for Bitcoins.
- HQER - High quality euro bills replicas / counterfeits.
- Hitman Network - Group of contract killers from the US/Canada and EU.
- Apples4Bitcoin - Cheap Apple products for Bitcoin.
- EuroGuns - Your #1 european arms dealer.
- Silkroad - Anonymous marketplace with escrow (Bitcoin)
- UK Guns and Ammo - Selling Guns and Ammo from the UK for Bitcoins.
- UK Passports - Original UK Passports.
- USfakeIDs - High quality USA Fake Drivers Licenses.
- USA Citizenship - Become a citizen of the USA, real USA passport.
- Kamagra for Bitcoin - Same as Viagra but cheaper!

Figure 1-6 *Darknet Marketing Sources*

> **Warning** Access the Darknet at your own risk! Because of the anonymous nature of hosting and accessing websites via Tor, many onion network resources contain malicious techniques not found on the Internet.

Business Challenges

In addition to the technical security threat landscape, legal and business-imposed decisions impact the way organizations operate information security. Examples of such decisions include moving services and information to the cloud; meeting compliancy requirements; the proliferation of bring your own device (BYOD); and the rise of the Internet of Everything (IoE), which brings people, processes, things, and data together by combining machine-to-machine (M2M), person-to-machine (P2M), and person-to-person (P2P) connections. For example, the IoE networked connection of people, processes, data, and things, shown in Figure 1-7, introduces challenges related to collecting, processing, storing, and analyzing large volumes of data generated at high velocity and with a variety of formats (that is, big data analytics, as discussed later in this chapter and in Chapter 2, "Overview of SOC Technologies."

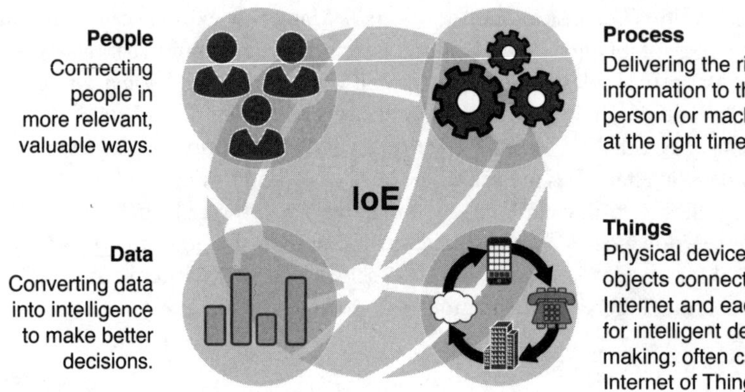

Figure 1-7 *Networked Connection of People, Process, Data, Things (Source: Cisco Internet of Everything Report[13])*

The Cloud

Cloud services are here to stay and evolve. Over the past decade, there has been a steady increase in the adoption of cloud services by small, medium, and large organizations from various industries. This trend maps to the economic gains expected from consuming cloud-based services.

According to various studies related to cloud adoption, security is one of the top concerns for chief information officers (CIO) for migrating their services to the cloud. For example, a study conducted by ChangeWave Research in April 2014[14] identified security concerns as being the leading reason why both large companies (more than 1000 employees) and small- to medium-sized companies (fewer than 1000 employees) are not moving to the cloud. Another study conducted by the firm McKinsey in conjunction with the World Economic Forum in May 2014[15] revealed that "some 70 percent of the respondents said that security concerns had delayed the adoption of public cloud computing by a year or more, and 40 percent said such concerns delayed enterprise-mobility capabilities by a year or more."

The exact security concerns vary from the ability of cloud service providers guaranteeing basic access control and confidentiality all the way to achieving audit and compliance requirements. Adoption rates also vary between the use of public and private cloud because private cloud tends to have more security based on being dedicated to a single client or company. What this book addresses is how to operate your SOC in an environment where cloud services are being consumed for business purposes regardless of the cloud model. You learn more about cloud services later in this book.

Compliance

Being compliant with mandatory or discretionary information security or privacy standards requires not only an investment in technology but also, in almost all cases, a fair amount of culture change. Required changes can also include a reform to the model by which information is managed and how security operations are conducted.

Typically, standards mandate reactive and preventive security measures to protect information. This means that all regulatory and discretionary security standards explicitly highlight the need for information security operations. In some cases, this is referred to as the need for continuous monitoring of the information security posture.

Examples of security standards many organizations must comply with include the following:

- The Payment Card Industry Data Security Standard (PCI DSS),[16] a standard set by the PCI Security Standards Council (PCI SSC) that applies to all entities that store, process, and/or transmit cardholder data, mandates a number of technical and operational security requirements. The standard mandates, under the "regularly monitor and test networks" control objective mapped to PCI DSS requirements 10 and 11, that organizations must regularly monitor and test networks to find and fix vulnerabilities.
- ISO/IEC 27001:2013, a standard that organizations can adopt to manage information security as a program, requires organizations to operate information security technical and nontechnical controls under the umbrella of an information security management system (ISMS) in which a plan, do, check, and act (PDCA) lifecycle is operated and maintained. Annex A.10.10 of the standard, titled "Monitoring," lists a number of important operation controls in the areas of audit logging, monitoring system use, and so on. The check phase of the PDCA lifecycle requires you to assess and, where applicable, measure process performance against ISMS policies, objectives and practical experience, and report the results to management for review.

PCI DSS and ISO/IEC 27001:2013, along with other information security and privacy standards, demand that security controls be properly monitored and that information security events and incidents be appropriately handled. Failure to comply with standards may lead to large fines or jail time for all persons held accountable for information assurance.

Privacy and Data Protection

In addition to business-centric standards, organizations must adhere to country-specific laws and regulations related to privacy and data protection. Examples of country-specific laws and regulations include the following:

- **United States:** US-EU Safe Harbor on Data Protection directive went into effect in October 1998 and prohibits the transfer of personal data to non-European Union countries that do not meet the EU-defined *adequacy* standard for privacy protection.

- **Germany:** The Federal Data Protection Act[17] (*Bundesdatenschutzgesetz* in German, BDSG) covers a range of data protection issues. For example, according to the act, organizations must have policies, procedures, and controls in place to protect all data types and categories that are under the BDSG umbrella. In addition, each German state has a data protection law of its own.
- **Japan:** The Act on the Protection of Personal Information[18] (APPI) prescribes the duties to be observed by entities handling personal information with the objective of protecting the rights and interests of individuals.
- **United Kingdom:** The Data Protection Act 1998[19] governs the protection of personal data in the UK.

Developing security operations capabilities is critical to supporting an organization's compliance state with such regulations; these same capabilities also allow organizations to react appropriately to security incidents that might result in an infringement of the law. Being compliant with these and other mandatory laws and regulations comes in direct support to ensuring that information is protected and monitored against potential attacks that would impact its availability, integrity, authentication, and confidentiality. In many cases, *reasonable effort* (as legally understood) must be used to protect sensitive data; otherwise, persons responsible for information assurance face potential fines or even jail time.

Let's now review the concepts underlying information assurance.

Introduction to Information Assurance

According to the U.S. Department of Defense (DoD) Directive 8500.01E,[20] information assurance (IA) refers to "measures that protect and defend information and information systems by ensuring their availability, integrity, authentication, confidentiality, and non-repudiation. This includes providing for restoration of information systems by incorporating protection, detection, and reaction capabilities." The National Institute of Standards and Technology (NIST) SP 800-59[21] and other NIST documents use the same definition for IA.

Taking a United Kingdom (UK) perspective to IA, the UK Home Office defines IA[22] as "the practice of managing information-related risks around the confidentiality, integrity and availability of information, particularly sensitive information. It covers information whilst in storage, processing, use or transit; and the risks created by both malicious and non-malicious actions." The UK Cabinet Office has a slightly different definition for IA, stating that "the confidence that information systems will protect the information they carry and will function as they need to, when they need to, under the control of legitimate users" and that "information systems include any means of storing, processing or disseminating information including IT systems, media and paper-based systems." Most requirements for IA will contain similar characteristics in the language used for protecting various aspects of data handled by your organization. It is extremely important to know exactly how IA is defined in your country and all associated requirements your organization must meet to avoid legal ramifications.

A question that is often asked is this: What is the difference between IA and information security? Taking NIST as our reference, NIST 800-53[23] defines information security as "the protection of information and information systems from unauthorized access, use, disclosure, disruption, modification, or destruction in order to provide confidentiality, integrity, and availability." You should notice that a close relationship exists between IA and information security. Considering the NIST definitions of IA and information security, you can think of IA as a superset that covers information security. In general, IA tries to address the different risks associated with information systems or media, encompassing technical, procedural, and human factor aspects involved in delivering physical and digital protection for information systems or media.

Before trying to address IA or information security requirements, it is imperative to understand the security risks associated with your environment. This is where the risk management discipline becomes relevant. It is worth noting that establishing a SOC supports the basic requirement of managing the security risk of an organization. So, the next section introduces risk management concepts.

Introduction to Risk Management

Let's start by defining what *risk* is. A common definition of risk is the *probability* of a *threat* executing on *vulnerability* and the *impact* resulting from successful exploitation. This definition of risk is similar to the one listed in the NIST guide for conducting risk assessments.[24] Dealing with risk cannot be achieved without understanding the organization-specific threat landscape and vulnerability status. This can be achieved using various types of security services such as a risk assessment.

A risk assessment is the process used to assign some value to risk associated with assets. The output of a risk assessment can then be used to make better-informed decisions on how to deal with risk. Decisions include one or more of the following: *mitigate*, *transfer*, *accept*, or *avoid*. Risk management involves combining the output of risk assessment with the decision on how to address risk.

Examples of frameworks that try to formalize the topic of risk management include ISO/IEC 27005:2010, ISO/IEC 31000:2009, NIST SP 800-39, OWASP Risk Rating Methodology, and the DoD Risk Management Framework (RMF). These frameworks use similar processes for managing risks, as shown in Figure 1-8, taken from the ISO/IEC 31000:2009 standard. Taking the DoD RMF as an example, the framework assumes a six-step process. The process starts with risk categorization and ends with effectiveness measurement through security controls monitoring.

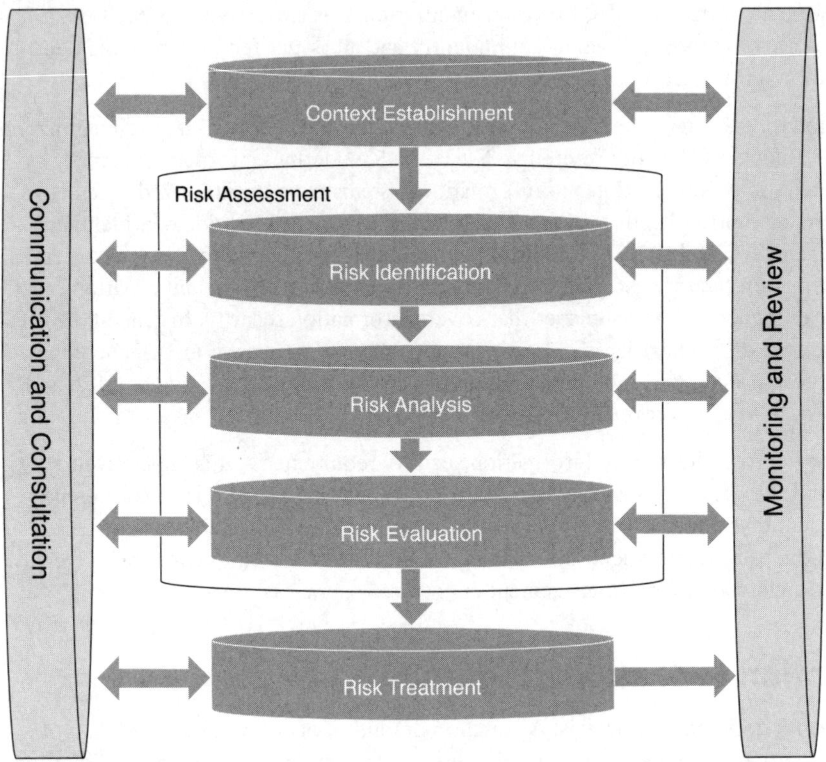

Figure 1-8 *Risk Management Framework (As per ISO/IEC 31000:2009)*

The task of assessing and managing risk should not be regarded as only a point-in-time exercise, but rather a continuous process that accepts input from various real-time and offline sources. Information generated by security operations is a vital source to the risk-assessment process. Consider the example in which security operations identified that a malformed IP packet destined for a critical system has caused this system to crash. The sequence of events should be investigated, and the risk associated with this system, and possibly other similar systems, should be reviewed. Changes made to the environment will have an effect on risk associated with individual assets and the overall security posture of the organization. For example, how should the organization react to the resignation of a system administrator who has responsibilities over privileged access systems? The proactive actions taken by the organization should be based on predefined processes that have been created to address new risk values introduced by this event. Another example is the public announcement of a new security vulnerability affecting a number of internal assets that are *not* publicly accessible. What should the new risk values associated with these internal assets be as a result of this vulnerability discovery? Let's consider the latter scenario to assess the risk associated with the internal assets based on the new security vulnerability announcement, using the Operationally Critical Threat, Asset, and Vulnerability Evaluation (OCTAVE) risk-assessment methodology that was first developed by the Software Engineering Institute (SEI)[25] at Carnegie Mellon University. Table 1-1 demonstrates going through an OCTAVE risk-assessment exercise.

Table 1-1 *Example of a Risk-Assessment Exercise*

Risk Component	Description
Vulnerability	A new vulnerability affecting internal assets has been announced. The analysis shows that a number of critical internal assets are indeed vulnerable.
Threat description	Vulnerable assets are classified as critical. The attack can be easily executed on an asset if the attacker can access the service over the network.
Existing controls	The internal assets are not connected to the Internet. The assets are protected by a firewall that allows internal users only. The assets are protected by an intrusion prevention system (IPS); however, the IPS vendor has not released signatures that can protect the assets from being exploited through the newly announced vulnerability.
Probability	Unlikely. The assets can be only exploited by internal users who have access to the assets over the internal network.
Impact	Critical. Exploiting the vulnerability results in the attacker gaining full administrative access to the system.

Next, we will map the information in Table 1-1 to a risk heat map that we can use to identify the priority of this event based on the *probability* of it occurring and *impact* to the business if the event occurs. The risk heat map is a simple color-based representation using a two-dimensional matrix calculating probability and impact levels to identify the organization's level of concern for the event. Figure 1-9 depicts a four-level severity risk heat map using low, medium, high, and extreme as the depth levels of concern.

In the next risk heat map example, we assessed the probability to be unlikely and the impact to be critical, resulting in a moderate priority course of action. It is important to note that the impact, probability, and the priority values presented in Figure 1-9 should be clearly defined and understood when designing your security assessment methodology. For example, a moderate action plan could be the implementation of the required system patches following the standard process of evaluating the patches in the test environment, following the standard change management process, and then applying the patches in production during a standard change window. You learn how to create different forms of heat maps and calculating different risk values in Chapter 7, "Vulnerability Management."

Probability		Impact			
		Negligible	Marginal	Critical	Catastrophic
	Certain	HIGH	HIGH	EXTREME	EXTREME
	Likely	MEDIUM	HIGH	HIGH	EXTREME
	Possible	LOW	MEDIUM	HIGH	EXTREME
	Unlikely	LOW	LOW	MEDIUM	EXTREME
	Rare	LOW	LOW	MEDIUM	HIGH

Figure 1-9 *Simple Risk Heat Map*

Information Security Incident Response

Detecting and responding to information security incidents is at the core of security operations. The team assigned to security operations is expected to monitor the organization's assets within scope and react to security events and incidents, including the detection and investigation of what would be considered indicators of compromise (IOC). IOCs are technical and nontechnical security compromise signals that could be detected with technology, processes, and people. For example, detecting a user accessing files from a USB memory device on an enterprise desktop machine can indicate that a policy related to restricting the use of USB memory devices has been violated and that a security control has been circumvented. Another example is detecting the IP address of an Internet botnet command-and-control server inside your network probably indicates that one or more of your systems have been compromised.

Responding to incidents starts by first detecting that an incident has actually occurred and is within the scope assigned to the security operations team. An example is capturing some IOCs with a monitoring system and either investigating the events or handing off the forensic tasks to another party. This process typically involves different internal and potentially external entities depending on factors such as the tools used, type of event, skills of parties involved, and location triggering the alarms.

Preparing a SOC to manage incidents extends to cover people, processes, and of course, technology. For example, a SOC is usually expected to educate users about how they must report security incidents and keep informed of the channels available for users to report what is perceived as a security incident. The exact sequence of steps to follow and the parties to involve depend on the nature of the incident. A typical incident-handling process follows the list of steps presented in the incident response (IR) timeline in Figure 1-10. Let's look at *detection*, which is the second stop on the incident response timeline.

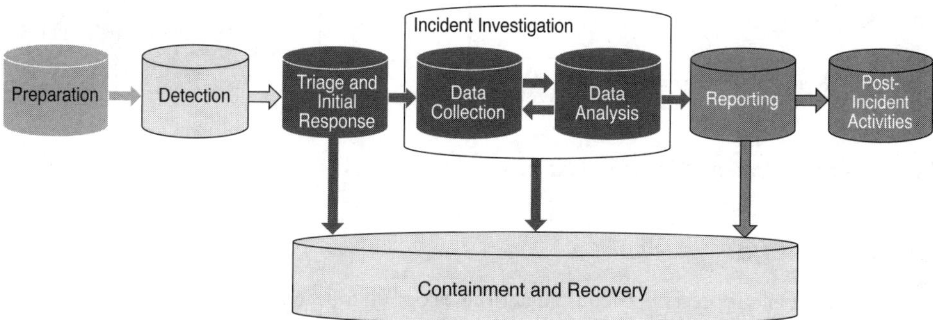

Figure 1-10 *Incident Response Timeline*

Incident Detection

Detection refers to the phase in which an incident is observed and reported by people or technology, and the process that handles the reporting aspects. A sample process for handling incoming incident reports is shown in Figure 1-11. For the process to be effective, the following must be documented and formalized:

- Identify the sources, such as people and technology, that are responsible for detecting and reporting computer security incidents.
- Identify the channels through which computer security incidents should be reported.
- Identify the steps that should be taken to accept and process computer security incident reports.
- Identify the requirements on people and technology for the process to work.

The steps described in the sections that follow outline the actions you expect to take after an incident has been reported, regardless of the channel through which the incident has been reported. Let's look at what follows detection, starting with triage.

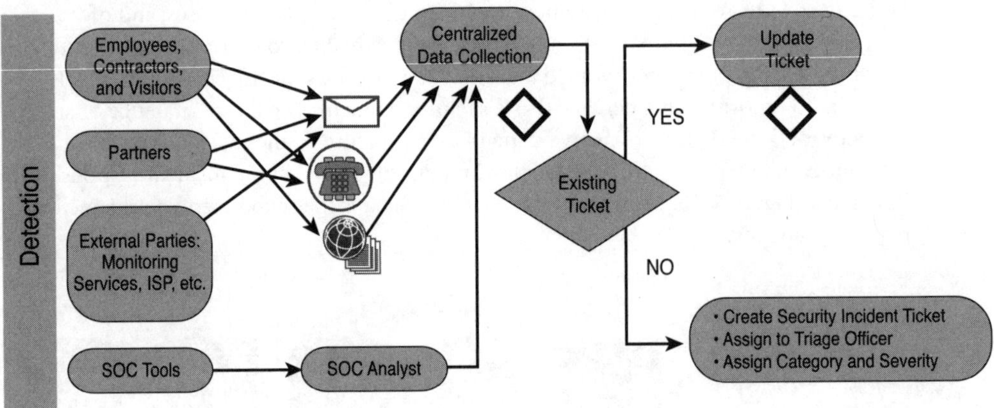

Figure 1-11 *Incident Detection Phase*

Incident Triage

Incident triage represents the initial actions taken on a detected event that is used to determine the remaining steps according to the incident response plan. The triage phase consists of three subphases: *verification*, *initial classification*, and *assignment*. An example of applying these phases is receiving an alert about an unauthorized system accessing a sensitive part of the network. The administrator would verify whether the alarm is something that should be investigated, classify the risk level for the event, and assign responsibility for handling the incident based on the level of associated risk.

The triage phase is concerned with answering questions such as the following:

- Is the incident within the scope of the program?
- Is it a new incident, or is it related to a previous reported one?
- What category should the incident be assigned to?
- What severity level should be assigned to the incident?
- Who should be assigned to analyze and investigate the incident (that is, the incident handler)?
- Is there a timeframe associated with the incident?

The triage process needs to be developed to prioritize incidents and move them along the incident response timeline to be analyzed and eventually conclude with some form of resolution. This usually involves placing the incident in a *category* for organization and assignment purposes along with applying a *severity level* so that incidents can be prioritized. Let's look at categorizing incidents and then at applying severity levels.

Incident Categories

All computer security incidents should be assigned a category. The category value identifies the type of the incident and its potential type of impact. Assigning a category value helps the SOC allocate the appropriate resources to analyze and investigate a computer security incident. Table 1-2 shows a sample list of categories that you could use for categorizing incidents.

Note that some incidents might have more than one category and that the category can change as the incident progresses or as the investigation of the incident unfolds new findings.

Table 1-2 *Computer Security Incident Categories*

Category Number	Name	Description
0	Exercise	This is used when conducting an approved exercise such as an authorized penetration test.
1	Unauthorized Access	This represents when an individual gains logical or physical access without permission to a client network, system, application, data, or other resource.
2	Denial of Service (DoS)	This is used when an attack successfully prevents or impairs the normal authorized functionality of networks, systems, or applications by exhausting resources.
3	Malicious Code	This identifies when there is a successful installation of malicious software, such as a virus, worm, Trojan horse, or other code-based malicious entity, that infects an OS or application.
4	Scans/Probes/ Attempted Access	This includes any activity that seeks to access or identify a client computer, open ports, protocols, service, or any combination for a future attack.
5	Investigation	This includes unconfirmed incidents that are potentially malicious or anomalous activity deemed by the reporting entity to warrant further review.

Incident Severity

Severity levels are based on the expected or observed impact of an incident. This is used for the prioritization of the incident, taking into account the amount of resources that should be assigned, and determines the escalation process to follow. Note that the severity level of an incident may change as the investigation unfolds. Chapter 7 covers calculating severity levels.

Table 1-3 shows a list of sample severity values. Levels can be more or less granular depending on your operational requirements.

Table 1-3 *Computer Security Incident Severity Levels*

Level	Description
High	Incidents that have severe impact on operations
Medium	Incidents that have a significant impact, or the potential to have a severe impact, on operations
Low	Incidents that have a minimal impact with the potential for significant or severe impact on operations

Once you categorize an incident and apply a severity level, you can decide how to resolve the incident. Let's review this stage of the incident response timeline.

Incident Resolution

The lifecycle of an incident should eventually lead to some form of resolution. This may include data analysis, resolution research, a proposed or performed action, and recovery. The objective of this phase is to discover the root cause of the incident, while working on containing the incident at the earliest stage possible.

During the analysis phase, the SOC team and the other teams should collaborate to achieve the quickest and best form of resolution. Access to some systems might be required to conduct necessary investigation activities. Figure 1-12 shows a sample process for handling the analysis tasks.

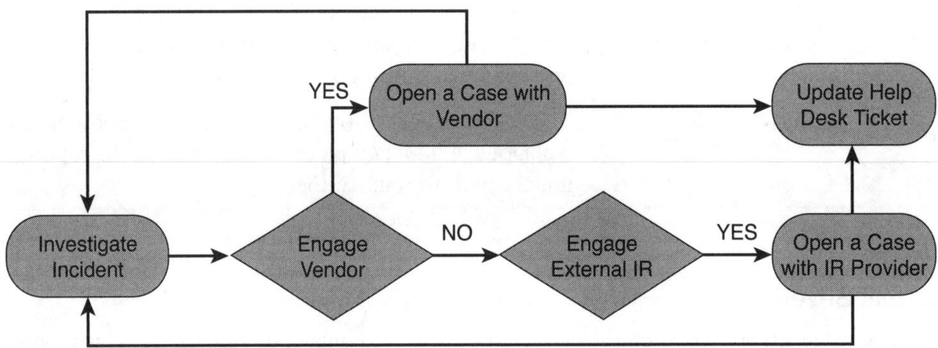

Figure 1-12 *Incident Analysis Phase Process*

The analysis and investigation phase involves the activities undertaken by SOC and by other teams for the purpose of

- Identifying compromised systems and accounts
- Understanding the impact of the computer security incident
- Identifying unauthorized access attempts to confidential data
- Understanding the chain of events that have led to the computer security incident

The containment phase involves the actions performed to quickly stop a computer security incident from escalating or spreading to other systems (that is, minimizing the potential damage caused by a computer security incident). Note that depending on the computer security incident and its impact, the containment phase can happen before, during, or after the analysis phase.

The process shown in Figure 1-13 is a sample containment process. You may, however, proceed with containment before or during the incident analysis.

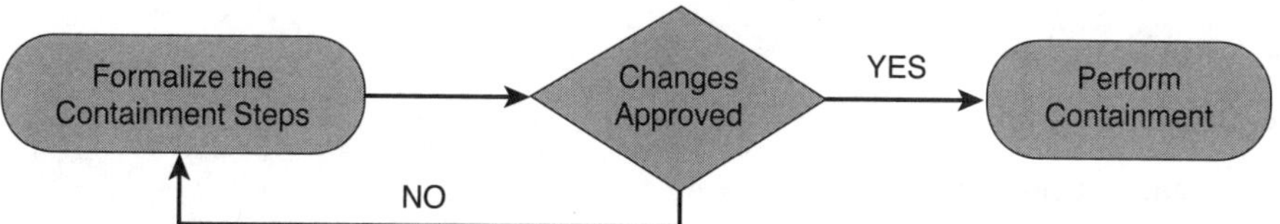

Figure 1-13 *Incident Containment Phase Process*

The exact steps to follow to contain a computer security incident vary depending on the nature of the incident and business criticality of the asset. Examples of containment actions include the following:

- Disconnecting a system from the network
- Moving an infected system to the quarantine network
- Stopping a service or a process
- Disabling an account
- Adding a firewall rule
- Adding an intrusion prevention system (IPS) signature/rule that would detect and block the attack's specific vector

Incident Closure

Closing a computer security incident refers to the eradication phase in which vulnerabilities that lead to the incident have been closed and all the incident traces have been cleansed. The closure process also includes testing systems to ensure that the eradication steps and controls were effective and that the vectors used by the attack do not exist anymore or are ineffective. Predefined actions to consider include applying any final information about the event, its final classification, any external notifications, and archiving information about the incident.

If the incident involved violating regulatory requirements or resulted in the infringement of law, the SOC might be obliged to notify external entities. The SOC should have processes in place so that this communication is timely, accurate, and contains all information required for such notification.

The exact steps to follow when eradicating a computer security incident will vary depending on the nature of the incident. Examples of eradication actions include the following:

- System reconfiguration
- System re-imaging or rebuild
- Patching of systems
- Software update
- Deletion of accounts
- Deletion of files

In many cases, the closure and containment phases are closely coupled.

Post-Incident

This is the "lessons-learned" phase in which you seek to improve the IR processes and reflect on other people, processes, and technology controls. Post-incident activities will vary depending on the severity of the computer security incident. Valuable knowledge gained from computer security incidents can be useful to prevent/mitigate future incidents in the form of proactive services such as enhancing security features of functions within defenses.

In general, the process of post-analysis starts after incident closure and mainly includes documenting proposals of improvements in linkage to the different areas of the SOC: people, processes, and technology. In addition, recommendations for improving the SOC capabilities might result from a scheduled or an ad hoc risk-assessment exercise.

In summary, following an incident response timeline, the SOC team would handle a number of critical tasks, from incident detection to closure. Each stage of an incident can have its own processes and involve other groups within the organization. It is important that the plan, design, and build phases for incident response be defined, documented, and sponsored by the right authorities within the organization. Incident response is all about timing, and the worst time to figure out responsibilities and incident-handling process is during an active attack.

Now that we have covered a general overview of the responsibilities of the SOC, let's take a look at the history of SOC generations to get a better idea of how SOCs have matured over time.

SOC Generations

Our understanding of SOC components and expected services has changed over time. This is a reflection to the adjustment in our perception of the criticality of information assurance and security operations. This transformation comes in response to the ever-changing security threat landscape, in addition to our increasingly adopting formal information security standards, requiring the establishment and management of a formal security operations model and review processes.

The SOC's journey for the past 15 years can be broken to four *incremental* generations, shown in Figure 1-14. Ideally, an organization that uses technologies from the fourth generation, such as big data security analytics, should have adopted most of the SOC services from the previous generations. This might not always be the case in practice, though.

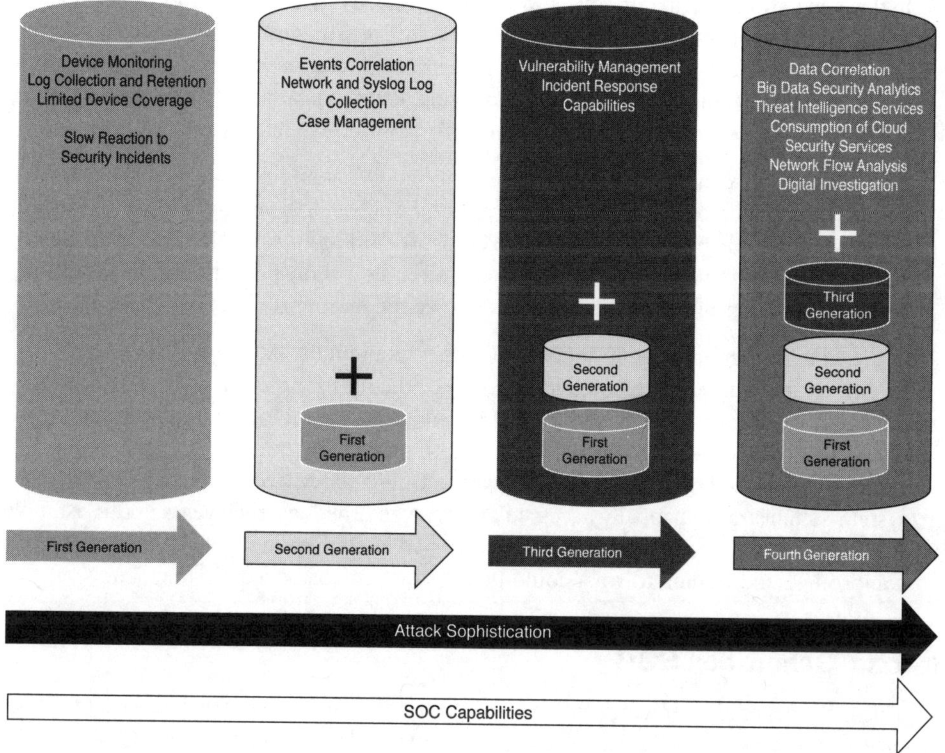

Figure 1-14 *The SOC: Four Generations*

The four generations reflect SOC capabilities in response to increasingly sophisticated attacks. Refer to the description of the generations to identify which SOC generation service your organization might be offering. Let's look at the details of the services offered in each SOC generation.

First-Generation SOC

In this generation, the wider IT operations team delivered what would be considered as SOC functions and services. This team was not necessarily skilled or trained to handle information security events and incidents. Security operations were not delivered by the establishment of a formal SOC, but in many cases by an IT operations individual or a team who focused on a blend of tasks. This could be responsibility for device and network health monitoring, managing antivirus security across the organization, and log collection. Log collection for the first-generation SOC was limited in the number of sources and types of devices capable of producing logs, such as firewalls. In many cases, storing logging messages was done locally. In other cases, a central logging facility was provisioned to receive log information, mainly in the form of unencrypted syslog or Simple Management Network Protocol (SNMP) messages.

In this generation, logging messages were rarely proactively analyzed, and were instead referred to if an incident was reported or some sort of troubleshooting was required. In addition, the concept of information security incident response was not formally established or appreciated. The process of identifying, communicating, and reacting to potential information security incidents was generally slow (and in many cases, ad hoc).

Let's look at an example of how a first-generation SOC would operate. Consider, for instance, that a number of systems have reported a substantial and relatively abnormal number of failed login attempts for the Microsoft Windows Active Directory domain administrator account within what is considered to be a short period of time. No evidence indicates suspicious activity or that a system compromise has been reported.

In the first generation of SOC, logging messages would most likely be locally saved on each system rather than stored on a centralized collection system such as a security information and event management (SIEM). The unsuccessful login attempt events would be saved to the local Windows security log store and buried under a large number of events generated by other various activities. Unless the Microsoft Active Directory system administrator manually accessed and analyzed the logs, the events in this example would have likely gone unnoticed, overlooking what could potentially be an account compromise and leading to what could be considered a major security incident.

Second-Generation SOC

This is the generation in which SIEM tools started to emerge. Early generations of SIEM providers such as netForensics, Network Intelligence (later acquired by EMC), and Cisco Security Monitoring, Analysis, and Response System (MARS) promised to detect network threats, releasing administrators from the complex and in many cases impossible task of manually analyzing huge amounts of log information. The early providers of such tools focused on security threat management (STM), also referred to as security event management (SEM), which delivers real-time log analysis for the purpose of threat detection. These tools accept log information generated by various sources in different formats, speeding up the process of detecting potential security incidents. The basic idea of SEM is to first aggregate log information in the form of events from various sources such as operating systems, security devices, and applications. Events are then correlated so that possible relationships between them are identified, indicating the potential occurrence of incidents. Incidents are then reported in the form of a dashboard alert to the operator to investigate further.

This SEM function was eventually consolidated with the security information management (SIM) function to produce what is known today as SIEM. SIM tools focused on searching through large amounts of acquired log data. This historical data could be then analyzed for different purposes, such as performing digital investigations or meeting a number of compliance requirements related to log retention and compliancy report generation.

Another important operational aspect introduced in the second-generation SOC was security incidents case management. SIEM operators can create and assign cases for security incidents reported by the tools. In some cases, this is integrated with the organization's service ticketing systems.

Taking the same multiple failed login attempts example used in the discussion about first-generation SOC, the Microsoft Windows systems would most likely be configured to forward logged events to a SIEM tool. The SIEM tool should be capable of receiving, parsing, normalizing, and correlating the different events and eventually alerting a security analyst that there have been multiple login failures for the account "administrator" on multiple systems. This behavior could indicate a possible brute-force attack, assuming that the SIEM tool is configured with correlation rules that can detect and assign a relevant and meaningful alert to this suspicious activity. You learn how correlation rules are created and tuned in Chapter 2.

Third-Generation SOC

As SIEM tools further established their importance, other security services started to find their way to the SOC. In this generation, the SOC team would handle tasks related to vulnerability management, in addition to being heavily involved in formalizing and executing tasks related to incident response.

Vulnerability management refers to the practice in which vulnerabilities are discovered and confirmed, their impact is evaluated, corrective measures are identified and executed, and their status is tracked and reported until closure. This definition is similar to the one used in the NIST SP 800-40 standard.[26]

It is critical that the impact evaluation phase for discovered vulnerabilities be associated with the organization's risk-assessment practice. This means referring to the whole process of managing vulnerabilities instead of running vulnerability scanning tools against IT assets only. Vulnerability scanning is an activity that is part of vulnerability management and is usually executed during the vulnerability discovery, confirmation, and tracking phases.

Some commercial products, such as Qualys[27], nCircle[28] (acquired in 2013 by Tripwire), and Rapid7 Nexpose[29] have evolved from being predominately vulnerability scanners to automating the vulnerability management process. The SOC team would either operate the vulnerability management process, working with other units, or would be assigned some of its tasks. You learn more about vulnerability management best practices in Chapter 7.

Fourth-Generation SOC

This generation of SOC introduces a number of advanced security services that attempt to tackle new security threats. The first new concept is expanding on the limited event correlation seen in previous generations of SIEM to big data security. Big data security analytics can be defined as "the ability to analyze large amount of data over long periods of time to discover threats and then present and visualize the results." Big data platforms are now being deployed to consume data from any source at high speed and with high volume, while being able to perform real-time or offline sophisticated security analytics. An example of using big data is ingesting large threat intelligence feeds about attacks seen all over the world rather than limiting event correlation to internal threats. Attack data could be website reputation data, malicious sources, volumetric trends for identifying distributed denial-of-service (DDoS) attacks, and so on. You learn more about big data security in Chapter 2.

Another new fourth-generation SOC concept is data enrichment through the use of sources such as geo data, Domain Name System (DNS) data, network access control integration, and IP and domain reputation service. Network telemetry information is also being used for sophisticated network and security monitoring, essentially turning common network equipment into security sensor ports.

New technologies are being used by the SOC for forensics and identifying network breaches also known as breach-detection solutions. Cross-product integration is being leveraged to automate remediation, such as an intrusion detection product identifying a threat and leveraging a network access control technology to automatically perform remediation.

In summary, fourth-generation SOC is expanding threat data sources, layering different security capabilities to battle more advanced threats, and automating security to improve reaction time to incidents. This generation of SOC also includes policies to evaluate their capabilities as a continuous process for optimization and enhancement purposes. To better understand the latest SOC generation, let's review the characteristics of an effective SOC.

Characteristics of an Effective SOC

To build and operate an effective SOC, organizations must account for a number of critical success factors. Some practices found in almost all organizations running a successful SOC are as follows:

- **Executive sponsorship:** The SOC program must have executive sponsorship. This sponsorship should be in the form of the sponsor signing the SOC mission, and the SOC team providing periodic updates to the sponsor, who is expected to be involved in major decisions taken by or for the SOC (for example, the acquisition of new tools or the expansion of the SOC team). The CIO and in some cases the CEO make ideal internal executive sponsors for the SOC program. There are also cases in which the SOC is established as part of the organization's risk management program. For these environments, the head of the security risk steering committee can oversee the SOC sponsorship.

- **Governance:** Establishing a governance structure is critical to the success of any security program. Metrics must be established to measure the effectiveness of the SOC capabilities. These metrics should provide sufficient and relevant visibility to the organization's management team on the performance of the SOC and should identify areas where improvements and investments are needed.

- **Operate SOC as a program:** Organizations should operate the SOC as a program rather than a single project. Doing so relies on the criticality and the amount of resources required to design, build, and operate the various services offered by the SOC. Having a clear SOC service strategy with clear goals and priorities would shape the size of the SOC program, timeline, and the amount of resources required to deliver the program objectives.

- **Collaboration:** The different units in an organization must collaborate during the plan, design, build, and operate phases of the SOC. The exact collaboration and interdepartmental relationships must be formally defined during the SOC design and build phases.

- **Access to data and systems:** Access to the required data and systems must be provided to the SOC team so that they can perform their tasks: before, during, and after a security incident. The exact definition of *access* must be established during the SOC design and build phases. This can be, for example, access to log data or extended to gaining access to system configuration. At a minimum, SOC tools should receive logging messages from various systems and applications.

- **Applicable processes and procedures:** The SOC team must be equipped with established processes and knowledge, augmented with the appropriate set of tools. The processes created during the SOC design and build phases should consider the current and desired capabilities.

- **Skill set and experience:** The SOC team must be equipped with the appropriate skill set that enables them to perform their tasks in terms of operating technologies and investigating incidents. The organization must consider training existing staff or acquiring the required skill set through a hiring process. This process should be continuous with the ability to rotate the SOC staff.

- **Budget:** The subject of budget is relative. The budget assigned to the build and operate phases would vary depending on a number factors, such as the following:

  - In-house versus SOC outsourcing

  - The services provided by the SOC

- The SOC operation hours
- The skill set gap
- The desired capability level roadmap

The characteristics of an effective SOC are connected such that the successful implementation of one is required to support the others. For example, the lack of executive sponsorship would lead to difficulties in implementing the required level of governance, establishing a collaborative environment, and allocating budget for the SOC. Figure 1-15 presents the relationship between the different characteristics.

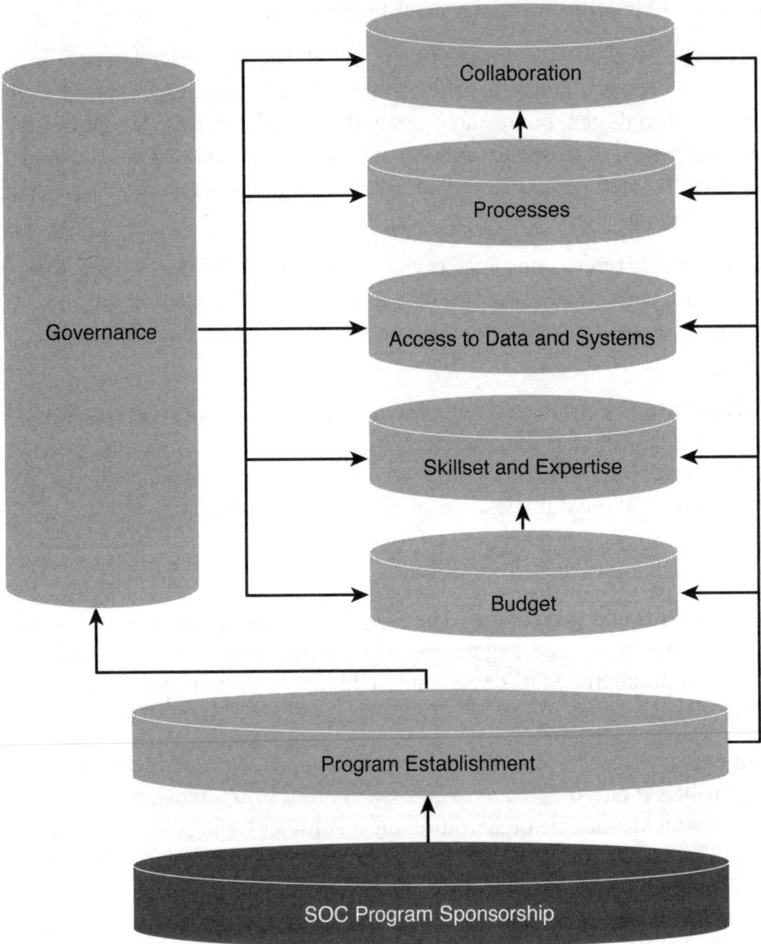

Figure 1-15 *The Characteristics of an Effective SOC*

Introduction to Maturity Models

Maturity models are IT governance tools used to describe management processes with respect to standardization, repeatable processes and results, and measurement of effectiveness. Examples of such models include the Control Objectives for Information and related Technology (COBIT) Maturity Model (MM), described in Table 1-4, and the Carnegie Mellon Software Engineering Institute (SEI) Capability Maturity Model[30] (CMM), now under the CMMI Institute, described in Table 1-5. Referring to Table 1-4 and Table 1-5, notice the slight difference between the two models.

Scores for the maturity model are based on an assignment of a 0–5 score. These scoring metrics are used in the next sections to provide a general understanding of maturity in each of the identified security management areas. Table 1-4 shows the maturity scores and associated descriptions for the COBIT MM.

Table 1-4 *COBIT MM Scoring*

Maturity Level	Process Criteria
0 Nonexistent	Complete lack of any recognizable processes. The organization has not recognized there is an issue to be addressed.
1 Initial/Ad Hoc	There is evidence that the organization has recognized that the issues exist and need to be addressed. There are, however, no standardized processes, but instead there are ad hoc approaches that tend to be applied on an individual or case-by-case basis. The overall approach to management is disorganized.
2 Repeatable but Intuitive	Processes have developed to the stage where similar procedures are followed by different people undertaking the same task. There is no formal training or communication of standard procedures, and responsibility is left to the individual. There is a high degree of reliance on the knowledge of individuals, and therefore errors are likely.
3 Defined Process	Procedures have been standardized, documented, and communicated through training. It is, however, left to the individual to follow these processes, and it is unlikely that deviations will be detected. The procedures themselves are not sophisticated but are the formalization of existing practices.
4 Managed and Measurable	It is possible to monitor and measure compliance with procedures and to take action where processes appear not to be working effectively. Processes are under constant improvement and provide good practice. Automation and tools are used in a limited or fragmented way.

Table 1-4 *continued*

Maturity Level	Process Criteria
5 Optimized	Processes have been refined to a level of best practice, based on the results of continuous improvement and maturity modeling with other organizations. IT is used in an integrated way to automate the workflow, providing tools to improve quality and effectiveness, making the enterprise quick to adapt.

Table 1-5 *SEI Maturity Levels*

Maturity Level	Process Criteria
0 Nonexistent	No security policy exists.
1 Initial: Process is unpredictable, poorly controlled, and reactive.	Processes are usually ad hoc and chaotic. The organization usually does not provide a stable environment to support processes. Success in these organizations depends on the competence and heroics of the people in the organization and not on the use of proven processes.
2 Managed: Process is characterized by projects and is often reactive.	The document exists, and has been validated and disseminated, but it is incomplete or does not fit the context of the organization.
3 Defined: Process is characterized as a defined process.	The document exists, is complete, has been validated and disseminated, and fits the context of the organization.
4 Quantitatively managed: Process is measured and controlled.	Controls are set up to assess the application of the validated document.
5 Optimized: Focus is on continuous process improvement.	A regular review process allows assessing the application of the previously validated document and enables the organization to regularly update it.

Using a maturity model helps you measure your current capabilities and track progress against goals. To achieve this, processes and capabilities must be first identified so that maturity level values are assigned and a roadmap is then formalized. The exact set of capabilities to measure depends on the discipline you are trying to evaluate. Figure 1-16 shows maturity level values assigned to a number of security operation capabilities.

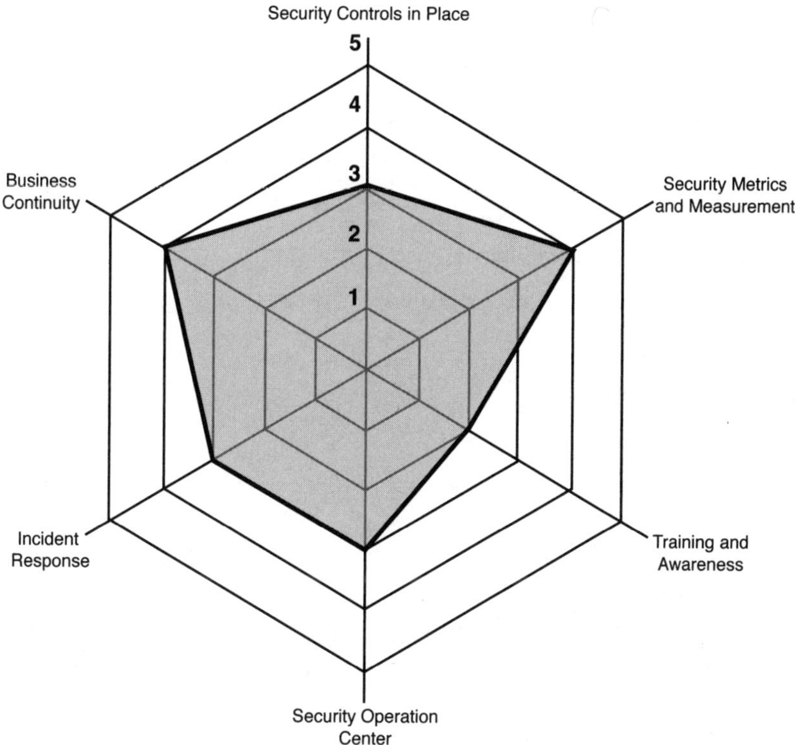

Figure 1-16 *Capability Level: Security Operations*

Applying Maturity Models to SOC

No single reference formalizes SOC capabilities. Here we propose a set of SOC-specific capabilities in three areas that could be evaluated. We use these capabilities as our reference for the rest of this book:

- **People**
  - Structure
  - Relative SOC knowledge and experience
  - Training and awareness
- **Process**
  - Incident triage
  - Incident reporting
  - Incident analysis

- Incident closure
- Post-incident
- Vulnerability discovery
- Vulnerability remediation

- **Technology**
  - Network infrastructure readiness
  - Events collection, correlation, and analysis
  - Security monitoring
  - Security control
  - Log management
  - Vulnerability assessment
  - Vulnerability tracking
  - Threat intelligence

Similar to Figure 1-16, the capabilities listed here can be graphically represented. For example, Figure 1-17 shows process-related SOC capabilities.

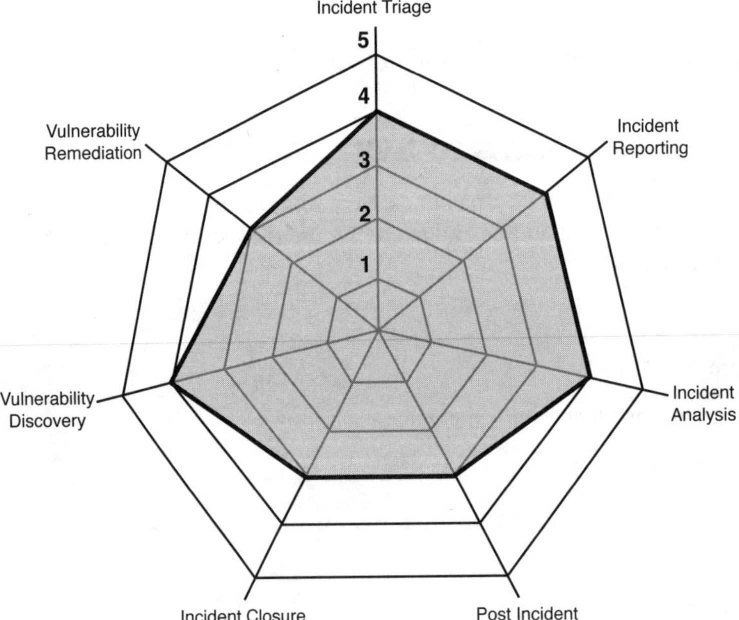

Figure 1-17 *SOC Capabilities: Process*

Phases of Building a SOC

This section introduces the sequence of phases that you expect to undergo when establishing a SOC: namely, plan, design, build, operate, and optionally, transfer. Each part of the book represents a SOC phase, with practices related to that phase. Although we use this chronological approach in the book to cover the different SOC topics, you can easily refer to any of these phases depending on where you are in your SOC program. For example, you might already be operating a SOC and looking to methodologies that you can use to assess your SOC's effectiveness in detecting and responding to various suspicious activity categories, or you might be looking to explore ideas related to people retention and skill development.

Delivering on each SOC phase requires having a set of relevant skills and the engagement of a number of internal and potentially external entities. The type of engagement varies from active involvement and actual service delivery to more of an executive and financial type of support.

A sequential approach in building a SOC does not necessarily mean following a rigid sequence of activities; instead, it gives you the opportunity to identify and consider the specific environment that your SOC will eventually operate within. How you plan and design your SOC will largely impact, positively or negatively, the time and cost you spend in deploying and operating your SOC. Properly planning for your SOC gives you enough visibility needed to formalize your SOC requirements before hiring resources or approaching technology vendors, some of whom are happy to sell you unnecessary modules of their SIEM solution, for example. In general, it is critical that SOC capabilities be developed and customized so that they are applicable to the organization's threat landscape, perceived risk, and compliancy needs.

Each phase consists of a number of activities that are performed in accordance with the organization's exact requirements. The list of phases is summarized in Figure 1-18 as an iterative process in which emerging security challenges introduced by the continuously evolving threat landscape are addressed. The following chapters extensively discuss each of these phases.

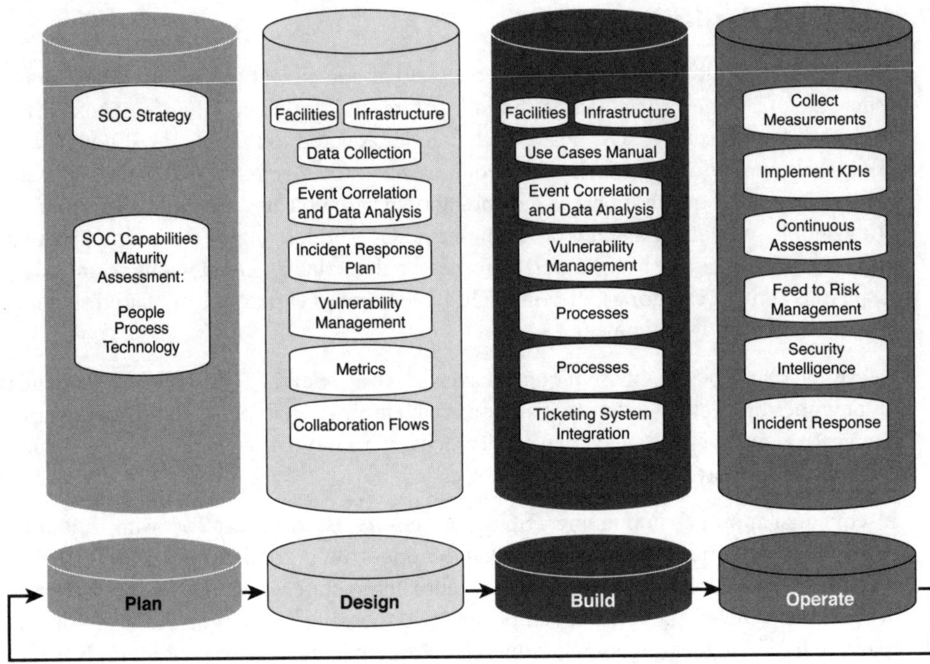

Figure 1-18 *Phases of Building a SOC*

Challenges and Obstacles

Although the success of any security program like the SOC relies heavily on proper planning, there are almost always challenges that are specific to the organization. These challenges are introduced because of issues related to governance, collaboration, skill sets, and so on. Such challenges must be identified and treated, or at least acknowledged, at an early stage of a SOC establishment program. They should be then tracked during each stage of the SOC. Chapter 3, "Assessing Security Operations Capabilities," discusses this topic in detail.

Summary

Establishing and maintaining a SOC is a continuous process of planning, designing, building, and operating a center that can detect and respond to security incidents. The establishment of the SOC requires developing various capabilities and maintenance related to people, processes, and technology. Understanding and formalizing the roles of the SOC program in the overall information security management system of an organization is paramount to the success of the SOC.

To set the stage for the rest of the book, this chapter provided a general overview of a SOC. Next we look at SOC operations, covering the tools and techniques found in most SOC environments.

References

1. The OODA Loop, http://en.wikipedia.org/wiki/OODA_loop
2. John Boyd_http://en.wikipedia.org/wiki/John_Boyd_(military_strategist)
3. The Lockheed Martin cyber kill chain model, http://www.lockheedmartin.com/content/dam/lockheed/data/corporate/documents/LM-White-Paper-Intel-Driven-Defense.pdf
4. Verizon 2015 Data Breach Report, http://www.verizonenterprise.com/DBIR/2015/
5. Backtrack Linux Distribution, http://www.backtrack-linux.org
6. Kali Linux Distribution, http://www.kali.org
7. http://www.networkworld.com/article/2164758/network-security/malware-detecting--sandboxing--technology-no-silver-bullet.html
8. VUPEN Security, http://www.vupen.com
9. Netragard, http://www.netragard.com
10. ReVuln Ltd., http://www.revuln.com
11. Endgame, http://www.endgame.com
12. The Known Unknowns Report by NSS, https://www.nsslabs.com/reports/known-unknowns-0
13. Internet of Everything, http://www.cisco.com/web/about/ac79/docs/IoE/IoE-AAG.pdf
14. Bitglass Cloud Adoption Report Summary, http://www.bitglass.com/company/news/press_releases/cloud-security-adoption-report-2014
15. The rising strategic risks of cyberattacks research by McKinsey, http://www.mckinsey.com/insights/business_technology/the_rising_strategic_risks_of_cyberattacks
16. PCI Quick Reference Guide, https://www.pcisecuritystandards.org/documents/pci_ssc_quick_guide.pdf
17. Germany—Federal Data Protection Act (*Bundesdatenschutzgesetz*, BDSG), http://www.iuscomp.org/gla/statutes/BDSG.htm
18. Japan—Act on the Protection of Personal Information, http://www.cas.go.jp/jp/seisaku/hourei/data/APPI.pdf
19. UK Data Protection Act 1998, http://www.legislation.gov.uk/ukpga/1998/29/contents
20. Department of Defense Directive on Information Assurance (IA), http://dodcio.defense.gov/Portals/0/Documents/DIEA/850001p.pdf
21. NIST Special Publication 800-59, http://csrc.nist.gov/publications/nistpubs/800-59/SP800-59.pdf
22. http://lincs.police.uk/Library/Freedom-of-Information/Publication-Scheme/Our-Policies-And-Procedures/Information-Management-Strategy.pdf

23. NIST Special Publication 800-53 Revision 4, http://nvlpubs.nist.gov/nistpubs/SpecialPublications/NIST.SP.800-53r4.pdf
24. Guide for Conducting Risk Assessments, http://csrc.nist.gov/publications/nistpubs/800-30-rev1/sp800_30_r1.pdf
25. Software Engineering Institute, http://www.sei.cmu.edu
26. NIST SP 800-40 Version 2.0 Creating a Patch and Vulnerability Management Program, http://csrc.nist.gov/publications/nistpubs/800-40-Ver2/SP800-40v2.pdf
27. Qualys, http://www.qualys.com
28. Tripwire, http://www.tripwire.com
29. Rapid7, http://www.rapid7.com
30. SEI Capability Maturity Model Integration (CMMI), http://www.sei.cmu.edu/cmmi

Chapter 2

Overview of SOC Technologies

"If all you have is a hammer, everything looks like a nail."—Abraham Maslow

Chapter 1, "Introduction to Security Operations and the SOC," provided a general overview of security operations center (SOC) concepts and referenced a number of technologies that offer SOC services such as vulnerability management, threat intelligence, digital investigation, and data collection and analysis. This chapter covers the details of these technologies using a generic and product-agnostic approach. This will give the fundamental understanding of how the technologies function so that these concepts can be related to products covered later in this book. This chapter also covers data collection and analysis, such as how a security information and event management (SIEM) collects and processes log data.

In this chapter, we continue to reference open source code deployments and industry-recognized architectures whenever applicable to illustrate how to deploy and customize SOC technologies. These technologies are used to develop a conceptual architecture that integrates the different SOC technologies and services. After reading this chapter, you should understand the technology and service expectations for most modern SOC environments.

Let's start by introducing the most fundamental responsibility for a SOC: collecting and analyzing data.

Data Collection and Analysis

You need to first acquire relevant data before performing any sort of useful analysis. In the context of security monitoring, data from various sources and in different formats can be collected for the purposes of security analysis, auditing, and compliance. Data of special interest includes event logs, network packets, and network flows. You might also want sometimes to actively probe or collect content such as the static content of a web page or the hash value of a file.

Generating and capturing event logs is crucial to security operation. Events can directly or indirectly contribute to the detection of security incidents. For example, a high-priority event generated by a properly tuned intrusion detection system would indicate an attack attempt. However, a high-link-utilization event generated by a router might not be a security event by definition but could indicate a security incident when correlated with other events such as a denial-of-service (DoS) attack or a compromised host scanning your network.

Every organization operates its own unique and continuously evolving list of services and systems. However, the basic questions related to data collection and analysis remain similar across all organizations:

- Which elements should you monitor?
- What data should you collect and in what format?
- What level of logging should you enable on each element?
- What protocols should you use to collect data from the various elements?
- Do you need to store the data you collect and for how long?
- Which data should you parse and analyze?
- How much system and network overhead does data collection introduce?
- How do you associate data-collection requirements with capacity management?
- How do you evaluate and optimize your data-collection capability?

Chapter 7, "Vulnerability Management," and Chapter 9, "The Technology," address many of these questions. The fundamental idea is not to monitor everything for the sake of monitoring, but rather to design your data-collection capability so that your technical and compliance objectives are met within the boundaries you are responsible for monitoring. For example, depending on your network topology and the elements you want to collect data from, you might want to distribute your data collectors and centralize your monitoring dashboard so that you have multiple visibility points feeding into one place to monitor all events. Another example is comparing the cost and return of investing in collecting and storing packets versus leveraging NetFlow in existing network assets for security forensic requirements.

Regardless of the technology and design that is selected, the key is that the final product not provide too much or little data. We find many failures experienced by a SOC results from poor data-collection practices. This could be caused by many factors, from blind spots based on how data is collected, to not correlating the right data such as identifying vulnerable systems that do not exist on the network. Sometimes the proper tools are enabled but their clocks are not properly synchronized, causing confusion when troubleshooting. We address these and other best practices for collecting data later in this chapter under logging recommendations.

In principle, the type of data to acquire and what the data originator supports determine the collection mechanism to deploy. For example, most enterprise-level network devices natively support the syslog protocol for the purpose of remote event logging, whereas other systems require the installation of an agent to perform a similar function.

Understanding your exact environment and identifying the elements that you acquire useful data from are the initial steps in the process of building a data-collection capability. The conceptual steps shown in Figure 2-1 represent this process. Data can be stored in a flat file, a relational database, or over a distributed file system such as the Hadoop Distributed File System (HDFS). The analyze step can use various techniques, such as statistical-based anomaly detection, deploying event correlation rules, or applying machine learning on data. Starting from the SOC design phase, you should formalize and document all processes and procedures, including your choices of technology.

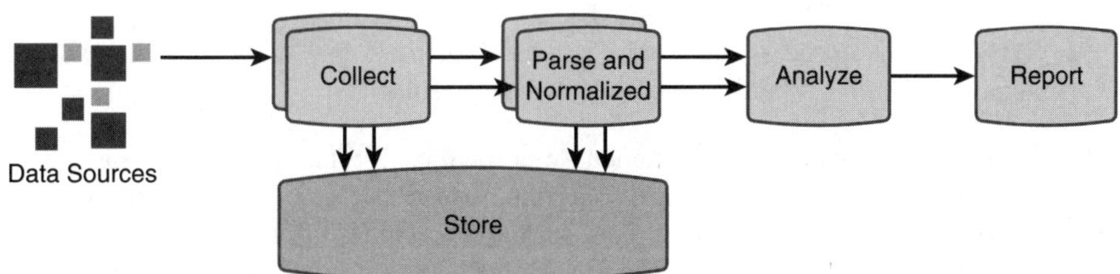

Figure 2-1 *Basic Data Management Workflow*

After data has been collected, you can decide whether to store it, parse it, or both. Although storing data in its original format can be beneficial for the purposes of digital investigations, out-of-band security analytics, and meeting compliance requirements, it is important to note that data at this point is regarded as being unstructured, meaning the exact structure is still unknown or has not been validated. To understand the structure of the data, parsing is required to extract the different fields of an event. For the data to have any use to the organization, be aware that when storing original data, regardless of the form, you must have a repository that can accept it and tools that can later query, retrieve, and analyze it. Many factors can determine what type and how much data the SOC should store, such as legal and regulatory factors, cost to manage the stored data, and so on. Let's look at the different types of data sources.

Data Sources

Logging messages are considered the most useful data type to acquire. Logging messages summarize an action or an activity that took place on a system, containing information related to an associated event. Depending on your environment, you might want to consider collecting logging messages from various forms of security, network, and application products. Examples of physical and virtual devices that could provide valuable logging messages include the following:

- Security elements such as firewalls, intrusion detection and prevention systems, antivirus solutions, web proxies, and malware analysis tools
- Network elements such as routers, switches, and wireless access points and controllers

- Operating systems such as the different releases of Microsoft Windows, UNIX, Linux, and OS X
- Virtualization platforms such as Virtual-Box, Kernel-based Virtual Machine (KVM), Microsoft Hyper-V, and VMware ESX
- Applications such as web servers, Domain Name System (DNS) servers, e-mail gateways, billing applications, voice gateways, and mobile device management (MDM) tools
- Databases
- Physical security elements such as security cameras, door access-control devices, and tracking systems
- Systems used in process and control networks, such as supervisory control and data acquisition (SCADA) and distributed control system (DCS)

In addition to logging messages, you might want to collect, store, and possibly analyze other forms of data. Examples include collecting network packets, NetFlow, and the content of files such as configuration files, hash values, and HTML files. Each of these data sources provides unique value, but each has its own associated costs to consider before investing in methods to collect and analyze the data. For example, storing network packets typically has a higher cost for collecting and storage but can provide more granular detail on events than NetFlow. Some industry regulations require storage of packet-level data, making capturing packets a must-have feature. For customers looking for similar forensic data at a lower price, collecting NetFlow can be a less-expensive alternative, depending on factors such as existing hardware, network design, and so on.

To better understand the cost and value of collecting data, let's look deeper at how data can be collected.

Data Collection

After you have an idea about the data you want to collect, you must figure out how to collect it. This section reviews the different protocols and mechanisms that you can use to collect data from various sources. Depending on what the data source supports, data can be pulled from the source to the collector or pushed by the source to the collector.

It is important to emphasize the need for time synchronization when collecting data. Capturing logs without proper time stamping could cause confusion when evaluating events and could corrupt results. The most common way a SOC enforces time synchronization across the network is by leveraging a central timing server using the Network Time Protocol (NTP). Best practice is to have all services and systems, including those that generate, collect, and analyze data, synchronize their clocks with a trusted central time server. Chapter 6, "Security Event Generation and Collection," discusses how to best design your NTP implementation for your SOC.

The Syslog Protocol

The syslog protocol, as defined in IETF RFC 5424,[1] provides a message format that enables vendor-specific extensions to be provided in a structured way, in addition to conveying event notification messages from a syslog client (originator) to a syslog destination (relay or collector). The syslog protocol supports three roles:

- **Originator:** Generates syslog content to be carried in a message
- **Collector:** Gathers syslog messages
- **Relay:** Forwards messages, accepting messages from originators or other relays and sending them to collectors or other relays

Figure 2-2 shows the different communication paths between the three syslog roles, noting that a syslog client can be configured with multiple syslog relays and collectors.

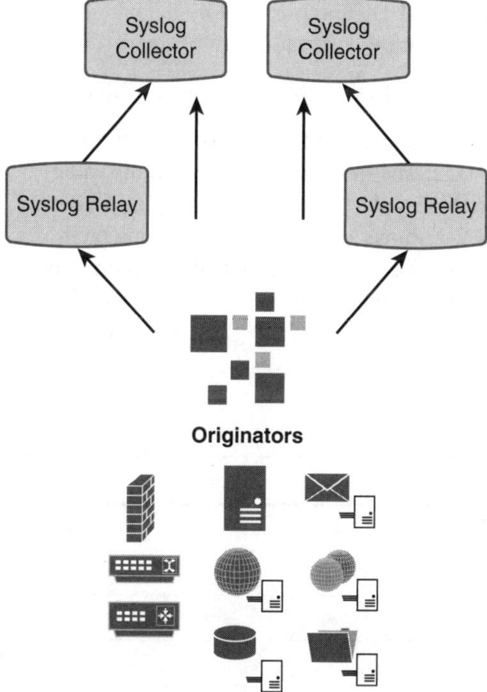

Figure 2-2 *Syslog Collection Design*

Implementations of syslog use User Datagram Protocol (UDP) with port number 514 to forward events. It is also possible to implement the protocol over a reliable transport protocol, for example, Transfer Control Protocol (TCP), as per IETF RFC 3195.[2] Syslog does not natively provide security protection in terms of confidentiality, integrity, and authenticity. However, these security features can be delivered by running syslog over a secure network protocol, such as Transport Layer Security (TLS) and Datagram Transport

Layer Security (DTLS), as described in RFCs 5425 and 6012, respectively. These approaches might be more secure, but typically at a cost of additional overhead and the risk that some systems might not offer support for these protocols. It is recommended to review the product's configuration guide to verify possible performance impacts and capabilities before implementing certain features.

Syslog is generally supported by network and security solutions for the purpose of event logging. UNIX and UNIX-like operating systems support syslog through the use of an agent such as rsylog and syslog-ng. Similarly, Microsoft Windows platforms require the installation of an agent to forward events in syslog format.

Regardless of the syslog client, you need to configure at least the following parameters:

- **Logging destinations:** The collector, relay IP addresses, or hostnames. Depending on the implementation, the originator can forward syslog messages to one or more destinations.
- **Protocol and port:** Typically these are set to UDP and port 514 by default. The option of changing this setting is implementation dependent.
- **Logging severity level:** Can be a value ranging from 0 to 7, as shown in Table 2-1.
- **Logging facility:** A value between 0 and 23 that could be used to indicate the program or system that generated the message. The default value assigned to syslog messages is implementation specific. For example, you can assign logging facility values to categorize your events. Table 2-2 shows an example of assigning facility values to asset categories. Other approaches could be designed based on your environment and requirements. The severity and logging facility values could be combined to calculate a priority value of an event, influencing the post-event actions to take.

Table 2-1 *Logging Severity Levels*

Level	Severity
0	Emergency: System is unusable.
1	Alert: Action must be taken immediately.
2	Critical: Critical conditions.
3	Error: Error conditions.
4	Warning: Warning conditions.
5	Notice: Normal but significant condition.
6	Informational: Informational messages.
7	Debug: Debug-level messages.

Depending on your setup and requirements, configuring other parameters beyond this list might be required. For example, the SOC may want more granular data by selecting which operating system or application events to log and forward.

Table 2-2 *Example of Mapping Facility Values to Categories*

Facility Value	Role
Local0	Databases
Local1	Core network devices (routers, switches, wireless controllers, and so on)
Local2	Other network devices
Local3	Operating system
Local4	Core applications
Local5	Not used
Local6	Not used
Local7	Other elements

Let's look at a few examples that demonstrate how to configure a syslog client. Example 2-1 shows how to configure a Cisco IOS-based router to forward events by specifying the logging destinations, level, and facility. Note that there are many other parameters available for syslog beyond what we used for these examples. You can find many comprehensive sources available on the Internet that provide a list of available parameters, such as http://www.iana.org/assignments/syslog-parameters/syslog-parameters.xhtml.

Example 2-1 *Configuring a Cisco IOS Router for Syslog*

```
Router# configure terminal
Router(config)# logging host1
Router(config)# logging host2
Router(config)# logging trap level
Router(config)# logging facility facility_type
```

With the configuration in Example 2-1, the router would generate sample messages similar to what is shown in Example 2-2. The log messages in Example 2-2 are for CPU and link status updates. Some administrators would consider these messages easy to read at an individual level. Now imagine receiving thousands or even millions of such messages per day from various network device types, each with a unique message structure and content. A firewall is a good example of a network security device that would typically generate a large number of logging messages, overwhelming a security administrator who operates a basic log collection tool.

Example 2-2 *Sample Syslog Messages Generated by a Cisco IOS Router*

```
Sep 9 03:34:57 ROUTER 23772: Sep 9 03:34:53.911: %SYS-3-CPUHOG: Task ran for 18428
  msec (22/9), process = IP SNMP, PC = 32976EC.Sep 19 10:25:32 ROUTER 77: Jun 19
  10:25:31.093: %LINEPROTO-5-UPDOWN: Line protocol on Interface Serial4/0, changed
  state to up.
Sep 19 10:26:02 ROUTER 78: Sep 19 10:26:01.093: %LINEPROTO-5-UPDOWN: Line protocol
  on Interface Serial4/0, changed state to down
```

Next, let's look at remote logging of Linux distribution messages. Remote logging of these events can be achieved by running syslog daemons. Examples are the syslogd and the use of commercial and open source logging daemons such as rsyslog or syslog-ng. In the case of Linux, most operating system log files, such as the ones shown in Example 2-3, are located in the /var/log/ directory. For CentOS (Community ENTerprise Operating System) using rsyslog, the, syslog configuration is maintained in /etc/rsyslog.conf, shown in Example 2-4. Once again, these logs might be able to be interpreted individually, but sorting through a large number of these types of log events would prove cumbersome for most administrators.

Example 2-3 *Linux Common Log Files and Directories*

```
messages : General message and system related stuff
auth.log : Authentication logs
kern.log : Kernel logs
cron.log : Crond logs (cron job)
maillog  : Mail server logs
httpd/   : Apache access and error logs directory
boot.log : System boot log
secure   : Access logs from the sshd process
```

Example 2-4 *rsyslog.conf Sample Configuration*

```
# Forward all messages, generated by rsyslog using any facility and
# priority values, to a remote syslog server using UDP.
# By adding this line and keeping the default configuration, the logs
# will be stored on the client machine and forwarded to the log
# server. To limit the log messages sent by rsyslog, you can specify
# facility and priority values.
# Remote host as name/ip:port, e.g. 192.168.0.1:514, port optional
*.* @log_serever

# You can use @@ for TCP remote logging instead of UDP
# *.* @@log_serever
```

Example 2-5 shows sample Secure Shell (SSH) access log messages for the user *root*. Note that, for many environments, allowing root to gain remote login access using SSH is not recommended.

Example 2-5 *Sample Linux Syslog Messages for SSH Access*

```
Sep  7 14:36:01 CentOS6 sshd[3140]: Accepted password for root from x.x.x.x
  port 65314 ssh2
Sep  7 14:36:02 CentOS6 sshd[3140]: pam_unix(sshd:session): session opened for user
  root by (uid=0)
```

Tip Pay attention to the log rotation settings for syslog files that are maintained locally on your system. In the case of CentOS, for example, the log rotation settings are maintained in the /etc/logrotate.d directory.

A syslog relay or collector must be ready to receive and optionally process (for example, parse, redirect, and/or enrich) logging messages as required. Your choice of the logging server is driven by a number of factors, such as your technical requirements, skill set, scalability of the platform, vendor support, and of course, cost of acquisition and operation. In addition to commercial log management tools such as Splunk and HP Arcsight ESM, a growing number of open-source code implementations are available, such as graylog2[3] and logstash[4] (part of the Elasticsearch ELK stack[5]).

Although some SIEM products manage security events, they might not be made for long-term event storage and retrieval. The reason why is that some SIEMs' performance and scalability are limited when compared to dedicated log management platforms such as Splunk or Logstash, especially as the amount of data they store and process increases. This is due to how legacy SIEM tools store and query events, which in most cases means the use of a relational database infrastructure. Note that some SIEM vendors are evolving their approach of managing events and deploying big data platforms for their data repository. SIEM vendors that have not made this move are sometimes referred to as *legacy*.

Logging Recommendations

Enabling logging features on a product can prove useful but also have an associated cost on performance and functionality. Some settings should be required before enabling logging, such as time synchronization and local logging as a backup repository when the centralized logging solution fails. When designing and configuring your syslog implementation, consider the following best practices before enabling logging:

- In the context of security operation, log events that are of business, technical, or compliance value.
- Configure your clients and servers for NTP, and confirm that clocks are continuously being synchronized.
- Time stamp your log messages and include the time zone in each message.
- Categorize your events by assigning logging facility values. This will add further context to event analysis.

- Limit the number of collectors for which a client is configured to the minimum required. Use syslog relays when you require the same message to be forwarded to multiple collectors. Syslog relays can be configured to replicate and forward the same syslog message to multiple destinations. This scenario is common when you have multiple monitoring platforms performing different tasks such as security, problem management, and system and network health monitoring.
- Baseline and monitor the CPU, memory, and network usage overhead introduced by the syslog service.
- Have a limited local logging facility, in file or memory, so that logs are not completely lost if the syslog collector is unavailable, such as in the case of network failure.
- On a regular basis, test that logging is functioning properly.
- Protect your syslog implementation based on evaluating the risk associated with syslog not providing confidentiality, integrity, or authenticity services.
- Ensure that log rotation and retention policies are properly set.
- Protect files where logs are stored: Restrict access to the system, assign proper files access permissions, and enable file encryption if needed. Read access to log files must be granted only to authorized users and processes. Write access to log files must be granted only to the syslog service. Standard system hardening procedures could be applied to operating systems hosting your logging server.

Logging Infrastructure

There are other elements to consider when designing a logging infrastructure. These include the type of data being received, expected storage, security requirements, and so on. Here are some factors that will influence how you should design your logging infrastructure:

- The logging level for which your systems are configured. Remember, configuring higher severity levels results in generating more logging messages. For example, configuring a firewall for severity level 6 (information) would result in the firewall generating multiple events per permitted connection: connection establishment, termination, and possibly network address translation.
- The amount of system resources available to the syslog client and server in comparison to the number of logging messages being generated and collected. An environment that generates a large amount of logging data might require multiple logging servers to handle the volume of events.
- The per-device and aggregate events per second (EPS) rates. This is closely related to the device type, available resources, logging level, security conditions, and the placement of the device in the network. You must consider the expected EPS rate in normal and peak conditions usually seen during attacks. Chapter 6 provides best practices for calculating EPS rates.

- The average size (in bytes) of logging messages.
- The amount of usable network bandwidth available between the logging client and the logging server.
- Protecting syslog messages using secure network protocols such as TLS and DTLS introduces additional load that must be accounted for.
- The scalability requirements of the logging infrastructure, which ideally should be linked to capacity planning.
- Consider collecting logging messages using an out-of-band physical or logical network. Separating your management plane—for example, by using a separate management virtual LAN (VLAN) or a Multiprotocol Label Switching (MPLS) virtual private network (VPN)—is a good network and system management practice that applies to most devices and systems. You might, however, encounter cases in which a system does not support having a separate physical or logical management interface, forcing you to forward logging messages in-band.

The preceding factors should influence your design decision related to the logging model: centralized, distributed, or semi-centralized.

Telemetry Data: Network Flows

Every network connection attempt is transported by one or more physical or virtual network devices, presenting you with an opportunity to gain vital visibility and awareness of traffic and usage patterns. All that is needed is a way to harvest this information from existing network devices such as routers, switches, virtual networking, and access points. This essentially is enabling additional visibility capabilities from common network equipment depending on how the network traffic is collected and processed. An example is looking at traffic on switches to identify malware behavior, such as a system passing a file that attempts to spread across multiple devices using uncommon ports, giving the administrator additional security threat awareness about the environment.

In many cases, capturing and transferring network packets is not required, desired, or even feasible. Reasons could include the cost for storage of the data being captured, skill sets required to use the data, or hardware costs for tools that can capture the data. This can be the case especially when multiple remote locations are connected by a wide-area network (WAN). The alternative to capturing packets is to collect contextual information about network connections in the form of network flow.

The IP Flow Information eXport (IPFIX) protocol, specified in a number of RFCs, including 7011,[6] is a standard that defines the export of unidirectional IP flow information from routers, probes, and other devices. Note that IPFIX was based on Cisco NetFlow Version 9. The standard ports that an IPFIX service listens to, as defined by IANA, are udp/4379 and tcp/4379.

A flow, according to the IPFIX standard, consists of network packets that share the same arbitrary number of packet fields within a timeframe (for example, sharing the same source IP address, destination IP address, protocol, source port, and destination port).

IPFIX enables you to define your own list of packet fields to match. In IPFIX, network flow information is exported (pushed) using two types of records: flow data and template. The template record is sent infrequently and is used to describe the structure of the data records.

Routers and high-end network switches are the most common devices that can capture, maintain, and update flow records using their cache. These devices can export a record when they believe that a flow has completed or based on fixed time intervals. Keep in mind that capturing, maintaining, and exporting network flow information could impact the system's overall performance depending on the platform being used. Best practice is working through a capacity-planning exercise and consulting with your network vendor on the impact of enabling the feature. Network device vendors generally maintain testing results per platform and are happy to share test results with their customers.

In addition to routers and switches, there is the option of using dedicated hardware appliances that can convert information collected from captured packets into network flow records that can then be exported. Similar to syslog, you can implement a distributed solution with relays that accept, replicate, and forward network flow information to various destinations such as SIEM tools and network flow analyzers. Some vendors, such as Lancope, offer sensor appliances that can add additional attributes while converting raw packets to NetFlow, such as application layer data that typically would not be included in a flow record.

Depending on your platform, a router (or any other flow-collection device) can support sampled/unsampled flow collection, as shown in Figure 2-3 and Figure 2-4, respectively. In the case of sampled flow collection, to update its flow records, the router looks at every *n*th packet (for example, 1 in every 128) rather than at every packet that traverses it. This behavior introduces probabilistic security threat detection, meaning some flows might be missed. In addition, relying on sampled flows would result in unreliable digital investigation, assuming network flows are part of your investigation artifacts. For these and other reasons, it is recommended to use only sampled flow collection if no other options are available. An analogy of comparing sampled and unsampled flow is knowing somebody has entered your house within the past few hours versus knowing a user entered your house a few minutes ago and currently is sitting in your living room. Unsampled details are much more valuable, and best practice is using the most current version if possible.

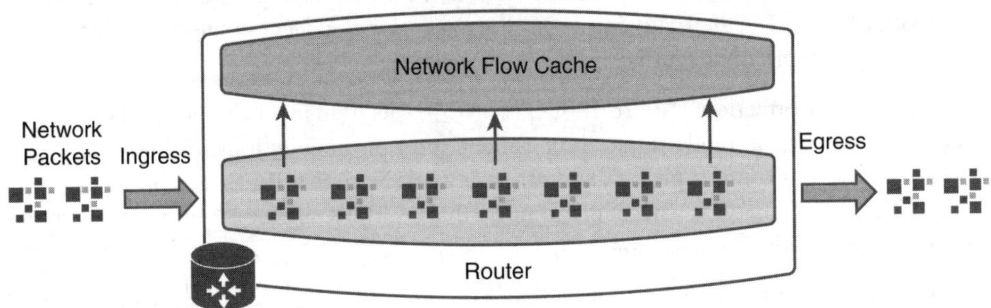

Figure 2-3 *Sampled Flow Collection*

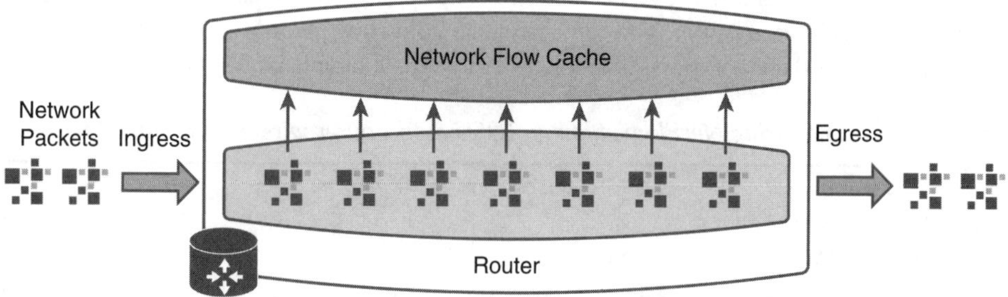

Figure 2-4 *Unsampled Flow Collection*

One major benefit of using flow-based detection for security is having "the canary in the coal mine" approach for identifying network breaches, meaning detecting unusual behavior that is not linked to an attack signature. An example is a trusted user performing network reconnaissance followed by connecting to sensitive systems that the user has never accessed before. Most common security products, such as firewalls and intrusion prevention system (IPS) technology, would probably ignore this behavior. A flow-based security product, however, could identify the user as being authorized to perform these actions but still flag the unusual behavior as an indication of compromise.

Another benefit of flow-based security is enabling the entire network as a sensor versus limiting visibility to security products. Typically, this also reduces investment cost in new products by leveraging capabilities within existing equipment. Security products may have limitations as to what they can see, because of traffic being encrypted or where they are placed on the network, thus causing security blind spots. It also might not be feasible to deploy security products at multiple remote locations. These and other scenarios are great use cases for using network flow for security analytics.

Let's look at a few examples of how to enable NetFlow on devices. Example 2-6 shows the steps to configure NetFlow v9 on a Cisco IOS-based router.

Example 2-6 *Configuring NetFlow v9 on a Cisco IOS-Based Router*

```
! Configure the NetFlow collector IP address and port
Router(config)# ip flow-export destination {ip_address | hostname} udp_port

! Configure the router to use NetFlow version 9
Router(config)# ip flow-export version 9

! Specifies the interface that to enable NetFlow on
Router(config)# interface type number

! Enables NetFlow on the interface:
! ingress: Captures traffic that is being received by the interface
! egress: Captures traffic that is being transmitted by the interface
Router(config)# ip flow {ingress | egress}
```

With IPFIX and NetFlow v9, you can do much more than what is shown in Example 2-6. On a Cisco IOS-based router, you can customize your flow records and define what to match and what data to export. Example 2-7 shows an example of this configuration.

Example 2-7 *Configuring NetFlow v9 on an IOS-Based Router with a Customized Record*

```
! Create a flow record that matches specific criteria and collect
! specific information
Router(config)# flow record MY_RECORD
Router(config-flow-record)# match ipv4 source_address
Router(config-flow-record)# match ipv4 destination address
Router(config-flow-record)# match transport source-port
Router(config-flow-record)# match transport destination-port
Router(config-flow-record)# match interface input
Router(config-flow-record)# collect counter packets
Router(config-flow-record)# collect counter bytes

! Configure your export settings
Router(config)# flow exporter MY_EXPORTER
Router(config-flow-exporter)# destination {ip_address | hostname}
Router(config-flow-exporter)# export-protocol netflow-v9
Router(config-flow-exporter)# transport udp udp_port

! Enabling flow monitor
Router(config)# flow monitor MY_MONITOR
Router(config-flow-monitor)# record record_name
Router(config-flow-monitor)# exporter exporter_name
Router(config-flow-monitor)# cache {entries number | timeout {active | inactive |
  update} seconds | type {immediate | normal | permanent}}
```

Chapter 6 delves deeper into NetFlow-based technologies. Now let's look at a different way to monitor the network using packet-capture technology.

Telemetry Data: Packet Capture

There are cases in which you need to go beyond collecting logging messages and network flow information. An example is the need for deep forensic capabilities to meeting strict regulation requirements for capturing raw network packets. Network traffic can be captured and forwarded to an intrusion detection system (IDS), a deep packet inspection engine (DPI), or simply to a repository where captured packets are stored for future use. Your choice of the packet capturing technology is influenced by the network and media type to monitor.

In the case of Ethernet, you can consider two techniques to capture network packets, each with its pros and cons:

- **Port mirroring:** This approach uses network switches to mirror traffic seen on ports or VLANs to other local or remote ports. This is a basic feature supported by most of today's enterprise-level network switches. The local Switched Port Analyzer (SPAN) configuration for Cisco switches can be used to mirror traffic locally, meaning within the same switch. The remote SPAN (RSAP and ERSPAN) configuration for Cisco switches can extend this feature by allowing remote mirroring of traffic across multiple switches if they are all configured for RSPAN. Note that based on the number of captured packets and state of your network, copying packets to a remote switch can have implications on the overall performance of the network. In addition, it is important to consider how much oversubscription you would allow when copying traffic. For example, you might not want to mirror traffic from multiple 10-Gbps interfaces on a switch to a single 1-Gbps interface. Best practice is carefully selecting the sources and destinations for port mirroring.
- **Network taps:** Another approach is connecting out-of-band devices in the form of network taps to monitor and capture packets from point-to-point links. Network taps capture and copy network packets without involving the active network components, making them suitable for most environments. Network taps, however, cannot capture some traffic, such as packets that are exchanged locally within a switch. It is also financially infeasible to connect taps to all network links. You would generally connect them to the most important locations in your network, such as your Internet gateways and data centers. Network taps are also ideal for on-demand troubleshooting.

Note Whether continuous or on demand, capturing packets is an expensive operation in terms of the amount of data to collect, transfer, analyze, and eventually store. The cost associated with capturing packets can be determined by the amount of data to acquire; the location in your network; and the network, system, and storage resources available for this purpose.

Capturing syslogs, network flows, and packets is not very useful if an administrator is manually shuffling through thousands of events. Even the most trained professionals could miss an important alert or not be able to associate events that look trivial as individual alerts but map out to a larger threat if pieced together. This is where centralized collection solutions show the most value, by parsing and normalizing data so that it can be used later for security analysis that helps administrators identify the most important events to focus on.

Parsing and Normalization

Data that requires further processing and analysis must be first parsed and normalized. *Parsing* refers to the process of taking raw input in string format and traversing the different fields based on a predefined schema, and *normalization* refers to the process of allowing similar extracted events from multiple sources to be uniformly stored or consumed by subsequence processing steps.

Let's look at an example of parsing a message generated by iptables (Linux host-based firewall) for dropped packets on a CentOS Linux host. Example 2-8 shows the original message saved to the local /etc/var/kernel.log file and the version of the same message represented in JavaScript Object Notation (JSON) format. The JSON form was created after being forwarded to and parsed by the log management platform Logstash. Notice that in this example the received syslog message is parsed, but this example does not extend parsing to extract the content of the iptables drop message. This means that in this example, we did not retrieve data such as the action, source and destination IP addresses, TCP ports, TCP headers, interface where the packet was dropped, and so on. This can be achieved by creating a parser that refers to the iptables logging message schema.

Example 2-8 *Event Generated by iptables and Processed by Logstash*

```
# Original logging message generated by iptables
DROP: IN=eth1 OUT= MAC= x:x:x:x:x:x:x:x:x:x:x:x:x:x SRC=10.x.x.28 DST=10.x.x.155
  LEN=48 TOS=0x10 PREC=0x00 TTL=55 ID=40590 DF PROTO=TCP SPT=61716 DPT=4433 WIN-
  DOW=65535 RES=0x00 SYN URGP=0


# Syslog message stored in /etc/var/kernel.log and received by the
# log collector (Logstash)
Sep 15 13:23:10 CentOS6 kernel: DROP: IN=eth1 OUT= MAC= x:x:x:x:x:x:x:x:x:x:x:x:x:x
  SRC=10.x.x.28 DST=10.x.x.155 LEN=48 TOS=0x10 PREC=0x00 TTL=55 ID=40590 DF
  PROTO=TCP SPT=61716 DPT=4433 WINDOW=65535 RES=0x00 SYN URGP=0


# The parsed syslog message, with fields shown in JSON format
{
  "_index": "logstash-2014.09.15",
  "_type": "syslog",
  "_id": "GDbzh5zJQw6VaWWO5CQAMg",
  "_score": null,
  "_source": {
    "message": "Sep 15 13:23:10 CentOS6 kernel: DROP: IN=eth1 OUT= MAC=
      x:x:x:x:x:x:x:x:x:x:x:x:x:x SRC=10.x.x.28 DST=10.x.x.155 LEN=48 TOS=0x10
      PREC=0x00 TTL=55 ID=40590 DF PROTO=TCP SPT=61716 DPT=4433 WINDOW=65535 RES=0x00
      SYN URGP=0 ",
    "@version": "1",
    "@timestamp": "2014-09-15T12:23:10.000Z",
    "type": "syslog",
    "file": "/var/log/kern.log",
    "host": "CentOS6.5",
    "offset": "1463891",
```

```
    "syslog_timestamp": "Sep 15 13:23:10",
    "syslog_hostname": "CentOS6",
    "syslog_program": "kernel",
    "syslog_message": "DROP: IN=eth1 OUT= MAC=x:x:x:x:x:x:x:x:x:x:x:x:x:x
      SRC=10.x.x.28 DST=10.x.x.155 LEN=48 TOS=0x10 PREC=0x00 TTL=55 ID=40590 DF
      PROTO=TCP SPT=61716 DPT=4433 WINDOW=65535 RES=0x00 SYN URGP=0 ",
    "received_at": "2014-09-15 12:23:06 UTC",
    "received_from": "CentOS6.5",
    "syslog_severity_code": 5,
    "syslog_facility_code": 1,
    "syslog_facility": "user-level",
    "syslog_severity": "notice"
  },
  "sort": [
    1410783790000,
    1410783790000
  ]
}
```


Parsing of messages such as event logs can make use of regular expressions also known as regex. Regex are patterns that you can use to extract information from some text input. A pattern can be expressed by a combination of alphanumeric characters and operators in a syntax that is understood by regex processors. An example is matching the string *root*, which is not case sensitive. This can be expressed using one of the regex patterns shown in Example 2-9. Both statements will match all possible lowercase and uppercase combinations of the string root (for example, rooting, -Root!-, or simply RooT).

Regex is commonly used for creating intrusion detection/prevention signatures, where you can quickly create custom regex-based signatures that match patterns of your choice. This allows you to alert and protect against attacks that try to exploit unpatched systems or alert and protect systems that could not be easily patched. An example is protecting legacy applications or devices used in process control networks.

Example 2-9 *Regex Pattern to Match the Non-Case-Sensitive String root*

```
[rR][oO][oO][tT]
OR
[rR][oO]{2}[tT]
```

Similarly, SIEM tools make use of regex. The schema or exact structure of the message must be known beforehand. SIEM tools must maintain a current schema library for all the different events they can process. In addition, the tools should allow creating custom parsers as required. Failing to property parse and normalize a message could result in being unable to analyze the data.

Many regex cheat sheets are available online, such as http://tinyurl.com/RgExCheatSheet, which you can use to reference regex commands.

Security Analysis

Security analysis refers to the process of researching data for the purpose of uncovering potential known and unknown threats. The complexity of the task varies from performing basic incident mapping to advanced mathematical modeling used to discover unknown threats. Revealing relationships between events within a context is achieved using machine learning-based techniques or knowledge-based techniques, such as rule-based matching and statistical anomaly detection.

Event correlation is the most known and used form of data analysis. *Security event correlation* refers to the task of creating a context within which revealing relationships between disparate events received from various sources for the purposes of identifying and reporting on threats. A context can be bound by time, heuristics, and asset value.

Correlation rules are packaged in SIEM tools. The vendors usually offer the option of performing regular updates to the rule sets as part of a paid support service. These rules can be tuned, or you can create your own rules; however, it is important to first know the use cases you are looking to address. Most correlation rules offered by SIEM vendors are based on experience they gain from their install bases and internal research teams, meaning that most likely they have developed rules for your business requirements. Examples of out-of-box correlation rules include flagging excessive failed logins, malware infection, unauthorized outbound connections, and DoS attempts. It is a good practice to have the SIEM vendor run through your business scenarios during a proof of concept to validate their correlation and reporting capabilities.

It is common practice to tune the out-of-the-box rules or create your own rules that meet your business requirements. Table 2-3 shows some of the use cases shipped with the Splunk SIEM application, referred to as Splunk Enterprise Security Application. Note that the thresholds are listed that you can adjust for each use case.

Table 2-3 *Splunk Enterprise Security Correlation Rules*

Correlation Search	Description	Default
Endpoint - Active Unremediated Malware Infection	Number of days that the device was unable to clean the infection	3
Endpoint - Anomalous New Services	Number of new services	9
Endpoint - Anomalous New Processes	Number of new processes	9
Endpoint - Anomalous User Account Creation	Number of new processes in a 24-hour period	3
Access - Brute-Force Access Behavior Detected	Number of failures	6
Access - Excessive Failed Logins	Number of authentication attempts	6
Endpoint - High Number of Infected Hosts	Number of infected hosts	100

Table 2-3 *continued*

Correlation Search	Description	Default
Endpoint - Host with Excessive Number of Listening Ports	Number of listening ports	20
Endpoint - Host with Excessive Number of Processes	Number of running processes	200
Endpoint - Host with Excessive Number of Services	Number of running services	100
Endpoint - Host with Multiple Infections	Total number of infections per host	> 1
Endpoint - Old Malware Infection	Number of days host had infection	30 days
Endpoint - Recurring Malware Infection	Number of days that the device was re-infected	3 days
Network - Substantial Increase in an Event	Number of events (self-baselines based on average)	3 St Dev.
Network - Substantial Increase in Port Activity (by Destination)	Number of targets (self-baselines based on average)	3 St Dev.
Network - Vulnerability Scanner Detection (by Event)	Number of unique events	25
Network - Vulnerability Scanner Detection (by Targets)	Number of unique targets	25

Correlation rules are meant to detect and report on threat scenarios, also referred to as use cases. Before you formalize a use case, you want to answer the following questions:

- What methodology should you use to come up with a use case?
- For a use case, what logging messages should you collect and from which devices?
- Can you achieve the requirements of a use case using existing security controls (for example, by using an existing intrusion detection/prevention system or a firewall)?
- How complex is the task of creating or tuning correlation rules?
- How do you associate use cases with your risk-assessment program?
- How complicated is the use case, and what impact will it have on the performance of your SIEM tool?
- Will the rule created for a use case result in an increase in false positives?

The exact use case and your choice of tools impact the complexity associated with creating or customizing correlation rules. For example, creating a rule that alerts on detecting the use of a clear-text management protocol such as Telnet could be straightforward compared to more complex rules that involve multiple sources, messages, and time periods.

Also, it is important to consider the performance impact on the SIEM as your rules grow in size and complexity along with management for customized functions.

Let's look at the example use case to create a correlation rule that triggers an alert when the same account was used to log in to more than ten data center servers, followed by one or more of these servers establishing one or more outbound TCP connections to external IP addresses within 5 minutes after the ten login attempts. The idea of using this example is to demonstrate how complex creating correlation rules can be for use cases that might sound simple. You can express this use case as a nested statement made of a combination of events (content) and operators such as **AND**, **OR**, **NOT**, and **FOLLOWED BY** (stateful context). In this use case, a context is nothing but an arbitrary set of parameters that describe a particular event of sequence of events. This nested statement to meet this use case is shown in Example 2-10.

Example 2-10 *High-Level Correlation Rule Statement*

```
[
     (More than ten successful login events)
     AND
     (Events are for the same user ID)
     AND
     (Events generated by servers tagged as data center)
     AND
     (Events received within a one-minute sliding window)
]
FOLLOWED BY
[
     (TCP connection event)
     AND
     (Source IP address belongs to the data center IP address range)
     AND
     (Destination IP address does NOT belong to the internal IP
      address range)
     AND
     (Protocol is TCP)
     AND
     (Events received within fives minutes)
]
```

After a custom statement has been created, the next step is to convert the statement to a rule following the syntax used by your SIEM tool of choice. Commercial SIEM tools provide a graphical interface for you to complete this task. An alternative is outsourcing rule creation to a third-party consultant or to the SIEM vendor's professional services. We recommend first verifying with the SIEM vendor that there is not an existing rule or rules that meet your needs before investing time and money into creating customized correlation rules.

Despite the fact that a use case might look simple, converting it to a rule might not be so easy. Even if you were to convert the previous example into a correlation rule, how about the more complicated ones? In addition, how much can you grow your rule base, and what impact on performance would it have on your tool? Let's look at some alternatives to creating correlation-based rules.

Alternatives to Rule-Based Correlation

Anomaly-based correlation is another approach that can be combined with rule-based correlation. Detecting anomalies relies on first statically profiling your environment to establish a baseline. After you have a baseline, the SIEM can identify activity patterns that deviate from the baseline, alerting on potential security incidents. Profiling an environment typically generates multiple baselines, such as the following:

- Traffic rate baseline such as average EPS and peak EPS per day of the week
- Network baseline looking at protocol and port usage per day of the week
- System baseline monitoring average and peak CPU and memory usage, average number of running services, user login attempts per day of the week

When it comes to profiling peaks, it is important to record not only the highest values reached but also the durations in which noticeable increase of usage were observed, thus adding statefulness to your profiling process. Figure 2-5 is a histogram that shows the distribution of syslog messages sent from Linux hosts in the past 24 hours. The distribution of events shows a spike in the number of events lasting for around 30 minutes. This type of event would generally trigger the interest of a security analyst. Figure 2-6 shows zooming in to this data to identify two different periods of high syslog activities corresponding to what was shown in Figure 2-5. In this specific example, the first period is short and corresponds to the installation of system patches on a number of hosts, and the second (and longer-lasting) period corresponds to a wider remote system compliance check. These might not have been malicious events; however, using anomaly detection can help administrators be more aware of changes in their environment. This proves useful for a response if users complain that the network is running slowly during the spike time periods.

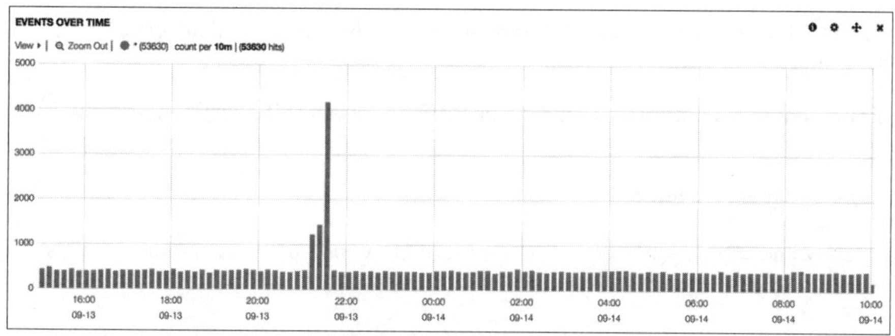

Figure 2-5 *Event Distribution Histogram Showing Two Different Peak Shapes*

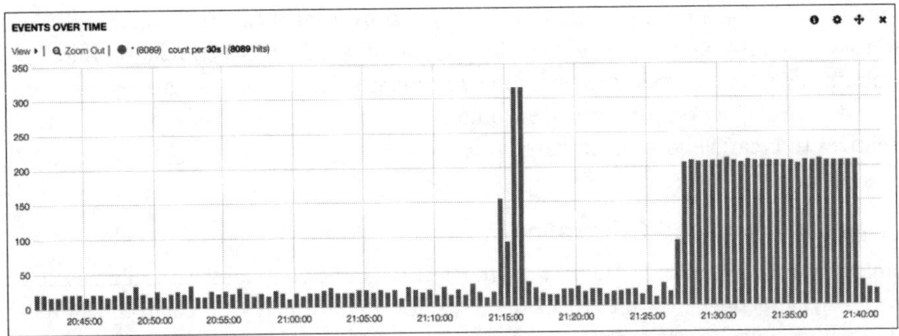

Figure 2-6 *Event Distribution Histogram Showing Two Different Peak Shapes: Zoom*

Another approach that could also be combined with rule-based correlation is risk-based correlation, also referred to as algorithmic. The basic idea is to calculate a risk score for an event based on the content and context of an event. Risk scores can be based on asset value, source IP address reputation, geolocation, reported user role (for example, a Lightweight Directory Access Protocol [LDAP] group), and so on. This approach is useful when you do not have much visibility on the use cases you require or when configuring correlation rules is complex. The challenge to this approach is the work required to design the risk formula and assigning values to input types that are being considered.

Note Risk scores do not include probability values. You learn how to calculate risk in Chapter 7, "Vulnerability Management."

There are other methods to improve network awareness beyond correlating events. Let's look at additional ways to improve data through data-enrichment sources.

Data Enrichment

Data enrichment refers to the practice of adding additional context to the data that you receive. Common examples of enrichment sources include the following:

- Geo information, allowing you to map IP addresses to geographical locations
- WHOIS information, allowing you to tap into further contextual information on IP addresses
- Reputation information on domain names, IP addresses and e-mail senders, file hash values, and so on
- Domain age information

This overlay knowledge you gain helps you make more informative decisions, increasing the accuracy of your threat-detection processes and tools.

Typically, enrichment is applied to post-parsed messages just before data is stored or processed in real time or off line. This can sometimes help security products save process power by blocking known attacks, such as sources with negative reputation, at a preprocess stage. Figure 2-7 shows a sample enrichment process. The figure also shows that enrichment information can be acquired in real time or from an existing cache.

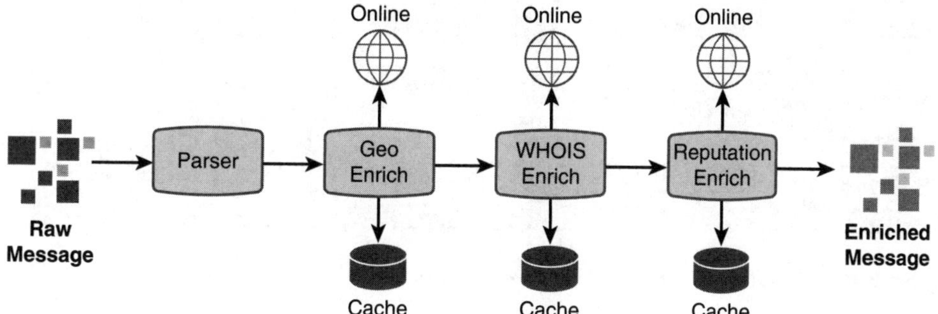

Figure 2-7 *Sample Enrichment Process*

Big Data Platforms for Security

Using relational databases to store and query data does not scale well and is becoming a huge problem for organizations as information requirements continue to increase. The solution is to use big data platforms that can accept, store, and process large amounts of data. In the context of security, big data platforms should not only be scalable in terms of storing and retrieving large amounts data but also support services offered by traditional log management and SIEM tools. This hybrid of capabilities and storage is critical for storing, processing, and analyzing big data in real time or on demand.

Most of today's big data platforms are based on Apache Hadoop. This framework allows for the distributed processing of large data sets across clusters of computers using HDFS, MapReduce, and YARN to form the core of Apache Hadoop. At the heart of the platform is the Hadoop Distributed File System (HDFS) distributed storage system. YARN is a framework for job scheduling and cluster resource management. MapReduce is a YARN-based system for parallel processing of large data sets. In addition, many Hadoop-related projects deliver services on top of Hadoop's core services.

Open source-based log management and processing tools are starting to present themselves as viable replacements to legacy the SIEM tools. This is not only the case of storage and offline processing of data but also for real-time processing using (for example, Apache Storm[7]). Figure 2-8 shows the architecture of the Cisco OpenSOC platform, which is based largely on a number of Apache projects, allowing data of various format to be collected, stored, processed (on-line and off-line), and reported.

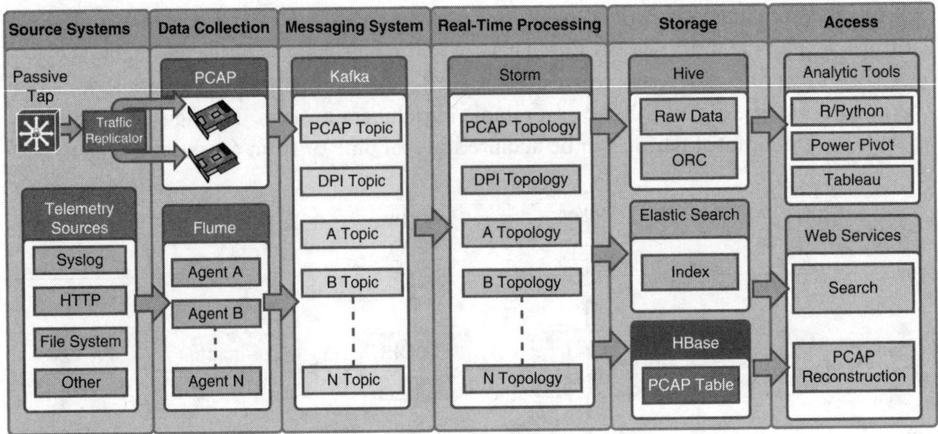

Figure 2-8 *The Cisco OpenSOC Platform Architecture*

Vulnerability Management

Vulnerability management refers to the process of discovering, confirming, classifying, prioritizing, assigning, remediating, and tracking vulnerabilities. Do not confuse vulnerability management with vulnerability scanning, the latter being part of the vulnerability management process, with emphasis on the discovery phase. It is also important to understand that risk management deals with all associated risks, whereas vulnerability management targets technology.

Vulnerabilities can be perceived as weaknesses in people, process, and technology. Vulnerability management in the context of SOC focuses on known technical weaknesses introduced in software and firmware. It is worth highlighting that the existence of a technical vulnerability could be the result of weaknesses in people and process such as the lack of a proper software quality assurance process.

Organizations with a mature security program integrate the closely linked vulnerability management and risk management practices. Sometimes this can be accomplished using tools that can automate this integration. Figure 2-9 shows the initial steps you would typically undertake to identify the scope and prepare your vulnerability management program. We will look deeper into preparing the SOC in Chapter 10.

The most critical element of vulnerability management is being faster at protecting the vulnerable asset before the weakness is exploited. This is accomplished by continuously applying a series of steps to identify, assess, and remediate the risk associated with the vulnerability. A good reference model that can be followed as a guideline for handling risk is the SANS Vulnerability Management Model shown in Figure 2-10. The details of each step are covered in Chapter 7.

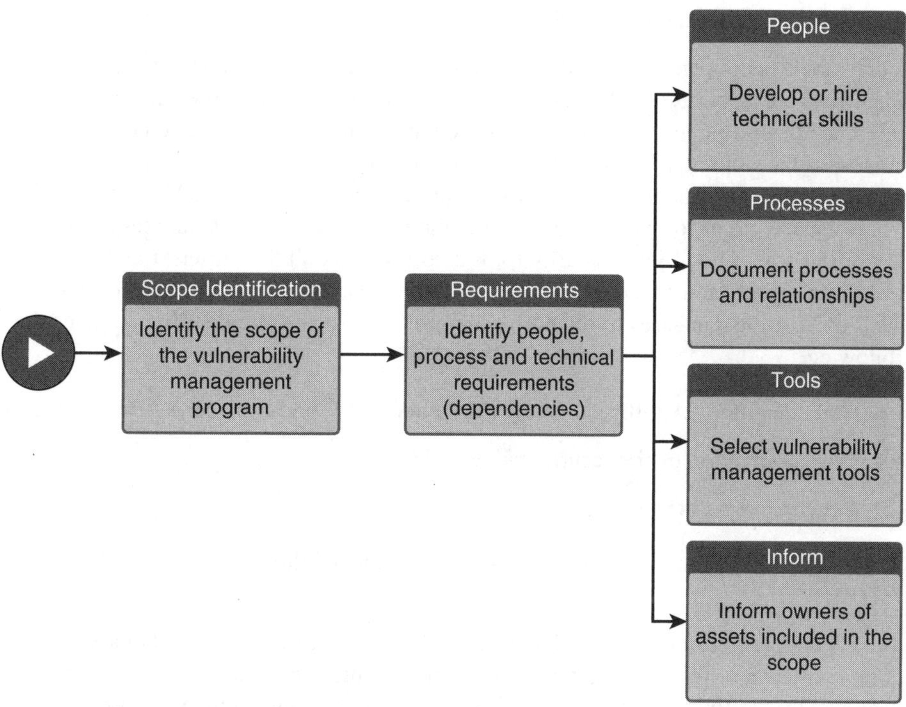

Figure 2-9 *Preparing a Vulnerability Management Program*

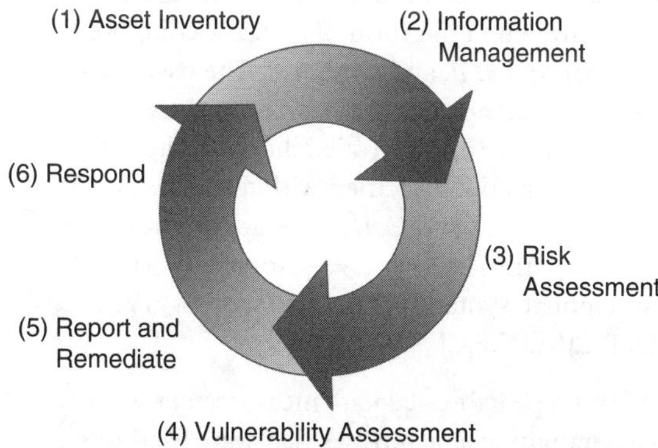

Figure 2-10 *SANS Vulnerability Management Model*

One of the most common methods to identify when a system is vulnerable is by monitoring for vulnerability announcements in products found within your organization. Let's look more into how this information is released.

Vulnerability Announcements

Vulnerabilities in open and closed source code are announced on a daily basis. Identifiers are associated with vulnerability announcements so that they can be globally referenced, ensuring interoperability. One commonly used standard to reference vulnerabilities is the Common Vulnerabilities and Exposures (CVE), which is a dictionary of publicly known information security vulnerabilities and exposures. CVE's common identifiers make it easier to share data across separate network security databases and tools. If a report from one of your security tools incorporates CVE identifiers, the administrator can quickly and accurately access and fix information in one or more separate CVE-compatible databases to remediate the problem. Each CVE identifier contains the following:

- CVE identifier (CVE-ID) number in the form of CVE prefix + Year + Arbitrary Digits
- Brief description of the security vulnerability or exposure
- Other related material

The list of products that use CVE for referencing vulnerabilities is maintained by MITRE.[8]

The CVE identifier does not provide vulnerability context such as exploitability complexity and potential impact on confidentiality, integrity, and availability. These are provided by the Vulnerability Scoring System (CVSS), maintained by NIST. According to NIST, CVSS defines a vulnerability as a bug, flaw, weakness, or exposure of an application, system device, or service that could lead to a failure of confidentiality, integrity, or availability.

The CVSS enables users to understand a standardized set of characteristics about vulnerabilities. These characteristics are conveyed in the form of a vector composed of three separate metric groups: *base*, *environmental*, and *temporal*. The base metric group is composed of six metrics: Access Vector (AV), Access Complexity (AC), Authentication (Au), Confidentiality (C), Integrity (I), and Availability (A). The base score, ranging from 0 to 10, derives from an equation specified within the CVSS. AV, AC, and Au are often referred to as exploit metrics, and C, I, and A are referred to as impact metrics. Figure 2-11 shows the base metrics used in CVSS (source: NIST CVSS Implementation Guidance). The vector template syntax for the base score is **AV**:[L,A,N]/**AC**:[H,M,L]/**Au**:[M,S,N]/**C**:[N,P,C]/**I**:[N,P,C]/**A**:[N,P,C].

CVSS is a quantitative model that ensures a repeatable accurate measurement while enabling users to see the underlying vulnerability characteristics that were used to generate the scores. Thus, CVSS is well suited as a standard measurement system for industries, organizations, and governments that need accurate and consistent vulnerability impact scores. Example 2-11 shows the information included in the vulnerability announcement labeled CVE-2014-4111 including the CVSS score of (AV:N/AC:M/Au:N/C:C/I:C/A:C).

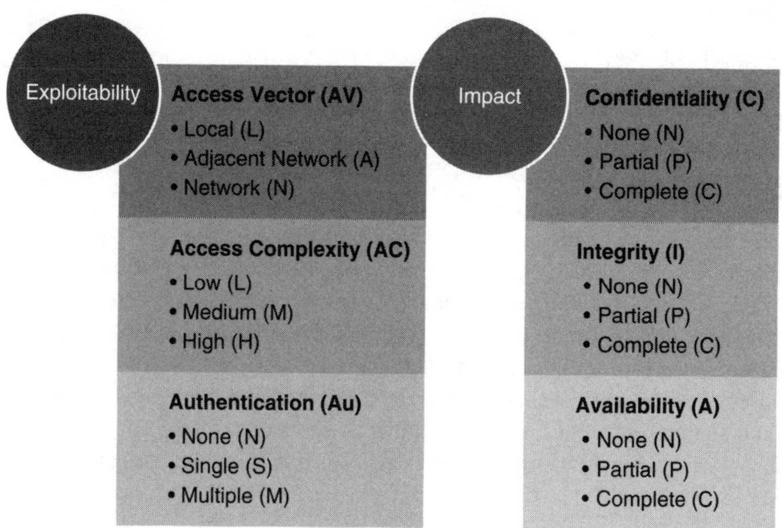

Figure 2-11 *CVSS Base Metrics (Source: NIST CVSS Implementation Guidance)*

Example 2-11 *Vulnerability Announcement CVE-2014-4111*

```
Original release date: 09/09/2014
Last revised: 09/10/2014
Source: US-CERT/NIST

Overview
  Microsoft Internet Explorer 6 through 11 allows remote attackers to execute
  arbitrary code or cause a denial of service (memory corruption) via a crafted
  web site, aka "Internet Explorer Memory Corruption Vulnerability."

Impact
CVSS Severity (version 2.0):
CVSS v2 Base Score: 9.3 (HIGH) (AV:N/AC:M/Au:N/C:C/I:C/A:C)
Impact Subscore: 10.0
Exploitability Subscore: 8.6

CVSS Version 2 Metrics:
Access Vector: Network exploitable; Victim must voluntarily interact with attack
  mechanism
Access Complexity: Medium
Authentication: Not required to exploit
Impact Type: Allows unauthorized disclosure of information; Allows unauthorized
  modification; Allows disruption of service
External Source: MS
```

```
Name: MS14-052
Type: Advisory; Patch Information
Hyperlink: http://technet.microsoft.com/security/bulletin/MS14-052
```

Threat Intelligence

The market's understanding of threat intelligence is evolving. According to Gartner, "Threat intelligence is evidence-based knowledge, including context, mechanisms, indicators, implications and actionable advice, about an existing or emerging menace or hazard to assets that you can use to inform decisions regarding the subject's response to that menace or hazard." Forrester defines threat intelligence as "details of the motivations, intent, and capabilities of internal and external threat actors. Threat intelligence includes specifics on the tactics, techniques, and procedures of these adversaries. Threat intelligence's primary purpose is to inform business decisions regarding the risks and implications associated with threats."

Converting these definitions into common language could translate to threat intelligence being evidence-based knowledge of the capabilities of internal and external threat actors. How can this type of data benefit the SOC? The idea is extending security awareness beyond the internal network by consuming intelligence from other sources Internet-wide related to possible threats to your organization. For example, you might hear about a threat that has impacted multiple organizations, and so you can proactively prepare rather than react once the threat is seen against your network. Do not confuse threat intelligence with enrichment data discussed earlier in this chapter. Providing an enrichment data feed is one service that threat intelligence platforms would typically provide.

Forrester defines a five-step threat intelligence cycle, shown in Figure 2-12, for evaluating threat intelligence sources: planning and direction, collection, processing, analysis, and production and dissemination.

In many cases, you will be the consumer for one or more intelligence feeds. A number of threat intelligence platforms that you might want to consider include the following:

- **Cyber Squad ThreatConnect:**[9] An on-premises, private, or public cloud solution offering threat data collection, analysis, collaboration, and expertise in a single platform. Learn more at http://www.threatconnect.com/.
- **BAE Detica CyberReveal:** A multithreat monitoring, analytics, investigation, and response product. CyberReveal brings together BAE Systems Detica's heritage in network intelligence, big data analytics, and cyberthreat research. CyberReveal consist of three core components: platform, analytics, and investigator. Learn more at http://www.baesystems.com/.
- **Lockheed Martin Palisade:** Supports comprehensive threat collection, analysis, collaboration, and expertise in a single platform. Learn more at http://www.lockheedmartin.com/.
- **MITRE CRITs:** Collaborative Research Into Threats (CRITs) is an open source feed for threat data. Learn more at https://crits.github.io/.

Figure 2-12 *Threat Intelligence Cycle According to Forrester*

In addition, a number of standards of schemas are being developed for disseminating threat intelligence information, including the following:

- **Structured Threat Information eXpression (STIX):** An express language designed for sharing of cyberattack information. STIX details can contain data such as the IP address of command-and-control servers (CnC), malware hashes, and so on. Learn more at http://stix.mitre.org/.
- **Open Indicators Of Compromise (OpenIOC):** Open framework for sharing threat intelligence in a machine-digestible format. Learn more at http://www.openioc.org/.
- **Cyber Observable eXpression (CybOX):** A free standardized schema for specification, capture, characterization, and communication of events of stateful properties that are observable in the operational domain. Learn more at https://cybox.mitre.org/.

Transport mechanisms, such as Trusted Automated eXchange of Indicator Information (TAXII), are used to exchange cyberthreat information represented by the previously discussed schemas.

You should define what threat intelligence is best for your security operation. Evaluation criteria could include the benefits it brings, do you plan to consume it, and how threat intelligence will integrate with your SOC technologies and processes, including the automation of this integration. Also, it is important to note that there are many open source and non-security-focused sources that can be leveraged for threat intelligence as well. Some examples are social media sources, forums, blogs, vendor websites, and so on.

Compliance

Monitoring the compliance of your systems against reference configuration templates or standard system builds gives you an opportunity to detect changes and existing configuration problems that could lead to a possible breach. Sometimes, these issues cannot be seen by common security tools such as vulnerability scanners unless the configuration problem is exploited, which is not the best time to identify the problem. There are also cases in which you might have a policy that forces you to follow some good security practices, such as continuously evaluating against benchmarks set by the Center of Internet Security (CIS) or meeting PCI DSS 2.0.

Many of today's vulnerability scanning tools, such as Qualys, Nessus, and Nexpose, include a compliance module that enables them to remotely log in to a system, collect its configuration, and then analyze that against a reference benchmark. You can also develop your own programs or scripts that can perform the same function.

Automating the system compliance process and then linking it to your risk management and incident response practices are key steps in any successful security operation. An example of including this in your practice is incorporating system compliance as part of the risk assessment and vulnerability assessment steps of the SANS Vulnerability Management Model shown earlier in Figure 2-10.

Ticketing and Case Management

The SOC team is expected to track potential incidents reported by tools or people. A case must be created, assigned, and tracked until closure to ensure that the incident is properly managed. This activity should be backed up by both, having the right tools, authority, and integration with incident response and case management processes.

SIEM, vulnerability management, and other SOC tools should either support built-in local case management or preferably integrate with your existing IT ticketing system such as BMC Remedy or CA Service Desk Manager, for central management and reporting of trouble tickets. You should work with the help desk team to create new ticket categories with meaningful and relevant security incident ticket fields and attributers.

A key point to consider is that remediation for some events may require resources outside the SOC analysts for business or other technical support. This is why assigning responsibilities that are sponsored by the proper authority is critical for the success of case management. The Responsibility, Accountable, Consulted, and Informed (RACI) matrix can be used as a model for identifying roles and responsibilities during an organization change process. Table 2-4 represents an example RACI chart, where R = Responsible, A = Accountable, C = Consult, and I = Inform.

Table 2-4 *RACI Matrix Example*

Function	Project Sponsor	Business Analyst	Project Manager	Software Developer
Initiate project	C		AR	
Establish project plan	I	C	AR	C
Gather user requirements	I	R	A	I
Develop technical requirements	I	R	A	I
Develop software tools	I	C	A	R
Test software	I	R	A	C
Deploy software	C	R	A	C

Typical steps to build a RACI matrix are as follows:

Step 1. Identify all the processes or activities known as functions on the left side of the matrix.

Step 2. List all the roles at the top of the matrix.

Step 3. Create values to reference, such as AR, C, I, and R, that will be assigned.

Step 4. Verify every process has an R and that there is only one R to avoid conflicts. If there must be more than one R, break up the function until there is only one R per function.

When multiple teams are involved, such as what could end up on your RACI matrix, collaboration between teams becomes mission critical. Let's look at how the SOC can leverage collaboration technologies.

Collaboration

The SOC should be equipped with a collaboration platform that allows the SOC team to centrally store, manage, and access documents, including system manuals, documented processes, incident response procedures, and so on. The platform can be based on commercial products such as Microsoft SharePoint, or can be a customized web-based platform that is developed to fit your exact needs. The platform should support role-based access control (RBAC) so that you can facilitate for various user-access requirements.

Communication is also important within the SOC and with external resources. Most likely, these tools already exist within the organization, such as e-mail, internal websites, conference products, and mailing lists that can be customized for specific purposes such as bringing together a tiger team when a high-priority incident is seen. An example is the Cisco Emergency Responder 9.0 architecture made up of voice, video, and web collaboration products and customized for incident response situations.

SOC Conceptual Architecture

To get the best out of your investment, you should operate the various SOC technologies under a cohesive architecture. The architecture should formalize the operation model of SOC in terms of components and relationships.

We propose a reference conceptual architecture in Figure 2-13. The proposed reference architecture formalizes the following:

- The input to the SOC in terms of categorized sources
- The output of the SOC in terms of alerts and actions
- The SOC's technologies
- The relationship between the technologies
- The areas where measurements can be collected in terms of type, value, and frequency

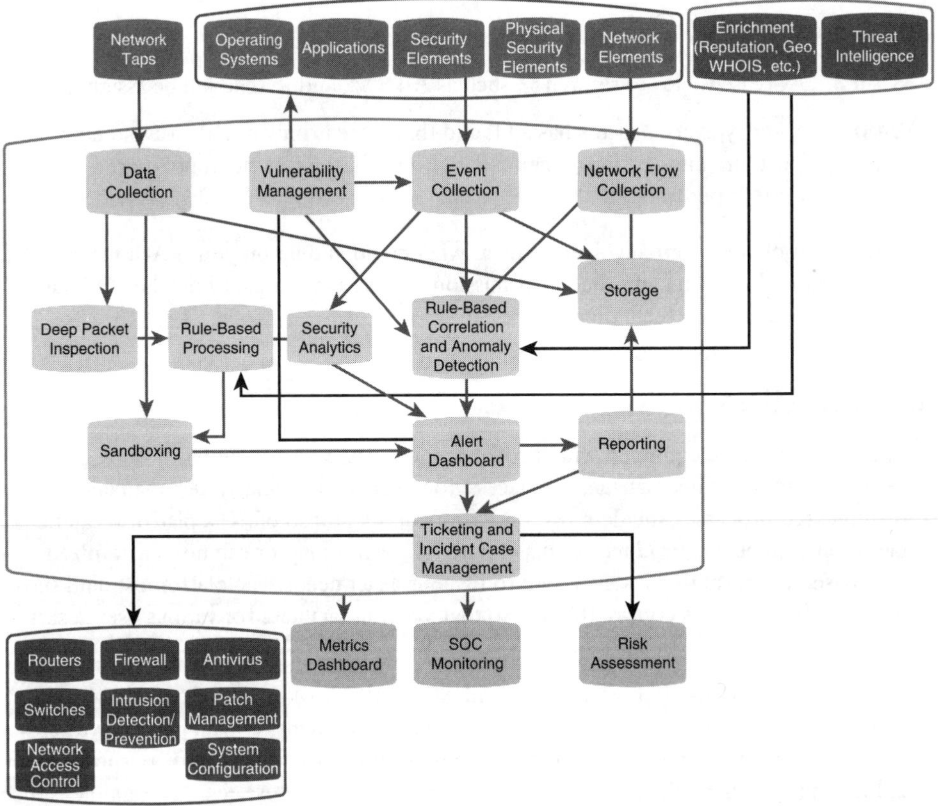

Figure 2-13 *SOC's Conceptual Architecture*

We will refer to this architecture and detail its different blocks in various chapters of this book. One other architecture to consider is looking at how SOC responsibilities could be outsourced to a managed service provider. Figure 2-14 represents the Cisco architecture for managed threat defense services targeting customers looking to outsource some or all of their SOC responsibilities.

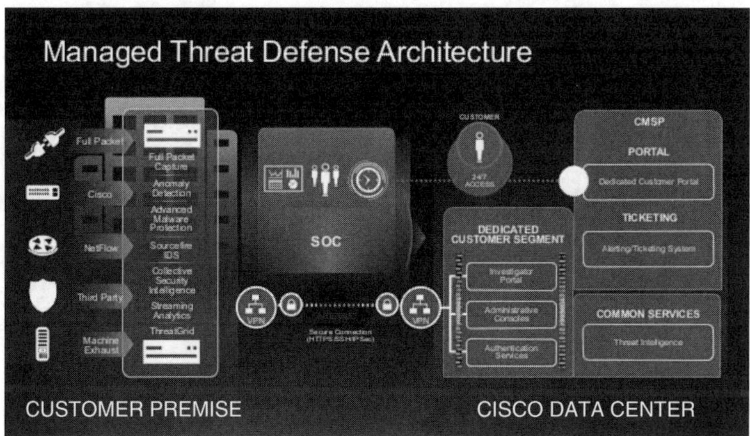

Figure 2-14 *Cisco Managed Threat Defense Architecture*

Summary

This chapter focused on the technology and services associated with most modern SOC environments. The chapter provided an overview of best practices for data collection that covered different data sources, such as syslogs, network telemetry, and packet capturing. The chapter then reviewed how data is processed so that it can be used for security analysis. We included different techniques that can also complement captured data, such as using data enrichment. The next topic covered was vulnerability management, following steps from the SANS Vulnerability Management Model. The chapter concluded with some operation recommendations, such as how to handle case management and collaboration between teams.

Now that you have a good idea about the technologies and services found in a SOC, it is time to look at how these can work together. Next up is Chapter 3, "Assessing Security Operations Capabilities," which focuses on assessing SOC operational capabilities.

References

1. The syslog protocol, http://tools.ietf.org/html/rfc5424
2. Reliable delivery for syslog, https://www.ietf.org/rfc/rfc3195.txt
3. Graylog2, http://www.graylog2.org

4. Logstash, http://www.logstash.net
5. Elasticsearch ELK, http://www.elasticsearch.org/overview
6. Specification of the IP Flow Information Export (IPFIX) Protocol for the Exchange of Flow Information, http://tools.ietf.org/html/rfc7011
7. Apache Storm, https://storm.incubator.apache.org
8. CVE-IDs - Products & Services by Product Category, https://cve.mitre.org/compatible/product_type.html
9. ThreatConnect, http://www.threatconnect.com

Chapter 3

Assessing Security Operations Capabilities

"Give me six hours to chop down a tree and I will spend the first four sharpening the axe."—Abraham Lincoln

Establishing security operations center (SOC) capabilities requires careful planning. The planning phase helps you decide on and formalize the objectives that justify having a SOC, and to develop a roadmap that you can use to track your progress against those predefined objectives. Before you can do any planning, the existing SOC or anything that will be used for the SOC must first be assessed to understand the current capabilities for people, processes, and technology. You can compare this existing environment baseline against the objectives for the desired SOC to establish the level of effort required to meet those future objectives.

This chapter describes a methodology for determining your SOC requirements and assessing your security operations capabilities against these requirements. The output of the assessment exercise helps you define your SOC strategy and formulate a supporting roadmap.

Assessment Methodology

A *capabilities assessment* is the first step to understanding how to develop a new or enhance an existing SOC operation. Findings from this assessment are used as the foundation that other chapters build upon, regardless if you are developing a new or modifying an existing SOC. The methodology of assessing the SOC requirements and capabilities should be relevant, documented, referenced, repeatable, monitored, and continuously improved, following the maturity models discussed in Chapter 1, "Introduction to Security Operations and the SOC." It is important to treat this as a continuous program so that the SOC can adapt to changes in business, technology, and threats.

The assessment methodology, shown in Figure 3-1, includes the following steps:

Step 1. Identify the SOC business and IT goals.

Step 2. Identify the capabilities that are to be assessed based on the SOC goals.

Step 3. Collect information related to people, processes, and technology capabilities.

Step 4. Analyze the collected information and assign maturity levels to the assessed capabilities.

Step 5. Present, discuss, and formalize the findings.

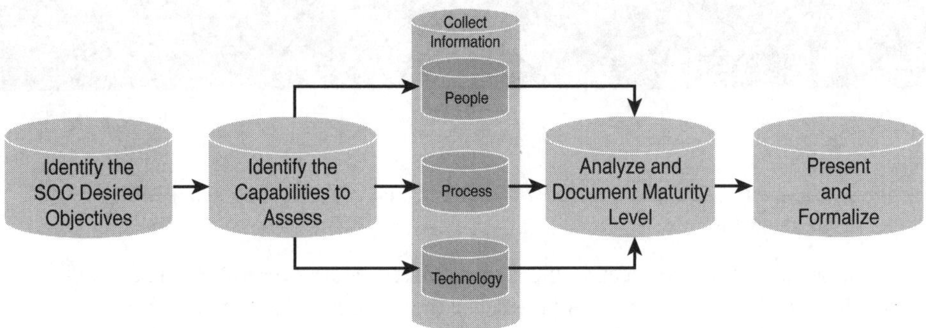

Figure 3-1 *Assessment Methodology*

The basic idea is to follow a process in which you collect, document, verify, and update information with the goal of providing a deliverable used to understand the current state of the SOC. The SOC assessment methodology considers activities to undertake and areas to assess without neglecting the importance of using tools that can automate the tasks of collecting, storing, and tracking information. The first two steps of the assessment methodology aim to understand what is important to the business. This is required before an auditor can gather information relevant to the organization. Step 3 starts the general collection of information that will be used along with the information from the previous steps to be analyzed for rating maturity levels of the SOC processes. The final step is reporting the results of the assessment, which is then used as the foundation for future SOC developments.

Many steps involve collecting information, which can be achieved through interviews, requesting documents, or simply observing how activities are being carried out. The collected information can have various representations that are associated with a reliability level. It is important that you separate personal opinions from facts by requesting supporting evidence, whenever applicable. You should also validate and crosscheck the information you receive from the various sources. Answers to some of the assessment questions might not be readily available, requiring you in some cases to facilitate discussions between team members to reach concessions. A general best practice is to collect as much data as possible to help validate results that end up in the final report.

First, you must focus on understanding the goals of the organization. This is accomplished by identifying the business and IT goals.

Step 1: Identify Business and IT Goals

Chapter 1 introduced the Control Objectives for Information and related Technology (COBIT)[1] Maturity Model (MM), which uses a scoring system to assess how maturely a specific IT process is handled by the SOC. The purpose of calculating a maturity level is to understand how well the SOC is performing. Before you can dive into the calculations for a SOC's maturity level, you first must identify the business goals for the organization. This is the foundation against which everything will be rated, so a maturity level can be justified. For example, a SOC could have very talented penetration testers, but if that skill set does not align with the business strategy, those skills might not have much value to the organization or could possibly even take away from another important responsibility that is being neglected.

Many organizations might not be able to clearly identify their business goals for technology. It is best to first identify the internal stakeholders who have the authority to represent the organization. Stakeholders might include any of the following titles:

Board	Human resource (HR) managers
Business executives	Internal audit
Business managers	IT managers
Business process owners	IT users
Chief executive officer (CEO)	Privacy officers
	Risk managers
Chief information officer (CIO)	Security managers
Chief risk officer (CRO)	Service managers

It is important to gather feedback from different ranks and departments of the organization to capture how the organization sees the business goals of IT. An assessment might show that a different message is being executed than delivered by leadership of the organization. Many questions can be asked to identify the business goals, and some questions might or might not be appropriate for the person being interviewed. The following list of questions shows examples of what can be used when interviewing leadership-level staff within an organization.

Stakeholder Questions

- How do I get value from the use of IT? Are end users satisfied with the quality of the IT service?
- How do I manage performance of IT?
- How can I best exploit new technology for new strategic opportunities?
- What are the (control) requirements for information in the organization?
- How am I addressing all IT-related risk?

- Am I running an efficient and resilient IT operation?
- How do I use IT resources in the most effective and efficient manner?
- Do I have enough people for IT? How do I develop and maintain their skills, and how do I manage their performance?
- Is the information I am processing well secured?
- How do I improve business agility through a more flexible IT environment?
- How critical is IT to sustaining the enterprise? What do I do if IT is not available?
- What critical business processes depend on IT, and what are the requirements of business processes?
- What has been the average overrun of the IT operations budgets? How often and how much do IT projects go over budget?
- How much of the IT effort goes to fighting fires rather than to enabling business improvements?
- How long does it take to make major IT decisions?
- Are the total IT effort and investments transparent?
- Does IT support the enterprise in complying with regulation-s and service levels? How do I know whether I am compliant with all applicable regulations?

The answers to many of these questions might not be technical; however, they involve people, processes, or technology for the business goal to be successful. The requirements to achieve a business goal translate to IT goals. This means that IT goals are actions that need to be accomplished to meet a business goal, and thus creating a SOC helps the business be successful. So, to understand how to accomplish business goals, you must break them down into IT goals. Table 3-1 shows a list of IT goals suggested by COBIT-5. Notice that the left side represents the IT business function.

Table 3-1 *COBIT IT Goals Example*

	Information Technology Goal
Financial	IT compliance and support for business compliance with external laws and regulations
	Manage IT-related business risk
	Transparency of IT costs, benefits, and risk
	Realized benefits from IT-enabled investments and services portfolio
	Commitment of executive management for making IT-related decisions
Customer	Delivery of IT services in line with business requirements
	Adequate use of applications, information, and technology solutions

Table 3-1 *continued*

	Information Technology Goal
Internal	IT agility
	Security of information, processing infrastructure, and applications
	Optimization of IT assets, resources, and capabilities
	Enablement and support of business processes by integrating applications and technology into business processes
	Availability of reliable and useful information for decision making
	IT compliance with internal policies
Learning and growth	Competent and motivated business and IT personnel
	Knowledge, expertise, and initiatives for business innovation

In many cases, multiple IT goals will make up one business goal. For example, a business goal of being Payment Card Industry Data Security Standard (PCI DSS) compliant may translate to various IT goals such as network segmentation, monitoring of sensitive systems, data-loss protection strategies, and so forth. The key thing to keep in mind is that all IT goals must align with a business goal so that they can be mapped to a strategy sponsored by leadership.

After all the business goals have been mapped to IT goals and have been assigned responsibility, you are ready to start breaking down IT goals into individual processes that can be evaluated for success rate. This is accomplished by assessing IT capabilities.

Step 2: Assessing Capabilities

Once the business and IT goals have been identified, the next step is to evaluate the IT processes involved with each IT goal. Just like business goals, IT goals are typically made up of multiple IT processes. For example, the previous example of the IT goal of having data-loss protection (DLP) requires specific products and people to make this happen. One IT process might be managing an RSA DLP technology, while another IT process is enabling DLP on a Cisco Email Security Appliance (ESA). Both of these IT processes are part of maintaining the IT goal of DLP, accomplished by protecting the network with RSA DLP technology and Cisco ESA DLP technology. This might seem confusing, but it is important to understand that IT processes can be evaluated for a maturity level. The average of all IT processes can be used to demonstrate the effectiveness of the IT goal. Figure 3-2 shows how *business goals*, *IT goals*, and *IT processes* are aligned with regard to how each impacts the result of the subcategory.

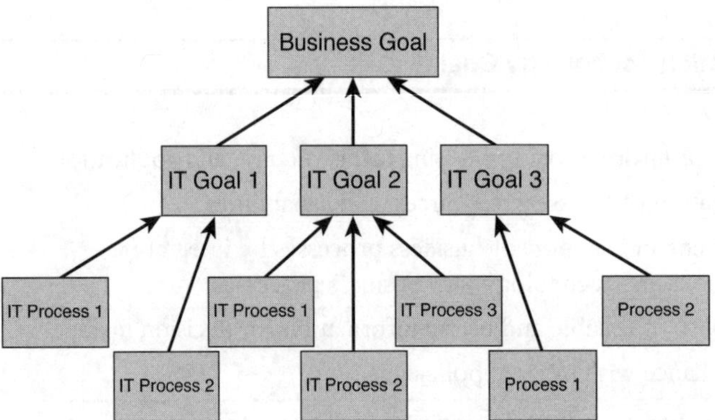

Figure 3-2 *Dependencies Between Business Goals, IT Goals, and IT Processes*

An IT process can be made up of specific requirements for people, processes, and technology. These elements should work in harmony to meet the IT processes aligned with an IT goal. For example, meeting the IT goal of DLP may be the responsibility of the server and network administrators monitoring data center traffic with a specific DLP product. Each task needs a process and to be mapped to an IT goal. So for this example, one IT process can be knowledge of the technology, and another could be maintenance of the Cisco ESA solution licensed for DLP. Both of these IT processes can be mapped to the IT goal of DLP for e-mail. The key is that these IT processes can be evaluated by an auditor for maturity, such as identifying a weakness in the person's skills who is responsible for the e-mail DLP product even though the technology is cutting-edge (resulting in the IT goal not properly monitoring data loss). By rating maturity levels of IT processes, you can quantify IT process effectiveness, which in this example means more training is required to improve the IT process of e-mail DLP. Calculating maturity levels for IT processes is handled during Step 4.

There are ways to validate alignment between dependencies to ensure that all aspects of the goal are covered. One method suggested by COBIT-5 is to place two dependencies on a graph, with one representing the X side and the other the Y side and with the level of responsibility as the values. The purpose is to identify that all goals have some form of primary and secondary reasonability assignment. Gaps in this type of report represent tasks that are not mapped back to a specific goal with proper sponsorship, meaning that they are either overlooked or not a requirement for the organization. Figure 3-3 shows a COBIT example of aligning IT processes with IT goals. Notice that *P* represents a primary responsibility and that *S* represents a secondary responsibility.

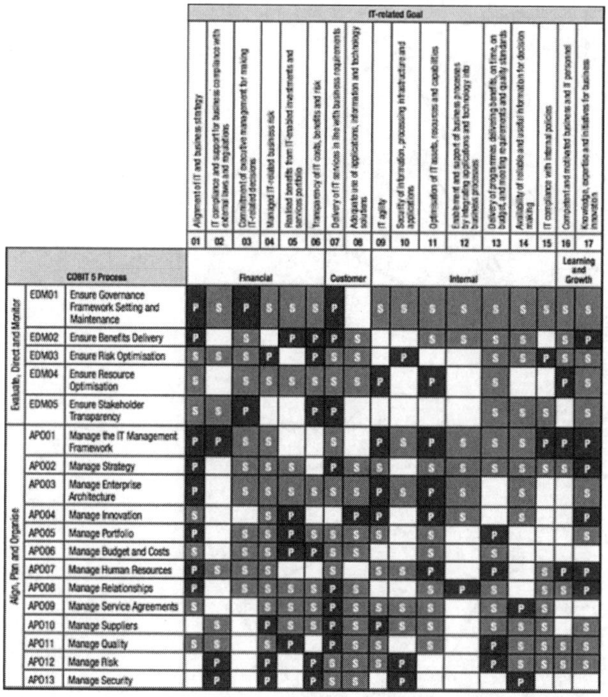

			IT-related Goal																
			Alignment of IT and business strategy	IT compliance and support for business compliance with external laws and regulations	Commitment of executive management for making IT-related decisions	Managed IT-related business risk	Realised benefits from IT-enabled investments and services portfolio	Transparency of IT costs, benefits and risk	Delivery of IT services in line with business requirements	Adequate use of applications, information and technology solutions	IT agility	Security of information, processing infrastructure and applications	Optimisation of IT assets, resources and capabilities	Enablement and support of business processes by integrating applications and technology into business processes	Delivery of programmes delivering benefits, on time, on budget, and meeting requirements and quality standards	Availability of reliable and useful information for decision making	IT compliance with internal policies	Competent and motivated business and IT personnel	Knowledge, expertise and initiatives for business innovation
			01	02	03	04	05	06	07	08	09	10	11	12	13	14	15	16	17
COBIT 5 Process			Financial						Customer		Internal							Learning and Growth	
Evaluate, Direct and Monitor	EDM01	Ensure Governance Framework Setting and Maintenance	P	S	P	S	S	S	P		S	S	S	S	S	S	S	S	S
	EDM02	Ensure Benefits Delivery	P		S		P	P	P	S			S	S	S	S		S	P
	EDM03	Ensure Risk Optimisation	S	S	S	P		P	S	S		P			S	S	P	S	S
	EDM04	Ensure Resource Optimisation	S		S	S	S	S	S	S	P		P		S			P	S
	EDM05	Ensure Stakeholder Transparency	S	S	P			P	P						S	S	S		S
Align, Plan and Organise	APO01	Manage the IT Management Framework	P	P	S	S			S		P	S	P	S	S	S	P	P	P
	APO02	Manage Strategy	P		S	S	S		P	S	S		S	S	S	S	S	S	P
	APO03	Manage Enterprise Architecture	P		S	S	S	S	S	S	P	S	P	S		S			S
	APO04	Manage Innovation	S			S	P			P	P		P	S		S			P
	APO05	Manage Portfolio	P		S	S	P	S	S	S	S		S		P				S
	APO06	Manage Budget and Costs	S		S	S	P	P	S	S			S		S				
	APO07	Manage Human Resources	P	S	S	S			S		S	S	P		P		S	P	P
	APO08	Manage Relationships	P		S	S	S	S	P	S			S	P	S		S	S	P
	APO09	Manage Service Agreements	S			S	S	S	P	S	S	S	S		S	P	S		
	APO10	Manage Suppliers		S		P	S	S	P	S	P	S	S		S	S	S		S
	APO11	Manage Quality	S	S		S	P		P	S	S		S		P	S	S	S	S
	APO12	Manage Risk		P		P		P	S	S	S	P			P	S	S	S	S
	APO13	Manage Security		P		P		P	S	S		P				P			

Figure 3-3 *COBIT Example of Process and IT Goal Alignment*

Assessing IT Processes

You should consider capabilities that are relevant to the SOC's model of operation in addition to the SOC services. Gaps in the SOC capabilities could mean requirements for training, recruiting new talent, or obtaining technology.

Creating a list of capabilities to evaluate a SOC against is difficult because every organization will have different technologies and differently skilled people. Figure 3-4 provides a general diagram of the different SOC capabilities you would typically evaluate; these are common in most SOC environments. The format of this approach breaks up capabilities into *people*, *processes*, and *technology* categories. The ideal situation is to have all the capabilities achieve desirable levels of maturity for that particular IT process (that is, meet maturity levels of 4 or 5 so that the average of all IT processes indicates that an IT goal is meeting or exceeding its intended effectiveness).

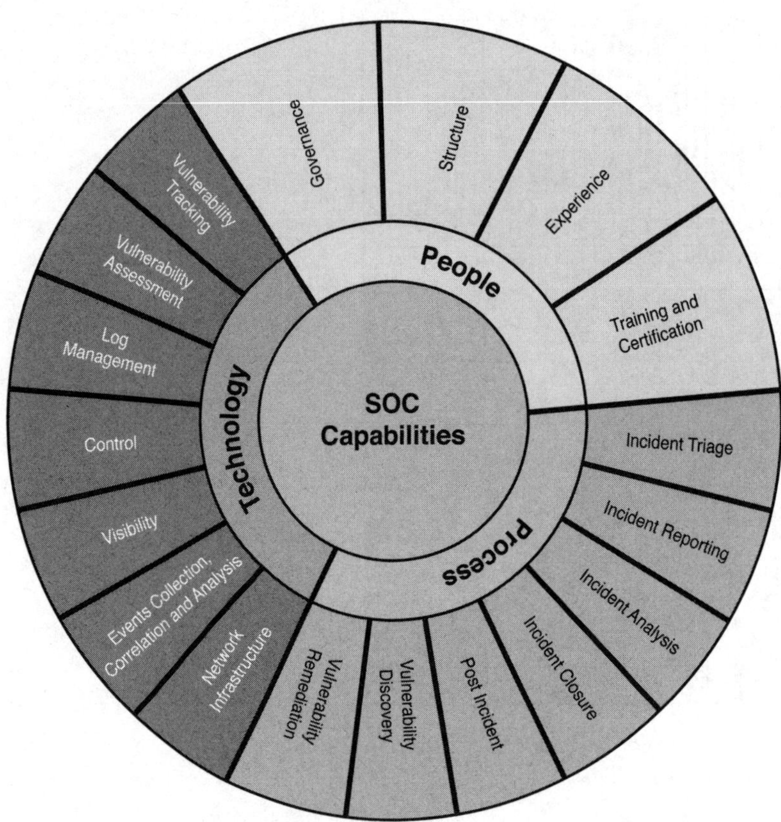

Figure 3-4 *SOC Capabilities to Evaluate*

The next section describes the various capabilities that you could use, following Figure 3-4, to evaluate an organization. For a real assessment use case, adjust this list to meet the IT goals established in Step 1 of the assessment process. Doing so ensures that your results map back to the business goals and therefore have the proper sponsorship. The results of these questions should provide a general feel for the maturity level of each capability. For example, a person's skill set could be documented as "has little experience," or if someone is properly trained, it could be "well versed" in some technology. We translate these generic findings into a quantifiable report at this end of the assessment.

Let's start with questions for the people category.

People

People are the core of any successful SOC. When evaluating people-related capabilities, you should consider areas that pertain to governance, structure, experience, and training and certifications. Here are some areas to consider when questioning people with regard to IT process capabilities.

Governance It is important to understand how the SOC is managed. It is also important to understand how the organization views and manages the SOC. Here are some governance assessment examples:

- Assess senior management's awareness level of the importance of the SOC.
- Evaluate the involvement and investment of senior management in supporting security operations projects and activities.
- Identify existing reporting capabilities with regard to meeting audits and identifying the current state of security.
- Document how management handles incident escalation with regard to classification and remediation.

Structure It is important to know how the organization is structured so that you can identify those who have the proper authority to answer your questions (and so that you can understand responsibilities for different tasks). Here are some structure assessment examples:

- Gain an understanding of the overall organizational structure and assess the reporting model, focusing on the department or unit that the SOC would operate within.
- Is the organizational structure formalized and documented? Is there a unit or a team that is tasked with security operations and monitoring security events?
- Are there cases of conflict of interest, in which, for example, the same individual might request, approve, and make changes to security-related tasks?
- Understand the relationships between the different roles and departments that are involved in security operations:
  - Examples of roles that you typically research include risk manager, security analyst, security investigator, and network security specialist.
  - Assess whether there are formal processes for exchanging security information between the departments.

SOC Experience Organizations typically have resources, whether in-house or outsourced, that can design and manage system and network security controls. Although these are valuable resources that you want to take advantage of in your SOC program, there are other critical and specialized areas of SOC experience that you should evaluate, including the following:

- Incident handling
- Digital investigation
- Vulnerability assessment
- Log management

- Working with security information and event management (SIEM) tools
- Threat intelligence
- Big data technologies
- People management
- Data analytics

Other aspects of SOC experience that should be assessed include the ability to work under pressure, especially during major security incidents, and skill sets. Most job roles have specific skill requirements; for example, people responsible for digital investigations should have forensic experience and knowledge of tools like EnCase. A quick search of the Internet will yield descriptions of common job roles, to give you an idea about what skills and technology are typically required.

Training and Certification Understanding training practices is important to identify how the SOC is adapting to changes and meeting employee job satisfaction needs. Many people want to have an opportunity to grow within their practice, and that typically requires training and obtaining certifications to validate new accomplishments. Here are some ways to look for this information:

- Collect information about relevant training courses that individuals have attended and certifications they have obtained.
- Assess whether there are processes that identify training courses required for information security operations. In many cases, you will find out that acquiring new knowledge relies on individual efforts rather than on a well thought-out training plan.
- Identify any regulations found within IT goals that require people to hold specific certifications. Assess whether certification for these requirements has been met.
- Align technologies from IT goals with training and certifications achieved or in process.

Processes

Processes are the enablers between people and technology. The security operations processes that you want to assess relate to how security incidents and vulnerabilities are handled. Understanding and documenting the current state of SOC processes is important to the development of a suitable and realistic SOC roadmap. SOC processes can be categorized into incident triage, incident reporting, incident analysis, incident closure, post-incident activities, vulnerability discovery, and vulnerability remediation and tracking. Here are some general discovery areas to consider when gathering information for these processes. Many of these processes are covered in more detail in Chapter 7, "Vulnerability Management."

Incident Triage

- Assess whether there is a computer security incident response plan that formalizes the triage process.
- Assess whether there are official channels and formats for reporting security incidents. Do the members of the organization know these channels?
- Assess whether there are processes to classify and prioritize incidents.
- Assess whether there are internal or external service level agreements (SLA) that the organization must meet.

Incident Reporting

- Assess whether there are processes to identify what reports are needed, the frequency of the reports, the structure of the reports, and who must be kept informed during the life of an incident.
- Assess automation from tools versus requirements for specific people during the incident reporting process.
- Assess incident reporting capabilities during business hours and after-hours.

Incident Analysis

- Assess whether there are processes to analyze security incidents mapped to the classification of the incidents.
- Assess whether there are procedures to retrieve and analyze data from various technical elements, and whether these processes are linked to the technology being deployed.
- Assess whether there are incident analysis processes linked to security use cases.
- Assess whether there are processes to involve internal and external parties in analyzing and investigating security incidents.

Incident Closure

- Assess whether there are processes to contain and then eradicate security compromises.
- Assess whether there are service level agreements (SLA) to contain incidents.
- Assess whether there are SLAs to eradicate incidents and eventually restore services.
- Assess whether there are processes to label incidents as closed.

Post-Incident Activities

- Is there a process to store the information collected and correspondence exchanged during an incident?
- Is there a lesson-learned exercise that feeds into the risk management program?

- Are major incidents being discussed during committee meetings (for example, the information security steering committee or the risk management committee)?

Vulnerability Discovery

- Assess whether there are processes to discover vulnerabilities.
- Assess whether there are processes to receive and consume vulnerability announcements.
- Assess whether there are processes to evaluate the impact of vulnerabilities and prioritize remediation activities accordingly.
- Assess gaps between discovery exercises and what part of the network is assessed.

Vulnerability Remediation and Tracking

- Assess whether there are processes to communicate vulnerabilities to system owners and operators.
- Assess whether there are processes to remediate and track the status of discovered vulnerabilities.

Technology

Similar to people and processes, using the right technology is critical to the success of the SOC. Technology categories that should be evaluated are related to infrastructure readiness, log collection and processing, system monitoring, security control positioning, and vulnerability management. Here are some areas to consider when collecting this information. Chapter 9, "The Technology," covers the SOC technology in more detail.

Network Infrastructure Readiness

- Assess whether a physical or logical out-of-band management network is used to manage and monitor systems. If one exists, assess the scope and coverage of this network.
- Assess capabilities for high availability of critical systems.
- Assess network performance levels, such as saturated devices or missing technologies causing user or customer dissatisfaction.

Events Collection, Correlation, and Analysis

- Assess whether an event collection design is in place.
- Assess the scalability of the event collection, correlation, and analysis platform.
- Assess whether systems are configured to forward their events.
- Assess whether there is a list of security use cases.
- Assess whether the event analysis and correlation platform is optimized for the list of use cases. Note that this is also looking at whether the system is tuned to events of interest versus gathering everything.

Monitoring

- Assess whether network flows are captured and analyzed.
- Assess whether network packets are captured and analyzed.
- Assess reporting capabilities.
- Assess gaps in monitoring, such as monitoring blind spots, delay between reporting, and so on.
- Assess monitoring capabilities during normal operation and after hours.

Control

- Assess whether the appropriate security controls are deployed. This is crucial so that events are generated by the security controls and captured by the SOC. For example, assess whether there are firewalls or intrusion detection/prevention systems protecting the data center servers (versus anybody inside the network being able to access these mission-critical devices).
- Assess whether security is properly configured so that the appropriate actions are taken and the corresponding events are generated.
- Assess whether role-based access control is enabled on all critical devices, ensuring that only authorized people have access.

Log Management

- Assess whether a log management platform is used to store the events in relation to the organization's log retention policy.
- Assess what devices are sending logs and any missing devices that would provide more value to the SOC.
- Assess the log management solution's reporting, alarming, and capability to share information with other systems.

Vulnerability Assessment

- Assess whether there are tools used to discover vulnerabilities.
- Assess whether the tools can detect the various types of vulnerabilities: network scanners, web scanners, and so forth. This includes understanding how far vulnerabilities are evaluated, such as scanning for vulnerability signatures versus executing an exploit against a vulnerability to validate it.
- Assess whether the tools are maintained.
- Assess whether the output of the tools is integrated with other security platforms such as risk management and SIEM.

Vulnerability Tracking

- Assess whether tools are used to track the status of discovered vulnerabilities.

Ticketing

- Collect information about the ticketing system and whether it is being used for security operations purposes.
- Assess whether the ticketing system is integrated with other tools, such as SIEM and vulnerability management tools.
- Identify whether business operations health can be measured based on the effectiveness of the ticketing system.

Collaboration

- Assess whether there is a platform that the SOC team can use to securely share and publish documents.
- Assess how quickly collaboration can be established between required parties during a security incident.
- Assess what teams outside the SOC collaborate with the SOC.

At this point, you should have defined the business and IT goals and identified the current capabilities of the SOC related to IT processes. Now you need to collect all this information so that it can be analyzed later. Next, we look at how to properly collect information during the assessment process. Note that we are continuing to follow the questions used in Step 2 that focus on people, processes, and technology.

Step 3: Collect Information

The first part of the assessment process generates lots of information about the capabilities of the SOC. This information must be collected in an organized manner so that it can be used to generate the results for the final assessment report. During Step 2, we looked at many general capability assessments that were categorized into people, processes, and technology. Now let's look at the type of data we should have obtained during this process so that we can be prepared to calculate the maturity level of the IT processes.

During the assessment process, you will be meeting and communicating with various roles within the organization. This might start with the head of the organization, typically the CEO or an equal role, and go all the way down to system operators. Earlier in this chapter, you saw a list of the types of people you should plan to meet with. You are not expected to be the expert in all the SOC topics, meaning that you might not understand the data being collected and could possibly misinterpret how the results should be recorded. To avoid contamination of data, consider yourself a consultant who is part of a team that offers different views of each subject being reviewed (so that you have authorized people validating the results). Having experts or multiple people contribute to the results will increase the potential for success of the final report.

People who you want to include in your extended assessment team can come from any of the following:

- Project management office (PMO)
- Security operations or the SOC if one exists
- Security architecture, planning, and engineering
- Information security governance
- Network and system engineering and operations
- IT help desk (and possibly external consultants)

Including these resources in your assessment can help you win support for the rest of the SOC establishment phases, because they would then feel involved with the design process. Involving input from other teams will also expand your understanding of the environment and possibly provide information that is known only inside that group. One final byproduct of extending the involvement beyond just the SOC is avoiding potential conflicts over the assessment results.

In some cases, individuals or entities might attempt to influence your assessment toward their desired outcome. Therefore, staying independent and demanding supporting evidence is crucial to the accuracy of the assessment outcome.

It might be difficult to identify the right people to speak with within an organization during the data-collection process. A good way to identify roles and responsibilities when job titles are not helpful is by using the Responsibility, Accountable, Consulted, and Informed (RACI)[2] matrix in Chapter 2, "Overview of SOC Technologies." Table 3-2 is an RACI matrix example.

Table 3-2 *RACI Matrix Example*

Function	Project Sponsor	Business Analyst	Project Manager	Software Developer
Initiate project	C		AR	
Establish project plan	I	C	AR	C
Gather user requirements	I	R	A	I
Develop technical requirements	I	R	A	I
Develop software tools	I	C	A	R
Test software	I	R	A	C
Deploy software	C	R	A	C

Other data to collect beyond people data is information about processes and technology. This is usually captured using various documents. Sometimes this data can be obtained from generated reports with currently available technology, whereas at other times it might be from documents that are manually maintained. It is important to validate the accuracy of this data because many reports can contain out-of-date results, such as an old network diagram containing systems that are offline. You should include the following processes and technology documents in an assessment:

- List of assets
- Risk registry
- List of existing security monitoring tools
- List of existing security control elements
- Processes and procedures associated with the technical components
- Network diagrams
- Configuration files
- Technical standards and templates
- High-level security model documentation
- The organization's help desk and ticketing system
- The organization's standard change control process

After all data about the organization has been collected, you need to calculate the effectiveness of the identified people, processes, and technology. These calculations are performed during the analyzing phase of the assessment process.

Step 4: Analyze Maturity Levels

Once data has been collected that supports the business and IT goals, the next step is to determine its effectiveness. You can do so by calculating the maturity level of an IT process and taking the average of all IT processes that directly relate to a specific IT goal. The rating of an IT process can vary in degree for scoring and weighing the importance of the process to the IT goal. Table 3-3 is a COBIT-5 example of evaluating an IT process for communication management aims and direction using a four-degree numbering system. Judging the effectiveness of a process is based on the auditor's personal opinion and will be better accepted if backed up with statements or documents collected during previous steps. Notice that the final value is the average of all processes.

Table 3-3 *COBIT-5 Example of Evaluating an IT Process*

	Process Name: Communicate Management Aims and Direction		**Do you agree?**				
	Process ID: PO6 **Maturity Level: 5**		**Not at All**	**A Little**	**To Some Degree**	**Completely**	
No	**Statement**	**Weight**	**0.00**	**0.33**	**0.66**	**1.00**	**Value**
1	The information control environment is aligned with the strategic management framework and vision.	1				✓	1.0
2	The information control environment is aligned, frequently reviewed, updated, and continuously improved.	1				✓	1.0
3	Internal experts are assigned to ensure that industry good practices are being adopted with respect to control guidance and communication techniques.	1				✓	1.0
4	External experts are assigned to ensure that industry good practices are being adopted with respect to control guidance and communication techniques.	1	✓				0.00
5	Monitoring, self-assessment, and compliance checking are pervasive within the organization.	1			✓		0.66
6	Technology is used to maintain policy and awareness knowledgebases and to optimize communication, using office automation and computer-based training tools.	1			✓		0.66
Total Weight		6	Compliance				0.72

Maturity level charts should be customized for the organization being evaluated. Table 3-4 shows a six-level scoring system that was introduced in Chapter 1. This could be used to create a variation of Table 3-3 that includes more granular maturity-level scoring options.

Table 3-4 *COBIT Capability Maturity Model Scoring Example*

Maturity Level	Process Criteria
0 Nonexistent	Complete lack of any recognizable processes. The organization has not recognized that there is an issue to be addressed.
1 Initial/Ad Hoc	There is evidence that the organization has recognized that the issues exist and need to be addressed. There are, however, no standardized processes, but instead there are ad hoc approaches that tend to be applied on an individual or case-by-case basis. The overall approach to management is disorganized.
2 Repeatable but Intuitive	Processes have developed to the stage where different people undertaking the same task follow similar procedures. There is no formal training or communication of standard procedures, and responsibility is left to the individual. There is a high degree of reliance on the knowledge of individuals, and therefore errors are likely.
3 Defined Process	Procedures have been standardized, documented, and communicated through training. However, it is left to the individual to follow these processes, and it is unlikely that deviations will be detected. The procedures themselves are not sophisticated but are the formalization of existing practices.
4 Managed and Measurable	It is possible to monitor and measure compliance with procedures and to take action where processes appear not to be working effectively. Processes are under constant improvement and provide good practice. Automation and tools are used in a limited or fragmented way.
5 Optimized	Processes have been refined to a level of best practice, based on the results of continuous improvement and maturity modeling with other organizations. IT is used in an integrated way to automate the workflow, providing tools to improve quality and effectiveness, making the enterprise quick to adapt.

Calculating the maturity level is very useful but needs to be documented in a usable format so that the information can be shared and understood. Step 5 concludes the assessment process by developing a delivery report based on the results from the previous steps.

Step 5: Formalize Findings

The last task for the capabilities assessment process is developing a final report. The final report should start by listing all identified business goals and map out how they relate to IT processes the SOC is responsible for. IT processes should contain a maturity rating so that their effectiveness is clearly identified and the current state of the SOC can be understood.

Let's walk through the format of the capabilities assessment report, including how each section should be organized. We start with the organization's vision and strategy, which should be part of the executive summary.

The Organization's Vision and Strategy

The organization's vision and strategy might only be business oriented, but it should call for information security to be a strategic goal. Many studies show that it is more expensive to add security after a process has been developed than to do so at the beginning while the process is being created. Also mandate and regulation requirements for security are increasing, which if not met could impact a business operation, brand, and profits. Organizations are taking security more seriously, with many CISOs having a seat on the board to ensure information security is part of the wider business model.

Make sure to capture the vision and strategy for the business and clearly state it as the focus for all findings in the final capabilities report. Also make sure to highlight information security elements or lack of security strategy in the vision and strategy statement, with notes about how this could affect the organization (positively and negatively). Having security incorporated in the organization's business strategies will dramatically improve the chances of the SOC getting the proper sponsorship.

The Department's Vision and Strategy

The strategy of IT (or any other department that will operate the SOC) should be closely aligned with the overall business strategy. This is why IT goals are created to support business goals and why the success of the IT goals indicates how well the SOC is performing. Security must be built in to the department-level processes and should be clearly defined in the department-level vision and strategy.

It is recommended to distinguish the department-level vision and strategy from the business version when providing a deliverable for the capabilities assessment. If security or other key elements differ between both versions of visions and strategy, the report should highlight this as a gap in business- and department-level alignment.

External and Internal Compliance Requirements

Compliance requirements must be included in the final capabilities report regardless of whether they are recognized by the organization. Most likely, compliance requirements will be included with the business strategy and make their way down to how the SOC should operate. However, you might find gaps in compliance requirement support that need to be highlighted. An example is identifying that an organization which has a small department that deals with customer financial transactions does not have PCI DSS identified as a business requirement. They need to be made aware of the legal implications of noncompliance, which might indicate a need for new services, people, or technology. According to PCI DSS requirement 11.2, for example, the organization must be able to "verify that internal and external vulnerability scans are performed as follows...".[3] This highlights the requirement to establish a vulnerability management capability, possibly operated by the SOC.

Another example where compliance requirements need to be highlighted is when trans-border data-flow restrictions enforced by data protection and privacy laws restrict the SOC outsourcing options to in-country providers. The situation is even more restricted when dealing with military or military-contracted organizations, which eliminates in many cases the option of outsourcing SOC services. Including this data in a capabilities report may either identify current practices that are breaching compliance requirements and should be adjusted or may impact future changes following capabilities assessment (such as in this example, limiting outsourcing options). Note that compliance limitations can also apply to other SOC factors, such as restrictions regarding citizenship requirements to work in the SOC.

We suggest placing the section listing compliance findings after the business strategy part of the capabilities assessment report.

Organization's Threat Landscape

Understanding the threat landscape of your organization helps you plan the appropriate security technologies to implement and operate. For example, monitoring and reacting to distributed denial-of-service (DDoS) attacks is more applicable to organizations that rely on the Internet to serve their customers and partners.

Including possible threat data that could impact the organization in the capabilities assessment report validates the reason why SOC capabilities are being assessed. You learned about the general threat landscape during the introduction in Chapter 1, but you could also search the Internet, news, or other sources for common threats seen in the same field as the organization operates within. In addition, industry security reports, such as the 2015 Verizon Data Breach Investigation Report (DBRI),[4] provide great data on top threats seen within different types of businesses. Figure 3-5 shows a diagram from the DBRI that clusters similar breaches across different industries.

History of Previous Information Security Incidents

Collecting information about previous security incidents helps you understand the areas in which the organization needs to focus security improvements. This also validates the reasoning for assessing the capabilities of the SOC: to improve on reacting to previously seen threats. You can obtain historical incident data from many parts of the organization, such as the SOC, audit team, groups with assurance functions, and so on. Historical security incident data should be placed close to the threat landscape data when developing the capabilities assessment report.

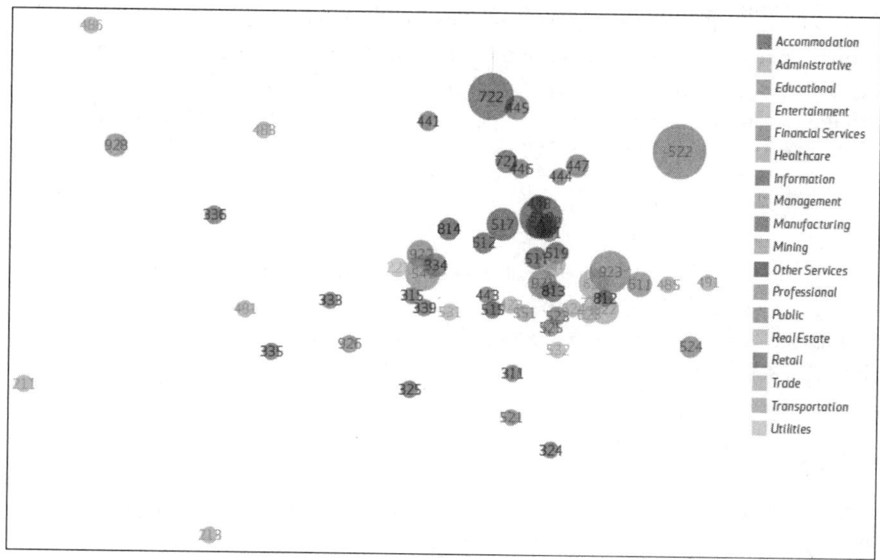

Figure 3-5 *DBRI Example Showing Clustering of Breach Data Across Industries*

SOC Sponsorship

It is important to identify the sponsor of the SOC program and specifically identify that person's business drivers and expectations for sponsoring the program. Usually this data can be associated with the business goals section of the capabilities assessment program, because all goals and processes enforced by the SOC should be mapped to a sponsored business goal. Identifying the people supporting the SOC program and business goals will ensure that the capabilities report is viewed as an exercise supported by the proper authorities.

Allocated Budget

In many cases, a budget is allocated for security projects such as the SOC even before a cost-benefit analysis is conducted. In other cases, you will be asked to develop a business case for your SOC program. In general, you are expected to deliver SOC services within the allocated budget or build a business case to justify further spending. This would impact some important decisions about the size of the SOC, the services offered, the choices of technology, and the timeline of offering the SOC services. Including budget figures will help leadership understand the costs associated with creating or improving SOC capabilities.

Presenting Data

The heart of the report should list data that backs up the results of the capabilities assessment. This includes a summary of the maturity rating for each IT goal, how that goal is mapped to a business goal, how the IT goal rating was calculated, and a summary of data collected during the capabilities assessment process. It is best practice to summarize key points with graphs and bullet points showing what was found to be strong and weak about the current SOC capabilities. Such a presentation makes it is easy to understand where investments in people, processes, and technology need to be focused to create or improve the SOC.

Closing

The end of the report should include references to sources used, such as who was interviewed, what tools were used to generate reports, and so on. In addition, including a summary statement will help wrap up the message you want to convey with the capabilities assessment report.

Summary

This chapter focused on the methodology to perform a capabilities assessment of a SOC to understand how successfully the SOC is operating. The process starts with identifying the business and IT goals for the organization. After goals have been recorded, data that maps back to those goals is collected. That data is analyzed to calculate maturity levels for IT processes associated with goals so that the organization can understand how successfully the SOC is operating. This data is organized and delivered in a report so that leadership can understand how the SOC (or the lack of one) is impacting the organization.

Once a SOC capabilities assessment is concluded, the organization can start to evaluate the current state for security and decide what investments are needed for the future SOC. Typically, the first thing to create or modify is the strategy for the SOC. Chapter 4, "SOC Strategy," focuses on developing an impactful SOC strategy.

References

1. ISAC's COBIT-5 Framework for Governance and Management of Enterprise IT. Principle 1: Meeting Stake Holder Needs, http://www.isaca.org/cobit/pages/default.aspx
2. RACI Matrix Explained by Duncan Haughey, PMP, http://www.projectsmart.co.uk/raci-matrix.php
3. PCI DSS 2.0, https://www.pcisecuritystandards.org/security_standards/
4. Verizon 2015 DBIR, http://www.verizonenterprise.com/DBIR/2015/

Chapter 4

SOC Strategy

"*Study the past if you would define the future.*"—Confucius

The output of the security operations center (SOC) assessment exercise, described in the preceding chapter, should provide you with a good understanding of your SOC objectives and your current security operation capabilities. This chapter describes how to craft a SOC strategy. The chapter also covers different SOC operation models and weighs the values of each approach. As the chapter concludes, you learn how to align the SOC strategy with a roadmap document so that the execution of the strategy can be monitored during the lifecycle of the SOC operation.

The first step in developing a SOC is to formalize a strategy. Let's start by looking closely at how to create a strategy.

Strategy Elements

Formalizing the SOC strategy and tracking its progress are key practices to achieve or extend a good governance program. The SOC strategy is based on the output of the capabilities assessment, as covered in Chapter 3, "Assessing Security Operations Capabilities," and aims to formalize the following aspects:

- SOC mission statement
- SOC strategic goals
- SOC scope
- SOC model of operation
- SOC services
- SOC capabilities development roadmap
- SOC key performance indicators (KPI) and metrics

The following topics should be recorded in a SOC strategy document, referencing the SOC assessment report and other documents such as the organization's strategy, the IT department's strategy, and possibly various high-level security policies:

- Who is involved?
- SOC mission
- SOC scope

Caution An inadequate or inaccurate SOC capabilities assessment exercise would typically produce a SOC strategy that does not properly address the actual requirements of the organization. This could negatively impact deployment timelines, budgets, and potentially cause frustration, dissatisfaction, and frictions between the different teams involved in the SOC program.

Who Is Involved?

Typically, a senior security architect or equivalent role would lead the development of the SOC strategy. Building a SOC strategy is a collective and collaborative effort that involves several decision makers from various teams, each with their own requirements, expectations, and level of influence. The roles that are involved in shaping the strategy document include the following:

- **SOC strategy leader:** This is a senior role that leads the strategy development efforts. Duties include coordinating with other roles to collect input and liaise discussions. In some cases, this role is outsourced to an external seasoned SOC consultant when internal resources with the proper skill sets are not available.
- **SOC strategy executive decision makers:** People involved with this role typically include the CIO, the CISO, and the SOC's executive sponsor. Depending on the organization, the CEO might be heavily involved in defining the SOC strategy; however, usually the SOC executive sponsor plays a major role in shaping the SOC strategy.
- **SOC strategy influencers:** These are usually the lead of IT units, business units, training department, HR department, and other departments that are impacted by the SOC. Typical IT units that would influence the SOC strategy include information security (infosec); security planning and engineering; network planning and engineering; system planning and engineering; system, network, and security operations, security risk management; and the project management office.

SOC Mission

The mission statement should be aligned with the organizational business vision and strategy, in addition to the department in which the SOC would eventually report to. When defining the mission statement, you should explicitly define the following:

- The scope of the SOC
- The roles of the SOC
- The department responsible for building, operating, and maintaining the SOC program

The SOC executive sponsor must approve and sign the mission statement.

The following is an example of a SOC mission statement:

> The security operations center monitors the overall security posture of the IT network. The security operations center reacts and tracks information security incidents with the objective of maintaining the overall security posture. The functions are performed around the clock in support of the organization operation model.

SOC Scope

Documenting the scope of the SOC helps the organization focus on what the SOC is tasked to perform. The scope should anticipate the level of effort and resources required to complete the project. This is critical because it is a common mistake to budget upfront costs but not include additional expenses for installation, maintenance, upgrades, support, tuning, and associated costs for turnover or canceling a service level agreement.

The scope for the SOC should consider the following:

- **Time period:** The strategy should be bounded by a time period in which the SOC strategic objectives and the SOC capability maturity roadmap are to be delivered. Delivering on these objectives is evaluated during and after the strategy period. Typically, the length of the SOC strategy period is aligned with its parent strategy (that is, the strategy of the department or unit in which the SOC function resides).
- **Locations:** The physical locations containing elements monitored by the SOC (for example, the headquarters, the regional offices, and the remote offices of an enterprise).
- **Networks:** These are the networks that are monitored by the SOC. Typical examples include data center networks, wide-area networks, local-area networks, extranets, and Internet points of access. Depending on your environment, other networks might exist. For example, a telecom company would typically operate an enterprise network in addition to the service provider network.
- **Ownership:** Ownership of systems and information influence the SOC scope in terms of which assets are going to be monitored and protected. For example, process and control networks or private networks that host industrial control systems are not typically managed by IT, and hence monitoring these assets might not be

in the scope of a SOC operated by IT. Depending on the information you collect during your SOC assessment, these networks might or might not be covered by the SOC.

- **Organization strategy:** The business goals for the organization and other department strategies should be factored into the overall SOC strategy. This will help other business units collaborate with the SOC and help the SOC better understand the requirements to keep each department secure.
- **Choice of technologies:** Depending on the elements you plan to monitor and the assets to protect, your choice of technologies will vary in terms of type, size, and design:
  - **Type:** The scope dictates the required technologies. The elements you monitor might require the implementation of specific technologies. For example, you might be required to implement packet-capturing and intrusion detection capabilities across multiple locations and networks.
  - **Size:** The deployed services should be able to handle the environment described by the SOC scope in terms of the amount of data to collect and process, impacting the required underlying hardware and the number and distribution of devices to deploy.
  - **Design:** Distributed versus centralized deployment of services such as log management and vulnerability-assessment tools.
- **Resources and expertise:** Some technologies might be more complex than others, possibly requiring specialized expertise. In addition, the larger the scope, the more resource you will require to design, build, and eventually operate the SOC.
- **Timelines:** The scope impacts the timeline of designing and implementing the SOC services.
- **Model of operation:** The scope may impact the model of operation, meaning when to outsource versus develop in-house capabilities.
- **Compliance:** Internal or external compliance requirements will be impacted by the SOC scope.
- **Budget:** Naturally, the larger the scope, the higher the cost associated with designing, building, and eventually operating your SOC.

Let's consider some SOC scoping examples from two industries.

Example 1: A Military Organization

Mission Statement

The SOC monitors the overall security posture of all networks operated by the organization, including general and tactical networks. The SOC reacts to information security incidents with the objective of maintaining the overall security of the organization, supporting the readiness of the organization's offensive and defensive capabilities.

SOC Scope Statement

The SOC scope covers all locations across the country hosting systems owned and managed by all units that are connected to the general and tactical networks. The services offered by SOC include around-the-clock security monitoring of systems, applications, and networks with the objectives of detecting and reacting to all external attacks and insider malicious behaviors. The services offered by SOC are handling incident response; collecting and correlating the various system events from the various networks; capturing, analyzing, and storing raw packet data from all the security enclaves; discovering, assessing, and tracking vulnerabilities; and consuming any threat intelligence information received from other alliance military forces.

Example 2: A Financial Organization

Mission Statement

The SOC monitors the security posture of networks, systems, and applications operated by IT, with the objective of detecting and reacting to information security incidents that could negatively impact the organization's business operation.

SOC Scope Statement

The SOC scope covers all systems that are managed and operated by IT, including these located in national and international offices. The SOC services are offered around the clock and include the collection and correlation of security events messages, handling distributed denial-of-service attack, detecting internal and external malicious activities, responding to information security incidents, leading the computer security incident response team, and conducting awareness sessions when required.

SOC Model of Operation

One important decision that the SOC architecture team needs to consider during the planning phase is whether to internally develop SOC capabilities, outsource capabilities, or leverage a hybrid of these two approaches. This decision should be based on a number of factors, including the following:

- Cost of internally developing, operating, and maintaining acceptable levels of SOC capabilities versus outsourcing them. This should include whether outsourcing costs can be spread over a period of time versus the upfront costs of developing an in-house SOC.
- The availability of a reliable SOC service provider that can meet or exceed your service level agreements (SLA).
- Available resources and weighing value of outsourcing versus the cost to maintain internally.
- Regulations that might prohibit outsourcing all or some of the SOC services.
- Time required for creating in-house SOC documentation and processes.

In-House and Virtual SOC

The traditional in-house SOC model of operation assumes all technology, processes, and people capabilities are developed and provided within a facility that hosts the SOC team and services. The organization is responsible for development, operation, and the maintenance of tools and processes and for making sure that the SOC resources are kept skillful. People can be employees or contractors, and technology can be local or cloud, but responsibilities for technology are configured and managed internally. Table 4-1 outlines the advantages and disadvantages of an in-house SOC operation model.

Table 4-1 *Advantages and Disadvantages of an In-House SOC Operation Model*

Advantages	Disadvantages
Local and dedicated staff.	More upfront investment
Familiar with the local environment.	Less likely than a outsourced SOC to identify patterns that impact multiple companies
Logging is usually stored locally.	High demand to show ROI to sponsor
Ownership of technology.	Hard to recruit talent and acquire proper technology

A virtual SOC is an implementation of the "SOC as a service" concept, in which organizations would outsource their SOC services. Some advantages to this approach are speeding up the creation of the SOC, minimizing process and technology development efforts, and acquiring the required SOC expertise. A virtual SOC is designed so that data is collected locally and managed by a specialized service provider handling the SOC facility and services, such as correlating events, managing vulnerabilities, and investigating security incidents. This SOC service provider typically supplies a management tool such as a web-based dashboard, though, so that the local team can view and track security incidents, view the status of vulnerabilities, and communicate with virtual SOC analysts who are based remotely. In this model, the local organization would typically operate a small team responsible for taking actions on alerts that are identified by the virtual SOC service. Table 4-2 outlines the advantages and disadvantages of the virtual SOC operation model.

Table 4-2 *Advantages and Disadvantages of a Virtual SOC Operation Model*

Advantages	Disadvantages
Less capital expenses because technology is outsourced	Less familiar with local environment
More data from different customers	Typically staff manages multiple customers
Typically less expensive than in-house	Log data stored off-premises
Unbiased, being outside company politics	Less customization options
Usually more flexible and scalable	Risk of data mishandling
On-staff experts	
SLA and outsourced documentation	

Another approach is using a hybrid of in-house and virtual SOC services. This would involve a blend of building a local SOC and outsourcing other services. One example of using a hybrid approach is outsourcing services for monitoring the perimeter or a remote site while using a local SOC to secure an internal network such as a data center or controlled environment for classified communications. Other reasons for a hybrid approach may be the requirement for specialized services or cost savings such as external monitoring that includes distributed DoS (DDoS) capabilities that are more economical to outsource than acquiring and managing technology locally. One important value of a hybrid approach is the possibility of collaboration between local and virtual teams. This can fill the gaps of an in-house model by having virtual team members collaborating with a local SOC.

In some cases, organizations would temporary outsource their SOC services while they develop their internal capabilities and slowly migrate to in-house SOC offering. When considering this strategy, the transition period should be well planned such that the security posture is maintained before, during, and after the cutover from virtual to in-house services. In addition, be aware that analysts and investigators operating virtual SOCs would usually be more seasoned in investigating security incidents, gaining experience from working with various clients. Recruiting and maintaining seasoned SOC staff is challenging and may be a reason to continue a virtual or hybrid SOC service.

It might be difficult to select the best SOC operation model for your organization. One way to qualify the in-house SOC approach is by answering the following questions, which tend to justify developing an in-house SOC or outsourcing this service:

- Do your current employees have the skills and knowledge to manage a SOC? Do you have enough employees to maintain the expected coverage level?
- How will you assess the skills to qualify whether the potential SOC member is competent?
- Do you have a resource that can architect a proper SOC? What about developing procedures and processes?
- Is there time and budget to develop the proper documentation for process and procedures?

If a virtual SOC services makes sense for your organization, it is recommended to qualify their capabilities. Some qualification questions/requests that will prove handy before signing an SLA are as follows:

- Ask for a copy of the service provider's operations manual.
- Research their reputation in the industry. How long have they been in business?
- Ask for reference customers in a similar industry and company size.
- Identify how long the reference customers have been using the virtual SOC services.
- What are the costs to terminate the services before the end of the SLA?

- How is data protected at the virtual SOC environment?
- What is the experience level of the state involved with the new SLA? What industry certifications are held?
- How trustworthy are all virtual SOC staff members working on your SLA? Have they had a background check? Do they sign strict confidentiality agreements? Are any staff members contractors?
- What is the employee turnover rate?

Effective virtual SOC services provide low false positive alerting by investing time to qualify incidents rather than just exporting alerts generated by the automatic tools. Effective virtual SOC providers also offer a continuous optimization process designed to share data and feedback on alert relevancy and fidelity. This is important because it is likely the virtual SOC would not have as much knowledge of the local environment as the onsite staff would have. When signing a contract with a virtual SOC provider, you should have service requirements such as how teams collaborate and expected reporting documented in the SLA model.

SOC Services

Developing a SOC strategy should end with a formal document stating the services that will be provided by the SOC. At this stage, you are not expected to explore the technical details on how services are delivered, but rather highlight the services and the value they bring to the organization. Some services that could be offered by SOC include the following:

- Detect, analyze, and manage the containment of information security incidents. The main objective is to be able to rapidly react and contain the incident, minimizing the possible impact.
- Perform compliance monitoring to meet internal and external requirements or standards. This includes legal, regulatory, and internal policies.
- Operate the vulnerability management program or work closely with system administrators who have vulnerability management responsibilities.
- Collect, analyze, and store events from relevant data sources with an objective of being able to perform detection and digital investigation of security incidents.
- Support security awareness sessions to educate users about the importance of being able to detect and report security incidents.
- Advanced digital investigation, including performing detailed and deep analysis of systems in a forensically sound manner.

When considering outsourcing SOC services, it is critical to have a well-defined SLA before committing to the agreement. This means having documented processes and time periods required for response to a security incident. The SLA should specify steps that are taken against an identified security incident, including procedures to protect from the same attack impacting the network in the future. There should also be some form of insurance for recovering losses in the event the provider does not deliver the agreed-upon services.

Once a SLA is signed, best practice is validating that you are receiving the proper service. Try calling during off-hours and identify the skill level of the support at that time. Request reports and verify your local team and leadership are satisfied with the format and level of details included. Test the service provider by setting off alarms to see how they react. Measure their ability to identify, address, and close the alarm you created.

SOC Capabilities Roadmap

Chapter 3 introduced a general diagram for SOC capabilities that is broken into three categories: people, processes, and technology. Capabilities must be continuously improved with targets to reach based on a measurable timeline. The first step is performing a capabilities assessment as covered in Chapter 3 to understand the current state of the SOC. The post-assessment tasks evaluate how the SOC should function in the future by identifying IT operations that could improve using maturity-level ratings. This quantifies the objectives so that the SOC can be measured every year to rate the progress of improving SOC capabilities. The new maturity-level goals should be formalized in a roadmap document that is agreed on by the SOC and associated sponsors. Figure 4-1 shows a general diagram of capabilities a SOC could assess for maturity so that a roadmap could be developed later.

Using Figure 4-1 as a guideline, a SOC could complete a capabilities assessment to establish maturity levels for the categories people, processes, and technology. Each of these categories can take the average of the maturity level for all the associated IT processes to develop an overall category maturity score. That score would represent the current state of the SOC for that particular category. An example is reviewing three IT processes for *governance* rated for maturity levels 0.33, 0.66, and .033, making a *people's governance category* maturity level of 0.44. So, every year, a .33 improvement could be the target SOC capabilities roadmap for the governance category for people. This could be represented as follows:

- **Area:** Governance under the people category.
- **Year 1:** Target maturity growth to be at least .55 by end of year.
- **Year 2:** Target maturity growth to be at least .66 by end of year.
- **Year 3:** Target maturity growth to be at least .77 by end of year.
- **Justification:** This section describes the plan to achieve the desired maturity level for this specific area after 3 years of operating the SOC.

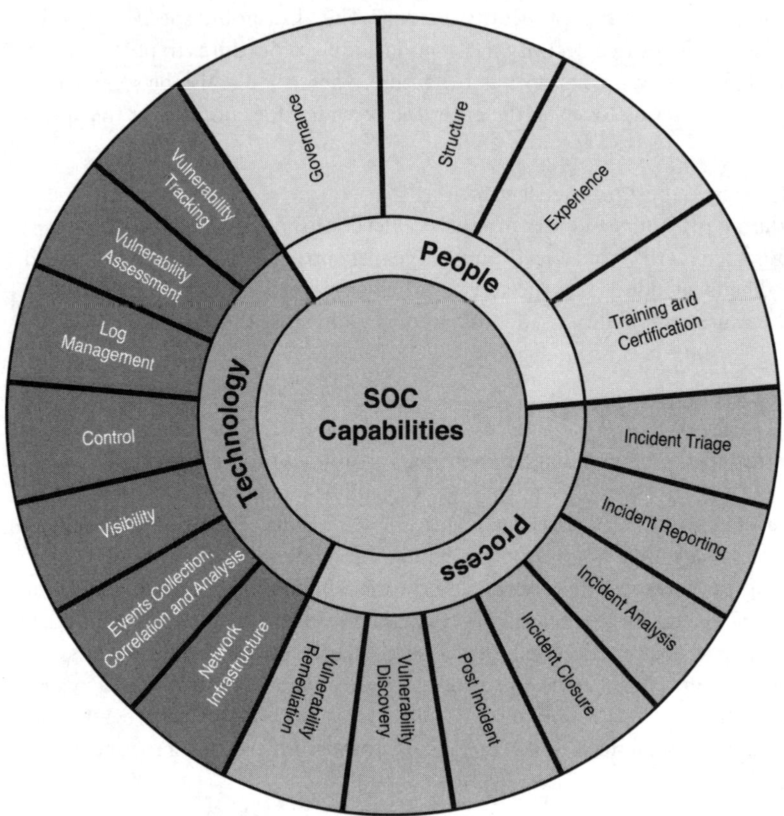

Figure 4-1 *SOC Capabilities*

For ease of presentation, you can tabulate these as shown in Table 4-3.

Table 4-3 *Example Table of SOC Capabilities Roadmap*

Category	Area	Year 1	Year 2	Year 3	Justification
People	Structure	.55	.66	.77	The initial SOC structure will be formalized during the build phase. We expect this structure to evolve as the SOC maturity increases. A recommendation for some modifications to the existing department structure has been proposed to address the requirements of the SOC program.

Some maturity-level growth rates may require acceleration through outsourcing services or investing in training or technology. These options have different costs associated, and therefore rely on the sponsor's support of the SOC program. This means that there must be a method to monitor progress to justify the funding required to continue progress toward improving the capabilities roadmap.

Evaluating your progress against the SOC strategic objectives and the SOC roadmap is key to the continuous success of the SOC strategy. Evaluating the strategy execution and presenting the results to the SOC sponsor provide you and the sponsor with important insight that can help guide the SOC operation toward the desired objectives that were originally set in the strategy document. Failing to deliver on key objectives may indicate some major deficiencies such as program management deficiencies, breakdown of communication between teams, technology gaps, or lack of investment in the SOC program. However, demonstrating success can help ensure support of the program and lead to additional benefits such as more budget, increase in staff, and access to more technology.

Summary

This chapter focused on developing a strategy and roadmap for SOC capabilities. This process starts with developing a mission statement and a supporting statement for the scope of support. The success of these statements is based on rating the maturity level of services the SOC is responsible for providing. To judge the success of a mission statement and scope of support, a capabilities roadmap must be developed stating how the mission should be accomplished during a specified timeframe. The roadmap can be used as a benchmark to justify future investments in the SOC program.

The next chapter covers what to consider when developing a SOC infrastructure.

Chapter 5

The SOC Infrastructure

"It is not the beauty of a building you should look at; its the construction of the foundation that will stand the test of time."—David Allan Coe

Security operations center (SOC) services should be accessed securely and reliably. Many of the systems used by a SOC contain confidential information that could negatively impact an organization if exposed. For example, network monitoring and vulnerability management tools could reveal weaknesses that an attacker could use to breach the organization and perhaps even to avoid detection. Data protection is also a requirement for many regulations that include processes for securing services associated with the SOC. Failure to meet such requirements could have negative legal and financial impact on the business.

This chapter reviews factors that impact the design of the SOC infrastructure. Important things to consider include the scope of the SOC, model of operation, timeline for establishing the SOC, and SOC services. Some infrastructure areas that must be addressed are the type of facility, networking, security, computing storage, collaboration, ticketing, and case management requirements. This chapter covers all these topics, but let's start with some general design considerations.

Design Considerations

During the course of designing a SOC infrastructure, the SOC architect must make decisions that should support the SOC roadmap and align with other related programs and projects. The first step following establishing the criteria for the SOC may be to speak with vendors to better understand the available technology and gather what the expected costs are going to be to meet the SOC objectives. We recommend starting these conversations with vendors that already supply equipment to your organization. This will help your organization take advantage of the same support model and in some cases the same support contract. If those vendors do not have the required technology, ask for recommendations for other suppliers or leverage the vendor evaluation questions that are covered in Chapter 6, "Security Event Generation and Collection" (in the "Data-Collection Tools" section).

Before evaluating technology, make sure to verify all hardware and connectivity requirements. In some cases, products may include proprietary components or require specialized configuration of network or power that might not be readily available or might be difficult to provide. Ensure that capacity planning is performed and documented based on acquiring the new technology. Capacity planning should not translate to oversizing requirements, but rather aligning the design and technology choices with the SOC roadmap. Capacity planning should also consider the expected growth while working within the allocated budget. It is important to be mindful that technology continuously evolves, so make sure to speak with vendors about their roadmaps, especially in areas that have direct impact on your SOC infrastructure design decisions.

Make sure that the SOC teams engages other business units, programs, and project teams early in the planning and evaluation cycle whenever possible. For example, the SOC architect should collaborate with the network, systems, and data center teams so as to make better design decisions on where and how to connect the SOC infrastructure components.

Many of these technology design decisions will be influenced based on whether you are developing an in-house SOC or leveraging virtual SOC services. Next, we look at how the SOC model of operation can impact the SOC design.

Model of Operation

The model of operation greatly influences the infrastructure required to provision SOC services. For example, outsourcing SOC services typically minimizes your capital investment, shortens the service deployment time, and potentially enables you to achieve a higher service delivery maturity level in a shorter period of time. Most deployments that outsource SOC services require minimal onsite hardware and software, which is usually used for data collection and vulnerability-assessment purposes. The remaining analysis portal services tend to live at the service provider locations. The possibility of outsourcing a SOC service is based on the decisions you made during the planning phase, as discussed in Part II of this book.

Chapter 4, "SOC Strategy," covered some factors to consider when preparing to outsource SOC services. Here are some questions to answer that cover SOC infrastructure design when considering virtual SOC services:

- How much bandwidth should you provision for the link between you and the SOC service provider?
- How many physical or virtual links should you provision to connect you to the SOC service provider, and what data-protection controls should you implement to safeguard data in transit?
- Where should you place devices supplied by your SOC service provider, and what remote-access privileges should they have?

- How should the organization integrate the managed service offering with internal ticketing systems?
- Where will the managed service provider components be installed?
- Would you be required to provide remote-access services to allow the service provider to manage onsite components?

The next part of this chapter breaks down common SOC infrastructure components. This includes everything from what is involved with designing a SOC to things an analyst will need to be productive. Let's start with selecting a SOC facility.

Facilities

The facilities discussion covers a number of topics related to preparing the suitable premises to host the SOC team and services. In general, the SOC should be designed to facilitate effective collaboration between the SOC members, while supporting a comfortable working environment. All systems and data held within the SOC should also be secured.

Depending on the size of the SOC, the services provided, and model of operation, there might be a requirement to establish a dedicated SOC facility that hosts the SOC team members and the SOC dashboards. In the case of a virtual SOC, a dedicated SOC facility might be required to distribute SOC members across the organization. The decision of having a dedicated facility is made during the planning phase, taking into consideration the cost and benefit associated with preparing, operating, and maintaining the facility.

A facility can be thought of as a location that can vary in type and size depending on the actual nature and size of the SOC. For example, a large service provider might choose to host their SOC along with their network operations center (NOC) and other operation teams in a separate building, whereas smaller organizations might host their SOC in a facility within the same premises that hosts corporate users. Other considerations would be including data-recovery locations for high availability, multiple large branches that may require their own local SOC team, local or country regulations that require local capabilities, and so on. The SOC facility structure should include the SOC internal layout, the analyst workstations layout, and other small but important details such as lighting preferences, the requirement for a raised floor, and soundproofing. The SOC structure does not have to be based on a science fiction scene or the NASA mission control center, but rather should be practical enough, allowing the SOC team members to function in the most optimal and effective setup possible. It is also worth considering investing in the aesthetics of the SOC to promote a positive workspace and to impress executive management and other sponsors who have invested in the location. We have found that many nontechnical executives are satisfied during an onsite tour seeing large monitors showcasing security data even though they do not understand its meaning. A good walkthrough impression could score additional future budget based purely on the look of the SOC workspace. A good first impression starts with the SOC internal layout.

SOC Internal Layout

A typical SOC layout consists of the following areas:

- **The SOC floor (also referred to as the operations room):** This is the area that SOC analysts occupy to conduct their day-to-day tasks, including monitoring the SOC dashboards, dealing with incoming incident cases, analyzing and investigating security incidents, and carrying out other administration tasks. The floor layout should provide all SOC analysts with unrestricted line of sight to the SOC video wall used to project or display various dashboards. The number of analyst consoles and the type and location of the video wall determine the size and dimensions of the floor. It is important that you do not end up with an overcrowded floor, which might negatively impact the SOC working atmosphere and obstruct communication between analysts.
- **The war room (also referred to as the situation room):** A room that is usually equipped with conference facilities and potentially a videoconferencing unit that allows the engagement of remote participants. The room is used by the SOC team to conduct their regular meetings, but is also used for situation management during major or high-severity security incidents.
- **The SOC manager and supervisor offices:** The SOC manager and supervisors oversee the SOC operation and the overall incident management process. It is recommended to have their offices located within the SOC facility and separated by glass windows so that they have visibility to the SOC floor and the video wall.
- **Computer room:** There might be a requirement for provisioning a computer room to host the SOC equipment, when they cannot be securely hosted in other locations such as the data center or a close computer/communication room. If a SOC computer room is required, the environment controls for computer rooms should be considered to ensure that heating, power supply, air conditioning, and other requirements are properly provisioned as per the organization's standards.

Figure 5-1 shows a standard SOC layout design. This design contains the SOC floor, a SOC war room, and a SOC manager office.

Figure 5-1 *Sample SOC Layout*

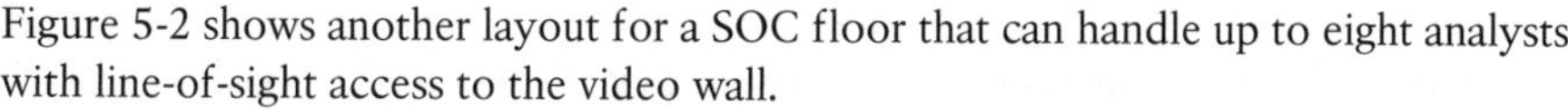

Figure 5-2 shows another layout for a SOC floor that can handle up to eight analysts with line-of-sight access to the video wall.

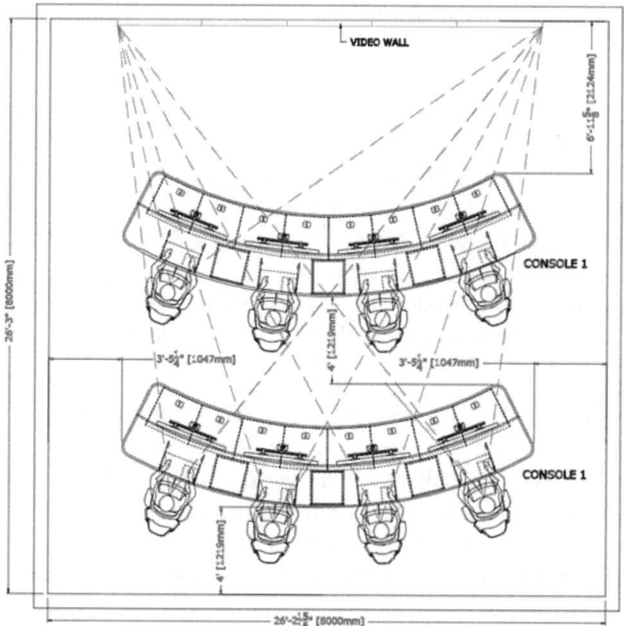

Figure 5-2 *SOC Floor Layout*

During the design phase, you should work closely with the facilities department or with an external SOC facility designer to develop schematics for the SOC layout. These schematics should formalize the various SOC layout features discussed earlier, along with other details such as power sockets, network and telephone points, and so on. The following subsections describe a few common features that you should include in design conversations.

Lighting

The floor of an operation center requires an overall dim illumination and higher levels of local illumination at the SOC analyst consoles. The level of details should be considered to ensure a comfortable working atmosphere in what can be regarded as a demanding operation environment, such as the one you expect in a SOC. There might also be additional lighting requirements, such as options to change the light color or additional warning lights to alert staff when there is a presence of personnel on the floor who are not authorized to view data managed by the SOC.

Acoustics

The noise level in a SOC should not be so high as to affect the operation of the SOC. Common sources of noise that you should consider include telephone conversations, operator conversations, and the noise generated by the SOC equipment. It is important that you identify the sources of noise during the SOC facility design phase so that you can work on reducing their effect. Possible options to reduce the impact of noise include installing equipment in a separate room and the installation of sound-deadening materials.

Physical Security

Access to the SOC facility should be restricted to SOC personnel. Door access control equipment should be used to restrict and log all access to the SOC. Your organization may also be required to maintain an access logbook for non-SOC personnel visiting the SOC. In addition, access to the SOC computer room located inside the SOC should have its own access control equipment allowing access to authorized SOC personnel only. If tailgating entry is a concern, there might be additional procedural controls or a two-door SOC entry system that can help prevent this from happening. A mantrap is an example of a way to prevent tailgating.

It is also a general practice to install CCTV cameras that monitor and record the areas of the SOC facility such as the SOC floor and the computer room. Footage from the CCTV system might be required for investigating incidents such as theft, unauthorized access to the facility, unwanted personnel access, and vandalism. It can also be used to evaluate the SOC performance and the overall interaction of the SOC analysts as part of a continuous improvement process. Note that some countries may have restrictions that apply to CCTV camera use.

Depending on the sensitivity level of the SOC operation, there might a requirement to install soundproof materials to protect internal SOC conversations related to SOC activities and incident investigations.

If forensically sound handling of evidence materials is required, a secure storage facility should be provided for electronic and nonelectronic material collected during an incident investigation. Make sure to identify the level of sensitivity for expected data, because some classified documents may require higher security controls such as a Sensitive Compartmented Information Facility (SCIF) design.

The installation of paper shredders or other destructive mechanisms might be required to ensure that material is adequately disposed of and in alignment with the organization's media-disposal policy.

Data-sensitivity requirements may lead you to question the use of external windows because of the risk of data leakage through tracking heat sources, also known as tempest. Walls may require specific materials such as metal plating to reduce the risk of attackers drilling into unauthorized locations or planting listening devices.

Video Wall

The various dashboards that SOC analysts use to monitor the security incidents are typically projected or displayed on a centrally accessible wall. SOC analysts should also have access to the same dashboards from their consoles.

Common video wall technologies include the use of projectors or having a dedicated video wall display system. The projector option can be economical and deployed quickly and requires less hardware and expertise to manage. This option, however, does not offer the same level of flexibility, reliability, and professional look provided by a decent video wall system.

The video wall should be placed high enough so that all the screens are comfortably accessible to the SOC analysts from their consoles when seated, while ensuring line of sight. You do not want your SOC analysts to have to stand up to be able to view parts of the video wall. Figure 5-3 shows a sample video wall design that achieves the required line of sight.

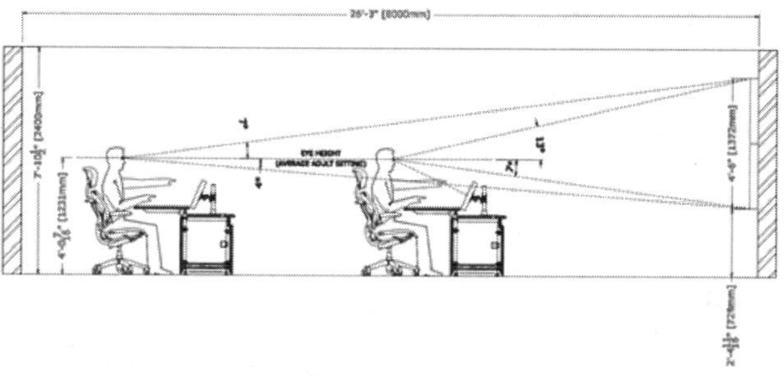

Figure 5-3 *Sample Video Wall Placement*

The number of screens that comprise the video wall or the video display is based on the dashboards that are displayed. Your choice of the video wall server should accommodate enough video outputs with sufficient free slots for future video wall expansion (that is, when more screens are added).

SOC Analyst Services

SOC analysts seated in the facility should have consoles that complement the SOC facility features, allowing effective access to information and a comfortable working space. SOC dashboards and tools should be displayed on flat-panel monitors properly mounted to provide more desktop space for the analyst. The monitor mounts should include a tilt functionality to adjust how data is viewed based on the personal preference of the analyst. Cables from devices and peripherals such as phones, monitors, and keyboards should be routed through properly designed grommets in the work surface. In addition, horizontal and vertical cable raceways should be fixed within the console to prevent sagging and ensure cables are secure. It is also recommended to include storage cabinets for securing personal items. SOC analysts should have their own standard enterprise workstation to carry out regular activities such as e-mail and other business activities and a second workstation to access the SOC tools. Analysts need telephony services for internal, local, and if needed, international calls. Incoming and outgoing SOC calls can also be recorded as per the organization's policy for quality assurance or other purposes.

Figure 5-4 shows a sample workstation design that can host four SOC analysts, each with two mounted monitors, a CPU tray, and a storage cabinet.

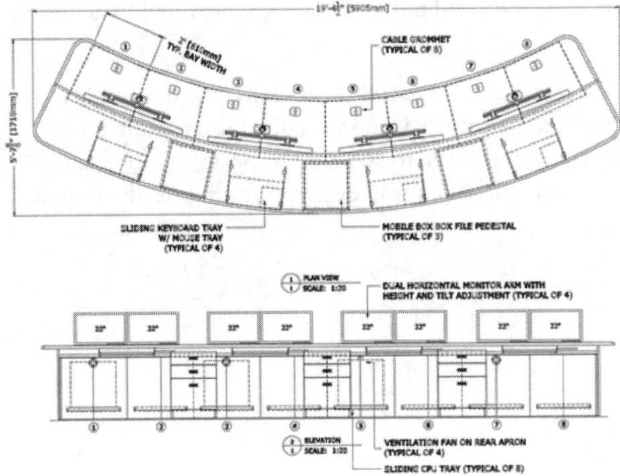

Figure 5-4 *Sample Analyst Workstation Design*

Active Infrastructure

The *active infrastructure* refers to the underlying IT hardware and software that supply network, security, computing, operating system, storage, collaboration, and case management services required to host the SOC applications such as data collection and analysis, vulnerability management, and so on.

A general good practice is to host the SOC components in an enclave that resides in an out-of-band network with dedicated secure logical/physical infrastructure servicing this enclave. The main advantage of separating the SOC infrastructure is to protect the SOC systems and information from incidents affecting various elements monitored by the SOC. The level of isolation is based on the criticality of the SOC to the organization and the risk associated with not doing so. For example, let's consider an organization hosting the SOC applications in a virtual LAN (VLAN) that resides on a network switch that also connects users and general servers. A risk to this approach could be a network administrator making a switch configuration error that allows uncontrolled access to the SOC applications. This could expose these applications to sources of threats that could have been avoided if SOC services had been provided by their own switches.

As shown in the preceding example, it is important not only to plan for properly segmenting SOC networking components but also to determine the level of isolation. In some cases, completely isolating the SOC from the rest of the network might not be practical or even possible. Best practice is reusing existing infrastructure services for low-security-related situations while investing in segmenting any services that should not be viewed by members outside of the SOC.

Network

A typical SOC network should include network segmentation. This will protect sensitive data and contain risk to a restricted space in the event of a compromise or other complication. All SOC tools should be hosted from a dedicated network segment that is separated from but permits access to the analyst workstations. There should be a separate network segment not connected to the SOC internal network for standard enterprise services such as e-mail and Internet traffic. Many SOCs also require an additional segment for malware-related tasks such as reverse engineering and sandbox or hosting systems used to conduct other high-risk activities.

Figure 5-5 shows a common SOC network design.

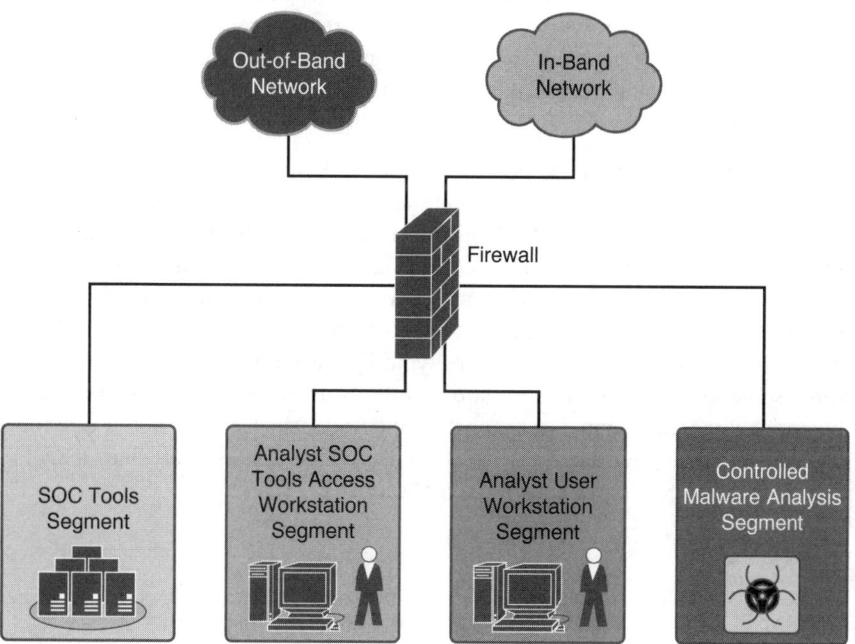

Figure 5-5 *Logical SOC Network Segmentation*

It is important that the SOC network be reliable by providing adequate levels of redundancy achieved using redundant network components. This can include planning for backup Internet service provider (ISP) connections, redundant networking hardware, and power generators in the event of a local power failure.

SOC personnel should have standard enterprise services segmented from SOC-related services. Standard enterprise services include e-mail, internal services, and Internet services. The SOC-related services such as the SOC console and dashboards should not be accessible by the common enterprise network, and a separate workstation should be provisioned to SOC personal for excusive access to such services. An option to provision restricted access to SOC services is to leverage a thin or a fat client to the console's network, such as Cisco AnyConnect VPN.

Some SOC tools require access to the Internet or other external networks. This includes, for example, access to threat intelligence information or downloading signatures and reputation information. Such access should be provisioned through a proxy or application layer firewall limiting access to necessary services only. This can be accomplished using a whitelist of destination domains and IP addresses, allowing the SOC tools to access only a predefined set of Internet destinations and protocols.

Access to Systems

The SOC enclave will be connected either in-band or using an out-of-band network with direct or indirect access to systems monitored by the SOC. It is recommended that devices be monitored using an out-of-band network allowing secure access that is not impacted by the in-band traffic, especially in the case of an attack. Today, most enterprise-level devices are provisioned with one or more management ports that can be connected to the logical or physical out-of-band management network. Access to this management network should be available only to authorized entities such as NOC and SOC members and devices.

Access to the network components should be authorized, preferably through a centralized authentication, authorization, and accounting (AAA) service and using network protocols such as Remote Authentication Dial-In User Service (RADIUS) or Terminal Access Controller Access Control System (TACACS). Using an AAA server guarantees that all access attempts are logged with an audit trail that can be retrieved during an incident investigation. Best practice is using as least two factors for authenticating users to SOC systems. Multifactor authentication solutions typically are a mix of something you know (password), something you have (access cards, hard or soft tokens), and something you are (fingerprint scanner). Communication between devices, such as from a user desktop to a SOC device, should leverage some form of encryption such as Secure Shell (SSH), Secure Sockets Layer (SSL), or Transport Layer Security (TLS).

Security

Protecting the SOC network, hosts, and applications is of topmost priority. Compromising the SOC network and systems undermines the objective of having a SOC and will negatively impact detection capabilities, organizational trust, and justification for future investments. Developing a SOC enclave using network segmentation and security controls can prevent a breach from happening.

Developing a SOC enclave starts with segmenting different trust levels of traffic using either physical separation or different variations of virtual network segmentation such as VLANs, access lists, or security group tags (SGT). Inbound and outbound connections from and to the SOC network segments should be monitored and controlled in support of the least privilege principle, in which access is limited to what a service or a user requires to operate.

When firewalls are used, firewall segmentation rules should provide standard network-based access control that applies to incoming, outgoing, and intra-SOC traffic. The rules should be managed and maintained by the SOC team and should follow a standard change management control process. Maintaining the firewall rule base should include regular reviews and updates. For example, expired rules should be manually or automatically disabled or deleted. All rules should also be properly documented. Each rule should be associated with a description that includes information such as the following:

- Requestor
- Purpose
- Creation and expiry dates
- Change management approval reference number

Intrusion prevention control should be integrated with the SOC enclave design such that traffic is inspected inline wherever possible. The intrusion prevention system (IPS) can be implemented as a standalone solution or can be integrated with the firewall. The IPS mode of operation can be set to fail-close or fail-open. When configured in fail-open, an IPS failure would result in the IPS acting as a network bypass, allowing traffic through with no inspection. Your security policy should identify the acceptable mode of operation based on understanding the risks associated with both options.

The IPS signatures and rules should be tuned such that irrelevant ones are disabled, while relevant signatures are manually or automatically enabled and tuned. It is also extremely important to consider the performance impact resulting from enabling too many rules and from operating the IPS and the firewall functions in the same system. Make sure to consult with your vendor on the performance impact before enabling multiple security features.

Note Some IDS/IPS solutions such as Cisco Firepower Management Center (FMC) offer autotuning or recommendations of IPS rules to enable or disable to assist with IPS rule management.

There might be a requirement to inspect traffic within the same network segment such as the same VLAN. One way to accomplish this is by implementing an IDS so that traffic from one or more VLANs is copied to a switch port configured where the IDS is connected, thus enabling you to monitor and inspect intra-VLAN traffic. In many cases, the same system can be configured in IPS and IDS modes of operation.

Figure 5-6 shows the implementation of the IPS and IDS functions within the SOC enclave shown in Figure 5-5.

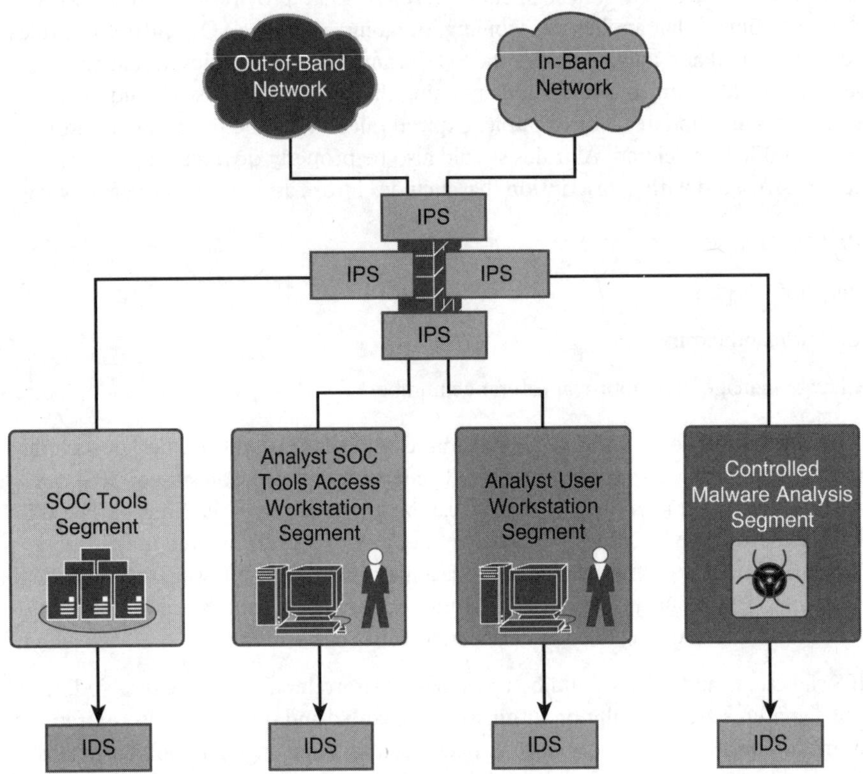

Figure 5-6 *Integrating IPS and IDS Functions in the SOC Enclave*

Another method to identify intra-VLAN traffic along with other areas of the network is by leveraging network telemetry, also known as NetFlow. For example, Lancope's StealthWatch can either digest NetFlow from existing networking equipment or place a StealthWatch NetFlow sensor that converts raw packets into NetFlow.

Additional network-based security tools such as breach detection can be used to identify network and security events within the SOC network. Chapter 9, "The Technology," provides more information about the technology options that are leveraged by and used to secure the SOC.

Another focus area for SOC security is protecting host systems and applications. For example, a security information and event management (SIEM) tool should have a web-based interface that is developed with the use of components like Tomcat,[1] JBOSS,[2] and OpenSSL.[3] Exploiting vulnerabilities in these components may result in a compromised SIEM that could provide an attacker with privileged access to other applications and systems in and out of the SOC.

- The first step to avoid host system compromise is to enforce security configuration benchmarks for operating systems and applications. Examples of secure configuration benchmarks include the U.S. Department of Defense (DoD) DISA Security Technical Implementation Guides (STIG)[4] and the Center for Internet Security (CIS)[5] set of benchmarks. You may also refer to the system provider for specific hardening recommendations.
- It is critical to stay on top of implementing the required and recommended security patches and fixes for operating systems, applications, and databases. Typically, the cycle of testing and implementing critical security patches can take a shorter time in the case of SOC when compared to other environments such as IT. Why is this so important? According to the 2015 Verizon Breach Investigation Report (VBIR),[6] studies showed that 99.9 percent of the exploited vulnerabilities were compromised more than a year after the CVE (method to patch) was published. This means that the majority of businesses that had a vulnerability exploited had over a year to fix it based on when the vulnerability was publicly announced. The same report showed that the most-exploited vulnerabilities for 2015 have been known since 2007. Chapter 7, "Vulnerability Management," covers best practices for vulnerability management.
- All host systems and servers should have protection software with signature-based and behavior-based protection features. Most vendors in this market space offer feature bundles that can include antivirus, antimalware, content filtering, host-based IPS, and so on.
- Another good practice is to enable process whitelisting or to use breach-detection applications to prevent unauthorized programs from running. These solutions offer capabilities beyond signature based antivirus by monitoring and controlling what processes are used by applications and processes and by looking for unusual endpoint behavior. Cisco Advanced Malware Protection and Bit9 are examples of breach-detection solutions.

Compute

Compute generally refers to the processing resources available on a system, represented in terms of processors, cores, and speed in gigahertz (GHz). For example, a quad-core 2-GHz processor contains four independent 2-GHz cores, where a core is a CPU that executes machine instructions. Common CPU architectures include x86 (32 or 64 bit), SPARC, and PowerPC. Note that the compute discussion is always coupled with the available system memory resources. Compute can also be carved up using virtualization technology to maximize the investment in the system. There are pros and cons to using virtualization versus dedicated compute.

Dedicated Versus Virtualized Environment

With today's technology, you have the choice of provisioning compute resources in dedicated and virtualized modes. *Dedicated* refers to deploying operating systems directly on bare-metal hardware. *Virtualization* enables you to host multiple guest machines that share the same underlying hardware, optimizing the allocation of resources in terms of processing power, memory, network connections, and so on. Examples of virtualization software include commercial products such as VMware vSphere,[7] Microsoft Hyper-V,[8] and open source products such as KVM,[9] Xen,[10] and VirtualBox.[11] Figure 5-7 is an example of how system virtualization can run multiple separate virtual systems on the same hardware.

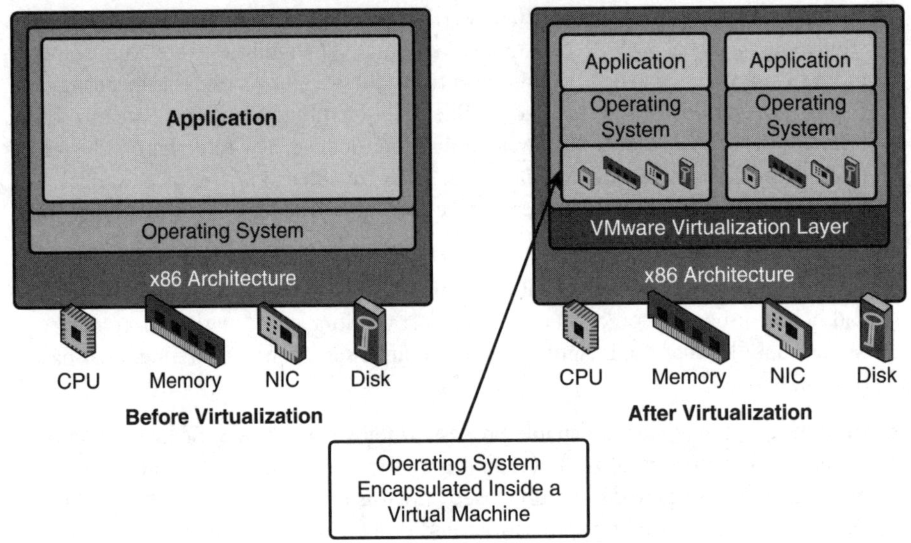

Figure 5-7 *System Virtualization*

Applications tend to perform slightly slower when operated in a virtualized environment. For example, according to the Splunk capacity-planning manual, the Splunk application can index data about 10 percent to 15 percent slower on a virtual machine than it does on a standard bare-metal machine. Similar performance drops are expected with other open source and commercial software.

When considering virtualized technology, it is important to verify that all applications can operate and are supported for virtualized environments. This includes identifying the performance impact that results when deploying the SOC application in the virtual environment, which may vary based on available resources on the hardware hosting the virtual services. Best practice is also to include logical segmentation of SOC and non-SOC applications and users in a virtualized environment to ensure data protection.

The amount and type of compute resources required to operate the SOC infrastructure depend on a number of factors such as the SOC services; the model of data collection; the location, type, and amount of data to collect, process, store; and the technologies of choice. Remote sites generally connect to the rest of the network using what is considered low-bandwidth links, limiting the amount of nonproduction traffic that can be sent to a central collection location. This typically forces you to deploy compute resources near the data for collection and possibly analysis purposes.

The amount of data can be expressed in terms of events per second (EPS) in the case of collecting logging messages, flows per second in the case of collecting network flows, and (K/M/G)bps in the case of capturing network packets. The amount of data to collect and process has a direct impact on how you design your compute infrastructure in terms of the number of collection engines to deploy to distribute the workload of processing incoming events and the number and speed of CPUs and the amount of memory to deploy per machine.

Let's take Splunk as an example. Figure 5-8 estimates the number of Splunk search heads and indexers to deploy based on the daily data volume processed by the indexers and the number of system administrators accessing the search head web interface. A Splunk search head is an instance with a web interface that accepts users and directs search requests to place the results into an index.

	Daily Indexing Volume						
	<2GB/day	2GB to 250GB/Day	250GB to 500GB/Day	500GB to 750GB/Day	750GB to 1TB/Day	1TB to 2TB/Day	2TB to 3TB/Day
Total Users: Fewer Than 4	1 Combined Instance	1 Search Head 1 Indexer	1 Search Head 2 Indexers	1 Search Head 3 Indexers	1 Search Head 4 Indexers	1 Search Head 8 Indexers	1 Search Head 12 Indexers
Total Users: Up To 8	1 Combined Instance	1 Search Head 1 Indexer	1 Search Head 2 Indexers	1 Search Head 4 Indexers	1 Search Head 5 Indexers	1 Search Head 10 Indexers	1 Search Head 15 Indexers
Total Users: Up To 16	1 Search Head 1 Indexer	1 Search Head 1 Indexer	1 Search Head 3 Indexers	1 Search Head 4 Indexers	2 Search Heads 6 Indexers	2 Search Heads 12 Indexers	2 Search Heads 18 Indexers
Total Users: Up To 24	1 Search Head 1 Indexer	1 Search Head 2 Indexers	2 Search Heads 3 Indexers	2 Search Heads 4 Indexers	2 Search Heads 6 Indexers	2 Search Heads 12 Indexers	2 Search Heads 18 Indexers
Total Users: Up To 48		1 Search Head 2 Indexers	2 Search Heads 3 Indexers	2 Search Heads 4 Indexers	3 Search Heads 8 Indexers	3 Search Heads 16 Indexers	3 Search Heads 24 Indexers

Figure 5-8 *Splunk Recommended Configuration*

Choice of Operating Systems

SOC tools are typically provided as software packages that have support for common operating systems such as Microsoft Windows and various UNIX and Linux implementations such as Solaris, AIX, Red Hat, and CentOS. There are many things to think about when considering an operating system for SOC analysts. You should first evaluate the operating system that has already been standardized across the organization. Most likely, there are already purchasing contracts in place and staff with expert knowledge on supporting those systems. Also review the support contract attached to the operating system, with an emphasis on service level agreements (SLA) and local support if applicable. Finally, verify that all expected applications to run on the operating system are supported.

Storage

One crucial technical function of a SOC is collecting, processing, and storing data of various formats and from various sources. The amount of data to collect and store can range from multiple gigabytes to multiple terabytes or even petabytes per day. The size and distribution of this data influence the technology and design used to efficiently store it. The storage infrastructure setup can range from the use of local disks to a distributed cluster-based storage solution. Tools that usually consume most of the storage resources are the logging servers, whether dedicated or integrated within the SIEM tool, and tools that perform packet capture and storage.

Deploying a new storage facility for the purpose of the SOC or making use of an existing storage implementation involves different design and operation options. Generally, it is preferable to deploy centralized storage using a storage-area network (SAN) or network-attached storage (NAS), rather than using attached storage. In the case of SAN, deploy SAN switches that allow you to connect multiple servers to the storage infrastructure using Fiber Channel (FC). The SOC team will probably not be the expert on managing storage solutions. Therefore, it might be preferable to hand over the operational aspects of the new storage platform to a team that is skilled in operating storage solutions. Make sure that they use best practices such as data access control to secure storage environments such as SANs and NASs.

Other important factors related to data storage are the cost of retaining large volumes of data and legal regulations. Cost is influenced by the type and amount of data, such as storing data packets versus network telemetry. A good practice is to store at least 1 year's worth of log data that is ready to access, while possibly archiving longer for data that would require additional effort to access. In addition, regulations such as Sarbanes-Oxley (SOX) and North American Electric Reliability Corporation Critical Information Protection (NERC CIP) impact the overall retention period for logs and the process for destroying logs that are no longer required. For example, NERC CIP 008-4 R2 requires at least 3 years of storage of documents related to cyber incidents. To be compliant, is critical to identify all associated legal requirements during the planning phase to plan for the additional associated costs.

Capacity Planning

Capacity planning is based on the SOC data-retention policy and what is required for incident investigation. A *data-retention policy* refers to the amount of time collected data must be kept. The higher the data-collection rate, the less amount of time it stays in your SOC disk storage facility, which is considered expensive when compared to other long-term, lower-cost storage options such as magnetic tape and optical disks. If the SOC disk storage capacity is lower than the specified data-retention policy requirement, it is recommended to implement a data backup facility or integrate the SOC with the existing organization's backup implementation.

During an incident, the SOC will require access to data that was previously collected by various elements such as logging messages of network packets. This data should be available during an incident investigation, and might require additional steps for uncompressing and reloading into the proper SOC tool. Design consideration should include when data should be transferred from short- to long-term storage based on business requirements and technical capabilities.

Figure 5-9[12] presents a projection for the cost of storage technologies, including the disk and tape options.

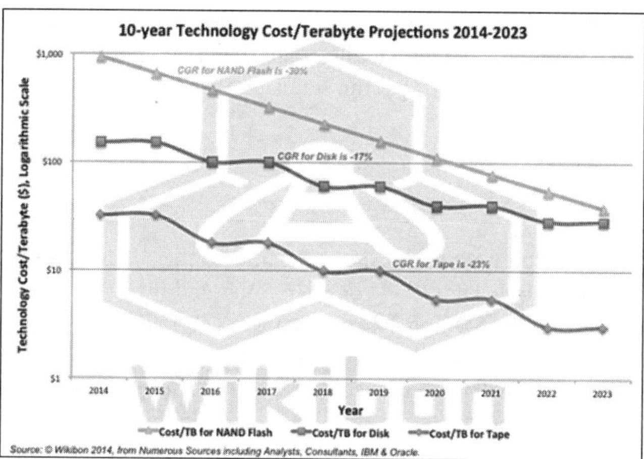

Figure 5-9 *Disk Technology Price Projections*

Collaboration

The SOC team requires quick and easy access to information about systems, tools, processes, policies, and so on. This is possible by provisioning an area where information is posted and discussion is facilitated. Various options can be considered when choosing a SOC collaboration platform. Options include the use of a wiki-style platform such as Mediawiki[13] or an enterprise-level collaboration application such as Microsoft SharePoint. Information that is generally shared on the SOC collaboration platform could be security policies, incident response plans, asset listings, contact information, network diagrams, and so on.

Access to the SOC collaboration platform or area should be controlled. Users should be authenticated and authorized before accessing SOC information posted on the collaboration platform. Authenticating against a centralized user database such as Lightweight Directory Access Protocol (LDAP) is recommended. In addition, traffic to and from the collaboration platform should be secured using Transport Layer Security (TLS).

Ticketing

Ticket management is directly connected to the security incident response program, where incident service requests are created, updated, and closed according to the incident handling process. Ideally, you want to make use of the organization's existing service request platform to keep track of security incidents. To separate SOC-related tickets, the system should assign a specific SOC tag to each ticket and the required security incidents fields should be incorporated in the service request tag. This will simplify the party responsible for handling the ticket.

The integration between the SOC tools and the service request platform can be implemented in a number of areas, including linking the SIEM and the vulnerability management tools with the service request platform. A SOC analyst should be able to open and populate a security incident service request from the SIEM tool, eliminating or possibly minimizing the manual effort required to raise and populate a new request. The service request fields should be aligned with the incident-handling plan such that important information is being appropriately captured and that the status of an incident can be continuously tracked.

Summary

This chapter covered various things you want to consider when designing a SOC infrastructure. The coverage started with some high-level considerations, and then delved into specific subjects such as the facilities, the SOC analyst environment, and different technology considerations. These topics were kept high level with a focus on what is needed for planning and design purposes. You will learn more about many of these topics, such as which technology to select and best practices for installation, later in this book.

The following chapter takes a deeper look at SOC technologies as you learn about best practices for data collection and analysis.

References

1. http://tomcat.apache.org
2. http://www.jboss.org
3. http://www.openssl.org
4. http://iase.disa.mil/stigs
5. http://www.cisecurity.org

6. http://www.verizonenterprise.com/DBIR/2015/
7. http://www.vmware.com/products/vsphere
8. http://www.microsoft.com/en-us/server-cloud/solutions/virtualization.aspx
9. http://www.linux-kvm.org
10. http://www.xenproject.org
11. http://www.virtualbox.org
12. http://wikibon.org/blog/why-tape-is-poised-for-a-george-foreman-like-comeback/
13. http://c2.com/cgi/wiki?MediaWiki

Chapter 6

Security Event Generation and Collection

"You will miss the best things if you keep your eyes shut."—Dr. Seuss

This chapter covers ways to collect data from various sources so that it can be converted into a useful format for the security operations center (SOC). The chapter provides many examples of data-producing sources, ranging from network firewalls to security software installed on end-user devices. Each data-generating source covered includes steps on how to export data to a centralized correlation utility. The chapter concludes with a discussion about how to use behavior analytics from NetFlow tuned to alert the SOC of top areas of concern, such as network breaches or systems reaching maximum capacity. This can be extremely useful, because many common network products that might not offer security features can support NetFlow.

It is absolutely critical that all aspects of data collection and analysis be designed properly to avoid gaps in how the SOC monitors the environment. A small blind spot could be a doorway to a future attack. For this reason, best practice is to layer security-monitoring points across the network and monitor all events from a centralized data-collection solution. This gives the SOC quick visibility across many systems and the ability to catch more advanced threats by using data correlation between what is seen by multiple products or through traffic-collecting taps. The value of data correlation was covered in Chapter 2, "Overview of SOC Technologies."

Best practice is to leverage a centralized data-collection solution to act as the SOC's first point of contact when investigating events. Let's start by looking at how the centralized data-collection system should be prepared before collecting data from security sensors.

Data Collection

Chapter 2 covered what *relevant data* means and how it is used to monitor for different types of events. Chapter 2 also touched on common tools used to obtain data and how to process syslog data using parsing and normalization so that it can be properly analyzed later for points of interest. Every solution functions a little differently; however, most will probably enable you to export syslog messages and follow common-practice logging security levels previously covered in Chapter 2.

It is important to properly size your data-collection solution for the number of expected data-generating products on your network. This includes considering how much data they will produce during normal and peak operation. To properly size a data-collection solution, you should answer three basic questions:

- How many devices are sending data?
- How many events per second (EPS) are generated by each device?
- What are the data-retention requirements for captured data?

Typically, the number of devices and data-retention terms is easier to prepare for than predicting EPS when developing a new network. It is critical to calculate an accurate EPS value to avoid oversizing or undersizing your data-collection solution. Oversizing could mean paying too much for your solution, and undersizing could crash the system or cause you to lose valuable event data. EPS also impacts storage requirements because very chatty devices will produce more data, which equals larger short-term and long-term storage needs.

Calculating EPS

There is not an official chart listing vendor devices and expected EPS because of the number of factors involved that impact the EPS number. The most accurate way to determine EPS is to place a syslog server on your network and measure your EPS for a specific time. For example, you can go to http://www.kiwisyslog.com to learn how to create a Kiwi syslog server, which may require some licenses (or you can use an Ubuntu environment to create a syslog server for this purpose). The goal is to run a syslog server for 24 hours and identify log trends during normal and peak times. Then you calculate the EPS by using the formulas covered later in this chapter. Those formulas not only assist with calculating EPS but also accommodate for unusual traffic behavior, such as spikes commonly seen during an incident.

Let's look at the steps to set up a simple Ubuntu syslog server for testing EPS.

Ubuntu Syslog Server

Ubuntu is an open-source Debian-based Linux operating system that runs everywhere, from smartphones to desktop environments. Ubuntu has a huge following, with many resources available to assist with customizing the software for almost any possible computing task. For this example, we use a default installation leveraging the 15.04 version of software.

The first step to build an Ubuntu-based syslog server is to install the syslog application on an Ubuntu system. Open a command-line terminal and type the following commands:

```
sysadmin@ubuntu:~$ sudo apt-get update
sysadmin@ubuntu:~$ sudo apt-get upgrade
sysadmin@ubuntu:~$ sudo apt-get install syslog-ng
```

This downloads and installs the syslog-ng application. It is important to note that the Ubuntu system must have Internet access for this command to trigger the software download. Also note that we are including running updates before launching the installation of syslog-ng.

When the installation is complete, you must configure the syslog server to receive messages from data-generating devices. We cover steps to export logs from various types of devices throughout this chapter. For this Ubuntu syslog exercise, we configure the syslog server to accept syslog messages from a specific firewall. There are many tuning options available; however, we will keep things simple for now. To configure the syslog server, we use the nano configuration utility. Once again, there are many editor utilities available as an alternative to nano; however, we use nano for our example.

Start by opening the syslog server configuration using the nano configuration utility:

```
sysadmin@ubuntu:~$ sudo nano /etc/syslog-ng/syslog-ng.conf
```

This brings up the syslog server configuration file. Now we need to configure our syslog server. For this example, we use an IP address of 192.168.1.50 to represent a firewall that will export syslog messages to our syslog server. We configure our syslog server to use the IP address 192.168.1.200 and listen on UDP port 241. We also need to specify a folder to store capture logs. That folder will be located at /var/log/eventdata.log. Figure 6-1 shows this setup and is followed by the configuration with explanations for each line of code.

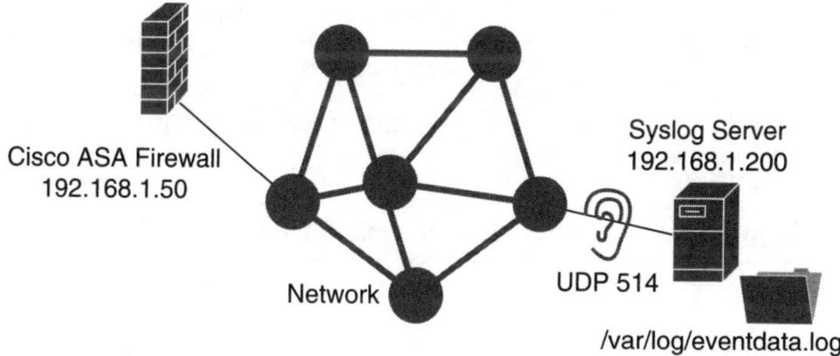

Figure 6-1 *Syslog Server Example*

Step 1. First, define the source for syslog events using the **source** command:

```
source source_example { udp(ip(192.168.1.200) port(514)); };
```

Step 2. Use the **filter** command to match traffic to all syslog messages from the firewall generating logs:

```
filter filter_example { host( "192.168.1.50" ); };
```

Step 3. Specify where to send syslog messages using the **destination** command:

```
destination destination_example { file("/var/log/eventdata.log"); };
```

Step 4. Bring the source, filter, and destination rules together with the **log** command:

```
log { source ( source_example ); filter( filter_example ); destination
  ( destination_example ); };
```

When the configuration is complete, you need to restart the syslog-ng process using the following command:

```
sysadmin@ubuntu:~$ sudo /etc/init.d/syslog-ng restart
```

This is just one approach to build a simple syslog server for testing EPS. You can learn more about using Ubuntu at http://www.ubuntu.com.

To measure EPS on an individual device, you can get a decent idea about how many EPS are being generated by setting up local logging. This will not give you network-wide EPS factors; however, it can give you an estimated EPS based on the security level of enabled logging for that device. For example, to enable local logging on the Cisco Adaptive Security Appliance (ASA) firewall, issue the command **logging buffered** *level* from the configuration level command prompt, where *level* is a value between 0 and 7 representing the security level. Many popular security products use the logging level values represented in Table 6-1.

Table 6-1 *Security Logging Level Values*

Level Number	Severity Level	Description
0	Emergencies	System is unusable.
1	Alert	Immediate action is needed.
2	Critical	Critical conditions.
3	Error	Error conditions.
4	Warning	Warning conditions.
5	Notification	Normal but significant editions.
6	Informational	Informational messages only.
7	Debugging	Debugging messages only.

When running this test, it is important to set the security level to what will generate similar log messages you would want to be sent to your centralized logging utility. The higher the level, the more logging you will generate because you will be enabling logs for that and any level lower than that security level. For example, logging at the warning level would use the command **logging buffered 4** and would enable logging for events that fall under levels 4 to 0. On many products, such as Cisco ASA firewalls, logging begins as soon as the command is executed.

Note Before testing for your EPS, it is critical that you first enable all security devices to generate their expected normal log information. Do not tune the network for a nonrealistic environment; otherwise, you will end up over- or undersizing your normal EPS.

The next step for testing EPS on a Cisco ASA is to use the logging buffer counter as a way to baseline your EPS. Use the command **show logging** to start the clock for monitoring the buffer logging, as shown in Example 6-1. You cannot reset the counters on a running ASA firewall; however, you can take the number of logs when you first ran the **show logging** command and subtract that from the number of logs generated after a set time to get an idea of how many logs you are generating. Figure 6-2 shows an ASA5512-X series firewall displayed zero logs when I first ran the **logging buffered 4** command, meaning my lab ASA did not have any level 4 or higher logs recorded. (It is a lab environment, so you should export more logs in an active environment.) I can come back 24 hours later and see what the final log count is to get an idea of how many logs this firewall will generate on a daily basis, assuming it is connected to an active network. I can also mathematically compute its EPS by using a formula covered later in this chapter.

Example 6-1 show logging buffered *Command on a ASA5512-X*

```
ciscoasa(config)# logging buffered 4
ciscoasa(config)# show logging
Syslog logging: disabled
    Facility: 20
    Timestamp logging: disabled
    Standby logging: disabled
    Debug-trace logging: disabled
    Console logging: disabled
    Monitor logging: disabled
    Buffer logging: level warnings, 0 messages logged
    Trap logging: disabled
    Permit-hostdown logging: disabled
    History logging: disabled
    Device ID: disabled
    Mail logging: disabled
    ASDM logging: disabled
ciscoasa(config)#
```

If you are preparing for a new network and cannot test live devices, your only option is to calculate an approximate EPS. This is not the most ideal approach because calculating EPS this way involves a lot of guesswork. Before making any calculations, you must first have expectations for how detailed you want each security device to be tuned for logging. For example, logging all successful and unsuccessful logging attempts would produce a lot less data than logging Network Address Translation (NAT) on firewalls. Use the logging severity levels covered in Chapter 2 and earlier in this chapter as a guideline for deciding the level of logging that will meet your organization's requirements. The higher the number means more expected logging, and therefore a larger estimated number should be used. It is critical to understand that coming up with this number without any live testing will be pure guesswork.

Once you get a general idea of the level of event messages you plan to enable, you can use *normal* and *peak EPS* formulas to come up with a generic number. For normal traffic, the EPS formula is calculated using the following:

EPS = Number of System Events / Time Period in Seconds

The number of events will vary depending on many factors, such as the time of day, an unusual increase in user count, or major security event. To accommodate for EPS fluctuation, peak EPS should also be calculated. Peak EPS is important to be concerned about because typically this is when an incident is taking place. Undersizing a system for peak EPS could mean having your SOC's key monitoring tools fail when they are needed the most.

Accommodating peak EPS can be done by taking into consideration the following factors:

- **Expected number of peaks:** This is a guess at how many peaks you may experience on your network. A good default number is three, taking into consideration morning logins, lunchtime return, and end-of-business wrap-up. Make sure to adjust this to the proper level of risk for your business.
- **Duration of a peak:** This number represents how long you predict a peak would last. A good default is 1 hour; however, you should adjust this based on possible reasons for peak EPS to your organization's network.
- **Deviation factor:** This is the average deviation between normal EPS. Peak EPS can be radically higher during a spike; however, this number should consider longer-term peaks such as an excessive distributed denial-of-service (DDoS) attacks or network congestion. A good default number is two to five times normal EPS, but this can vary depending on possible reasons for peak EPS.

When looking at peak EPS, it is usually calculated based on daily expectations because common peaks tend to happen during specific hours of operations. To calculate the total peak events per day, use the following formula:

Total Peak EPS per Day = Normal EPS * Expected Number of Peaks * Duration of a Peak (Seconds) * Deviation Factor

There are 86,400 seconds in a day, so divide the total peak EPS per day by 86,400 to get your peak EPS.

Peak EPS = Total Peak EPS per Day / 86,400

Calculating normal and peak EPS requires guesswork and will be different for every environment. Regardless if you are using real numbers or estimating, it is best practice to build in at least 20 percent margin to ensure that you have enough space and process power on your data-collection solution. If you are unsure about your final calculations, it is highly recommended to stick with data from measuring active traffic or over estimate numbers so you include room for growth before designing your collection tool around your findings. You will be better off oversizing your investment and later cutting back after you are operational rather than not having enough storage or performance power to handle your environment.

One other factor in additional to sizing a centralized data-collection solution that must be correctly configured is accurate time synchronization between products. Let's look at how Network Time Protocol (NTP) can be used for solving this requirement.

Network Time Protocol

Having a centralized solution to collect data is invaluable, but there must be some order to how data is categorized; otherwise, the end result will not be useful to the SOC. We covered the general steps used by data-collection tools such as security information and event management (SIEM) systems to process data in Chapter 2; however, one key element that is required when collecting data is proper time synchronization. Logs must be time stamped to trace back the events and correlate findings against what other systems are seeing. Best practice to ensure that all systems are on the same time schedule is to use an NTP server. There are many publicly available NTP servers, or you can host your own NTP servers for clock synchronization of trusted systems.

Note We have seen environments where microsecond delays in time stamps cause major logging problems. It is critical to verify device capabilities for time stamping of events along with the SIEM used to collect the data to be sure the expected delays are acceptable.

NTP functions as a client/server model where the server is centralized trusted system clock for other systems. Some systems also contain a calendar used to initialize the system clock when the system is restarted. It is also common that the calendar function leverages NTP from another system to compensate for the inherent drift in calendar time. When setting the time of an individual system, there are four methods it can use to retrieve the proper time:

- Network Time Protocol (NTP)
- Simple Network Time Protocol (SNTP)
- Virtual Integrated Network Service (VINES) Time Service
- Manual Configuration

SNTP is a client-only limited version of NTP, meaning systems using SNTP can only receive time from NTP servers. SNTP typically provides time within 100 milliseconds of the actual time and does not offer any ability to authenticate traffic outside of configuring extended access lists. For these reasons, it is recommended to use NTP over SNPT whenever possible.

NTP typically runs over User Datagram Protocol (UDP), using port 123 for both source and destination. An NTP network usually gets its time from an authoritative time source, such as a radio clock or an atomic clock attached to a server. NTP reads the time from the authoritative resource and distributes it across the network so that all devices are in proper synchronization for time. An NTP client uses a polling interval to connect with an NTP server, which can range from 63 to 1024 seconds. Most clients do not need more than one NTP transaction per minute to synchronize with an NTP server.

Stratum describes how many NTP hops a client is from the authoritative time source. NTP clients use the NTP server with the lowest stratum number to identify the closest authoritative time source. Multiple authorized NTP sources can be configured on a client creating a list of NTP sources from which to select. Typically, this is statically configured and seen as an association of NTP servers. The recommended minimal number of servers is three to apply an agreement algorithm and detect inaccuracy between the three authoritative time sources. Some LAN environments may use IP broadcast as an alternative approach; however, the accuracy of timekeeping is marginally reduced because the information flow is one-way.

NTP can perform over nondeterministic path lengths of networks because it takes into consideration network delay, clock error between hosts, and the required clock offset between the server and client. Levels of accuracy such as within a 10-millisecond window can be maintained between a server and client separated by large distances 2000 km or longer, while local clock synchronization for most LANs tend to fall in the 1-millisecond level of synchronization.

NTP includes two checks to validate a system before syncing. First, it will not connect to a system that is not synchronized. Second, NTP compares the time reported from several systems and will not synchronize to a source that has a significantly different time from the other sources, regardless of whether it has a lower stratum number.

Best practice is leveraging the security features included with NTP because misconfigured time could spoil the accuracy of reporting and disrupt some services. Security features available for NTP are an access list-based restriction scheme and an encrypted authentication mechanism.

Deploying NTP

When deploying NTP, there are three association modes:

- **Client/server:** When using client/server mode, the client or dependent server is synchronized to a group member, but no group member is synchronized to the client or dependent server. This provides protection against protocol attacks or malfunctions with the NTP service.

- **Symmetric active/passive:** This mode uses a group of low stratum peers operating as mutual backups for each other. Each peer has one or more primary reference sources, and if a peer loses all reference resources, other peers automatically reconfigure so that time values can flow from surviving peers to others in the group. Peers operate by pushing or pulling the time values depending on the configuration.
- **Broadcast:** This mode uses a broadcast server to broadcast time over a local subnet address. A broadcast client is configured, allowing the broadcast client to respond to broadcast messages received. Using this approach is not as accurate as other modes and it is highly recommended to include authentication to avoid a malicious party from impersonating a broadcast.

Public NTP time servers and fully qualified domain name (FQDN) servers for NTP can be found at http://www.ntp.org. This is made up of over 50 public primary servers synchronized directly to coordinated universal time (UTC) by radio, satellite, or modem. These lists are updated frequently; however, there are also other sources available to the public for time synchronization.

For our next example, we cover configuring NTP on Cisco IOS devices such as routers and switches. We use the Cisco IOS device's hardware calendar for synchronization purposes. The first step is to verify what the current time is on the device. You can view the time using the command **show clock**. The following example shows my clock is set at 11:01 on Friday March 1 in 2002. This is obviously not correct:

```
NTPServer# show clock
*00:11:01.639 UTC Fri Mar 1 2002
NTPServer#
```

If this device is going to act as an NTP server, I need to configure the clock to the current time. To set the clock, we must first configure the time zone of the clock using the **clock timezone** *zone hours_offset* [*minutes_offset*] command. The default time zone is UTC, so if you select another zone, you must accommodate for the offset difference. This device is currently in Washington, D.C., so that means I should use the eastern standard time (EST) time zone with an offset of –5 hours from UTC. So for my example, I will use the command **clock timezone EST -5**. You can identify your current time zone by using websites such as http://everytimezone.com.

Another thing to consider about setting your IOS clock is daylight savings time, also known as summer time. To set the IOS clock to consider summer time, use the command **clock summer-time** (*time_zone*) **recurring** to specify when summer time should start and end for the corresponding specified days every year under the (config) interface. Note that for my example, the time zone would be EST. The next step is to configure the time under the # command line level by using the command **clock set** *hour:minute:second day month year* followed by the **clock calendar-valid** command under the (config) interface to specify this system is a authoritative time source. Here are the configuration steps for a Cisco IOS device configured for Washington, D.C., time:

```
NTPServer(config)# clock timezone EST -5
NTPServer(config)# clock summer-time EST recurring
```

```
NTPServer# clock set 09:16:00 24 Apr 2015
NTPServer(config)# clock calendar-valid
```

Doing a **show clock** confirms that my NTP server clock is now correct:

```
NTPServer# show clock
09:18:46.859 EST Sat Apr 25 2015
NTPServer#
```

The next step is to make this IOS device a master NTP server by setting the stratum number. I will go with a value of 3 for this example using the command **ntp master** *value*, where the value variable is 3. I want to specify where I am sourcing the NTP packet. I will use the loopback interface of my IOS device by using the command **ntp source** *interface*, where the *interface* value is loopback0 for my example. To view logging for troubleshooting purposes, I can use the command **ntp logging.** Here are these commands in action:

```
NTPServer(config)# ntp master 3
NTPServer(config)# ntp source loopback0
NTPServer# ntp logging
NTPServer(config)#
```

The last step that is highly recommended is enabling authentication. To do this, we first create an authentication key using the command **ntp authentication-key** *key_number* **md5** *your_key*. Next, we must tell the NTP server which key to trust by using the command **ntp trusted-key** *key_number*. Because we are using the client/server approach in this example, this is all you need because the server will not authenticate against a client. To create a key called cisco on an IOS NTP server, enter the following:

```
NTPServer(config)# ntp authentication-key 1 md5 cisco
NTPServer(config)# ntp trusted-key 1
NTPServer(config)#
```

Now I am ready to configure other Cisco IOS devices as clients that will use my NTP server for time synchronization. The first step on my client is to set the clock time zone and summer time just like we did with the NTP server. Next, we specify where the client should go to get its NTP information using the **ntp source** *location* command. The location can be a VLAN, interface, or so on. Because we have authentication configured on the NTP server, we need to specify the authentication key using the command **ntp authentication-key** *key_number* **md5** *your_key* on all clients before they can receive NTP information. Specify the trusted key by using the command **ntp trusted-key** *key_number* followed by the command **ntp authenticate** telling the client to first authenticate the server before using the NTP information. Example 6-2 shows the commands to set up an ASA5520 firewall as an NTP client that will be accessing my NTP server using the NTP server loopback IP address of 1.1.1.1.

Example 6-2 *Configuring a Cisco IOS Device for NTP Synchronization*

```
ASA-003fw(config)# clock timezone EST -5
ASA-003fw(config)# clock summer-time EST recurring
ASA-003fw(config)# ntp authentication-key 1 md5 cisco
ASA-003fw(config)# ntp trusted-key 1
ASA-003fw(config)# ntp authenticate
ASA-003fw(config)# ntp server 1.1.1.1
```

To verify my ASA5520 is now using the NTP server for time synchronization, I can use the command **show ntp associations.** Example 6-3 shows the NTP server 1.1.1.1 with a stratum of 3 is being used for time synchronization on this Cisco ASA.

Example 6-3 *Configuring a Cisco IOS Device for NTP Synchronization*

```
ASA-003fw(config)# show ntp associations
   address         ref clock      st  when  poll  reach  delay  offset      disp
*~1.1.1.1           127.127.7.1       3  20    64    17      0.9  431439    899.3
 *~200.100.34.4  127.127.7.1       8  28    64    360     0.9  -73.78    1600.
 * master (synced), # master (unsynced), + selected, - candidate, ~ configured
ASA-003fw(config)#
```

Many security and network products offer graphical user interface (GUI) managers that have a process to point the system time synchronization to an external NTP server. Typically, the setup is simply entering in the IP address for the trusted NTP resource. In the next example, we configure a Cisco FirePOWER Management Center to leverage an NTP server located at 198.18.133.1.

The first step is to log in to the FirePOWER Management Center and access the System Policy menu by going to the System tab and selecting the **Local** tab. Then from the drop-down menu, select **System Policy.** The left panel shows different menu options. Select **Time Synchronization.** This brings up an option for enabling NTP from a source you specify, as shown in Figure 6-2. Make your changes and click **Save Policy and Exit.**

And that's all there is to it. You can verify the time by clicking **System** and selecting **System Configuration** under the Local menu. Under the Configuration tab, select **Time** to verify the current time and where NTP data is being obtained.

One important point is to make sure to synchronize time on all devices before attempting to export logs to your centralized data-collection solution. Having devices out of sync for any time can cause massive logging complications and cause alerting to not be valid. If your existing network equipment is not capable of providing NTP master services, it might be ideal to leverage a dedicated atomic clock or hardware device for this purpose.

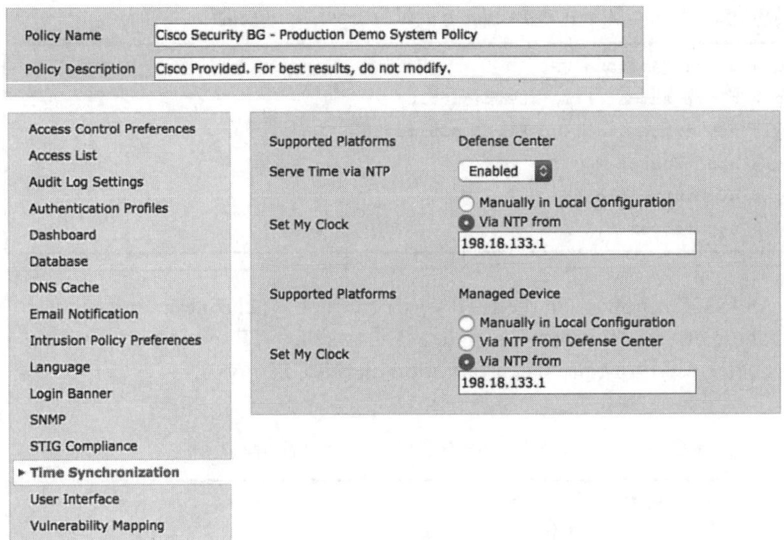

Figure 6-2 *Accessing Type Synchronization in FirePOWER Management Center*

Regarding data-collection solutions, you have many different vendors to choose from. Let's review how to evaluate different product offerings to get an idea of how each vendor can charge for sizing, what are possible capabilities, and other factors that could impact your decision for what would be the best solution for your SOC environment.

Data-Collection Tools

Chapter 1, "Introduction to Security Operations and the SOC," covered the different generations of SOCs. During that overview, SIEM technology was highlighted as a key element as the SOC's capabilities improved over time to handle events. Some environments may have generic syslog servers or vendor-specific threat intelligence managers that can serve as a data-collection tool, but the most common data-collection tool used in a SOC is a SIEM based on how a SIEM is designed to be vender neutral.

In summary, a SIEM is a blend of security information management (SIM) and security event management (SEM). SIMs focus on digesting larges amount of log data and making it easy to search through collected data, hence the name *security information management*. A SEM's goal is to consolidate and correlate large amounts of event data so that an administrator can prioritize events and react appropriately. Most SIEM vendors tend to specialize in SIM or SEM even though they offer both event and information management features. Figure 6-3 offers a breakdown comparing SIM and SEM technology and the blend of the two with regard to the general SIEM offering.

Security Information Management and Security Event Management Products	
Security Information Management (SIM) Search many logs, archiving, historical reporting, forensic investigations, data mining, operations focused.	Security Event Management (SEM) Real-time threat analysis, normalizing, correlation, aggregation, visualization, and incident response. Security operations focused.

Security Information and Event Management Products
Data mining, archiving, historical reporting, visualization, normalization, correlation, aggregation, forensic investigation, incident response. Security and operations focused.

Figure 6-3 *Comparing SIM, SEM, and SIEMs*

We covered the different generations of SIEM technology in Chapter 1, showcasing how SIEMs have evolved over time. When evaluating a SIEM vendor or other data-collection solution using technology available today, consider the following areas for identifying the best solution for your SOC.

Company

It is important to trust who you are doing business with. This means verifying that the solution provider is financially stable so that they will be around to support any possible issues you may encounter. Financially stable vendors can also invest in researching new features and provide a solid roadmap for improving solutions being offered.

Many industry analyst reports, such as Gartner, Forrester, NSS Labs, and so on, grade manufacturers, which can help with rating different vendors; however, it is extremely important to be aware of how the report is funded. Some vendors may be highlighted based on their financial contributions rather than real capabilities. Make sure to validate the research behind a report to avoid being fed false information about a product's capabilities. We recommend NSS Labs because they do not charge for vendors to be involved, publish how they test products, and are not afraid to publish when a vendor's product has poor performance according to their tests.

If you decide to do the research on your own, make sure to look at how long the vendor has been in the industry, marketplace opinions about the offering, money spent on R&D, financial performance, reference customers, and partnerships or alliances. Usually a little research can identify whether a vendor is worth your investment.

Product Options and Architecture

Vendors will have different flavors of a solution, so it is important to know how flexible their deployment architecture can be. Do they offer appliances, virtualized appliances, software, or any Software as a Service (SaaS) options? How is high availability designed, and what happens when components fail? How is the solution licensed, and does the cost model accommodate for growth without becoming too expensive? Is there additional required infrastructure such as storage, networking, and so on that is needed for the system to function properly? Be careful to capture the entire project's cost to become operational for a specific range of time, such as 5 years, rather than just the price to purchase the solution from the vendor. It is common to miscalculate the total cost of a project and not be able to properly bring the solution into operation due to unexpected expenses.

When looking at different SIEM vendors, look to see how data is collected. Are there agents involved, and what operating systems are supported? For agentless features, are industry standard formats such as syslog, SNMP, SQL, APIs, and so on supported? What are the EPS limitations? How well does the offering scale to your physical and logical environment? What APIs are available? Does the solution allow for local and remote storage? Can data that is stored be compressed and if so at what rate? How long can data be on box before it must be exported? How easy is it to bring old data back into the system to be evaluated? These are just a handful of architecture and product questions that you should answer before making a decision.

Installation and Maintenance

It is important to know what the difficulty level is to install and maintain the solution. Sometimes the most challenging part is the installation, which can be outsourced and is typically a one-time cost. Operational costs, on the contrary, are ongoing and can be extremely expensive if part of the project's cost is staffing for skills outside of your team's ability. Some vendors offer training courses and knowledge-transfer options to overcome the learning curve, along with periodic health checks to ensure the system is functioning properly. The requirement for training should rely on how intuitive the product is to use. Remember that in the end, it will be your network analysts who are responsible to use the system, so they must be properly prepared; otherwise, the solution might never be used to its full potential.

User Interface and Experience

How easy is it to use the product interface? Can the desired results be found quickly, and can a similar experience be flexible enough for the different operational groups that will use the system? Will the solution support role-based access control and the needs of a tier-based SOC analyst, incident handlers, responders, and so on? How detailed are the reporting features? Can data be controlled to only what should be seen by the authorized administrator?

Compliance Requirements

Some industries must have products that meet specific requirements. For example, any system that touches financial transactions in terms of credit card payments must be able to meet Payment Card Industry Data Security Standard (PCI DSS) requirements. Another example is how the U.S. Department of Defense requires the Joint Interoperability Certification (JITC) certification for products used on certain parts of the military network. If you have such requirements, make sure to request that the vendor provide evidence of certification or a written letter specifying when the solution will meet certification. Sometimes, having a letter justifying the technology is being tested with a expected data of certification is enough to meet a security audit; at other times, you need the actual certification.

Another compliance consideration may be legal and regulatory requirements. An example is a requirement to properly protect log files in the event they are needed for a civil/criminal proceeding because of a security incident. Many countries are adding these specific types of requirements, such as Europe's Network and Information Security (NIS) directive emphasizing reporting requirements.

This should give you a pretty decent checklist for evaluating solutions, but many other things could also impact your decision outside of these recommendations. The most important thing is that the people who will be using the solution support the product choice and that the end result is the best option for the mission of the SOC.

When your data-collection solution is ready and all systems have their clocks properly synchronized, it is time to start exporting log data on different devices from your centralized collection solution. Let's look at how to enable logging for common security and network devices so that data can be exported to your SIEM or other data-collection solution.

Firewalls

Webopedia.com defines a *firewall* as "a system designed to prevent unauthorized access to or from a private network."[1] This is the general definition of the purpose for a firewall; however, not all firewalls offer the same functionality. As firewalls have matured over time, they have added many more features, which in turn can provide greater logging details to a SOC centralized data-collection solution. Let's look at some different versions of firewalls to get an idea of what type of data we can expect to collect when exporting logs.

Stateless/Stateful Firewalls

The first firewalls to hit the market were based on static packet filtering. These worked by viewing each packet entering or leaving the firewall and either passing or rejecting the traffic based on a set of rules. They were not concerned with the trust of a connection, meaning verifying where packets came from or should be going, and hence they were stateless in nature. This made these firewalls vulnerable to IP spoofing, where an attacker could gain access by sending an IP address indicating it is on a trusted network to bypass the firewall's protection.

Stateful packet inspection was later added to examine the packets rather than only applying filtering. So, an incoming packet would be matched with the outbound request before being permitted. If the outbound request does not exist, that packet is dropped.

Many organizations are running stateful firewalls today. Logging options may contain the following data that could be exported to a SIEM or other centralized data-collection solution:

- Permitted connections by the firewall
- Denied connections
- Denied rule rates
- User authentication and command usage
- Cut-through-proxy activity
- Bandwidth usage broken down by connection, user, etc.
- Protocol and port numbers
- Network Address Translation (NAT) or Port Address Translation (PAT) auditing

We review stateful firewall architectures in Chapter 9, "The Technology" (because the focus of this chapter is on collecting data). Now let's look at Cisco's stateful firewall offering and learn how to export data to our data-collection solution.

Cisco Adaptive Security Appliance ASA

Cisco's most popular stateful firewall is the Adaptive Security Appliance (ASA) platform. The ASA was first introduced in 2005 as a replacement to the PIX firewall and VPN 3000 concentrator, combining firewall and VPN features from both platforms. The first generation of the ASA series also offered room for different security modules or blades such as antimalware and intrusion prevention, giving more options for additional security features. Figure 6-4 shows the front and back of a first-generation ASA 5520, which offered one physical module space for additional security features.

Figure 6-4 *Front and Back of an ASA5520*

The latest ASA models known as the second-generation ASA are labeled as the 5500-X series, offering an internal virtualized space capable of running additional features such as application layer firewalling, intrusion prevention, and malware defense rather than space for physical modules. Figure 6-5 is a logical diagram of how the second-generation ASA-X series separates ASA processing from the virtualized security module and how traffic can be routed between the ASA and security module using policy maps.

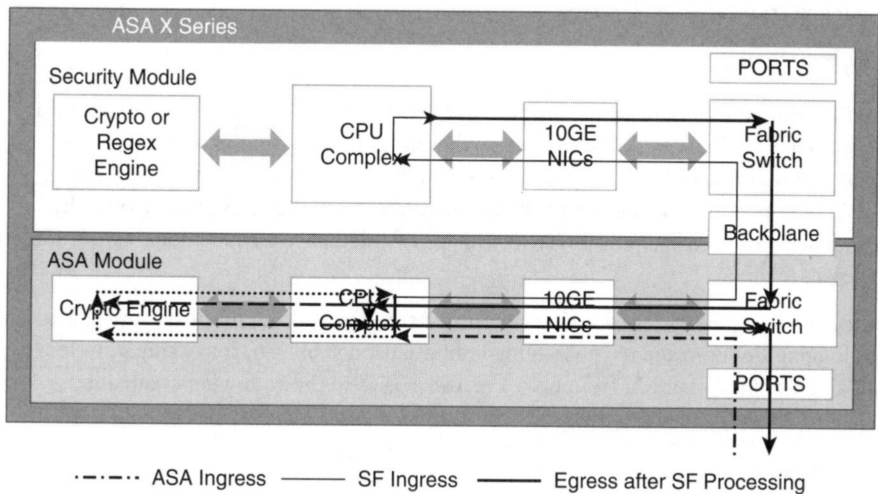

Figure 6-5 *Logical Diagram of ASA5500-X Traffic Flow*

The ASA5500-X series does not have spaces for modules because the additional features are installed in the virtualized space internally. Figure 6-6 shows the back of an ASA5525-X, which is part of the second-generation ASA series.

Figure 6-6 *Back of an ASA5525-X*

Managing the ASA can be accomplished locally using the command line or a Java-based GUI known as ASDM. Cisco also offers a centralized security manager known as Cisco Security Manager (CSM) capable of managing multiple ASAs. For the examples in this chapter, we showcase one method of enabling a feature: using the command line. However, most features have other tools available that can accomplish the same tasks.

Exporting ASA Data

The method to capture data from an ASA is to enable logging. Previously in this chapter, we demonstrated how to enable local logging to identify that system's EPS using the local memory. The command to enable local logging is **logging buffered** *level*, where *level* is the desired security level ranging from 0 to 7. Most likely, you will want to send these logs to an external data-collection tool such as a syslog server or SIEM. Let's review how this can be done.

To export logging to an external data-collection tool, use the following commands:

- **logging host** *interface_name ip_address* [*tcp*[*/port*] | *udp*[*/port*]] [*format embled*]
- **logging trap** *severity_level*
- **logging facility** *number*

The ASA sends syslog data on UDP port 514 by default, but the protocol and port can be modified as desired. If TCP is chosen as the logging protocol, this causes the ASA to send syslogs via a TCP connection to the syslog server. If the server is inaccessible, or the TCP connection to the server cannot be established, the ASA will, by default, block all new connections. This behavior can be disabled if you enable **logging permit-hostdown.**

To add debug log messages to syslog output for troubleshooting purposes, use the command **logging debug-trace** to the logging configuration steps. So, for example, to log debugging level information from host 192.168.1.15, use the following commands:

```
logging trap debugging
logging debug-trace
logging host inside 192.168.1.5
```

Syslog messages can also be sent to customize message groups using the message **list** command. This is can be useful to group alerts and send them to specific systems with additional information such as a work group identification number or the party responsible for viewing the logs. To configure a message list, use the following commands:

- **logging list** *message_list | level severity_level* [*class message_class*] creates a message list that includes messages with a specified severity level or message list.
- **logging list** *message_list* **message** *syslog_id-syslog_id2* adds additional messages to the message list.
- **logging** *destination message_list* specifies the destination of the message list created.

For example, to create a list called Critical_Syslogs that is concerned with level 2 or higher messages and have alerts forwarded to the SOC help desk's system located at 192.168.1.15, use the following commands:

```
logging list Critical_Syslogs level 2
logging list Critical_Syslogs message SOC_Helpdesk
logging host 192.168.1.15
```

You can do a similar export for all syslogs associated with a class using the message **class** command. The command is as follows:

```
logging class message_class destination | severity_level
```

Or you can use combinations of message lists and message classes such as the following:

```
logging enabled
logging timestamp
logging list my-list level debugging class vpn
logging trap my-list
logging host inside 192.168.1.15
```

Syslog messages can also be sent as e-mails using the following commands:

- **logging mail** *severity_level*
- **logging recipient-address** *e-mail_address*
- **logging from-address** *e-mail_address*
- **smpt-server** *ip_address*

Note A Simple Mail Transfer Protocol (SMTP) server is required to ensure successful relay of e-mails when you send ASA syslog messages by e-mail.

The commands to send syslogs to an external SNMP management station are as follows:

- **logging history** *severity_level*
- **snmp-server host** [*if_name*] *ip_address*
- **snmp-server location** *text*
- **snmp-server contact** *text*
- **snmp-server community** *key*
- **snmp-server enable traps**

Note An existing Simple Network Management Protocol (SNMP) environment is required in order to leverage this approach.

These are just some of the logging features you can enable on a Cisco ASA. Now let's look at the next generation of firewalls that appeared after the stateful firewall.

Application Firewalls

As firewalls became more relevant for security operations, a new generation of capabilities hit the market. Administrators needed to see and control more than traditional stateful firewalls, including traffic at the application layer of the OSI model. For example, administrators not only want to know whether an authorized computer is sending traffic over port 80 but also control how that connection is used. A common scenario is permitting social media such as Facebook but denying Facebook games, which could not be accomplished by a stateful firewall. Later in this chapter, we cover web proxies that can also accomplish this task; however, application firewalls cover all ports and protocols, whereas web proxies are limited to the ports they can monitor. This gives application layer firewalls an advantage at truly enforcing policies such as blocking applications like Skype that can tunnel over ports web proxies do not have visibility or control over.

Application firewalls act as a gateway or proxy by intercepting connections for each Internet protocol so that they can perform security inspection. The proxy function evaluates data sent by clients and either permits or denies, meaning that the firewall sits between client communications. The value of this approach is the ability to capture more details about traffic, such as user Raylin Muniz is on the inside network using a Windows XP computer to access the FarmVille application from http://www.facebook.com using a Firefox browser. So from a logging viewpoint, application firewalls can provide much richer data to the SOC about how the network is being used.

There are challenges to overcome, such as performance bottlenecks, when considering application firewalls. Many vendors can offer high-throughput point products; however, as different security features are enabled for unified products, process power is consumed and delays are introduced because of the time needed to inspect traffic. For example, many vendors can take a huge performance hit by enabling Secure Sockets Layer (SSL) decryption of all traffic crossing the application layer firewall. SSL decryption is becoming more of a requirement as popular websites such as Google and Facebook enhance security. So, bundling features such as intrusion prevention, antivirus scanning, SSL decryption, and so on can dramatically impact the actual throughput offered by a fully licensed application layer firewall. The easiest workaround for performance bottlenecks is to separate functionality as higher performance is needed, but this varies based on what is offered by the vendor.

Let's look at Cisco's application layer firewall offering and how to export data from it.

Cisco FirePOWER Services

Cisco first introduced application layer firewall capabilities as a software option that could be installed on the second-generation ASA or ASA-X series using the internal virtualized security module space. The first security module software packages known as CX was replaced with technology obtained during the Sourcefire acquisition in 2013. Today, Cisco's application layer firewall offering is known as FirePOWER services. Figure 6-7 shows various Cisco FirePOWER-capable devices.

Figure 6-7 *Examples of ASA FirePOWER -Capable Products*

FirePOWER series can be enabled on a second-generation ASA-X series or come as a physical or virtual FirePOWER appliance. All modules offer the same features based on three different license options.

FirePOWER license options are as follows:

- **Application Visibility & Control (AVC):** The default system supports over 3000 application layer and risk-based controls, in addition to visibility and control over geo locations, users, and websites. This also includes the ability to enforce usage and tailor detection policies based on custom applications and URLs. AVC comes with the default system.
- **URL Filtering Subscription:** The URL filtering license adds the capability to filter more than 280 million top-level domains by risk level and more than 82 categories. The URL Filtering license can be added alone or as part of a bundle by combining IPS and Apps or combining IPS, Apps, and AMP licenses
- **IPS Subscription:** The IPS license provides highly effective threat prevention and full contextual awareness of users, infrastructure, applications, and content to detect multivector threats and automate defense response. IPS licenses can be added alone or bundled in combination with either AMP or with the AMP and URL Filtering licenses.
- **AMP Subscription:** Advanced Malware Protection (AMP) delivers inline network protection against sophisticated malware. The AMP license option can be added as an individual license or bundled individually with either IPS or Apps or as one larger bundle with IPS, Apps, and the URL Filtering licenses.

All versions of FirePOWER, regardless of whether run on an ASA or as a dedicated physical or virtual appliance, are managed by a centralized physical or virtual manager known as FirePOWER Management Center (FMC). Individual sensors are accessed only by command line for the initial setup, and once they are added to the FMC, the FMC performs all configuration and management functions. This means that all reporting and logging information can be obtained from the FMC.

> **Note** New versions of ASDM are adding some management capabilities for when FirePOWER is run on an ASA-X series appliance. These capabilities will not be as feature rich as using an FMC, and therefore the recommendation is to use an FMC for centralized management whenever possible.

Figure 6-8 shows an FMC displaying details on what applications are being used, where people are going on the Internet, what type of servers are on the network, and the type of devices such as Windows laptops. Dashboards can be developed to focus on different administrative roles and responsibilities such as IPS threat data, network performance, identified malware, and so on. Dashboards can be exported as reports, as covered in the next section.

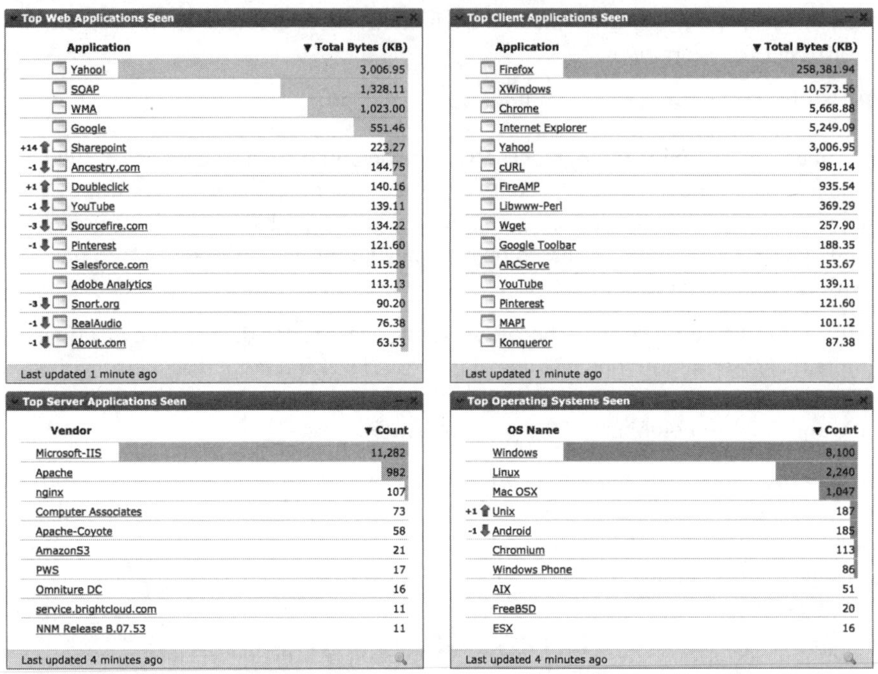

Figure 6-8 *FirePOWER Management Center Dashboard Example*

Exporting Data from FirePOWER

Although the FMC provides many great methods to view security events along with granular reporting capabilities, most SOC teams are going to export logging to an external data-collection solution for constant monitoring across all systems. The FMC can generate an e-mail, SNMP trap (SNMPv1, SNMPv2, or SNMPv3), or syslog when one of the following is triggered:

- A network-based malware event or retrospective malware event.

- A connection event that is triggered by a preconfigured access control rule.
- An intrusion event is triggered.

The first step to enable external alerting is to configure where and how the FMC should send alerts. This is called an *alert response*. After creating an alert response, you associate the alert response with the event that should trigger the specific alert. It is important to note that associating alert responses with events is different depending on if it is a malware event or connection event. Malware events use their own configuration page while connection events use access control rules and policies.

Some alerts require specific FirePOWER features to be licensed. Those alerts are as follows:

- Intrusion events are based on the IPS functionality and therefore require the IPS subscription.
- Malware-based events are based on the AMP license and therefore require the AMP subscription.
- Connection events are based on access control policies and therefore available with the base FMC license.

To create an alert response, log in to the FMC and go to the Alerts page found at **Configuration > Policies** tab **> Action** tab and select **Alerts**. The slider under the Enabled heading indicates whether the alert is active, and the In Use heading indicates whether the alert is being used in a configuration, such as an alert tied to a access control rule. Clicking a column header sorts the alerts when looking through multiple alert configurations. Figure 6-9 shows an alert response for e-mail and syslog that are not enabled or associated with a configuration.

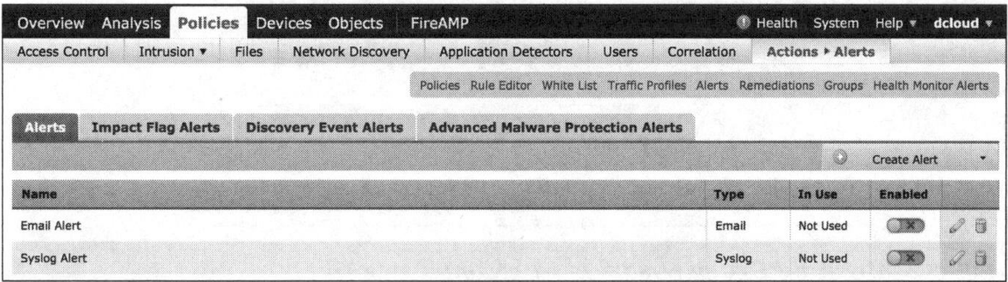

Figure 6-9 *Alert Response Configuration Example in the FMC*

To create a new alert, click the **Create Alert** button and select either **Create E-mail Alert**, **Create SNMP Alert**, or **Create Syslog Alert**. After you fill out the appropriate information and click **Save**, the alert response will automatically be enabled, but it will not be associated with a configuration. Figure 6-10 shows the form that pops up when selecting to create an SNMP alert.

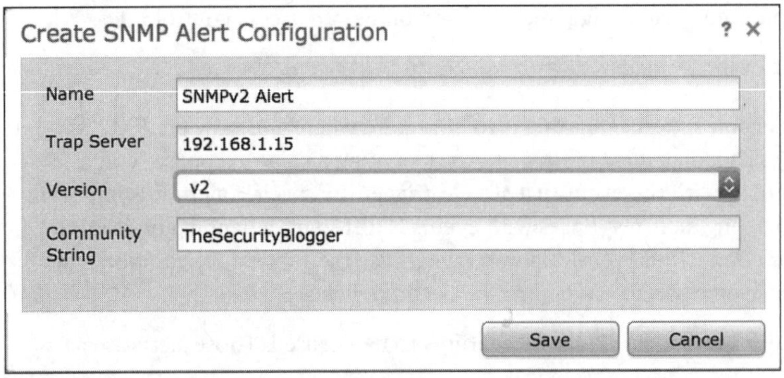

Figure 6-10 *SNMP Form Example in FMC*

Configuring a syslog alert response has a slightly different form. The default port field is 514, but can be customized as desired. The available syslog facilities and security levels are straightforward and available using the drop-down menus on the syslog forum. Figure 6-11 shows configuring a debug-level syslog alert.

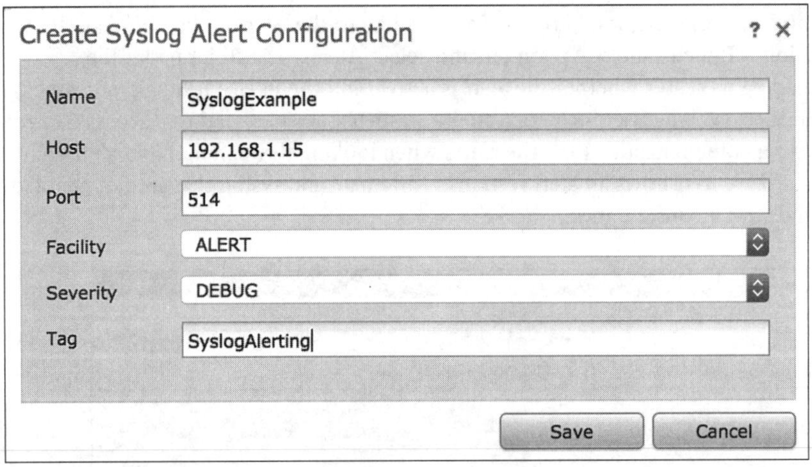

Figure 6-11 *Configuring Debug Syslog Alert Example in FMC*

To associate a connection-based alert with an access control policy, you must select the alert response you created under the Logging tab found when building the access control rule. To view the FMC access control rules, go under the **Policies** tab and select **Access Control.** You should see all the access control policies configured for your system. Figure 6-12 shows four different policies.

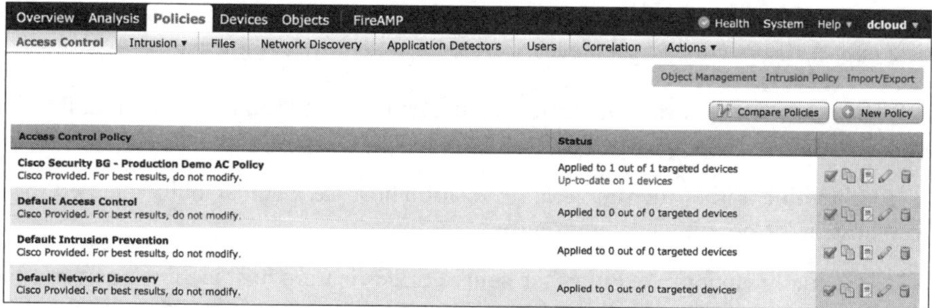

Figure 6-12 *Access Control Policy Examples in FMC*

Tip You can download a report showing your access control policy settings by clicking the report icon.

Select the pencil icon for the access control policy you want to edit, and that will bring up all the access control rules for that particular policy. You can create a new access control rule or edit an existing rule by selecting the associated pencil icon. When creating or editing a rule, there will be a Logging tab found on the right of the configuration window. Selecting the **Logging** tab brings up logging options for the access control rule. Here you can specify to log at the beginning and/or end of a connection, if you want to generate a file and specify where to send the logging. Selecting defense center (now called FMC) will store the logs locally, while syslog and SNMP are used for external systems. By selecting syslog or SNMP trap, you can use the alert responses created earlier in this chapter. Figure 6-13 shows a sample access control rule that will leverage both syslog and SNMP alert responses we used in the previous example demonstrating how to create alert responses.

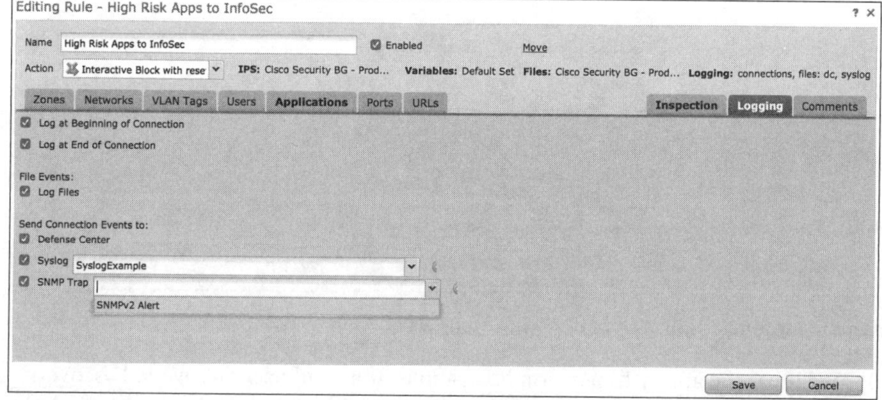

Figure 6-13 *Sample Access Control Rule in FMC*

You can use Impact Flag Alerting to generate alerting whenever an intrusion event with a specific impact flag occurs. Impact levels can be any one of the following:

- **(0) Unknown:** Neither the source nor the detination host is on a network that is monitored.
- **(1) Vulnerable:** Either the source or destination host has a vulnerability mapped to the host and is potentially compromised.
- **(2) Potentially vulnerable:** Either the source or destination host is using a server application protocol or host is using the protocol.
- **(3) Currently not vulnerable:** Either the source or destination host does not have the port open or not using the protocol.
- **(4) Unknown target:** Either the source or destination host is on the monitored network, but there is not an entry for the host in the network map.

Impact flag alerts are found by going to the **Policies** tab, selecting the **Actions** tab, and choosing **Alerts.** Under the Alerts section, select the second tab called **Impact Flag Alerts.** You can select to be notified via syslog, e-mail, or SNMP using the alert responses we previously created. Figure 6-14 shows enabling all impact flag alerts for syslog and SNMP notifications.

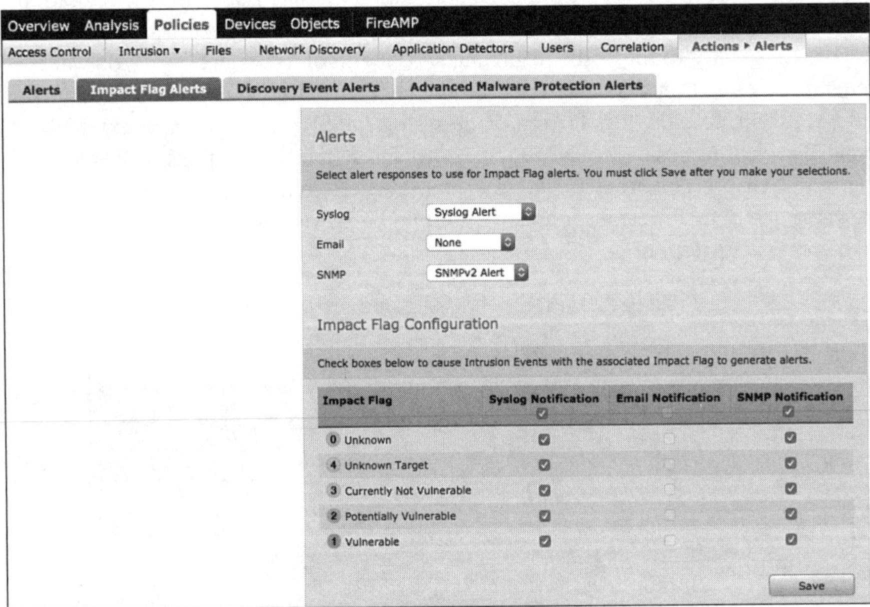

Figure 6-14 *Enabling Impact Flags Example in FMC*

FirePOWER has the ability to perform host, application, and user discovery. Discovery is used to create an up-to-the-minute profile of your network by monitoring traffic and determining the number and types of hosts, operating systems, active applications, and open ports on hosts. You can also configure a user agent to monitor user activity such as login data. Discovery data can be used to perform traffic profiling, assess network compliance, and respond to policy violatons.

Network discovery can be configured by going to the **Policies** tab and selecting the **Network Discovery** tab. This will show all network discovery rules being monitored by FirePOWER. To create a new rule, click **Add Rule**, which brings up the rule configuration page. You can specify different network ranges, call existing network objects or zones, and exclude different port types. At the top of the rule is the ability to either discover or exclude all the items selected along with the ability to include hosts, users, and applications in the discovery. Figure 6-15 shows creating a discovery rule for anything on the 192.168.1.0 /24 subnet.

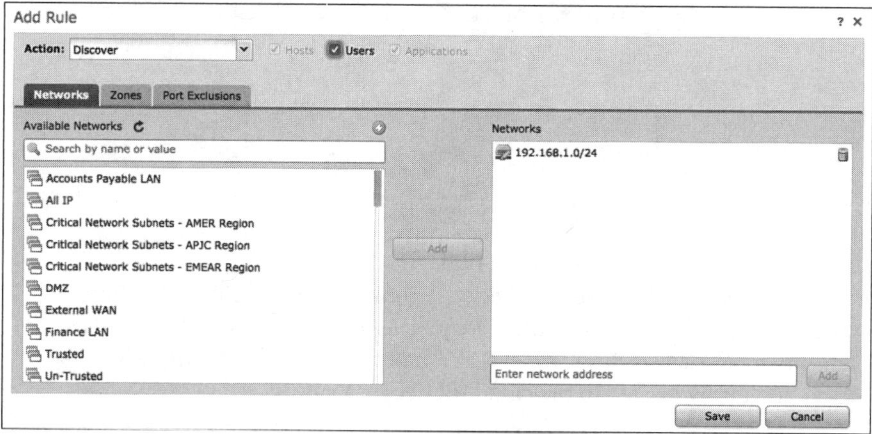

Figure 6-15 *Example of Creating a Discovery Rule in FMC*

Discovery event alerts can be configured to be triggered as different attributes about devices are identified by the FirePOWER solution. For example, you could create a syslog notification anytime a new device is discovered on a sensitive part of your network. There are a ton of event options to choose from, and you can specify a specific alert response to trigger for any event item selected. To create discovery event alerts, go under the **Policies** tab and select the **Actions** tab. Then select **Alerts.** Select the third tab for **Discovery Event Alerts.** Fill out the form to generate the desired alerts. Figure 6-16 shows using the syslog and SNMP alert responses created earlier in this chapter.

The last option under the Alerting tab is exporting alerts for AMP alarms. The focus of AMP is to identify unknown threats, meaning threats that would potentially bypass signature-based security such as antivirus or IPS detection. This is accomplished by using a combination of network and cloud analytics providing the following:

- **File reputation:** Analyze files inline and block or apply policies
- **File sandboxing:** Analyze unknown files to understand true file behavior
- **File retrospection:** Continue to analyze files for changing threat levels

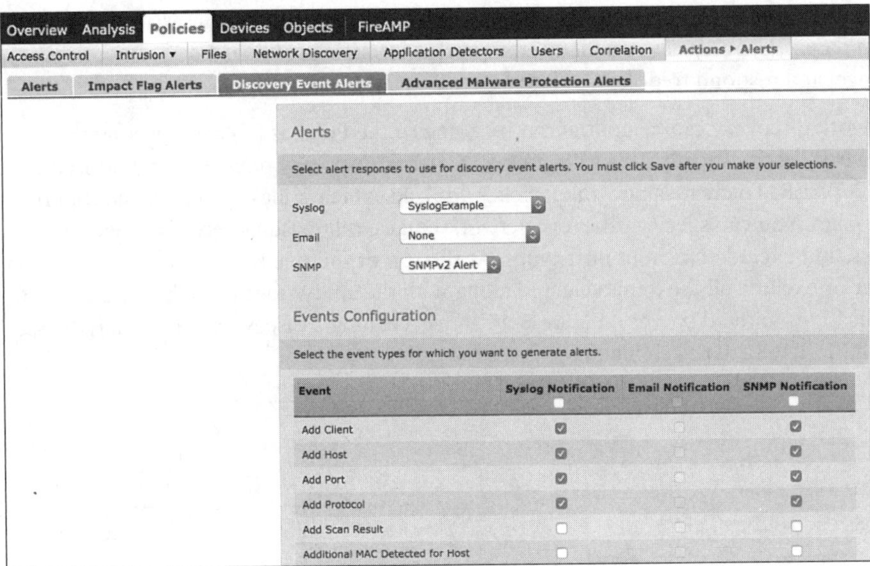

Figure 6-16 *Discovery Event Alert Example in FMC*

Figure 6-17 summarizes the different checks performed on every file by FirePOWER when the AMP licensed is enabled. Malware policies can be configured to view specific files category types such as PDFs, executables, and so on and also control what type of files could potentially be sent to the cloud for deeper analysis.

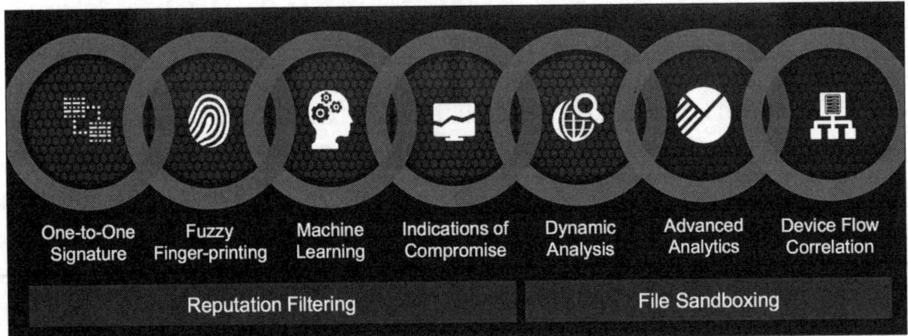

Figure 6-17 *Cisco AMP Detection Methods*

When a breach is identified, the associated SHA-256 hash of the file is tracked back to identify how the file first got on the network and identify all systems that contain the infection. This is called *retrospective security*, and is defined as the ability to go back in time to identify the entire lifecycle of the threat. Figure 6-18 shows an executable file identified as malicious, along with all systems that have the malicious file.

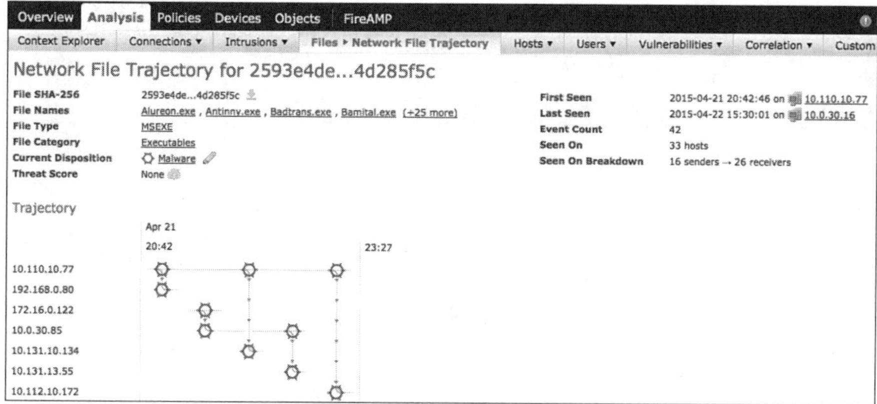

Figure 6-18 *Malicious File Tracked by Cisco AMP*

By clicking the first device in the attack timeline, we can identify who introduced the infection to the network (a.k.a. patient zero), along with how that user obtained the file. Figure 6-19 shows user 10.110.10.77 downloaded the indexing-intimidation.msexe malware using a web browser.

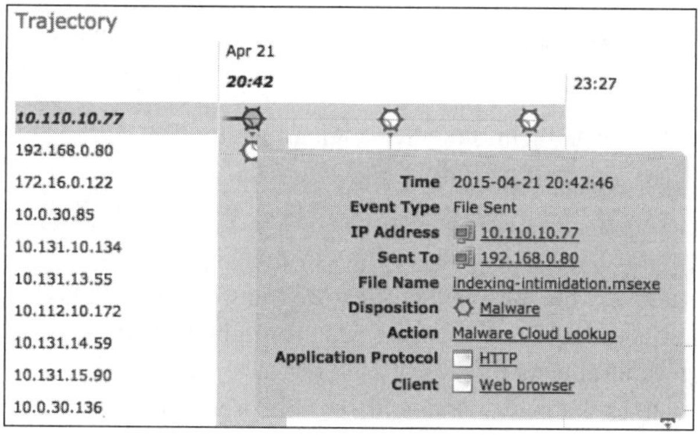

Figure 6-19 *Identifying Who Brought a Malicious File onto the Network with Cisco AMP*

Most likely, your SOC will want to know when a breach has been detected. You can configure AMP alerts using the alert responses we created earlier in this chapter. For example, you could have a syslog event and SNMP alert generated anytime a retrospective and network-based AMP alarm is triggered. Figure 6-20 shows how to configure this AMP alerts use case.

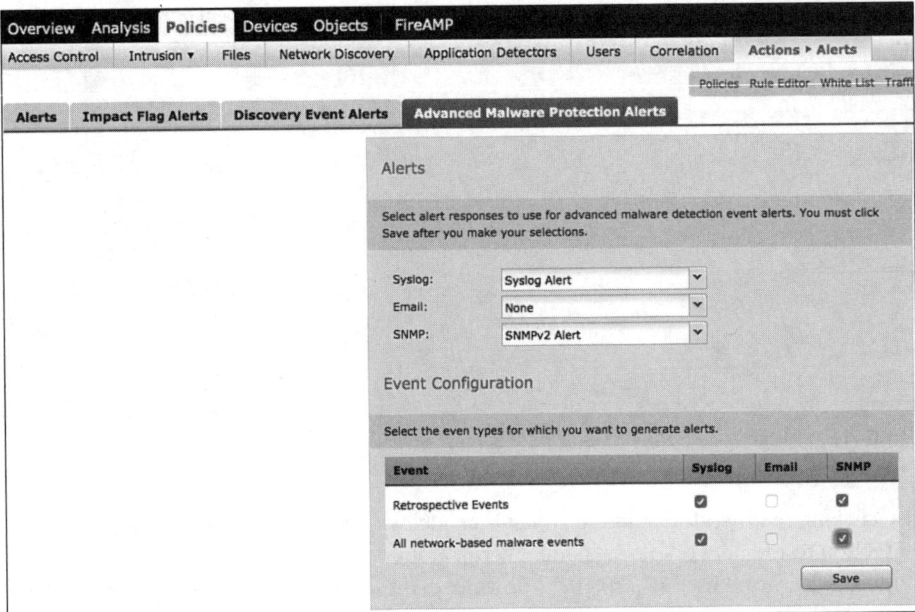

Figure 6-20 *Configuring AMP Alerts in FMC Example*

These are a few methods to export data from a FirePOWER solution to a centralized data-collection solution.

Now let's look at another form of firewall technology leveraging the cloud.

Cloud Security

As all technology becomes Internet capable, business models are transforming. Classic deployment strategies involving lots of hardware and laborious configuration are being replaced with outsourcing requirements to cloud-based services. Sometimes, specific pieces of the solution, such as the management, are cloud based while other solutions are 100 percent cloud offerings also known as Software as a Service (SaaS). An example of a full cloud offering from Cisco is the Cloud Web Security service that proxies all traffic from a connected device to the nearest Cisco cloud-based security enforcement point. No additional hardware is required as all features are licensed on a subscription basis.

Hybrid cloud technology is when part of a solution is delivered through a local component, while other components are part of a cloud service. The common use case is having management features handled through a cloud service to centralize controls and outsource any maintenance requirements. An example of this is the Cisco Meraki product line that offers onsite appliances that are managed through the cloud.

There are advantages to using a cloud and hybrid cloud versus dedicated appliances. Some advantages of using cloud technologies are as follows depending on the vendor's offering:

- Centralized manager for all products globally deployed.
- Simplified deployment because configurations are done using the cloud.
- Predeployment configuration can be sometimes be accomplished before technology arrives at its specified location.
- Maintenance such as firmware updates and feeds can be automatically applied.
- Compliance for mandates such as PCI and HIPPA can be met with a compliant cloud infrastructure.
- Web management typically is easier than command-line tools to master, lowering training requirements for administrators.
- Some offerings can reduce costs as physical components are replaced by cloud services.
- Technology upgrades could be less frequent depending on what components are managed by the cloud.
- Scalability and high availability can be simplified depending on what components are cloud-based services.

Some customers have concerns about sending sensitive data to a cloud-based solution. Our recommendation is to verify what industry certifications have been meet by the locations hosting the services and what type of encryption is leveraged to protect data in transit. For example, Cisco Meraki's solutions leverage SSL-encryption and have met level 1 PCI audits, and data centers hosting data have met SSAE16/SAS70 two II certifications. Cloud-based security solutions may not be ideal for some situations, so it is best to speak with a cloud consultant for more information.

Let's look a little deeper at the Cisco hybrid cloud security appliances, which include application layer firewall features.

Cisco Meraki

The Cisco Meraki product line is a catalog of network and security solutions that are centrally managed from the cloud. Cloud networking works by deploying either wireless access points, switches, or security appliances and connecting them to an Internet-capable network port. The device automatically establishes an encrypted SSL connection back to the Cisco network and downloads its configuration. All firmware updates and feeds such as application signatures are continuously deployed over the web, simplifying maintenance for the equipment. System administrators can manage all equipment from the Internet using the meraki.cisoc.com GUI manager.

The Cisco Meraki product line includes cloud-managed security solutions featuring similar capabilities as the ASA and FirePOWER services. Meraki security solutions offer features such as stateful as well as application layer firewalling, IDS, VPN, content filtering, antimalware, and antiphishing. Models range from the MX64 targeting small offices to the MX600 offering up to 1 Gbps of firewall throughput. More on the Meraki product line can be found at meraki.cisco.com.

Exporting Logs from Meraki

Log data can be exported from any Meraki offering by setting up exporting of logs from the Meraki cloud dashboard. The Meraki MX security product line supports sending four categories of messages. Those are Event Log, IDS Alerts, URLs, and Flows. Examples of logs are as follows:

- URL logs specifying any HTTP GET requests.
- Inbound or outbound flows will generate syslog messages showing source and destination along with port numbers and firewall rules they matched.
- Events such as leasing an IP address can generate event logs.
- Security events identified by the IDS will generate syslog messages.

Let's look at how to export logging from the Meraki cloud dashboard.

To access the Meraki cloud dashboard, open an Internet browser and go to https://meraki.cisoc.com. Click the **Login** option at the top-right corner and log in with your administration information. Once logged in, information about all managed Meraki equipment will be displayed on various dashboards. The management of networks can be divided into different organizations or seen as one large business depending on how the Meraki network is architected.

The logging functions can be found by going to the **Network-wide** tab, under the **Configure** section, and selecting **General**. This brings up different general configuration options for your Meraki environment. Scroll down to the section titled Reporting. The top of this section lists any existing syslog servers that are configured to receive messages. To add a new syslog server, click the **Add a Syslog Server** link. This brings up the option to provide a syslog server IP address, port (default value is 514), and a drop-down used to specify the types of syslog events to send. Figure 6-21 shows configuring a syslog server at IP address 192.168.1.200 and the available options for syslog event types to be sent.

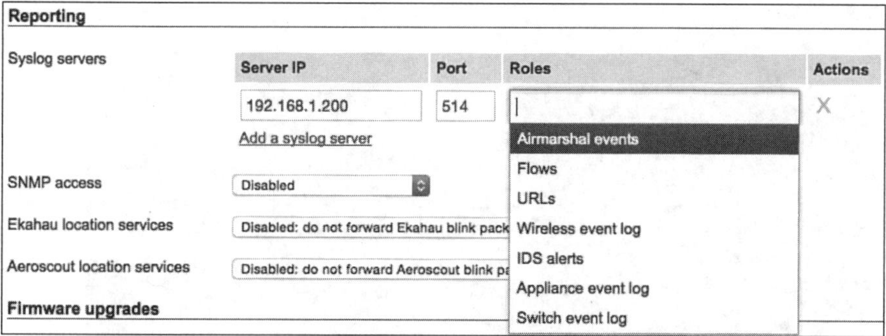

Figure 6-21 *Configuring a Syslog Server in Meraki Example*

Meraki also offers SNMP Version 1, 2, and 3, along with Ekahau and Aeroscout reporting support. That is all there is to it. You can repeat the process to add multiple syslog servers and rules for different types of alerts.

Now that we have covered different types of physical and cloud-managed firewall options, let's look at firewalling for virtualized environments.

Virtual Firewalls

A virtual firewall (VF) is a network firewall service or appliance that operates within a virtualized environment and provides similar security features of a physical firewall. For virtual networks, a VF controls communication between virtual machines in a virtual environment providing client-to-client or "east-west" traffic segmentation along with other features. Some virtual switches have firewall capabilities, and some dedicated VFs can manage kernel processes running with the host hypervisor.

It is extremely important that firewalls dedicated to data center traffic be architected to accommodate the existing data center design and not introduce additional packet loss. Traditional networks see the majority of traffic entering or leaving, whereas data centers typically operate in a reverse fashion, having most of the traffic take place internally. Common mistakes in data center security strategies are not considering security solutions for internal compute (that is, just focusing on what enters and leaves the data center) and assuming any vendor firewall can function properly for a data center environment. Figure 6-22 showcases the general concept of data center traffic.

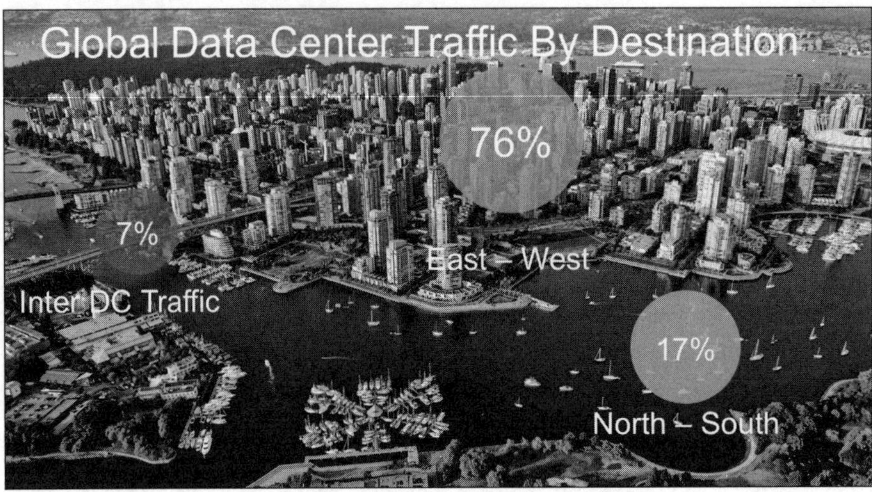

Figure 6-22 *Data Center Traffic*

We will dive deeper into data center architecture best practices, such as when to use a virtual versus physical firewall, in Chapter 9. Let's look at the Cisco offering for data center security and how to export event data.

Cisco Virtual Firewalls

Cisco Systems has a large catalog of data center products that range from virtual switching to network storage. Part of the data center catalog is security components that make up validated designs for security best practices. The core security products for these reference designs are virtual and physical firewalls that you can use for segmenting networks down to the virtual machine level. One option is using the Cisco ASA 5500-X series covered earlier in this chapter for this purpose. Other options are using a virtualized version of the Cisco ASA firewall or an integrated firewall option with the Nexus 1000v product line. Here is a description of these virtualized options:

- **Cisco Adaptive Security Virtual Appliance (ASAv):** Cisco ASAv brings the full ASA series firewall capabilities to virtual environments. The ASAv is optimized for vSwitches and can be deployed in Cisco, or other environments.
- **Cisco Virtual Security Gateway (VSG):** Cisco VSG is a virtual appliance available on the Nexus 1000v switch series used for controlling and monitoring traffic between trust zones using security policies.

You can find Cisco-validated designs covering best practices for leveraging virtualized firewalls at http://www.cisco.com/c/en/us/solutions/enterprise-networks/secure-data-center-solution/index.html. Chapter 9 covers data center security best practices for architecture. Now let's review how to export logs from these products.

Exporting Syslog Messages

The steps for exporting syslog data from an ASAv are similar to a physical ASA-X appliance because all versions of ASA use the same software. See the steps previously covered under exporting syslog data from an ASA-X appliance for more details on exporting syslog messages from an ASAv.

Exporting syslogs from a Cisco VSG can be performed using the Cisco Prime Network Services Controller. Let's review the steps to set this up:

Step 1. Go to **Policy Management > Device Configurations > A-Tenant > Policies** and select **Syslog**. Next, click **Add Syslog Policy**. This brings up a window with options to fill out. Specify the IP address of the syslog server, port (default 514), protocol (default UDP), level of logging, interface to send logs, and so on. Then click the **OK** button.

Step 2. Assign the syslog policy to a device profile. Go to **Cisco Prime Network Services Controller > Policy Management > Device Configurations > Device Profiles > A-Tenant > Device Profiles** and select **Add Device Profile**. This brings up a window for creating a new firewall device profile. One of the options under this window is to select a syslog policy. Use the drop-down window to select the syslog policy you previously configured.

Step 3. Assign the device profile to Cisco VSG. Do this by going to **Cisco Prime Network Services Controller > Resource Management > Managed Resources > Tenant > Compute Firewall** and selecting **VSG-Firewall**. The panel on the right side shows firewall settings. Select the device profile you previously created for syslog and save the configuration.

And that is all there is to it. Now let's move on to host-based firewalls.

Host Firewalls

Another version of virtual firewalls can be found on host systems. Most modern operating systems have virtual firewalls enabled by default designed to monitor and control incoming and outgoing traffic. Firewall features are either managed by the host administrator or through a centralized desktop management platform. It is rare for a SOC to collect host system firewall logs unless the administrator is troubleshooting the particular system. We cover securing host systems later in this chapter.

Intrusion Detection and Prevention Systems

An intrusion detection system (IDS) is used to monitor a network or system activities for indications of malicious behavior or policy violations. An IDS does not prevent attacks so it is purely a monitoring solution. Adding the ability to stop or block an attack is known as an intrusion prevention system (IPS). Today, most security products with IDS capabilities can also be configured to perform IPS depending on how the solution is deployed. Network IPS solutions are always deployed inline with the traffic of interest. This is a requirement to drop packets and defend against attacks before the malicious traffic hits the network or preventing unauthorized connections from leaving the network. Network IDS solutions can also be inline, but it is more common to place an IDS off a tap or SPAN port that views a copy of the traffic of interest.

Figure 6-23 shows some diagrams displaying common types of IPS and IDS deployments.

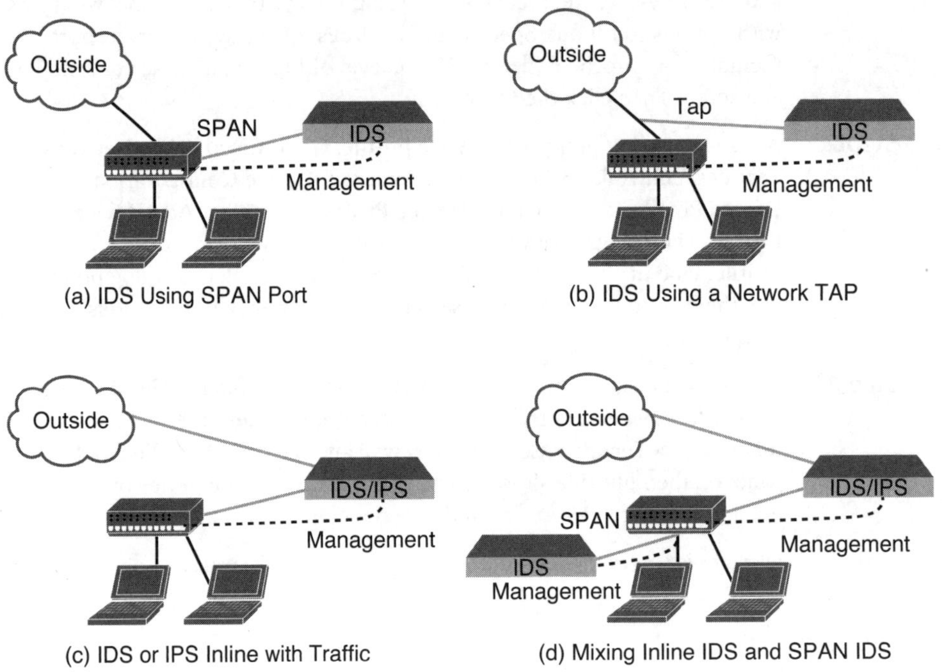

Figure 6-23 *Common IPS/IDS Deployments*

A security solution running as an IPS can also function as an IDS when it is designed to prevent traffic that is inline while simultaneously monitoring other traffic that can be seen from the IDS interfaces. An example of this is placing an IPS at the gateway to deny inbound and outbound inline attacks while monitoring traffic between hosts inside the network that never crosses the gateway. Figure 6-24 is an example of this type of design.

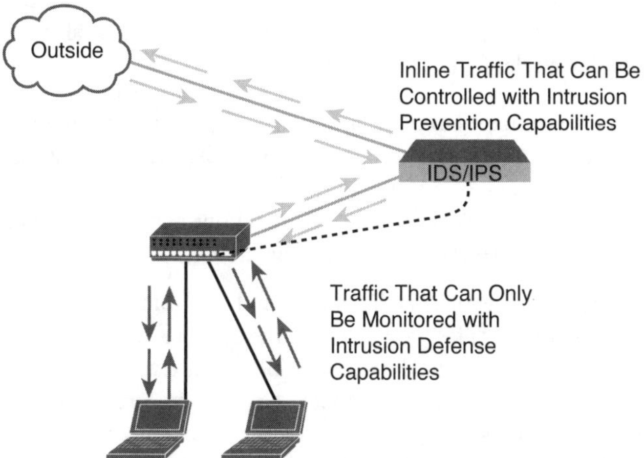

Figure 6-24 *IPS and IDS Example*

For an IPS or IDS to monitor for security events, it must be able to see the traffic. Visibility requirements vary between solutions, so at a minimum, the IPS/IDS must have network reachability to a system to include it in its reporting. It is common for administrators to not take into consideration Network Address Translation (NAT) or other design challenges that prevent an IDS/IPS from viewing the traffic. For example, a Citrix environment can accommodate multiple systems accessing a network and show all traffic from those systems as one internal IP address. An IDS/IPS monitoring the inside network would associate all traffic from the Citrix network to the only viewable IP address, causing difficulty when attempting to track back alarms to specific devices hidden by the Citrix NAT. Another example is how Google uses QUIC elliptical crypto, which makes it almost impossible to perform man-in-the-middle (MitM) inspection of encrypted traffic. Chapter 9 covers network IDS and IPS deployments in more detail.

Other types of IPS and IDS solutions can be found on hosts and in virtual environments. Host-based IPS solutions act similar to antivirus, but tend to offer more than signature-based detection. Usually IPS/IDS functionality for host systems is bundled with other features such as firewall, antimalware, and so on.

In general, an IPS and IDS uses the following methods to detect threats:

- **Signature-based detection:** A signature is a known attack pattern, meaning a threat that has been seen before and documented. Signature-based detection compares traffic, files, or behavior against a known list of attack signatures. If the matching signature is not enabled for an attack or the attack is unknown, that attack will bypass a signature-based security solution. Typically, signatures are published and shared between different parties to improve the overall industry's ability to block a known attack.
- **Statistical anomaly-based detection:** Statistical detection, also known as behavior-based detection, looks for abnormal behavior from network trends. Examples could be alarming when spikes in bandwidth are seen, unusual ports being used, shifting

traffic patterns at unusual hours, and so on. Statistical detection is not always accurate and requires proper tuning to avoid either being bombarded with false alarms or not being sensitive enough to detect events of interest.

By combining signature- and behavior-based detection, an IPS/IDS technology can be very effective at catching known and unknown threats. The key to the success of using an IDS or IPS, however, is how it is tuned. Not enabling the proper signatures or not aligning statistical anomaly settings to match accepted traffic on your network will result in useless logging and probably not be effective against certain attacks.

When evaluating IPS/IDS vendors, one key fact is that all IPS and IDS solutions are not created equally when it comes to how detailed you can tune the system. For example, the Cisco hybrid cloud security solutions from Meraki offer IPS but are very limited in tuning capabilities, as covered later in this chapter. In contrast, the Cisco FirePOWER IPS offering is very customizable, with granular tuning capabilities, including the ability to autotune or adapt when vulnerabilities are identified on devices being monitored.

Let's look at the different IDS/IPS options from Cisco and see how to export data to our data-collection solution.

Cisco FirePOWER IPS

Earlier in this chapter, we introduced the Cisco FirePOWER solution as an application layer firewall. One of three license options for FirePOWER is enabling intrusion detection and prevention used to identify and block attacks. This can be enabled on a Cisco ASA-X series appliance running the FirePOWER services or on a standalone FirePOWER physical or virtual appliance.

There are a handful of functions used by FirePOWER to identify threats effectively. The first function is leveraging a subscription to the latest attack signatures. As explained earlier in this chapter, signatures are known attack patterns. So when a new threat is seen in the industry, vendors or security researchers publish signatures describing characteristics of the attack so that any security product with the signature can identify the threat if it is seen on the network.

The second function used by the Cisco FirePOWER IPS to identify threats is leveraging the FMC's visibility of devices, users, and applications. This gives the IPS a more accurate understanding of what is being protected so that it can adjust protection to only systems and protocols that exist on the network. Adjustments can happen automatically or comes as a list of recommendations that can be manually enabled. This feature is known as FirePOWER recommendations.

A third function that further improves the FMC's recommendations is leveraging either a built-in vulnerability scanner or importing vulnerability scans from third-party products. This can map a potentially vulnerable system to the appropriate signature file so that defenses can be enabled using the IPS while the system is waiting to be patched. Figure 6-25 shows an example of running the FirePOWER built-in vulnerability scanner and identifying systems that could potentially be exploited.

Overview Analysis Policies Devices Objects FireAMP Health System Help dcloud

Context Explorer Connections Intrusions Files Hosts Users Vulnerabilities ▸ Vulnerabilities Correlation Custom Search

Bookmark This Page Report Designer View Bookmarks Search

Vulnerabilities

Table View of Vulnerabilities › Vulnerabilities on the Network › Vulnerability Detail

No Search Constraints (Edit Search)

Jump to...

SVID	Bugtraq ID	Snort ID	Title	Date Published	Vulnerability Impact	Remote	Available Exploits	Description
100358	0	30,761	Integer overflow in the abc_set_parts function in ...	2013-09-16 15:14:38	pending	FALSE	FALSE	Integer overflow in the abc_set
100358	0	30,762	Integer overflow in the abc_set_parts function in ...	2013-09-16 15:14:38	pending	FALSE	FALSE	Integer overflow in the abc_set
100358	0	30,763	Integer overflow in the abc_set_parts function in ...	2013-09-16 15:14:38	pending	FALSE	FALSE	Integer overflow in the abc_set
100358	0	30,764	Integer overflow in the abc_set_parts function in ...	2013-09-16 15:14:38	pending	FALSE	FALSE	Integer overflow in the abc_set
100357	0	30,770	Multiple stack-based buffer overflows in the cff_d...	2010-08-16 14:39:40	pending	FALSE	FALSE	Multiple stack-based buffer over
100357	0	30,771	Multiple stack-based buffer overflows in the cff_d...	2010-08-16 14:39:40	pending	FALSE	FALSE	Multiple stack-based buffer over
100356	0	30,774	** RESERVED ** This candidate has been reserved by...	1979-01-01 00:00:00	pending	FALSE	FALSE	** RESERVED ** This candidate
100355	0	30,526	Multiple cross-site scripting (XSS) vulnerabilitie...	2014-01-30 13:55:03	pending	FALSE	FALSE	Multiple cross-site scripting (XS
100355	0	30,527	Multiple cross-site scripting (XSS) vulnerabilitie...	2014-01-30 13:55:03	pending	FALSE	FALSE	Multiple cross-site scripting (XS

Figure 6-25 *FMC's Vulnerability Scanner*

The FirePOWER IPS can inspect anything within network reachability as long as its part of the network discovery configuration and there is an associated inspection rule. This includes the ability to be both an IPS for inline traffic and IDS for other parts of the network. Chapter 9 covers design details and recommendations.

Exporting IPS/IDS inspection data from the FMC follows the same steps covered in the "Application Firewalls" section earlier in this chapter. In summary, you must first create an alert response specifying how and where to export data. The next step is to create network policies under the access control section and enabling logging referencing the alert responses previously created.

Figure 6-26 shows creating an IDS inspection rule. The Logging tab is where you enable logging and link alert responses to the rule, as shown earlier in this chapter in the "Application Firewalls" section. See the FirePOWER overview in the "Firewalls" section of this chapter for more detail.

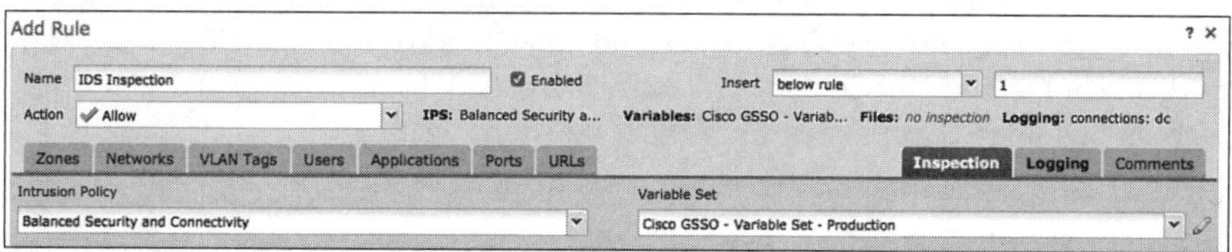

Figure 6-26 *Creating an IPS Inspection Rule*

Meraki IPS

Earlier in this chapter, we covered the Cisco hybrid cloud product line from Meraki. Meraki security solutions, also known as the MX-Series, offer stateful as well as application layer firewalling, IDS, VPN, content filtering, antimalware, and antiphishing. The IDS feature leverages Sourcefire for its rule set and detection capabilities. Tuning is limited to three different operation levels, labeled Connectivity, Balanced, and Security. Figure 6-27 shows the configuration page for the Meraki MX IDS functions.

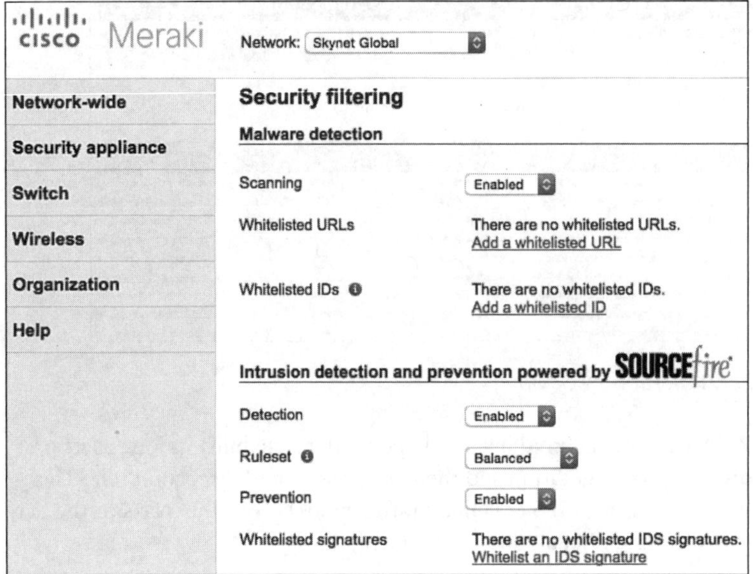

Figure 6-27 *IPS Options Within the Meraki MX Product Line*

Steps for exporting Meraki syslogs were previously covered in the "Cisco Meraki" section of this chapter. IDS events are just one of the available options when creating a policy for exporting syslog messages.

Snort

Snort is a free and open source IPS and IDS originally created by the founder of Sourcefire and later acquired by Cisco. Snort can perform real-time traffic analysis, packet logging, protocol analysis, content searching, and content matching. Snort has three configuration modes: sniffer, packet logger, and network intrusion detection. Each mode offers different methods for Snort to collect, analyze, and display data. You can learn more about building a Snort system at http://www.snort.org.

Host-Based Intrusion Prevention

Host-based IPS and IDS technology typically complements antivirus with signature detection, along with adding additional behavior detection capabilities. Typically, host-based security software packages offer a combination of antivirus, firewall, and IPS features as one application installed to monitor all traffic coming and leaving the system. Some common examples of vendors offering host security software packages are Symantec, Sophos, and McAfee. Other examples are open source host firewalling such as using IPTables or IPCop, both used in Linux environments.

We cover host security products later in this chapter.

Routers and Switches

Routers and switches are the key elements to almost every network. By general function, a switch forwards data looking at a physical device address, whereas a router forwards packets by locating a next-hop address. Many network appliances offer both routing and switching elements today and many other features such as voice over IP (VoIP), various security features, and so on. Administrators sometimes overlook the value from router and switch logs, which can assist with fault notification, network forensics, and other auditing functions.

The Cisco bread-and-butter product lines are its extensive routing and switching platforms. There are products that range from home office to enterprise-level networks accommodating various architecture requirements. Regardless of the product line, the available operating system tends to offer similar commands to export log messages. Typically, logs are exported because most Cisco switches and routers lack large internal storage space for such data.

In general, there are five different ways to export log messages on Cisco routers and switches, as follows:

- **Console logging:** Messages are sent to the console by default and only viewed by having physical access to the device's console port. This is a default setting for Cisco routers and switches. The router does not verify whether a device is attached and monitoring these messages.

  To stop console messages for security reasons or save CPU load, use the global configuration command **no logging console.** You can also limit the amount of logging sent to the console using the **logging console** *level*, such as **logging console informational.**

- **Terminal logging:** Messages are sent to the vty lines just like how they are sent to the console port. This is not enabled by default. To display VLAN Trunk Protocol (VTP) messages, use the **terminal monitor** command.

- **Buffered logging:** Uses a device's RAM for storing log messages instead of just displaying them on the console port. This is a first-in, last-out process, having the router delete old messages from the buffer as new log messages are created. Use the **logging buffered informational** command to enable this. You can also set the log size using the **logging buffered** *size* command, such as **logging buffered 64000.** Example 6-4 shows some of the options available for buffered logging on an iOS router.

Example 6-4 *Show Buffered Logging Options Example*

```
R5(config)# logging buffered
 <0-7>            Logging severity level
 <4096-2147483647>   Logging buffer size
 alerts              Immediate action needed                       (severity=1)
 critical            Critical conditions                           (severity=2)
```

```
 debugging          Debugging messages                               (severity=7)
 emergencies        System is unusable                               (severity=0)
 errors             Error conditions                                 (severity=3)
 informational      Informational messages                           (severity=6)
 notifications      Normal but signification conditions              (severity=5)
 warnings           Warning conditions                               (severity=4)
 xml                Enable logging in XML to XML logging buffer
<cr>
```

- **Syslog server logging:** Messages are forwarded to an external syslog server for storage. This is not enabled by default. To enable exporting syslog data, use the commands shown next. Be sure to first verify that the time settings are correct before enabling syslog logging. This can be corrected locally with the **set clock** command or by leveraging an NTP server by using the **ntp server** *IP_address* command, as covered earlier in this chapter. It is also important to enable logging time stamps to include the date and time with each log generated.

Steps for enabling syslog on a Cisco IOS switch or router are as follows:

```
service timestamp // sets the system to time stamp messages
logging host (IP Address of Syslog server)
logging trap (0-7)  // set this based on desired level of logging messages
logging source (interface to monitor for logging)

logging on // enables logging
```

Example 6-5 shows how to export level 4 event logs to a syslog server located at 192.168.1.200.

Example 6-5 *Enabling Logging Example*

```
R5(config)# service timestamp
R5(config)# logging host 192.168.1.200
R5(config)# logging trap 4
R5(config)# logging source FastEthernet 0/0
R5(config)# logging on
R5(config)#
```

- **SNMP trap logging:** Device uses SNMP traps to send log messages to an external SNMP server. There are two global commands on a Cisco iOS device to enable this.

Specify the external system to receive SNMP:

```
snmp-server host host-addr [traps | informs] [version {1 | 2c | 3 [auth | noauth |
  priv]}] community-string [udp-port port] [notification-type]
```

Enable the system to send traps:

```
snmp-server enable traps [notification_type] [notification_option]
```

To configure a Cisco IOS device to report on syslog and TCP connections, you enter the following:

```
R5(config)# snmp-server host 192.168.1.200 string config syslog tty
R5(config)# snmp-server enable traps syslog

R5(config)# snmp-server enable traps tty
```

To display the state of the system logging and contents of the standard system logging message buffer, use the **show logging** command. To clear logging from the router's internal log buffer, use the **clear logging** command.

> **Note** Before exporting syslog data, it is critical to make sure that the proper date, time, and time zone are configured.

Example 6-6 shows a Cisco IOS device set up for logging various items such as sending console messages, sending logs to the buffer, and exporting logging to a 192.168.1.200.

Example 6-6 *Exporting Various Logging Example*

```
R5(config)# show log
Mar 1 03:56:07.852: %SYS-5-CONFIG_I: Configured from console by console.
Syslog logging: enable (1 message dropped, 0 messages rate-limited,
                0 flushes, 0 overruns, xml disabled, filtering disabled)
       Console logging: level debugging, 15 messages logged, xml disabled,
                        filtering disabled
       Monitor logging: level debugging, 0 messages logged, xml disabled,
                        filtering disabled
       Buffer logging: level debugging, 1 messages logged, xml disabled,
                        filtering disabled
       Logging Exception size (4096 bytes)
       Count and timestamp logging messages: disabled
       Trap logging: level warnings, 18 message lines logged
               Logging to 192.168.1.200(global) (up port 514, audit disabled, link
  down), 0 message
                       filtering disabled
Log Buffer (64000 bytes):

Mar 1 03:56:07.852: %SYS-5-CONFIG_I: Configured from console by console
```

Access control lists (ACL) can be used with logs, but there is an associated performance hit when enabled. Log-enabled ACLs are useful for troubleshooting or adding controls to how log data is used.

There are many variations of tuning exporting event data using the methods covered. See the device configuration guide for more details on configuration options.

Another valuable data stream that can be exported from switches and routers is NetFlow. We cover exporting NetFlow later in this chapter. Now let's look at host systems.

Host Systems

Host systems are computing systems participating in networks that are assigned a network layer host address. Typically, host systems are end-user laptops or mobile devices, but as everything is becoming Internet capable, also known as the Internet of Everything (IoE), administrators are seeing other variations of host systems appear on the network, such as IP-enabled watches and glasses. This increases the challenge to enforce security policies such as proper access control as new device categories bring with them new possible threat vectors.

Securing host systems typically involves a combination of properly configuring native security features and installing additional security applications, such as antivirus, from a trusted security vendor. Sometimes you can use open source host applications, such as IPTables, as a host-based firewall.

Manufacturers of host security solutions typically support the most widely used operating systems and device types such as Windows, Apple, and Android. Less-popular operating systems such as Linux might not have as many options from commercial security vendors such as Windows; however, these operating systems tend to see fewer attacks. Open source options can be used for environments such as Linux and tend to have strong support communities that can be referenced for configuration examples; however, they do not usually offer the same level of support as commercial products.

Popular host security products tend to offer the following features:

- Firewall
- Intrusion detection/prevention
- Antivirus/antimalware/antispam and other "anti" bad stuff
- Web security

There are many other host security features, such as data-loss prevention and virtual private networking (VPN), used to protect host system data. Popular vendors that offer such products include Symantec, Sophos, and McAfee.

Most SOCs tend to collect data from host systems using a centralized system versus pulling from individual devices. These systems tend to support exporting event data as syslog, SNMP, and other common file types accepted by SIEM solutions. The steps to export such data vary depending on the vendor and product.

Mobile Devices

Mobile devices tend to be treated differently regarding management and security versus desktops and laptops due to their mobile nature and limitations inherited from the manufacturer. The most common security platforms used for managing policies on mobile devices are Mobile Device Management (MDM) platforms. MDMs tend to take two different approaches to enforcing policies for mobile devices:

- **Sandbox approach:** This strategy involves creating an isolated environment that limits what applications can be accessed and controls how systems gain access to the environment. Sometimes this is accessed through VPN technology; other times access is controlled by a MDM solution. The secure container can include various policies such as data-loss prevention, encryption, and limit data access, which all can be delivered through MDM-issued access methods versus features native to the endpoint. The value of this approach is that nonsecure devices can access sensitive data because all security controls are contained within the sandbox. Once the end device leaves the sandbox, the history of the session can be deleted, including activity inside the sandbox.
- **Endpoint management:** This strategy requires an agent to be installed on the mobile device to control applications and to issue commands such as remotely wiping sensitive data. Having an agent means that the device owner is allowing MDM administration to have access to that device. So from a user acceptance viewpoint, device owners must agree to opt in to the security program. The goal of the endpoint management approach is to secure the device so that it can access approved data and applications.

Both of these approaches for securing mobile devices have pros and cons, which cater to different business requirements. The good news is that many MDM vendors offer flavors of both approaches as the MDM technology continues to mature. Unlike hardware vendors, most MDM vendors are continually developing new features at a rapid pace, making it difficult to compare one offering to another. To choose the right MDM for your organization, use the same checks as covered earlier in this chapter for identifying the right SIEM offering.

In general, MDM offerings by leading vendors typically include the following:

- Mandatory password protection
- Jailbreak detection
- Remote wipe
- Remote lock
- Device encryption
- Data encryption
- Geo location
- Malware detection

- VPN configuration and management
- WiFi configuration and management

MDM offerings leverage a form of centralized management to create and enforce policies. These managers usually offer a way to export event data such as syslog messages. For example, MobileIron provides the following support:

> "MobileIron Core collects over 200 fields of data with device, application, user metrics, and status which administrators can use to analyze, visualize, and get actionable insights into their mobile infrastructure. This data can be exported natively to Splunk, or other third party reporting tools like Tableau, Crystal Reports, and QlikView."[2]

See the configuration manual for the management of the MDM offering for more information about how to export messages. It is uncommon for a SOC to export data from individual mobile devices unless troubleshooting problems with the device.

Breach Detection

Breach-detection capabilities focus on identifying activity of malware inside a network after a breach has occurred. This is becoming very relevant to administrators, as attacks increase in sophistication and volume. Breach detection can be part of common host security packages such as antivirus, but many feature-rich breach-detection offerings tend to complement other security products that heavily leverage attack signatures.

A best practice for breach detection is to view both network and application behavior. Network monitoring looks for indications of compromise, such as a trusted user scanning ports. Application monitoring looks for unusual software activity, such as applications attempting to mask its activity or files changing names. The combination of network and application aims to identify attacker behavior and the tools typically involved with a breach. This can be enforced through network appliances and software applications. Vendors with breach-detection offerings include Bit9, FireEye, and Mandiant.

Let's look at the Cisco breach-detection offerings for multiple types of host systems.

Cisco Advanced Malware Prevention

Cisco Systems made a few acquisitions to enhance breach-detection capabilities. The first breach-detection features came from Sourcefire, which covers both network and endpoints known as Advanced Malware Protection (AMP). Network AMP is enabled on an appliance running FirePOWER services and continuously evaluates all files seen on all networks being monitored. AMP uses a multisource indication of compromise approach, leveraging both network intelligence and cloud security research, which includes sandboxing files of interest and comparing hashes of files with data from other networks. You learned about AMP for networks earlier in this chapter.

AMP for endpoints requires a lightweight connector to be installed on host devices such as laptops and mobile tablets, providing visibility of all applications and process. Like

AMP for networks, the goal is to detect malware and retrospectively identify where it came from. AMP for endpoints can also offer autoremediation of threats seen by AMP for network and by the AMP for endpoint client. Figure 6-28 shows AMP for endpoint quarantining multiple malicious files on an Apple laptop owned by Michael Korten.

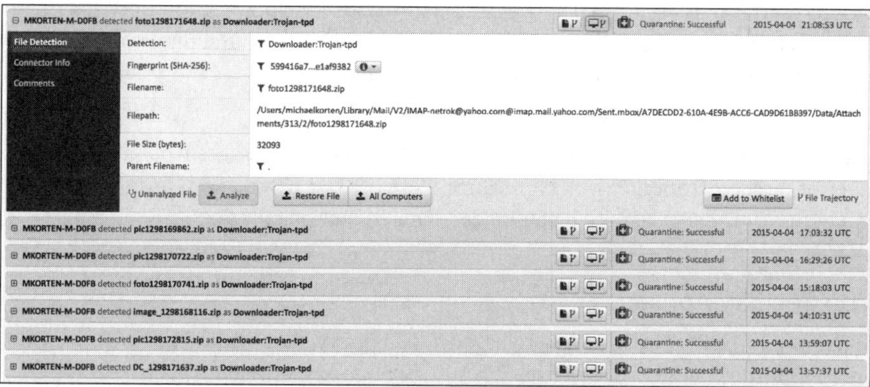

Figure 6-28 *Example of AMP for Endpoint Quarantining Multiple Threats*

AMP for networks is available on most Cisco security products, including e-mail, web, and cloud-based security. AMP for endpoints is a complementary component or sold as an independent solution managed through the cloud as bundles of agents for endpoints.

You learned how to export syslog messages from FirePOWER in the "Application Firewalls" section earlier in this chapter. AMP logs are just one of the available options when creating a policy for exporting syslog message.

Another solution for breach detection is to identify threats using network telemetry. We cover this topic later in this chapter. Now let's look at web proxies.

Web Proxies

Web proxies act as an intermediary between a host systems and the Internet. The most common use case for a web proxy is facilitating access to the Internet; however, there are other benefits depending on the model. Web proxy use cases examples include improving network performance through website caching, masking internal communications with an external address, server load balancing, authentication verification for web resources, security scanning, and so on.

Web proxies work by intercepting traffic between two sources such as the inside network and Internet. This can be accomplished by placing the appliance inline between two networks, routing traffic through the proxy using a method such as Web Cache Communication Protocol (WCCP) or configuring a host system's web browser to send traffic to the proxy. It is critical that the web proxy solution be configured properly before pushing traffic to it to avoid end-user interruption of services. This includes identifying all ports and protocols that will be associated with the web proxy.

Web proxies and application firewalls that have content controls enabled can accomplish similar goals but are different depending on the model. In general, an application firewall can cover all ports and protocols, whereas a web proxy can only interact with certain ports such as 80, 443, 25, and so on. Some web proxies include a protocol check to ensure that traffic is for the Internet, in addition to intercepting and replacing traffic if needed. Web proxies tend to have better performance than application firewalls based on how they process and cache websites. Popular web proxy manufacturers include Blue Coat, Websense, Cisco IronPort, and Barracuda. Chapter 9 covers web proxy design in more detail.

Most proxies offer ways to export event data such as syslog messages from a centralized manager or directly from the proxy appliance. Let's look at Cisco's web proxy offering and how to export event data to a centralized data-collection solution.

Cisco Web Security Appliance

Cisco acquired IronPort in 2007 and released a web proxy series called the Web Security Appliance (WSA). At its core, WSA is a web proxy providing many feature licenses that can be enabled for a specific term, such as 1, 3, or 5 years. Features of the WSA include threat defense using different antivirus and antimalware scanning engines, AMP, outbreak controls, application visibility/controls, and Layer 4 traffic monitoring targeting phone-home communication from malware.

A Cisco WSA can provide valuable data to the SOC based on what features and logs are enabled. There are a few ways to view WSA logs. The first option is to log in directly to the CLI and use the **grep** command. This brings up a list of logs on the WSA. You can select a specific log category that is listed or leave it blank to search for everything. Example 6-7 shows running the **grep** command to see some of the available options.

Example 6-7 *Running the* **grep** *Command on the WSA Command Line*

```
Poll
19. "ocspd_logs" Type: "OCSP Logs" Retrieval: FTP Poll
20. "pacd_logs" Type: "PAC File Hosting Daemon Logs" Retrieval: FTP Poll
21. "proxylogs" Type: "Default Proxy Logs" Retrieval: FTP Poll
22. "reportd_logs" Type: "Reporting Logs" Retrieval: FTP Poll
23. "reportqueryd_logs" Type: "Reporting Query Logs" Retrieval: FTP Poll
24. "saas_auth_log" Type: "SaaS Auth Logs" retrieval: FTP Poll
25. "shd_logs" Type: "SHD Logs" Retrieval: FTP Poll
26. "snmp_logs" Type: "SNMP Logs" Retrieval: FTP Poll
27. "sntpd_logs" Type  "NTP Logs" retrieval: FTP Poll
28. "sockslog" Type: "SOCKS Proxy Logs" Retrieval: FTP Poll
29. "sophos_logs" Type: "Sophos Logs" Retrieval: FTP Poll
30. "status" Type: "Status Logs" Retrieval: FTP Poll
31. "system_logs" Type: "System Logs" retrieval: FTP Poll
32. "trafmon_errlogs" Type: "Traffic Monitor Error Logs" Retrieval: FTP Poll
```

```
33. "trafmonlogs" Type: "Traffic Monitor Logs" Retrieval: FTP Poll
34. "usd_logs" Type: "UDS Logs" retrieval: FTP Poll
35. "updater_logs" Type: "Updater Logs" retrieval: FTP Poll
36. "wbnp_logs" Type: "WBNP Logs" Retrieval" FTP Poll
37. "webcat_logs" Type: "Web Categorization Logs" retrieval: FTP Poll
38. "webrootlogs" Type: "Webroot Logs: Retrieval: FTP Poll
39. "welcomeack_logs" Type: "Welcome Page Acknowledgement Logs" Retrieval: FTP Poll
Enter the number of the log you wish to grep
[]>
```

Another option to view logs is from the GUI manager. Once you log in to the GUI, you can find the log options under **System Administration > Log Subscriptions.** This brings up a list of log subscriptions featuring various types of log data. You can select any existing log subscription and modify it to export data or create a new subscription. There are dozens of log types available when creating or editing a log subscription. Figure 6-29 shows creating an access control log subscription that includes informational level data.

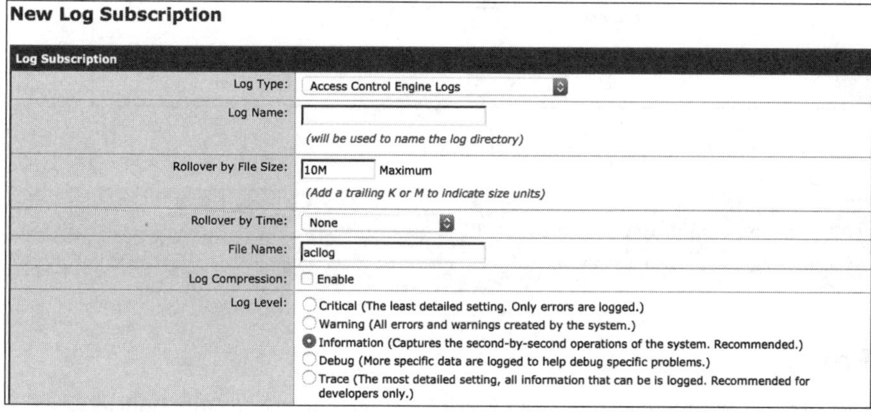

Figure 6-29 *Access Control Log Subscription in the WSA GUI*

Both new and existing log subscriptions offer File Transfer Protocol (FTP), Secure Copy (SCP), and syslog exporting of log subscriptions. Figure 6-30 is an example of these available options for exporting log events.

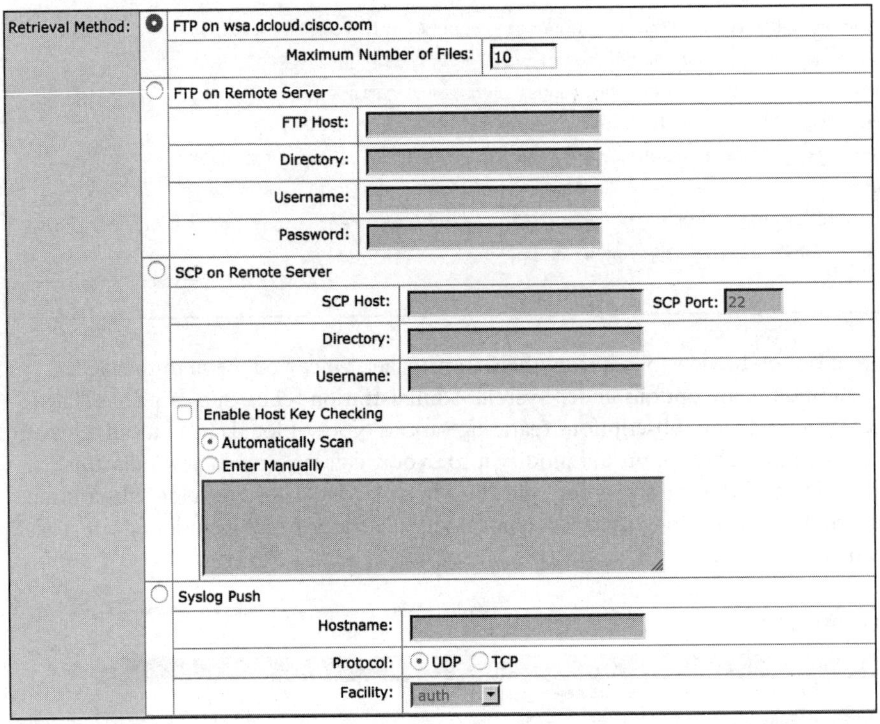

Figure 6-30 *Options for Exporting Logs in WSA*

> **Note** The steps are similar if you are using the Cisco M-Series Security Management appliance to centralize all WSA logging.

Cloud Proxies

Another option for adding web security is using SaaS to enforce security policies. As with proxy appliances, this can be accomplished by having traffic routed through the security solution. For SaaS offerings, however, the proxy technology is outsourced. Traffic can be routed through a VPN, sent from a network device such as a router, firewall, and so on, or routed from the host through local proxy configuration settings. Some advantages to this approach are outsourcing maintenance tasks, simplified deployment, reduction of hardware costs, and scalability.

Cisco Cloud Web Security

Cisco Cloud Web Security (CWS) offers similar capabilities as WSA; however, enforcement of functions is performed by a Cisco SaaS enforcement point. Features include controlling web usage based on signature, reputation and content analysis, and malware scanning. CWS also offers AMP for breach detection.

Logging can be exported from the device connecting the network to Cisco CWS service such as a Cisco ISR router using the **logging** command under the **parameter-map type content-scan global** settings.

There is also a log-extraction application programming interface (API) available that consists of more than 20 attributes and available within 2 hours of an event. This feature requires an additional license and targets customers with 4000 or more seats.

DNS Servers

A Domain Name System (DNS) server is a database that provides mapping between hostnames, IP addresses (both IPv4 and IPv6), text records, mail exchange, name servers, and security key information defined in resource records. The most common use case for DNS is mapping domain names to IP addresses and vice versa. Domain names were designed to help people remember how to find websites without having to remember the IP address. Instead, domain names are used but need to be translated to IP by a DNS server before a computer can find website. Each query message to a DNS server contains three pieces of information, specifying a question for the server to answer:

- A fully qualified domain name (FQDN)
- A query type that can be a specific resource record by type or specialized type of query operation
- A class for the DNS name

DNS servers can resolve requests a few different ways. If the request has been seen before, the DNS server can use its cache records to resolve the request. A DNS server can connect with other DNS servers on behalf of the client to resolve the name, which is known as recursion. The client may also resolve its request using its own cache or send requests to more than one DNS server. The process typically works by first attempting to resolve the name using the client's cache, and if it is not found, a request is sent to the DNS servers. If the preferred DNS server does not have the name in its local cache, it reaches out to other DNS servers to resolve the name.

DNS servers around the globe look to a central registry, also known as a domain name registrar, for the latest DNS information. New domains on average take around 12 to 36 hours to be updated on DNS servers worldwide. DNS servers can use UDP or TCP and typically uses a destination port of 53.

DNS can be vulnerable to certain attack such as DNS cache poisoning, DNS amplification and reflection attacks, and resource utilization attacks. One downside of using DNS is that it can generate a considerably large number of logging messages. Chapter 9 covers DNS design best practices.

Exporting DNS

DNS logging can be extremely valuable to a SOC for a handful of reasons. The most important value is being able to accurately view all Internet activity from users and devices. This includes domain-level visibility for any port or protocol used and all external domain requests. There are also security benefits from DNS, such as being able to respond quicker to incidents, identify network failures, validate DNSSEC, and mining hostnames that have visited a website of interest such as one that has been identified as malicious. Many SIEMs can leverage DNS to identify abnormal behavior, such as a system sending queries to both internal and external systems. This type of behavior is likely an indication of compromise.

One challenge to gathering DNS logs is that most Internet service providers (ISP) do not offer DNS logging capabilities. Another challenge is that internal DNS servers are usually used for authoritative DNS resolution for intranet domains rather than as a primary DNS source. In addition, DNS is typically constructed from multiple servers that could format DNS logs differently.

One way to capture outbound DNS traffic is to leverage a Switched Port Analyzer (SPAN) port for such data. This data could be exported directly to a centralized data-collection solution and parsed to log IP addresses making requests, names being requested, DNS server taking the request, response generated, time, and dates. The steps to create a SPAN port and parse data vary by manufacturer and model of equipment involved.

Windows-based DNS servers store event messages in their system event log. This log can be accessed using the DNS Manager or Event Viewer utilities. Event Viewer can be used to view and monitor client-released DNS events. These events appear in the System log and are written by the DNS Client service. You can also use DNS Manager to enable additional debug logging options for temporary trace logging to a text-based file of DNS server activity. The file Dns.log is used for this and stored in the %systemroot%\System32\Dns folder.

Network Telemetry with Network Flow Monitoring

Chapter 2 introduced the concept of using telemetry data as a way to identify behavior-based events. Network flow monitoring, commonly called NetFlow, can be enabled on standard network and security products, essentially turning your network into a giant sensor. This can be extremely useful by extending the SOC visibility across anything that handles network traffic rather than limiting data collection to just designated security tools and chokepoints.

It is important to note that all NetFlow is not created equal, meaning that each version provides different capabilities and levels of detail. For example, comparing JFlow to NetFlow Version 9 is similar to knowing that somebody has entered your house sometime in the past 24 hours versus Joseph Muniz entered your house 10 minutes ago and is currently sitting in your living room watching your television. The same concept for visibility is also dependent on how much of your network has NetFlow enabled, leaving blind spots in areas not generating NetFlow. Chapter 9 covers the different versions of NetFlow.

NetFlow Tools

NetFlow security tools rely on trends found from monitoring network behavior. For this reason, most NetFlow tools require at least a week's worth of data before they can distinguish what is considered normal and unusual behavior. Once a network baseline is established, NetFlow tools can use different algorithms to convert data into different types of reports.

Note A network baseline is not required for all NetFlow-based alarms. For example, monitoring for reconnaissance behavior such as a host launching Nmap would immediately trigger a NetFlow alarm regardless of the amount of NetFlow collected.

Typically, NetFlow tools offer different types of performance, security reports, and alarms depending on the focus of the manufacturer. For example, SolarWinds's NetFlow Traffic Analyzer is known for providing charts and tables displaying how the network is being used for performance purposes, while Lancope's StealthWatch and Plixer's Scrutinizer also use NetFlow but focus heavily on security. Many SIEMs can also accept NetFlow data directly but tend to be limited in how NetFlow is used. The key to deciding which NetFlow tool is right for your organization is to identify which NetFlow tools provide the right data for your SOC's mission.

NetFlow tools can see data from many sources and need to be tuned to understand the environment being monitored. This means that best practice is to define what is considered internal traffic and different sensitivity levels of each network segment. If you do this, the NetFlow tool will react when tracking external IP addresses and can have specific alarms when security zones are penetrated and if critical internal systems are being overutilized. For example, Figure 6-31 shows defining a sensitive and nonsensitive security zone within StealthWatch with the purpose of monitoring for unauthorized access to or from the sensitive network, known by StealthWatch as a host lock violation.

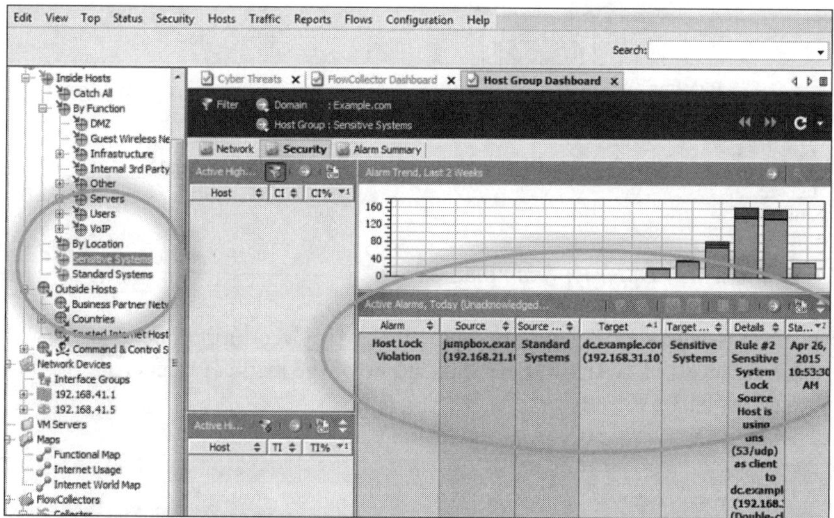

Figure 6-31 *Security Zones in StealthWatch*

One of the most important values obtained when using NetFlow-based tools for security purposes is the ability to turn common network devices that typically offer little security awareness into security sensors. This fills the visibility gap between these common network devices and dedicated security sensors such as firewalls and IPS/IDS solutions that are limited to what they can touch. Using network tools as security sensors also helps further validate an event, meaning that it is more likely something is a real event if a bunch of network devices are seeing a similar event as that seen by the dedicated security product. This also can provide additional value to other centralized event management tools, such as SIEMs, by giving broader visibility into possible events. Figure 6-32 shows the use of NetFlow as both a network and security tool by monitoring throughput between locations and whether any location is communicating with a command-and-control server. Note that although the locations refer to a physical topology, the objects referenced by the command-and-control server group could be located anywhere.

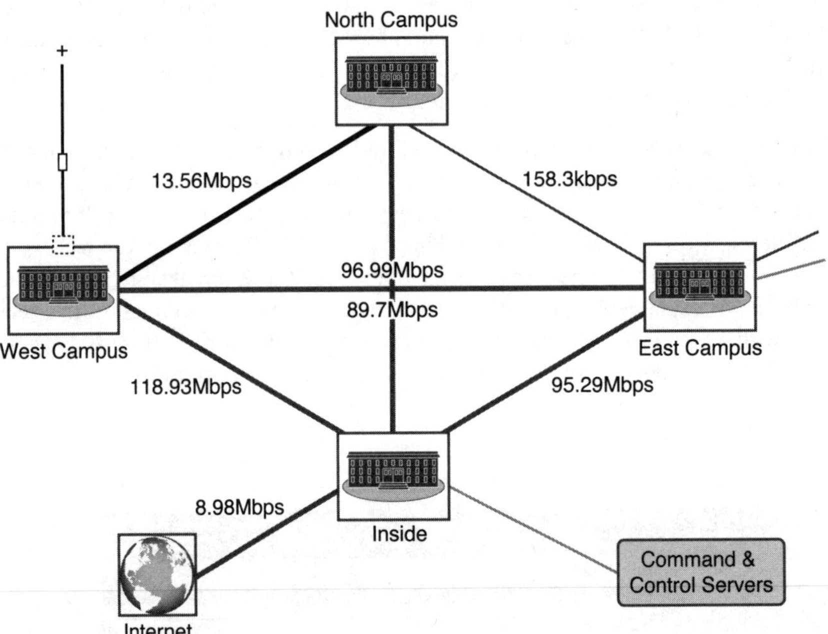

Figure 6-32 *StealthWatch Diagram Example*

Chapter 9 covers NetFlow architecture best practices. Many vendor products can produce different levels of NetFlow. Let's look at one of the market leaders for providing NetFlow-based security.

StealthWatch

Lancope first released StealthWatch as a probe-based tool like an IDS. After a few years, Lancope refocused the tool on NetFlow and behavioral analytics instead of deep packet inspection probes. Lancope has partnered with Cisco Systems and offers StealthWatch as a Cisco catalog item and part of Cisco's Cyber Threat Defense offering.

The StealthWatch solution is made up of several components, as follows:

- StealthWatch Management Console (SMC)
- StealthWatch FlowCollector
- StealthWatch FlowSensor
- StealthWatch Identity
- UDP Director
- SLIC Threat Feed

The *StealthWatch Manager*, or SMC, is the centralized manager used to view all data collected by the solution. *Collectors* are used to consume NetFlow from systems capable of producing flow. Later in this chapter, we look at how to enable NetFlow on various systems that support flow. For devices that cannot produce NetFlow, Lancope offers *sensors* that convert raw data into NetFlow that later can be sent to a collector for analysis. Sensors can also add additional information such identifying applications and protocols used across the network, details normally not obtained using standard NetFlow.

Enabling NetFlow on some networks can be a cumbersome process depending on the number of devices, different device types, tools used to manage configuration changes, and so on. Part of enabling NetFlow is specifying a destination for the flow data. Many flow-producing devices are limited in the number of destinations to which they can send flow and must be updated if the destination changes. The StealthWatch portfolio includes a *UDP Director* that receives flow from multiple devices and then forwards it to one or many destinations. This means that only the UDP Director needs to be configured when new NetFlow collecting tools are added to the network, which also increases the number of destinations to which the SOC can send flow data.

The last part of the StealthWatch offering is linking authentication information to IP addresses seen on the network. A StealthWatch Identity server is used to integrate common authentication systems such as an active directory or Lightweight Directory Access Protocol (LDAP) with StealthWatch. This links user data to IP but does not determine the device type. To add more authentication data to an identified IP address, StealthWatch offers an alternative to the StealthWatch Identity by integrating with Cisco's Identity Services Engine (ISE). The additional value of using ISE over the StealthWatch Identity server is having device context, meaning the determination of the device's operating system and the associated identity. For example, ISE can determine whether a device is an iPad versus an iPhone based on various network attributes such as ARP, DHCP, DNS, and so on. That information is passed over to StealthWatch so that IP addresses are tagged with the device type and user authentication information originally captured by Cisco ISE. These identity solutions also gather the monitored host's interface MAC address. StealthWatch can also use ISE to quarantine devices identified as having a high concern index, meaning devices that are very likely compromised. This can prove extremely useful to a SOC because automation of remediation can dramatically improve the reaction time to threats.

One additional feature of the StealthWatch offering is a subscription to a threat feed that monitors communication to known command-and-control servers, also known as CnCs. This feed is continuously updated and is shown in Figure 6-33.

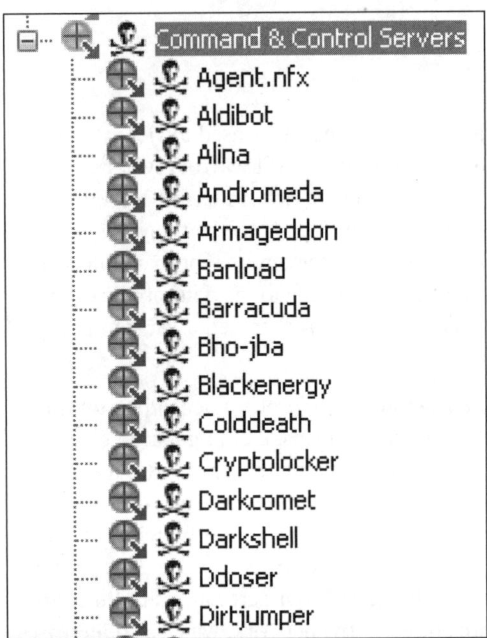

Figure 6-33 *A Small Part of the StealthWatch SLIC Feed*

The big value from StealthWatch is its ability to use proprietary algorithms designed to look for malicious behavior, also known as a concern index or indications of concern, from standard NetFlow traffic. For example, a default module focuses on events such as malware, botnets, data loss, and reconnaissance and requires minimal tuning to produce relevant data. Alerts are based purely on behavior, meaning that StealthWatch can identify unknown attacks or attacks that do not have signatures associated with them (commonly referred to as day-zero breaches). Figure 6-34 shows the cyberthreat dashboard identifying the spread of malware based on NetFlow behavioral monitoring.

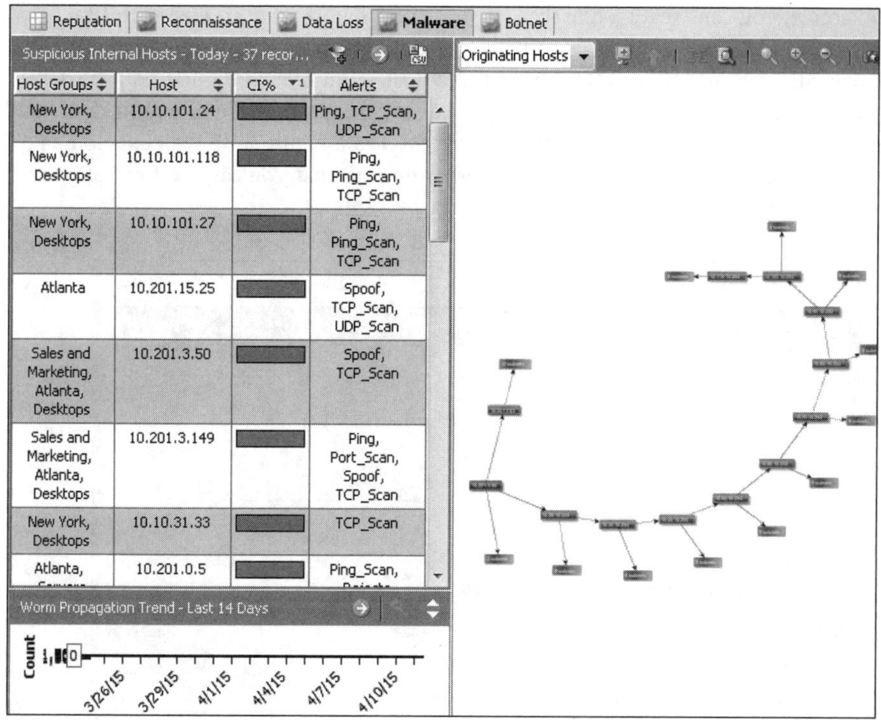

Figure 6-34 *StealthWatch Cyberthreat Dashboard Example*

Exporting Data from StealthWatch

StealthWatch can provide significant value to a centralized data-collection tool by giving the "network's" view of an event. For example, a SIEM may highlight an attack alarm generated by an IPS, but that alarm can be further qualified by comparing it to what StealthWatch is seeing from the rest of the network regarding the possible security event. The SMC is where data is processed and can export events to an external data-collection tool such as a SIEM.

Exporting data from StealthWatch is configured by accessing the Response Management option found under the Configuration tab. This brings up a window with options for adding rules, actions, and syslog formats. Rules represent the types of alarms you can set up to export data. Rule options are as follows:

- StealthWatch Management Console System Alarm
- FlowCollector System Alarm
- Exporter or Interface Alarm
- Host Alarm
- Host Group Relationship Alarm

For example, you can create a rule that exports event data anytime a host with IP address 10.0.2.100 sets off a trivial or higher severity alarm. To create this, click **Rules**, and then click the **Add** button. This brings up a host alarm rule configuration page. Give the rule a name and specify which host events would trigger this rule to export data such as specifying the IP address 10.0.2.100 and severity level. Figure 6-35 is an example of configuring this host alarm rule and shows other options that you can use to trigger the exporting of data.

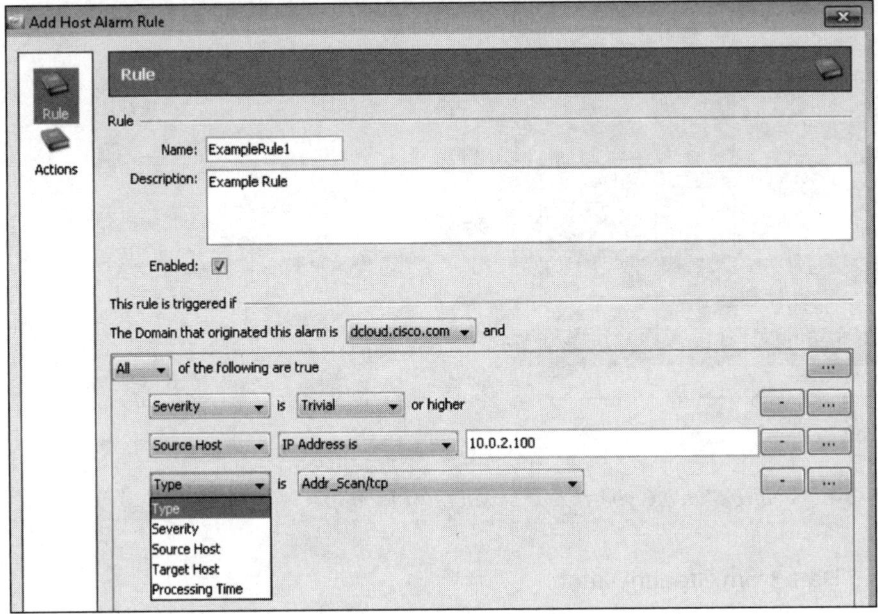

Figure 6-35 *Example Host Alarm for Exporting Events*

Actions are how the data will be exported. There are five different ways to export data from StealthWatch:

- Using Common Event Format (CEF). This was intended for exporting data to Arcsight and deprecated.
- E-mail. This requires an SMTP server configuration and userid@gomain.com for destination.
- QualysGuard. Export designed to send data to the QualysGuard.
- SNMP trap.
- Syslog (legacy StealthWatch and general syslog options).

So for our host alarm example, we could specify to have a syslog event sent by clicking **Actions** and the **Add** button. In the pop-up window, name the rule and specify the external data-collection tool's IP address, along with which port to use. Figure 6-36 shows an example of this configuration.

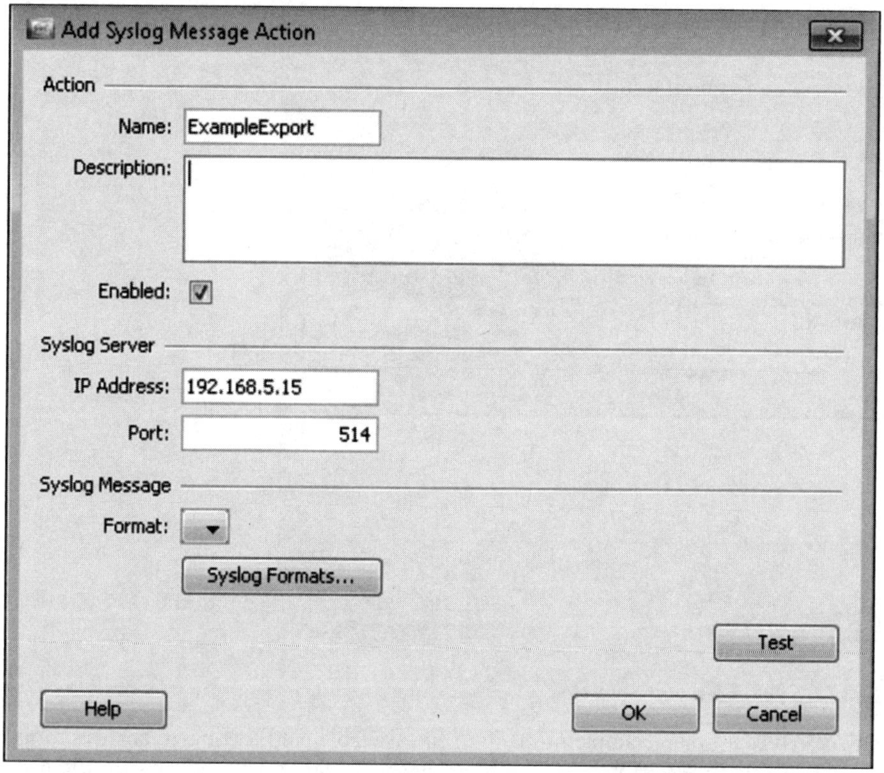

Figure 6-36 *Example of StealthWatch Action Configuration*

The last option is to select the syslog format, which can be selected within the action rule or during the main Response Management window. You have many options for the types of syslog information that can be exported from StealthWatch. Figure 6-37 shows an example of creating a syslog format for a specific facility type, severity level 3, and various types of syslog variables. Chapter 2 covered what facility types, severity levels, and syslog variables are available. The action rule will reference the syslog format you create and export data according to which fields are selected.

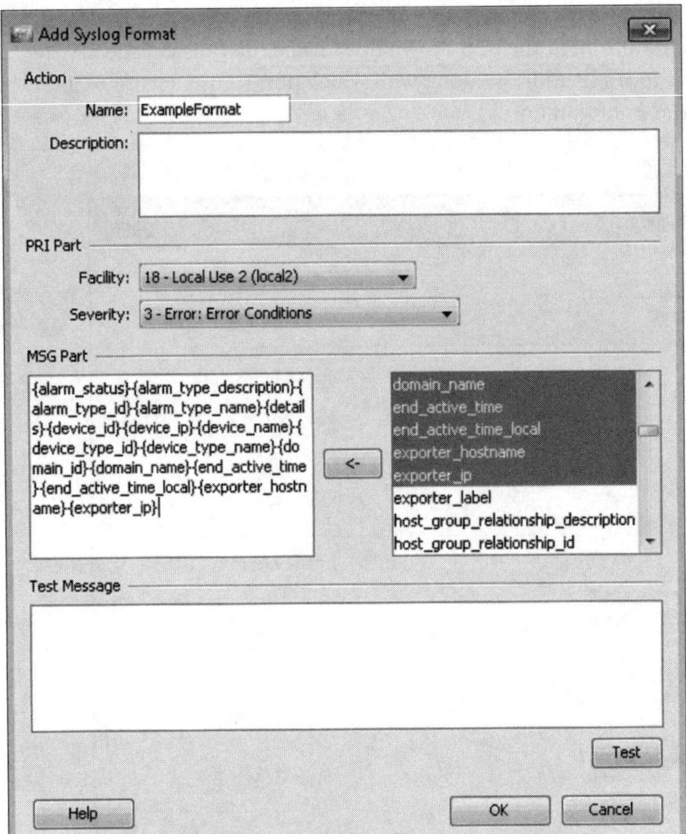

Figure 6-37 *Syslog Format Selection*

StealthWatch is just one example of many of the available NetFlow-based analysis tools. To learn more about StealthWatch, visit http://www.lancope.com. Now let's look at how we can enable NetFlow on common network devices so that flow can be leveraged from tools such as StealthWatch.

NetFlow from Routers and Switches

As specified in Chapter 2, NetFlow has been around for a while and continues to improve on the value it can provide as each new version is released. As of this writing, NetFlow 9 is the latest and most data-rich version of NetFlow available on network equipment. It is also important to note that the Internet Protocol Flow Information Export (IPFIX) covered in Chapter 2 derives from NetFlow 9 and is available for non-Cisco hardware. One value of leveraging Cisco for networking is that most of the current products support NetFlow 9, including some of the newer virtual switching available today.

Table 6-2 shows the Cisco NetFlow feature support history.

Table 6-2 *NetFlow Feature History*

Release	Modification
12.0(24)S	This feature was introduced.
12.3(1)	This feature was integrated into Cisco IOS Release 12.3(1), and output of the **debug ip flow export** command was modified to show NetFlow Version 9 information.
12.2(18)S	This feature was integrated into Cisco IOS Release 12.2(18)S.
Supported Platforms	
Cisco 2600 series, Cisco 3600 series, Cisco 7100 series, Cisco 7200 series, Cisco 7300 series, Cisco 7400 series, Cisco 7500 series, Cisco 12000 series	

You learned how to enable NetFlow 9 on a standard IOS-based router in Chapter 2. If we were planning to point NetFlow at a StealthWatch NetFlow collector, we would use that IP address for the destination IP address of the collector. Example 6-8 shows the general steps to enable the export of NetFlow from a Cisco router to a external NetFlow tool. This Cisco-specific configuration toolset, using custom flow records and separate monitors and exporters, is known as Flexible NetFlow.

Example 6-8 *Configuring NetFlow 9 on an IOS-Based Router with a Customized Record*

```
! Create a flow record that matches specific criteria and collect
! specific information
Router(config)# flow record MY_RECORD
Router(config-flow-record)# match ipv4 source_address
Router(config-flow-record)# match ipv4 destination address
Router(config-flow-record)# match transport source-port
Router(config-flow-record)# match transport destination-port
Router(config-flow-record)# match interface input
Router(config-flow-record)# collect counter packets
Router(config-flow-record)# collect counter bytes


! Configure your export settings
Router(config)# flow exporter MY_EXPORTER
Router(config-flow-exporter)# destination {ip_address | hostname}
Router(config-flow-exporter)# export-protocol netflow-v9
Router(config-flow-exporter)# transport udp udp_port
```

```
! Enabling flow monitor
Router(config)# flow monitor MY_MONITOR
Router(config-flow-monitor)# record record_name
Router(config-flow-monitor)# exporter exporter_name
Router(config-flow-monitor)# cache {entries number | timeout {active | inactive |
  update} seconds | type {immediate | normal | permanent}}
```

Using our StealthWatch example, if the Cisco router is configured properly to send NetFlow to the StealthWatch collector, we should see traffic from our new device, and the device should appear on the Network Device tab. Figure 6-38 shows StealthWatch reporting flow from a collector after traffic has been sent to it.

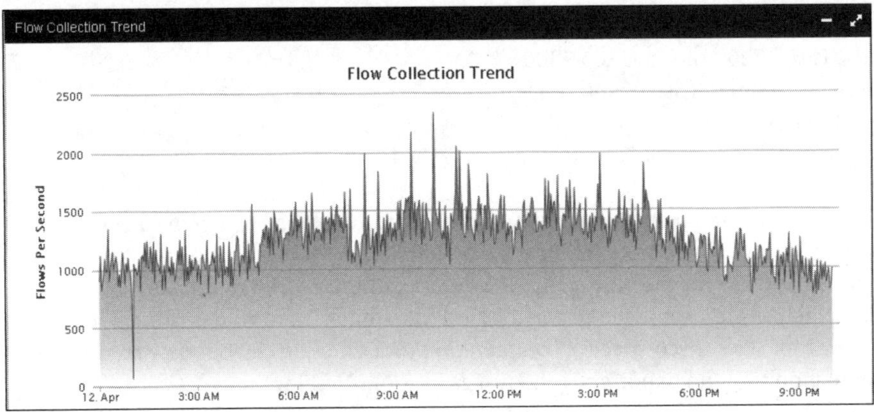

Figure 6-38 *StealthWatch SMC Showing Captured NetFlow*

NetFlow from Security Products

Many security products such as firewalls and intrusion prevention solutions produce NetFlow. It can be valuable to leverage NetFlow as a method to expand the solution's detection capabilities and fill in the gaps between network segments. For example, a security solution may be able to detect various forms of attack, yet not recognize a possible unauthorized data breach based on data leaving a critical system for the first time to an unusual system.

The steps for enabling NetFlow can vary depending on the manufacturer and product type. For the next example, we walk though how to enable NetFlow 9 on a Cisco Adaptive Security Appliance (ASA) firewall. If we were to use StealthWatch as our NetFlow analysis tool, we would either use the NetFlow collector or UDP Director as the destination IP address for this example.

For this example, we will use the ASA's web GUI manager known as ASDM to enable NetFlow. Once logged in, click the **Configuration** tab and select the **Device**

Management section. From the Logging drop-down, select **NetFlow.** This brings up the NetFlow configuration page, as shown in Figure 6-39. You can adjust different aspects of how NetFlow will be transmitted and specify where to send NetFlow via external NetFlow collectors. Click the **Add** button to add a new NetFlow collector. ASDM will ask you to specify through which interface the collector can be reached, its IP address, and which UDP port to use. For our example, we have specified two collectors using port 2055 because that is the default port used by StealthWatch.

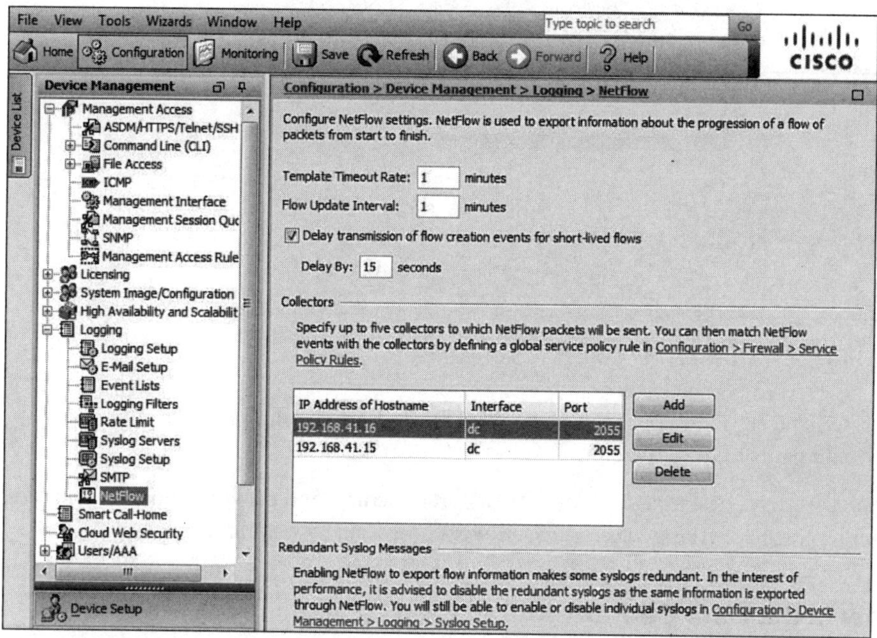

Figure 6-39 *ASDM NetFlow Configuration Example*

The next step is to create a firewall policy by clicking the **Configuration** tab and then the **Firewall** tab on the left and selecting **Service Policy Rules.** You will see any service policy rules that are running on your ASA. For this example, I create a new service policy by clicking the **Add** button. This brings up a wizard that asks where to apply this service policy rule. I select **Global – Applies to All Interfaces** and then click **Next.** This will prompt to create a new traffic class. I'll call it **NetFlow**, check the check box to match **Any traffic**, and then click **Next.** This brings up rule action tabs to choose from. I select the **NetFlow** tab showing all NetFlow collectors that are receiving NetFlow from this policy. None are showing, so to add my two collectors I configured previously, I click the **Add** button and check the boxes next to the collectors, as shown in Figure 6-40.

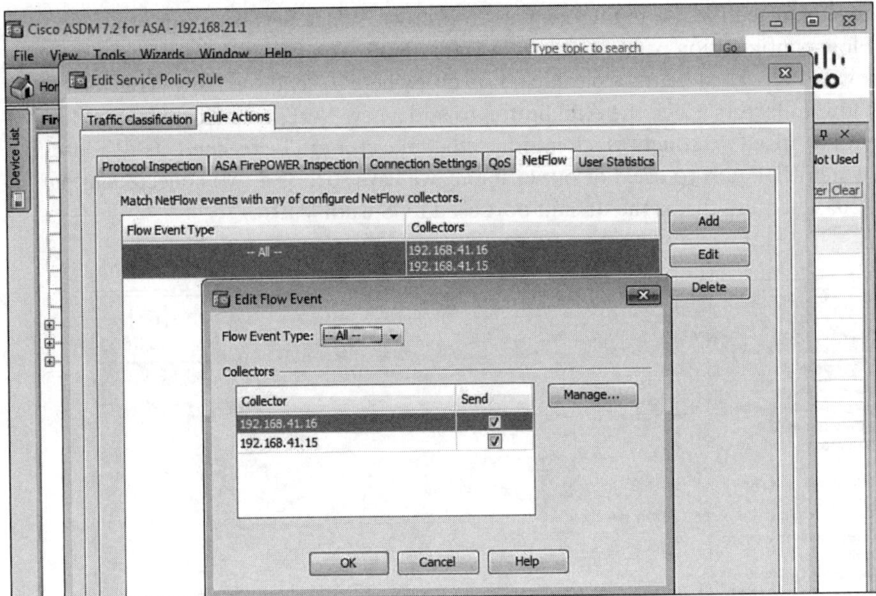

Figure 6-40 *ASDM NetFlow Collector Selection*

Click **OK** and finish to apply this new policy. Now NetFlow should begin streaming to your external NetFlow collector.

Chapter 9 covers best practices for network architectures and provides more information about leveraging NetFlow to enhance network and security visibility.

NetFlow in the Data Center

Earlier in this chapter, you learned how data center traffic is typically heavier between servers inside the data center, or "east-west" traffic, versus traffic entering or leaving the data center, also known as "north-south" traffic. It can be challenging to provision visibility for security events inside the data center with today's advanced virtual switching environments, which can produce very high throughputs. Typically, virtual firewalls and IDS solutions can be placed to monitor traffic, but this could leave blind spots depending on where these security systems are placed inside the data center.

Another approach to adding visibility inside a data center is to leverage NetFlow. Cisco Nexus 3000 and 7000 series switches support NetFlow 9. Let's look at the steps to enable NetFlow for these product lines.

The first step is to enable the NetFlow feature and set the active and inactive timeouts:

```
switch(config)# feature netflow
switch(config)# flow timeout active 60
switch(config)# flow timeout inactive 15
```

Next, you can either create a NetFlow record or leverage a predefined template called netflow-original. We use the predefined template for this example. Now, we create a flow exporter to specify where and how NetFlow will be sent:

```
switch(config)# flow exporter Exporter_Example1 // Name your exporter
switch(config-flow-exporter)# description My Exporter Example // can be anything
switch(config-flow-exporter)# destination <NetFlow collector IP address>
switch(config-flow-exporter)# source <interface that will be sending NetFlow>
switch(config-flow-exporter)# transport udp 2055 // This example uses
  StealthWatch's default port
switch(config-flow-exporter)# version 9 // specify NetFlow v9
```

Now we need to create a flow monitor that will link the flow record to the flow exporter:

```
switch(config)# flow monitor Monitor_Example1 // Name your monitor
switch(config-flow-monitor)# record netflow-original // using the predefined
  template
switch(config-flow-monitor)# exporter Exporter_Example1 // exporter we previously
  created
```

Next, we assign the flow monitor to some interfaces. Best practice is assigning monitoring to every Layer 3 interface for full visibility of the environment. This is repeated for every interface on which you want to enable monitoring:

```
switch(config)# interface <interface name you are enabling flow on>
switch(config-if)# ip flow monitor Monitor_Example1 // the monitor we created
```

To validate your work, use the following commands:

```
switch# show flow record netflow-original
switch# show flow monitor Monitor_Example1 statistics
switch# show flow monitor Monitor_Example1 cache
```

Enabling NetFlow on other data center products such as Nexus 1000v is similar. See the configuration guide for those solutions for more details.

Other Cisco products designed for the data center that support network are the ASA physical and virtual firewall series, physical and virtual FirePOWER service platforms, Catalyst vSwitches, and the latest Unified Computing System (UCS) devices. For specific information about equipment support, check out Cisco.com or search the product name followed by “NetFlow support.”

Summary

This chapter covered various tools used to produce and collect security data. It is critical that you design visibility across the network using a layered approach to avoid gaps in monitoring. For example, having network devices such as switches verify threat data seen by a security sensor is ideal to further qualify alarms, provide gaps in defense techniques, give more accurate location data, and so on. Topics covered included how to select and prepare a data-collection solution, exporting data from various security products, and using NetFlow as another way to gather security and network intelligence from common network devices.

The following chapter covers best practices for identifying, managing, and remediating vulnerabilities.

References

1. http://www.webopedia.com/TERM/F/firewall.html

2. https://www.mobileiron.com/en/resources/faq

Chapter 7

Vulnerability Management

"The weakest link in a chain is the strongest because it can break it."—Stanislaw Jerzy Lec

Attackers need to exploit just one vulnerable system to gain access to your network. Once inside, they can establish multiple doorways to the outside, making it extremely difficult to completely remediate the breach. This is known as *establishing a foothold* according to Mandiant's *Targeted Attack Lifecycle*.[1] From there, the attacker can move about the network, causing havoc through internal attack campaigns, stealing data, and so on. Figure 7-1 shows the targeted attack lifecycle.

Many breaches discovered are caused by a system having a known vulnerability exploited before it is properly patched. The 2015 Verizon Breach Investigation Report (VBIR)[2] showed that 99.9 percent of the exploited vulnerabilities were compromised more than a year after the CVE (method to patch) was published. That's right, 99.9 percent of compromised systems using vulnerabilities could have been prevented if proper vulnerability management was enforced! This research shows us organizations are not keeping up with patch management or more likely just focusing on the latest threats. The lesson learned from this research is that organizations must continuously audit for new and old vulnerabilities because any vulnerability is relevant. Unfortunately, being 100 percent for patch management is usually impossible to achieve for most organizations because new vulnerabilities found daily make this goal a moving target.

The challenge for a SOC is to identify and remediate vulnerabilities before a malicious party takes advantage of the exposed weakness. The 2015 VBRI found that half the organizations surveyed discovered a malware event within a 35-day (or fewer) timeframe, which is not good. This is why proper vulnerability management can make or break a SOC's effectiveness at battling threats.

This chapter looks at best practices for identifying and remediating vulnerabilities. The chapter covers popular tools used for assessment services and how to qualify the risk caused by identified vulnerabilities. These concepts are leveraged to define best practices for managing vulnerabilities. The chapter concludes with a discussion about how to pull in threat intelligence from other external sources to expand vulnerability awareness beyond what is seen by the internal network.

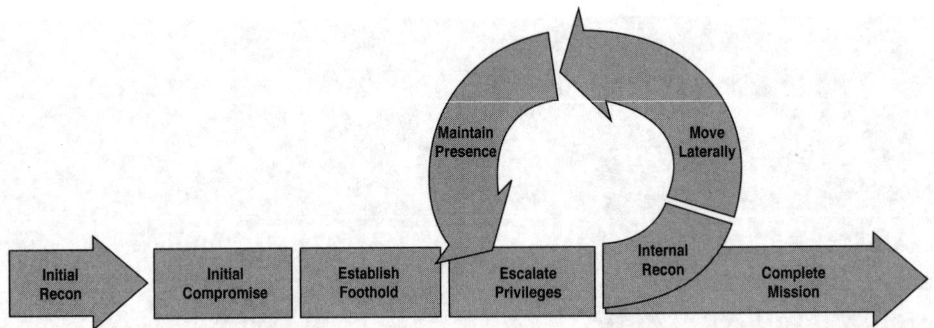

Figure 7-1 *Targeted Attack Lifecycle*

Let's start by defining what it means to be vulnerable to an attack.

Identifying Vulnerabilities

Chapter 2, "Overview of SOC Technologies," defined *vulnerabilities* as a perceived weakness in people, processes, and technology. Being vulnerable means the potential for an attack, but it does not mean that the system has been exploited. For example, there might be systems that are considered vulnerable to a certain type of attack, such as exploiting web-based services; if those systems do not connect to the Internet, however, the risk of being exploited is potentially low. An important objective for the security operations center (SOC) is qualifying vulnerabilities and determining which is the highest risk to the organization so that those can be prioritized over other remediation tasks.

As networks grow and expand in use, more new vulnerabilities tend to be introduced. Vulnerabilities can be any of the following, plus many more possibilities:

- Misconfiguration of software or error in network architecture
- Weak security policies such as using short, predictable passwords
- Manufacture flaw in hardware or software
- Lack of education about possible threats
- Weakness in ports or protocols in use

The list of possible vulnerabilities is endless, and the range of targets can be anything from computing systems to people. It is pretty much impossible to not have vulnerabilities in your network, so it is critical to have a clear definition of how your SOC manages vulnerabilities, along with having the support of leadership for enforcing associated policies.

In general terms, *vulnerability management* is the cyclical practice of identifying, classifying, remediating, and mitigating vulnerabilities. Vulnerability management is an ongoing process that must adapt to changes and scale to all areas of the network and to any associations with your business. This is a key point, because we have seen very secure companies become compromised by vulnerabilities with business associations such as vendors they do business with. An example is a company purchasing authentication systems from an outside vendor that happens to be vulnerable during their shipping cycle, from the warehouse where gear is created, to the company that sells the products. A malicious party could intercept a shipment and plant malware on the products before they are delivered with the goal of having a back door into any company's network that installs the solution. *This is why vulnerability management must extend to all aspects of your business, have multiple layers of checkpoints, and be continuously monitoring for possible weaknesses.* We look deeper at vulnerability management best practices later in this chapter.

How does a SOC discover vulnerabilities within systems or processes? There are many services and tools available, ranging from contracting professional services for a vulnerability assessment to utilizing a scanning application. Typically, internal or contracted services leverage certain types of tools to automate and standardize the process of searching for known and unknown weaknesses. Before covering the tools, let's review the different types of services used to identify vulnerabilities and when each should be leveraged.

Security Services

Many organizations and solution providers use terms such as *audit*, *penetration test*, or *assessment* to describe similar services that identify vulnerabilities. This can cause confusion about requirements for the level of effort and the expected results when contracting externally or training a SOC's organization to handle such responsibilities. In general, the industry uses the following services to identify vulnerabilities:

- **Compliance and audits:** Compliance and audits can focus on evaluating the risk level of a system or application, network architecture design risks, or evaluating existing controls against a set of standards or baselines. Standards and baselines could be security requirements or the minimal acceptable level of security that a corporation is validating against that are internally published or following external recommended architectures (that is, published policies and architectures). For example, some security audits validate against a required regulation such as being Payment Card Industry Data Security Standard (PCI DSS) compliant or being hardware Joint Interoperability Test Command (JITC) certified. Sometimes they are based on testing the effectiveness of a control or identifying design flaws. An example is an intrusion prevention system (IPS) that does not have visibility into some network segments, making those segments more vulnerable to attacks due to the lack of protection. Reasons for providing this high-level audit service range from being legally obligated for meeting legal requirements to simply passing cooperate security policies. For this reason, audits could provide a false sense of security based on the simple fact that many industry regulations or cooperate policies take time to publish requirements. Cyberattacks are rapidly changing tactics, outpacing many industry regulations for minimal security standards. It is best practice to leverage audits to prove compliance with specific controls or regulations; however, use more rigorous baselines and deeper vulnerability scanning practices for securing your network.

- **Vulnerability assessment:** This service focuses on scanning devices, operating systems, and applications for known and potentially unknown vulnerabilities. Typically, this is accomplished by using a tool or set of tools that automates the scanning process. Vulnerability assessments stop once the vulnerability is found, meaning that vulnerabilities are not validated. Findings represent a potential security weakness; however, they do not confirm all vulnerabilities identified could be exploited. Vulnerability assessments are great for establishing a list of new vulnerabilities that can be used to calculate risk to the business and validate existing security controls; these can also be positioned as a target list for deeper analytics, such as using penetration testing services.
- **Configuration assessment:** Like a vulnerability assessment, a configuration assessment focuses on scanning devices, operating systems, and applications; however, a configuration assessment could evaluate the architecture and configuration against industry best practices or the organization's policies and standards. Examples include identifying the use of features not recommended for a proper security setup (such as Telnet or Simple Network Management Protocol [SNMP] Version 1), design flaws in how systems are configured, lack of enabled features, and so on. A vulnerability assessment may catch configuration issues; however, the results of that service are from a pure vulnerability viewpoint instead of identifying the configuration issue causing the unwanted risk. Audits and vulnerability assessments may include configuration assessment tasks as part of the scope of service.
- **Penetration test:** Penetration testing further evaluates identified vulnerabilities by attempting to exploit the weakness in a similar method of a real malicious attacker. This means identified vulnerabilities are validated before they are included in a report, providing a shorter but more accurate list of vulnerabilities the SOC should consider. Penetration testing is usually more targeted and involves more services and a higher cost than a vulnerability assessment designed to test the strength of the security in place. This means that *penetration testing is not designed to make your network more secure*. It is best to use penetration testing when you have exhausted investments in improving security and need to verify that you have enough protection from anticipated threats or further evaluate known threats such as a weakness discovered during a vulnerability assessment.

Each service offers different forms of benefits and costs to consider. Audits may not provide enough data to protect your network; however, they can help justify compliance with mandated regulations. Audits also can help justify budget for future projects because many mandates have legal implications if not met. It is important to include a strategy to generate audit data when validation is required.

Vulnerability and configuration assessments are great for monitoring for vulnerabilities and capturing a general overview of the current state of security risk for your environment. Assessments should be a continuous process, because the threat landscape for the SOC's environment will change as soon as an assessment is concluded. Assessments should extend across the entire network and consider all aspects of the business. This should be blended with the SOC's information assurance goals and backed by leadership to give it authority.

Penetration testing could be used to validate any potentially high-risk vulnerability, but should be well defined to avoid exhausting budget and time. A good use case is using penetration testing to validate findings from a vulnerability assessment or testing the security capabilities of specific critical systems. A bad use case is using a penetration test to break into the network any way possible. The reason why is that the penetration tester may spend countless hours (and bill you for it if outsourced!) researching areas that most SOCs would not consider critical to the business, such as social media sources. Another bad outcome is breaching your network using tactics that will not improve the SOC's practice. An example is hiring consultants for a penetration test and finding out that they went through the hiring process, spent two weeks stealing data as a new hire, and then delivered stolen data, all while employed and billing you for the penetration testing services. This weakness could be useful to know; however, most SOCs could probably find more value investing in other methods to identify vulnerabilities.

Yes, the core goal of penetration testing should be to use unorthodox tactics that the SOC is not prepared for to evaluate incident response; however, the reality of this service is that budget can limit the scope depending on the desired results. Best practice is to make sure that the approving resource clearly defines whether the penetration testing engagement is black box (completely unknown environment attacking without any knowledge of the targets), white box (very specific environment with specific targets), or gray box (some knowledge of environment and targets but nothing specific and possible limited attack domain) before engaging penetration testing resources to get better results.

You could use a penetration test to justify budget by validating weaknesses through real-world exploitation. An example is showcasing a penetration test deliverable report providing various methods to access company sensitive data. A smoking gun report typically captures the right people's attention regarding how vulnerable the business is to an attack. This tactic is best used in conjunction with an audit that the organization is mandated to comply with.

We reference these services later in this chapter when covering how a SOC can provide vulnerability management. Now let's look at some of the tools used when providing security services.

Vulnerability Tools

As stated earlier in the chapter, vulnerability management is all about the reaction time for identified high-risk weaknesses. Tools can dramatically improve reaction time through automation and can simplify complex tasks. Security services can use a range of tools, both open source and commercial. Here are a few popular tools used by SOCs to identify vulnerabilities.

- **Nmap:** Nmap, short for "Network Mapper," is one of the most popular open source tools used for network discovery, network inventory, monitoring connectivity, and security auditing. Nmap can determine which hosts are connected to the network, what services (including application names and versions) are running, which operating system is installed, existing firewalls in use, and many other details depending on the type of scan run. You can learn more at https://nmap.org. Figure 7-2 shows performing a basic Nmap scan on host system 10.0.2.62.
- **OpenVAS:** Open Vulnerability Assessment System (OpenVAS) is a free software package used for vulnerability scanning and vulnerability management. The security scanner feature is updated daily and contains more than 35,000 (and growing) network vulnerability tests. Learn more at http://www.openvas.org.
- **Nessus:** Nessus is a popular vulnerability scanner developed by Tenable Network Security. Nessus can provide scanning features found in Nmap and can apply exploits to validate potential vulnerabilities. There is a free home use version limited to 16 IP addresses, in addition to subscriptions for scanning larger networks. Learn more by visiting https://www.tenable.com.
- **Metasploit:** Rapid7 created the Metasploit project as an open source framework used for developing and executing exploit code against a remote target machine. Metasploit is great for validating possible vulnerabilities identified by the built-in tools such as Nmap or other external vulnerability scanners. Many researchers validate vulnerabilities by identifying exploits found within the Metasploit framework. You can learn more about Metasploit by visiting https://metasploit.com.
- **Kali Linux:** Kali Linux is one of the most widely used open source penetration testing and digital forensics platforms used by security professionals. There are over 600 penetration testing programs, including Nmap, OpenVAS, and Metasploit. You can learn more at https://www.kali.org.

```
root@kali:~# nmap 10.0.2.62

Starting Nmap 6.47 ( http://nmap.org ) at 2013-09-19 21:59 EDT
Nmap scan report for 10.0.2.62
Host is up (0.0091s latency).
Not shown: 996 filtered ports
PORT     STATE SERVICE
135/tcp  open  msrpc
139/tcp  open  netbios-ssn
445/tcp  open  microsoft-ds
5357/tcp open  wsdapi

Nmap done: 1 IP address (1 host up) scanned in 4.78 seconds
root@kali:~#
```

Figure 7-2 *Basic Nmap scan*

- **Core Impact:** Core Impact is just one example of many companies providing tools for vulnerability identification and management and other capabilities such as penetration testing. This includes multivector testing capabilities across network, web, mobile, and wireless. Check out http://www.coresecurity.com/ for more information.

This is just a generic list of tools; many others are available. Also, it is common to find skilled professionals within a SOC using customized scripts or homegrown tools developed for their specific environment. For those situations, it is important to ensure proper support is available for updates and change of ownership as developers leave the organization.

Selecting the right tools should be based on the goal of the service being delivered and on available skill sets within the organization. For example, many audit tools are designed for specific regulations that could save your organization many hours of manually labor if the network is compliant. Note that for our example, to avoid inaccurate results, make sure to validate the selected audit tool being used is aware of the latest policies associated with the regulation it is measuring your network against.

Vulnerability-assessment services tend to leverage automated scanners such as Nessus and Nmap or security packages from companies such as Core Impact and Rapid7. Outsourcing vulnerability-assessment services could be done to ramp up capabilities; however, vulnerability-assessment services should be ongoing from the service provider or internal SOC team to avoid long gaps between delivering services. Penetration testing tends to leverage attack arsenals such as Kali Linux or real malware customized to breach systems regardless of the impact.

Note It is highly recommended that the people responsible for all systems involved with security services have approved the service in writing prior to executing the engagement. Some security services could cause negative impact to systems or processes. All associated risks with security services should be reviewed and signed off on by the proper authorities to avoid unwanted outcomes that are not accounted for by the owners of the system or processes.

We reference security services and tools we just covered in this book as part of a *vulnerability-assessment service*, but note the various types of services this really could include. A vulnerability assessment is one of the steps used during a vulnerability management process covered later in this chapter.

Next, let's look at the methodology behind handling identified vulnerabilities. We use these concepts to develop a vulnerability management process.

Handling Vulnerabilities

Discovering vulnerabilities is important; however, that is just the first step in the vulnerability management process. It is absolutely critical to have a well-defined process on how to handle vulnerabilities, which centers on estimating *risk*. Calculating the amount of risk associated with vulnerabilities helps determine the possible impact and likelihood of the vulnerability being exploited. Risk can be measured against the asset value and cost for remediation to determine the best course of action. Examples of risk management frameworks were introduced in Chapter 1, "Introduction to Security Operations and the SOC." It is important to note that some organizations will have another team outside the SOC manage risk for the organization, whereas other SOC environments may have this responsibility. Even when another team handles risk, the SOC is still responsible for identifying, assessing, and communicating identified risks.

There are four general ways a SOC can identify risk:

1. **Mitigate:** Provide a countermeasure that reduces or alters associated risk.
2. **Transfer:** Purchase insurance to transfer some or all of the potential cost of loss.
3. **Accept:** Acknowledge the associated risk and accept the potential loss if the risk occurs.
4. **Avoid:** Do not acknowledge, and pretend that there is no risk.

Most SOCs use variations of all four of these options during normal operations. For example, a SOC may determine there is a risk for earthquakes; however, the best course of action depends on location. Offices in Florida would probably accept or ignore the risk, whereas offices in California would probably choose to reduce or transfer risk based on known frequencies of earthquakes for the area.

One way to help determine the best course of action is to perform a *quantitative risk analysis* according to (ISC)². (ISC)² recommends handling risks by calculating the *annualized loss expectancy* and comparing it against the possible *safeguard value* to decide whether it is worth protecting. Let's look at how to calculate these values and the associated variables:

- **Asset value (AV):** An asset is anything the SOC's is responsible for protecting. The value of the asset used for calculations can be a ballpark number, but it should consider depreciation.
- **Exposure factor (EF):** The exposure factor represents the loss or cost that an organization would suffer from a specific asset being compromised by an identified risk.
- **Single loss expectancy (SLE):** This formula calculates the loss from one identified compromise against a specific asset. The formula for calculating SLE is as follows:

  SLE = AV * EF

- **Annualized rate of occurrence (ARO):** This relates to how often a threat would occur within a year timeframe.
- **Annualized loss expectancy (ALE):** The ALE considers the yearly cost of all loss expectancies from an identified compromise to a specific asset. The formula for calculating ALE is as follows:

  ALE = SLE * ARO or ALE = AV * EF * ARO

- **Annualized cost of safeguard (ACS):** This is the cost to reduce the risk for a specific asset within a year timeframe.
- **Safeguard value (SV):** The SV represents the benefit from investing in an ACS. This can help determine whether the best course of action is investing or avoiding an ACS. For example, if the safeguard costs more than the asset, most likely it is not worth the investment unless there are other factors such as mandated regulations requiring the additional protection. The formula for determining SV uses the cost before and after applying the safeguard:

  SV = (ALE pre-safeguard) – (ALE post-safeguard) – ACS

This might seem like a lot of work to calculate for every incident, and therefore it is not expected to know values such as the ALE for every asset on the network. Best practice is to use quantitative risk analysis to help justify or avoid large expenses to reduce or transfer risk from identified vulnerabilities. Values used for some of these formulas are estimated, so it is recommended to use conservative values for assets and loss when calculating these formulas. The final goal is taking the annualized loss expectancy and seeing how it compares to the safeguard value to decide whether it is worth investing in reducing the risk, transferring the risk, or accepting the risk but not doing anything about it.

Before performing efforts such as quantitative risk calculations for vulnerabilities, it is best practice to first perform a risk assessment by assigning a *risk rating* to a new vulnerability. This rating system can be used to prioritize remediation efforts and to decide on the best course of action such as determining the SV to protect the asset. A good model to follow for determining risk ratings is the *OWASP risk rating methodology*.[3] The end goal is to develop reoccurring reports such as a risk heat map introduced in Chapter 1.

Let's look at how risk rating can be calculated using the OWASP methodology.

OWASP Risk Rating Methodology

The Open Web Application Security Project (OWASP) is a community founded in 2001 that focuses on web application security. Over the years, OWASP has been involved with many projects, including offering best practices for handing risk associated with vulnerabilities. The standard risk model starts with a simple formula:

Risk = Likelihood * Impact

Typically, the calculated value is broken down into a ranking such as low, medium, or high, but can be more granular depending on the SOC policy requirements. That ranking can be placed into a chart that the SOC can use to determine the severity of the associated risk. This helps to justify how to handle the risk associated with the new vulnerability.

First, we need to determine the *likelihood* of the risk. Likelihood means how likely it is that the particular vulnerability will be uncovered and exploited. OWASP uses *threat agents* and *vulnerability factors* as a method to factor how likely it is that a vulnerability will be exploited. The sections that follow demonstrate how to calculate threat agent and vulnerability factors.

Threat Agent Factors

Skill level: What skill level of attacker is required to exploit the vulnerability? Can anybody with a computer exploit the vulnerability, or does it require a unique expert level of knowledge?

Points: Advanced penetration skills (1), network and programming skills (3), advanced computer user (4), some technical skills (6), no technical skills (9)

Motive: What is the level of motivation to exploit the vulnerability? High-value targets attract very motivated attackers.

Points: Low or no reward (1), possible reward (4), high reward (9)

Opportunity: What tools, resources, and opportunities are required to be successful in exploiting the vulnerability? A threat agent's risk increases as the effort required to exploit a vulnerability decreases. For example, cracking a password might require as little as a basic laptop, or it might need a very large supercomputers and a lot of time depending on the length, complexity, and lifetime of the password. Everything risks exploitation, but low-opportunity situations tend to discourage attempts.

Points: Expensive resources and time (0), special access or resources required (4), some access or resources required (7), no access or resources required (9)

Size: How many types of attackers could be aware or have access to the vulnerability? More people means a higher risk that somebody will figure out how to exploit the vulnerability.

Points: Limited group such as developers or administrators (2), intranet users (4), partners (5), authenticated users (6), anonymous Internet users (9)

Each threat agent factor has a point system rating from 0 to 9. Points are added up and used along with points collected from the vulnerability factors to calculate the likelihood of the risk. Vulnerability factors can be calculated using the concepts described in the next section.

> **Note** The point value systems described here are just examples of different variations that you can use.

Vulnerability Factors

Easy of discovery: How easy is it for an attacker to discover the vulnerability?

Points: Practically impossible (1), difficult (3), easy (7), automated tools available (9)

Ease of exploit: What level of effort is involved to exploit the vulnerability?

Points: Theoretical (1), difficult (3), easy (5), automated tools available (9)

Awareness: How well known is this vulnerability to possible attackers?

Points: Unknown (1), hidden (4), obvious (6), public knowledge (9)

Intrusion detection: What is the likelihood of an attack being detected?

> **Points:** Active detection in application (1), logged and reviewed (3), logged without review (8), not logged (9)

Likelihood can be calculated by taking the average score of both the threat agent factors and vulnerability factors. The final value for calculating likelihood and impact levels can be placed into rankings representing the severity level, such as low, medium, high, or extreme. This can be adjusted to be more or less granular depending on the SOC requirements. Figure 7-3 shows associating severity with likelihood and impact levels using a four-category severity table.

Severity Ranking for Likelihood and Impact	
0 < 3	LOW
3 < 5	MEDIUM
5 < 7	HIGH
7 < 9	EXTREME

Figure 7-3 *Four-Category Security Table*

Figure 7-4 shows calculating the likelihood of a threat based on dividing the sum of eight different values by eight. Note that the final value shown in this example has a medium-level risk associated with it.

Threat Agent Factors				Vulnerability Factors			
Skill Level	Motive	Opportunity	Size	Ease of Discovery	Ease of Exploit	Awareness	Intrusion Detection
1	7	5	2	6	3	2	9
Likelihood of Threat = 4.375 MEDIUM							

Figure 7-4 *Calculating the Likelihood of Threat*

Next, we need to calculate the *impact* if the vulnerability is successfully exploited. This can be considered from a *technical* and *business* viewpoint. That is, what are the technical risks associated with a threat, and how will it impact the business? Business impact will most likely be more important; however, it might not be clear how a threat can impact the business. For these situations, you can use technical impact to develop a risk score for the vulnerability.

Impact can be calculated using the technical and business impact factors described in the sections that follow.

Technical Impact Factors

Loss of confidentiality: This looks at the amount of data and sensitivity level of the data that could be lost.

> **Points:** Nonsensitive data loss (2), sensitive data loss (6), critical data loss (7), all data loss (9)

Loss of integrity: Loss of integrity means evaluating how much data could be corrupted and the level of damage from being corrupted.

> **Points:** Slight data corruption (1), minimal data corruption (3), serious data corruption (5), extensive data corruption (7), all data corrupted (9)

Loss of availability: Availability means how many services could be lost and how important it is if it goes down.

> **Points:** Minimal secondary services interruption (1), minimal primary services interruption (5), serious secondary services interrupted (5), serious primary services interrupted (7), all services interrupted (9)

Loss of accountability: This targets whether threat agents can be traced back to the attacker.

> **Points:** Full traceability (1), possible traceability (7), completely anonymous (9)

Business Impact Factors

Financial damage: How much could exploiting the vulnerability cost the business?

> **Points:** Damage less than remediation cost (1), minor impact on annual profits (3), major impact on annual profits (7), possible bankruptcy (9)

Reputation damage: This considers the negative impact on the business reputation. An example is the negative business impact experienced by the company RSA Security due to the publicity following a security breach from a cyberattack. RSA announced, "This information could potentially be used to reduce the effectiveness of a current two-factor authentication implantation,"[4] meaning that the two-factor technology could be ineffective. The fallout from this breach is estimated to be around $66 million.

> **Points:** Minor damage (1), major accounts lost (4), customer trust lost (5), brand damage (9)

Noncompliance: What is the business impact of not being compliant? Are there large fines or jail time associated with not meeting mandated regulations associated with risk from the vulnerability?

> **Points:** Minor violation (2), major violation (5), high-profile violation (7)

Privacy violation: How much and what is the business impact of sensitive data such as privacy information being exposed due to the exploitation of a vulnerability?

> **Points:** Individual (3), hundreds of people (5), thousands of people (7), millions of people (9)

Calculating impact is similar to calculating likelihood; however, the technical and business impacts are kept separate because an associated risk may technically be high but not necessarily impact the business or vice versa. Having both viewpoints when calculating risk helps quantify things for different purposes. Because each section has four factors, the impact is calculated by dividing the sum of the four factors by four. The final number is compared against the severity chart to determine the severity rating.

Figure 7-5 shows calculating the technical and business impact for an identified vulnerability. This example shows a threat that could have an extreme technical impact but lower business impact.

Technical Impact				Business Impact			
Loss of Confidentiality	Loss of Integrity	Loss of Availability	Loss of Accountability	Financial Damage	Reputation Damage	Non-Compliance	Privacy Violation
8	9	7	5	2	2	1	5
Technical Impact = 7.25 EXTREME				Business Impact = 2.25 LOW			

Figure 7-5 *Example of Calculating Technical and Business Impact*

Risk heat maps can be developed based on aligning impact and likelihood for X and Y coordinates of a graphical representation of the risk associated with vulnerabilities. The scale of the heat map is determined by the level of granularity for breaking out the severity levels used by the organization. Figure 7-6 shows an example from Chapter 1 representing a four-category rating severity system used when calculating impact and likelihood.

Once risk ratings are assigned to vulnerabilities, the SOC can review all identified vulnerabilities and prioritize which risks to address first.

At this point, we have covered how to identify vulnerabilities, how to rank the vulnerabilities according to risk ratings, and how to calculate risk values for new vulnerabilities. Now let's look at applying these concepts to a vulnerability management process.

Likelihood		Impact			
		Negligible	Marginal	Critical	Catastrophic
	Certain	HIGH	HIGH	EXTREME	EXTREME
	Likely	MEDIUM	HIGH	HIGH	EXTREME
	Possible	LOW	MEDIUM	HIGH	EXTREME
	Unlikely	LOW	LOW	MEDIUM	EXTREME
	Rare	LOW	LOW	MEDIUM	HIGH

Figure 7-6 *Four-Category Risk Heat Map*

The Vulnerability Management Lifecycle

The primary goal of vulnerability management for a SOC is reducing the risk from a technical weakness to an acceptable level. There will always be risk within the organization, so it should be understood that like risk management, vulnerability management is a continuous process of risk reduction rather than efforts to prevent risk. Note that vulnerability management targets technical weaknesses; however, the existence of a technical vulnerability could be the result of a weakness in people and processes.

Chapter 2 introduced the SANS Vulnerability Management Model as a six-step process to manage vulnerabilities. Figure 7-7 shows this model.

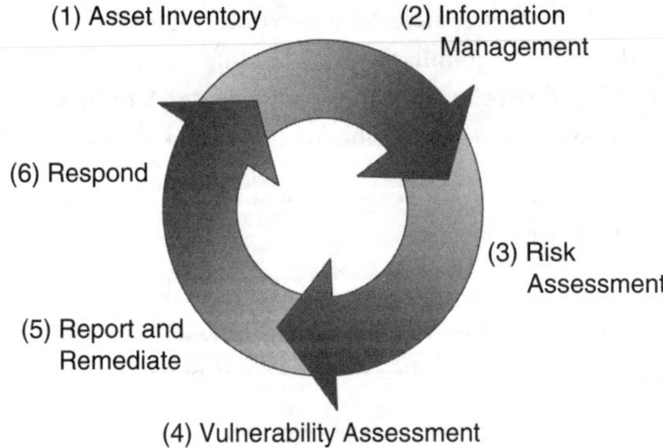

Figure 7-7 *SANS Vulnerability Management Model*

Let's define each step of this vulnerability management model to better understand how this could be applied to a SOC vulnerability management process:

1. **Asset inventory:** The first step of this model is to develop and maintain an accurate list of inventory. This way you have a defined set of systems with associated users that can be evaluated for vulnerabilities. Developing and maintaining an asset inventory list is a huge challenge for most organizations because they lack visibility and access control to network resources. Best practice is to assign a specific team responsible for maintaining the asset inventory list and provide that data to other groups such as the SOC to validate vulnerabilities against. Chapter 8, "People and Processes," covers best practices for role assignments, such as who should be responsible for asset inventory.
2. **Information management:** Maintaining information such as being alerted about the latest known attacks or results from a vulnerability assessment requires a process to manage how this sensitive data is handled by the organization. Most organizations would not want vulnerabilities identified within the organization posted to the public, because of possible negative business impact and the potential to increase the likelihood of the vulnerability being exploited. Best practice to control sensitive risk data is to assign incident response tasks to a specific team. Usually this is the responsibility of the SOC, but some organizations may have a separate Computer Security Incident Response Team (CSIRT) that focuses on interfacing with the public and internal staff about possible vulnerabilities. It is critical to have these responsibilities well defined before starting any later steps involving identifying risk and vulnerabilities within the organization.
3. **Risk assessment:** Before you start evaluating systems for vulnerabilities, it is best practice to first establish a baseline for the known risk in your environment. This will help the SOC prioritize where to focus services such as vulnerability assessments and be more prepared to handle next steps for remediation. For example, there might be two network assets of concern; however, one may have more risk associated based on its value to the business. Knowing the risk will help determine which asset to focus on first. You learned about the process for delivering risk assessments earlier in this chapter.
4. **Vulnerability assessment:** Once you have a general idea of the associated risk with assets that the organization is responsible for, the next step is to evaluate those systems for vulnerabilities. This should start with the highest risk factors to the business and work down to lower-priority threats. Timing is a critical element, so the SOC may need to include external services or acquire solutions that improve efficiency so that all systems are evaluated quickly enough to meet the business's tolerance level for risk. Vulnerability assessments can range in services from basic audits to tactical penetration testing depending on the factors such as the value of risk identified during the risk assessment or available resources.
5. **Report and remediate:** This step is the follow up to the results from risk and vulnerability assessments. Reporting is critical to track and assign the responsibility to remediate any vulnerabilities deemed a high enough priority to address. Other

areas where reporting can be used include verifying compliance, validating the current security state of the organization, justifying budget for improving areas that are challenging to remediate, and measuring remediation effectiveness. Not reporting and remediating findings from risk and vulnerability assessments negates any value from having those services.

6. **Responding:** The final step in this Vulnerability Management Model before repeating the entire process is how to respond to a vulnerability. This might include remediation as one step, but takes into consideration the entire response plan when addressing new vulnerabilities such as how the vulnerability impacts the business rather than one particular system. An example is identifying a particular vulnerability in a protocol used by different types of systems in the organization. The response plan may be a method to roll out patches based on prioritizing high-risk systems followed by systems showing less risk. Patches may not be available for some systems, requiring contacting the vendor or placing temporary additional security in place while the systems remains vulnerable. This example would run the vulnerability management cycle for each system and link them to the appropriate response plan.

Each phase of the vulnerability management lifecycle can involve different teams or be the sole responsibility of the SOC. Regardless of responsibility, it is critical to publish a plan for handling each step with assigned roles. Gaps in any step could negatively impact the results of other steps. For example, not having a current asset list could result in vulnerability and risk assessments of devices that do not exist on the network. Another example is not having the risk associated with a system may cause investment in patching a system that offers little business relevance while leaving a mission-critical system exposed to threats.

Part of developing a vulnerability management plan should include the process for establishing communication between all parties with responsibilities. One example is having an emergency e-mail or phone list that can quickly be leveraged when needed. Response time is mission critical for vulnerability management, so best practice is to have a few methods for bringing the appropriate team members together. We find that many organizations' biggest problem with regard to response time for threats is not having the right people involved quickly enough versus being technology related.

Another best practice is to develop a list of relevant contacts such as vendor support lines, trusted security consultants, and legal authorities to pull from if additional resources are required outside of the SOC team. In some situations, it might be more cost-effective to leverage a consultant who specializes in a specific vulnerability or use the help of a developer of a technology to properly address a new vulnerability. The worst time to hunt for contact information is when there is a time-sensitive issue at hand, such as a critical vulnerability on your network. This is why this list should be proactively developed by the SOC.

Each step can be performed with manual steps, but may be very time-consuming and possibly unrealistic based on factors such as network size, security policies, and diversity. Tools are available to help automate and consolidate findings from each step to simplify executing the vulnerability management process.

Let's take a look at the different types of tools that can assist with vulnerability management.

Automating Vulnerability Management

As stated earlier in this chapter, reaction time is one of the most critical steps to prevent vulnerabilities from being exploited. Vulnerabilities can happen at any time, so best practice is to use tools to automate enforcement at any hour of the day. Automation can also speed up tedious tasks and include a record of everything for the reporting step of the vulnerability management process.

Let's look at tools that could improve a SOC's capability to deliver the six steps of the SANS Vulnerability Management Model.

Inventory Assessment Tools

Automating the process of maintaining a current inventory can be accomplished in a few ways. The first option is to use network access control (NAC) technology that validates users and devices before they are permitted specific network access. Cisco Identity Services Engine (ISE) not only provides such features but also continuously profiles devices to ensure that you have a accurate list of what is on the network. For example, a hacker may try to sneak onto the network by spoofing the MAC address of an authorized device such as a network printer. Cisco ISE would also monitor other network attributes seen from the device, such as Dynamic Host Configuration Protocol (DHCP), Domain Name System (DNS), Address Resolution Protocol (ARP), and so on, which would validate that the asset is really a Windows laptop with a fake MAC address and apply the correct security actions toward that device. Figure 7-8 shows user bob accessing the 802.1X protected network using an Apple iPad.

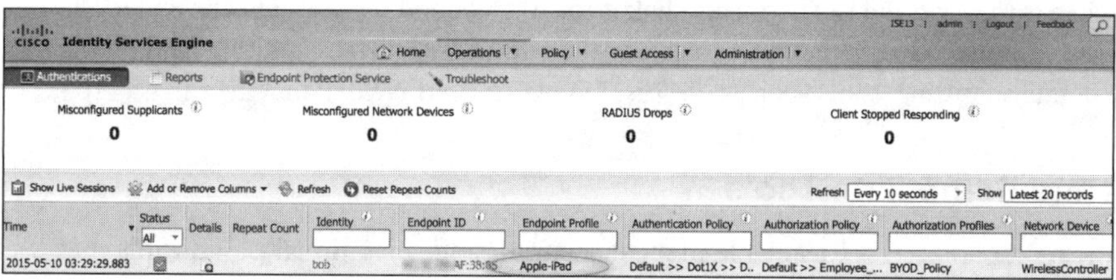

Figure 7-8 *ISE 1.3 Identifying an Apple iPad*

Another approach to managing asset inventory is to use an asset management tool that includes network discovery features. Network discovery can be accomplished by different methods such as monitoring for ARP broadcasts or integrating with a wireless controller to identify when any device associates with the network. Asset management tools tend to offer other features such as capturing software licenses, developing network diagrams, and compliance reporting. Some examples of vendors that offer tools with asset management features are Peregrine, LANDesk Management Suite, Latis Networks, and many security information and event management (SIEM) vendors.

Information Management Tools

Information management is all about communication. Most likely, the SOC has existing tools to meet the technology requirements for this step of the vulnerability management process. Communication tools can be e-mail, internal websites, conference products, and mailing lists.

Cisco offers various conferencing products such as WebEx and TelePresence that can be configured for emergency response functions such as automatically dialing people and alerting through web and e-mail. Learn more at Cisco.com, where you can check out available validated designs such as the Emergency Responder 9.0 datasheet.

Risk-Assessment Tools

The risk-assessment process involves lots of calculations that can be performed manually or automated with the right tool. One approach is to use a governance, risk, and compliance (GRC) solution that performs automated management and monitoring. GRC tools such as RSA's Archer platform can record steps taken when an event occurs and tie them to triggers so that future processes are automated. There are also open source tools with risk management features such as OpenFISMA, which includes a Risk Management Framework.

Another approach is to create worksheets that have the risk-assessment formulas built in so that only specific variables are needed to calculate risk values. Excel or scripting programming languages could easily accomplish basic risk-assessment calculations but may be challenging for more advanced formulas and operational upkeep.

Vulnerability-Assessment Tools

We covered various types of vulnerability-assessment tools earlier in this chapter. The best approach is to select the right tool and link it to the intended service being provided. If assessing vulnerabilities is the main focus for the current task versus auditing for compliance or penetration testing, tools such as Nessus, OpenVAS, and NMAP may be the way to go.

Report and Remediate Tools

Reporting capabilities are available in most security- and operational-based tools that can be leveraged for this step of the vulnerability management process. Best practice is to centralize data collection using methods covered in Chapter 6, "Security Event Generation and Collection," and leverage reporting from that centralized tool. Many SIEMs offer both reporting and remediation capabilities through integration with internal or external tools. An example is the SIEM Splunk's ability to leverage Cisco's access control technology ISE as the method to quarantine systems posing high levels of risk.

One feature that should be a requirement when selecting a tool for remediation is tracking and notification of actions taken by the tools being used. This way, the SOC can assign and track which vulnerabilities are being remediated and avoid wasting time on systems that have already been remediated or overlapping resource assignments. There are ticketing and case management applications available such as TeamSupport, Mhelpdesk, and Microsoft Dynamics CRM designed for help desk services. Many security tools such as SIEMs also include ticketing and case management capabilities.

Responding Tools

A SOC's response to managing vulnerabilities is based on corporate policies and the outcome from other steps of the vulnerability management process. This means the response to vulnerabilities will follow a documented response plan and leverage people using the tools and tactics from the other steps in the management model, instead of requiring additional tools. For example, the same collaboration tools from the information management phase could be used to bring together responsible parties required to decide the best course of action for a list of high-risk vulnerabilities. Other useful reports that would be used during this phase are the risk heat maps and results from security services.

The SANS Vulnerability Management Model is just one example of a best practice for how a SOC can manage new vulnerabilities. Many vendors or security organizations offer variations of vulnerability management models such as Cisco's Rapid Risk Vulnerability Response Model[5] and Core Security's Threat and Vulnerability Management Maturity Model.[6] Figure 7-9 and Figure 7-10 show diagrams of these models.

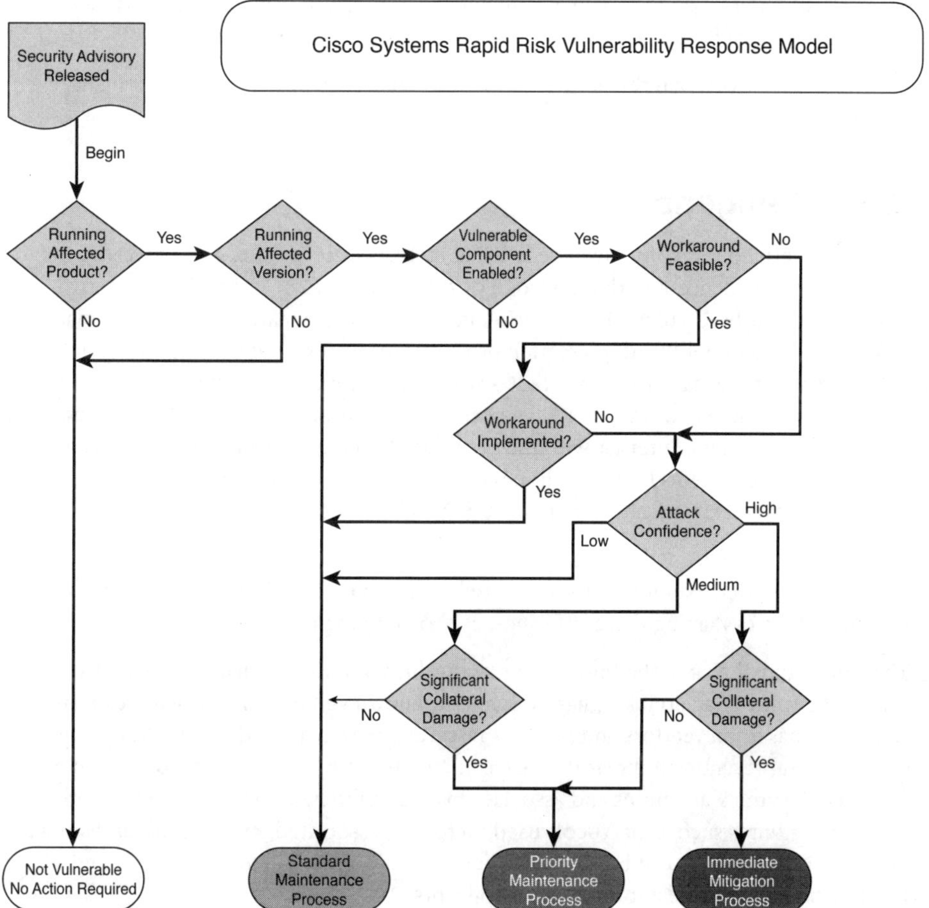

Figure 7-9 *Cisco Rapid Risk Vulnerability Response Model*

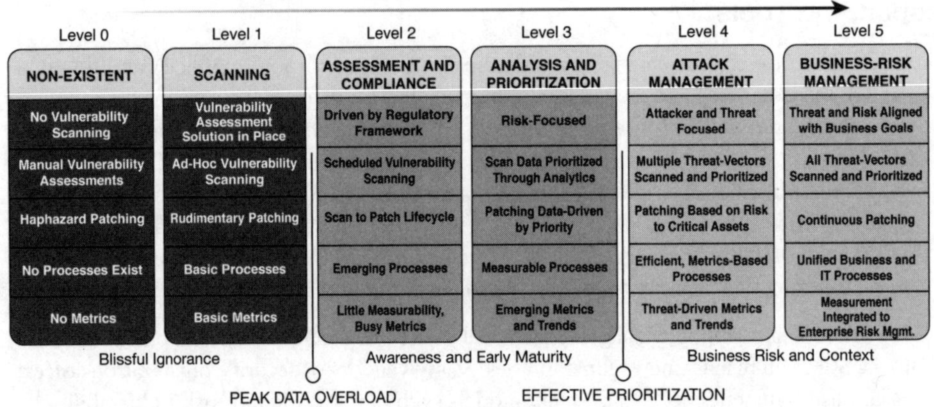

Figure 7-10 *The Threat and Vulnerability Management Maturity Model*

These models are based on SOC internal capabilities, but many external sources could be used with internal data to dramatically enhance the effectiveness of SOC vulnerability management capabilities.

Let's review how external threat intelligence can complement SOC efforts to manage vulnerabilities.

Threat Intelligence

Chapter 2 defined threat intelligence in using references to Gartner and Forrester. In summary, it is evidence-based knowledge of the capabilities of internal and external threat actors. As SOC vulnerability management capabilities mature, they accumulate attack trends that could lead to creating proactive measures to prevent future attacks. Other organizations have their own SOCs with attack trend data containing threats that your organization may or may not have encountered. Also, some research firms focus on placing systems on the Internet with the purpose of collecting attack data such as monitored vulnerable systems known as honeypots. Threat intelligence feeds could combine all this data, thus dramatically expanding a SOC's knowledge of the threat landscape.

Various threat intelligence sources are available as open source or paid services. Chapter 2 provided examples of threat intelligence sources and showed Forrester's five-step model for evaluating these offerings, as shown in Figure 7-11.

The first external source that most security products leverage is sharing threat information in the form of an attack signature against a known vulnerability. The attack signature concept is based on vendors and security researchers from around the world posting a signature representing a threat they have encountered so that other products can be aware of the attack attributes and associated vulnerabilities. There are different variations of attributes such as protocols used, behavior, associated applications, and so on. For simplicity sake, we can break attack signatures into two categories: atomic and stateful signatures. Let's take a look at these concepts.

Figure 7-11 *Threat Intelligence Cycle According to Forrester*

Attack Signatures

Let's first define the two types of attack signatures leveraged by signature-based security solutions:

- **Atomic signatures** are the most basic signature type representing a single packet, activity, or event to trigger the alarm. This means that these signatures do not require a system to correlate knowledge of historical or future data because they are based on a single event.
- **Stateful signatures** are more advanced signatures requiring a sequence of events to trigger the alarm. This means that these signatures require a system to correlate knowledge of historical or future data because multiple events must be identified to trigger the alarm.

Many vendors offer a source listing their signature knowledgebase to verify whether specific signatures exist within their products. Examples include Cisco's Product Security Incident Response Team (PSIRT) portal[7] and Symantec's Attack Signature portal.[8] We covered the standard used for releasing vulnerabilities, known as the Common Vulnerabilities and Exposures (CVE), in Chapter 1. CVE updates are usually free, but vendors may charge to have their products automatically provide updates to attack signatures based on the latest CVE announcements. An example is the Heartbleed bug associated with CVE-2014-0160. For owners of the Cisco products, this threat is defended with Snort system identifiers (SID) 30510 through 30517, along with 30520 through

30523. Snort is an open source product that can provide this protection, but Cisco Next-Generation Intrusion Prevention System (NGIPS) charges for a subscription for the IPS capabilities that leverage these attack signatures.

Threat Feeds

Threat feeds are another external source that the SOC can use to obtain attack data to be more aware of threats seen by other customers and researchers. This goes beyond attack signatures or data seen within the SOC, meaning concepts like new or abnormal events can be a lot more accurate when data is based on threat characteristics validated on multiple networks. Also correlating threats across multiple networks means that events can be targeted down to a specific IP, URL, or payload pattern even if there are different variations hitting different customers. Most important, many advanced threats remain undetected for long periods and can be detected only when they become active. Having data from compromised customers could help the SOC search for sleeper threats inside the local network before having them execute the attack.

Here are some questions you should consider when evaluating a threat feed source:

- What is the number and type of sources used to create the threat intelligence feed?
- How often is the feed updated?
- How are threats evaluated regarding severity ranking?
- Can you verify that an identified threat is real?
- What is the format of the threat intelligence feed?
- How does the threat data complement your environment?

Threat feeds continue to grow in number and range from open source to paid services. We referenced examples of both options in Chapter 2 under the "Threat Intelligence" section. The most important value from leveraging a threat feed service was shown in the previous last question about how the feed complements your environment. Most feeds are designed to feed into a centralized data-collection tool such as a SIEM, but many other threat intelligence tools can benefit from intelligence feeds. The typical goal is to import the threat feed and verify whether threats added are found in your environment.

Cisco offers a few paid threat intelligence feeds such as the ThreatGrid prepackaged and custom threat feeds. These feeds offer a unique repository of malware analysis content that can be customized for your industry and threat environment. ThreatGRID sees 200,000+ samples submitted every day, meaning that these are willingly sent to Cisco for evaluation mixed with other malware research. An example of a custom feed is subscribing to threats seen in banking environments for customers in that market. Figure 7-12 shows how an administrator can submit anything, such as .exe, .dll, .jar, .pdf, .rtf, .doc, .ppt, .zip, URLs, and so on, to be analyzed by Cisco ThreatGRID.

Figure 7-12 *ThreatGRID File Upload Option*

Threat feeds can also be part of subscriptions for a particular product. Chapter 6 introduced Lancope's StealthWatch as a NetFlow solution using network telemetry as a method to identify threats. StealthWatch offers a threat intelligence subscription service known as SLIC that populates StealthWatch with the latest command-and-control (CnC) attack data. This data is based on Lancope's research and on data collected from other customers using the StealthWatch solution. Figure 7-13 shows a StealthWatch alarm triggered when an internal host was identified communicating with a CnC based out of Russia.

Start Active...	Alarm	Source	Details	Target Host ...	Target
May 11, 2015 3:59:30 PM	Host Lock Violation	209.182.184.8	Rule #86 Suspicious Internet Connection Source Host is using http (80/tcp) as client to 195.93.180.252 (Double-click for details)	Russian Federation, CnC, Zeus	195.93.180.252

Figure 7-13 *Lancope CnC Detection*

Other Threat Intelligence Sources

There are many ways to share threat intelligence across different platforms. Some method use exchange languages such as the Incident Object Description Exchange Format (IODEF), Real-time Internet Defense (RID), or one growing in popularity known as STIX. MITRE developed Structured Threat Information Express (STIX) as an express language designed for sharing of cyberattack information. STIX details can contain data such as the IP address of CnC servers, malware hashes, and so on. Information is shared using a Trusted Automated Exchange of Indictor Information (TAXII) agent, which is used for transporting STIX data in an automated manner. So essentially, companies are sharing STIX data using TAXII. An example of using STIX could be identifying a phishing attack and sharing the phishing information to an external party in the STIX format. You can learn more about STIX and TAXII at http://stix.mitre.org/.

Many vendors provide data feed services that can be part of a product or feed you import into your own toolsets. You should expect to pay at least $2000 to $3000 per month for a single data feed, but that cost can increase depending on the type of feed, vendor billing model, and additional required hardware. Examples include Symantec charging approximately $28,000 per year for 1 to 2499 managed users as a feed, and FireEye changing 20 percent to 30 percent of the purchased appliance price for the feed. (Appliances start around $18,000 and go over $150,000 per unit.) Here is a list of some popular threat intelligence offerings:

- **AlienVault.com:** Offers multiple sources, including large honeynets that profile adversaries.
- **CrowdStrike.com:** Advanced threat intelligence as part of their threat protection platform.
- **Cyveilance.com:** Feed focusing on indications of criminal intent from threat actors.
- **EmergingThreats.net:** Proofpoint threat intelligence feed.
- **FireEye.com:** Threat intelligence service.
- **InternetIdentity.com:** Threat feeds from their big data solution ActiveTrust.
- **iSightPartners.com:** The ThreatScape threat intelligence series.
- **MalwareCheck.org:** Provides intelligence on any URL.
- **MalwareDomains.com:** A list of domains known to be associated with malware.
- **RecordedFuture.com:** Organizes information from the Internet for real-time threat intelligence.
- **SecureWorks.com:** Provides feeds and also instruments networks.
- **Symantec.com:** DeepInsight feeds on a variety of topics, including reputation.
- **Team-Cymru.com:** Offers threat intelligence plus bogon lists.
- **ThreatConnect.com:** Focused on information sharing.
- **ThreatGrid.com:** Unified malware analysis. Now part of Cisco.
- **ThreatStop.com:** Block botnets by IP reputation.
- **ThreatStream.com:** Multiple sources in interoperable platform.
- **ThreatTrack.com:** Stream of malicious URLs, IPs, and malware- and phishing-related data.
- **Verisigninc.com:** Defense feeds highly regarded by some key institutions.

One interesting trend is how the security industry is leaning more on threat intelligence as a way to keep up with threats and a tool used to offload process-intensive features. Hardware and software can only analyze so many things locally before the solution has to let the traffic proceed without impacting business. It makes sense to outsource certain types of checks to block threats before they hit the security solution, thus giving more process power for a smaller range of threats that have passed the first checkpoint. An example is Cisco blocking websites preconnection based on reputation security, also known as *credit scoring*, so that every website seen by a solution is not required to be scanned and thus saving local process power. Figure 7-14 shows the website ihaveabad-reputation.com being blocked based on a –9.5 reputation score by Cisco Web Security Appliance (WSA).

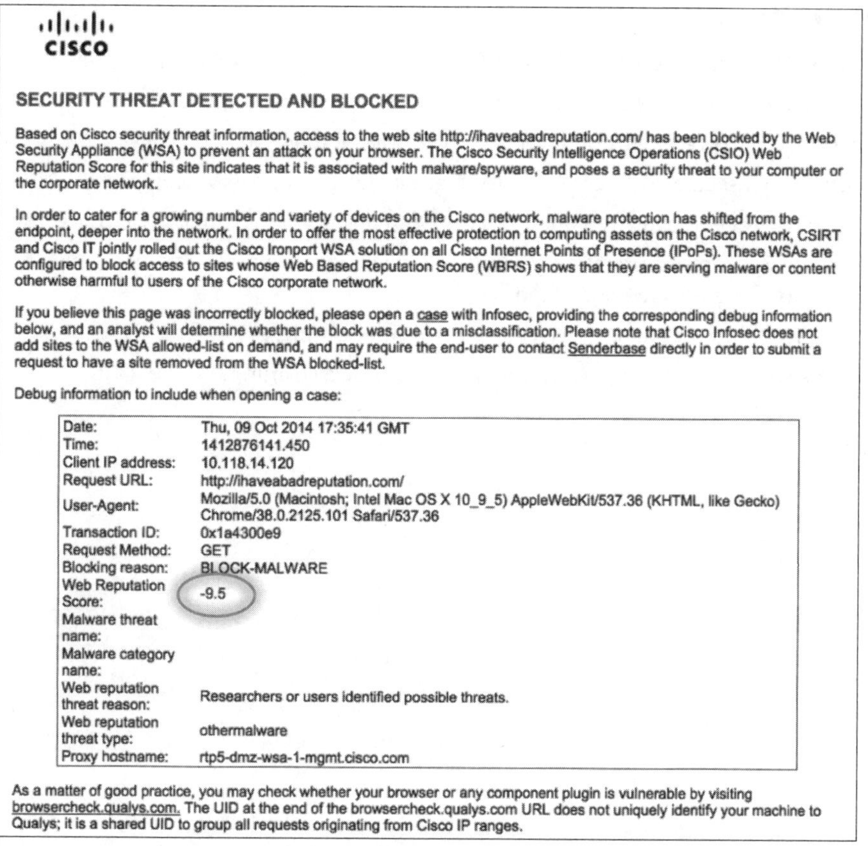

CISCO

SECURITY THREAT DETECTED AND BLOCKED

Based on Cisco security threat information, access to the web site http://ihaveabadreputation.com/ has been blocked by the Web Security Appliance (WSA) to prevent an attack on your browser. The Cisco Security Intelligence Operations (CSIO) Web Reputation Score for this site indicates that it is associated with malware/spyware, and poses a security threat to your computer or the corporate network.

In order to cater for a growing number and variety of devices on the Cisco network, malware protection has shifted from the endpoint, deeper into the network. In order to offer the most effective protection to computing assets on the Cisco network, CSIRT and Cisco IT jointly rolled out the Cisco Ironport WSA solution on all Cisco Internet Points of Presence (IPoPs). These WSAs are configured to block access to sites whose Web Based Reputation Score (WBRS) shows that they are serving malware or content otherwise harmful to users of the Cisco corporate network.

If you believe this page was incorrectly blocked, please open a case with Infosec, providing the corresponding debug information below, and an analyst will determine whether the block was due to a misclassification. Please note that Cisco Infosec does not add sites to the WSA allowed-list on demand, and may require the end-user to contact Senderbase directly in order to submit a request to have a site removed from the WSA blocked-list.

Debug information to include when opening a case:

Date:	Thu, 09 Oct 2014 17:35:41 GMT
Time:	1412876141.450
Client IP address:	10.118.14.120
Request URL:	http://ihaveabadreputation.com/
User-Agent:	Mozilla/5.0 (Macintosh; Intel Mac OS X 10_9_5) AppleWebKit/537.36 (KHTML, like Gecko) Chrome/38.0.2125.101 Safari/537.36
Transaction ID:	0x1a4300e9
Request Method:	GET
Blocking reason:	BLOCK-MALWARE
Web Reputation Score:	-9.5
Malware threat name:	
Malware category name:	
Web reputation threat reason:	Researchers or users identified possible threats.
Web reputation threat type:	othermalware
Proxy hostname:	rtp5-dmz-wsa-1-mgmt.cisco.com

As a matter of good practice, you may check whether your browser or any component plugin is vulnerable by visiting browsercheck.qualys.com. The UID at the end of the browsercheck.qualys.com URL does not uniquely identify your machine to Qualys; it is a shared UID to group all requests originating from Cisco IP ranges.

Figure 7-14 *Cisco WSA Reputation Block Page*

Summary

This chapter covered how a SOC can create and deliver a vulnerability management process. The chapter covered common security services and associated tools typically used to identify and manage vulnerabilities. You learned how to calculate risk and develop risk ranking to properly prioritize which vulnerabilities to address first and to decide the appropriate plan of action. You also learned how to combine this to formulate a vulnerability management best practice following the SANS recommended model, with references to other models. The chapter concluded by reviewing threat intelligence as a way to gather additional security information to improve a SOC's ability to understand the threat landscape.

The next chapter covers the people and processes involved with a SOC. This will help designate roles and responsibilities for the topics covered in this book.

References

1. https://dl.mandiant.com/EE/library/BH2012_Aldridge_RemediationPaper.pdf
2. http://www.verizonenterprise.com/DBIR/2015/
3. https://www.owasp.org/index.php/OWASP_Risk_Rating_Methodology
4. http://www.secureworks.com/cyber-threat-intelligence/threats/rsacompromise/
5. http://www.cisco.com/web/about/security/intelligence/vulnerability-risk-triage.html
6. http://www.coresecurity.com/system/files/attachments/vulnerability-management-maturity-model-white-paper_0.pdf
7. http://tools.cisco.com/security/center/publicationListing.x
8. http://www.symantec.com/security_response/attacksignatures/

Chapter 8

People and Processes

"The key is to keep company only with people who uplift you, whose presence calls forth your best."—Epictetus

A strong team is critical to the success of any security operations center (SOC). As the front line for most security incident investigations and responses, they are expected to deliver a consistently robust set of services, often under great pressure and constraint. Individuals within such teams often require a wide range of technical and nontechnical skills, in addition to the ability to work effectively as a cohesive unit. In some SOCs, this also means a seamless stitching of many organizations, both internal and external, to deliver on the SOC's core mission.

This chapter focuses on developing an appropriate governance and staffing model based on the range of services that the SOC will provide. This includes common roles and responsibilities. This chapter starts by covering various resourcing strategies for recruiting and developing SOC personnel and leveraging internal resources, contractors, outsourcing, and managed service providers. The chapter also delves into the processes and procedures used to guide or constrain the work that professionals perform within the SOC. Failing to produce proper processes and procedures can damage the effectiveness and long-term sustainability of your SOC.

Key Challenges

As with most elements that make up an effective and functioning SOC, you must address a number of challenges for the SOC to operate successfully. This includes a wide range of challenges as you develop and maintain your SOC team and related processes. Let's start by focusing on the most important asset to any organization: its people.

Wanted: Rock Stars, Leaders, and Grunts

One fear shared by many SOC leads is the responsibility of building a SOC team. The technology may be complex, but even world-class automated systems will fail if not monitored and maintained by the right people. Good SOC team members should have a combination of deeply specialized skills and general security knowledge. They need to be able to interpret and investigate potential security incidents with a limited amount of data as quickly as possible with high fidelity. These skills are usually developed as the team builds a thorough working knowledge of the organization's assets and the threats they will likely experience.

The lifestyle of a SOC team member consists of long periods of daily operational tasks and short periods of high crisis. The best team members will be highly driven and goals focused, using slow operational periods for improving security processes, analyzing logs, proactively engaging other teams for collaboration efforts, and for self-study. It is important to be aware that although technology can be taught, the internal drive to want to learn and be great is something people either have or do not have. So, you want to select a hungry engineer over somebody with more certifications but less enthusiasm for cybersecurity.

There are some general characteristics that are not listed on a security rock star resume. They must be personally driven but work well with other teammates. They must be able to be leaders one moment and grunts the next. They must be able to communicate with nontechnical executives one minute and technical IT staff the next. Communication must be effective and patient, even in the midst of the worst and most panicked situations.

The last important characteristic of great SOC team members is that they must be pleasant to work with, most of the time. Unfortunately, such people with all of these characteristics can be extremely difficult to find or develop. They are usually even more difficult to retain. One reason it is challenging to retain great team members is the impact of SOC processes limiting how effectively they can perform their job. Another reason is limitations in available tools make it difficult to perform required tasks. Let's look deeper at these concepts.

The Weight of Process

Inexperienced SOC leaders tend to believe that solid, mature processes and procedures will solve many people problems. After all, consultants and their own peers have likely told them that a well-defined, thorough process is a cure for SOC team inexperience or a team member's lack of skill. Unfortunately, processes and procedures have limited effectiveness in a SOC.

This might seem somewhat heretical given our industry's current fascination with strategies guided by process maturity models within IT. There is an implication that a mature process that is well defined, consistently followed, and measured is somehow just *better* than the alternative. It also, however, carries the implication that such processes can make up for inexperienced or unskilled staff or that just about anyone can do SOC work. (After all, they just need to follow the process.)

Paradoxically, we have found that too many well-defined processes and procedures (what one customer called "the weight of process") actually hampers the effective SOC. Processes and their related procedures do have a place in any SOC, but they often negatively impact key SOC services and the ability to develop and retain SOC personnel.

Right about now you might be thinking, "How do we make up for inexperience if not through appropriate process?" The short answer is that you need to build a strong core cadre of experienced SOC analysts not only to handle more advanced investigation or hunting activities but also to mentor junior staff. The mix of more-experienced and less-experienced analysts will be required regardless of whether you choose more traditional tiered delivery models or small agile teams. In most environments, processes are developed for junior analysts, while senior members handle more advanced investigations that require freedom from restrictions.

The Upper and Lower Bounds of Technology

Outside of the impact of process, another unforeseen challenge for the SOC team is associated with the technologies that could underpin SOC services. For example, security information and event management (SIEM) technologies tend to be limited in ways that impact the perceived effectiveness of the SOC. On the lower bound, the SIEM may either not see certain events from key systems or be unable to provide a long-term view into such data. On the upper bound, the SIEM may simply not alert the team to real security incidents because it either misinterprets event data or has been configured to ignore some events in favor of others. The SIEM might not have sufficient information about assets or the environment it is monitoring to distinguish serious attacks. In some organizations, the SOC may have little control over the technologies they rely on, and have less ability to influence improvement. Not having the right tools can be frustrating for the SOC team and could lead to a failure for which the team will be held responsible.

There are challenges even when the SOC has full control of their technology estate. The SOC team may find itself in need of a wide range of technical experts to maintain the technology, which could include duties for tuning, product updates, and other manual efforts. This could lead to not only monitoring the environment for threats but also monitoring security vendors and suppliers to keep the solutions in use operational.

The next section provides an example that presents a fictitious SOC team that has a very inclusive mission. This SOC group must not only provide "typical" SOC services related to security event monitoring and security incident response but also a wider range of SOC services such as threat intelligence, analysis, and breach discovery, and also has the responsibility to deploy and maintain the SOC technology infrastructure. As you will see as you follow this example presented later in this chapter, there are many ways to address technology challenges within the scope of the SOC team.

Designing and Building the SOC Team

When designing a SOC team, it is always a good idea to start with the SOC's mission, the detailed requirements to deliver the SOC services in scope, and your chosen resourcing strategy. When building the team, you must be able to define a clear recruitment and development strategy to guide the development of a long-term, sustainable SOC. Let's walk through this process.

Starting with the Mission

It might seem obvious, but the makeup of a sound SOC team depends entirely on the SOC team's mission. That mission may be relatively narrow or broad, but what is most important is that it be clearly defined. Chapter 4, "SOC Strategy," covered how to build a mission statement.

Usually captured within an executive-ratified charter, the SOC team's mission may include a wide range of responsibilities within the enterprise. It clearly distinguishes the responsibilities of the SOC within the larger security operations capability and how those responsibilities compare or contrast with other parts of the organization. It also describes who is ultimately accountable for SOC services and lists the expectations of the executives who are investing in the SOC.

For example, consider the following SOC mission statement derived from a real-world example:

"Under the Director (Security Operations), the security operations center (SOC) team is responsible for continuous security monitoring and response for cybersecurity incidents on the organization's infrastructure. SOC aims to detect and contain attacks and intrusions on the shortest possible timeframe through

1. Real-time monitoring and analysis (that is, collection of security relevant events from the organization's systems and networks and selection of items that could represent an actual security incident or breach).

2. Primary response to security incidents (that is, analysis of incident characteristics, triage, definition of a suitable response strategy, and coordination of actual responsive action).

3. Discover and coordinate the remediation of breaches on the organization's systems."

This SOC mission statement is not a bad start. From this statement, we can quickly determine that core SOC services must be "real-time" security monitoring, "primary" security incident response, and breach discovery. The team we construct must therefore focus on these services, almost to the exclusion of all others, with the understanding that other services will be provided outside of the SOC team. For example, the SOC will only provide primary security incident response, implying that someone else will provide advanced security incident response. They will provide breach discovery services, but apart from coordinating breach remediation, they will not be responsible for actually remediating breaches. With this information, the new SOC director can focus on building the SOC team around specific services and related service levels.

In other cases, such mission statements can be much more broad and may include a wider variety of services to the enterprise. Consider the following real-world example:

> "The security operations center (SOC) delivers enterprise security services providing best-in-class security monitoring, security incident response, security intelligence, and certificate and key management, as well as the deployment and ongoing management of key IT security technologies within the organization. The SOC provides value to the organization by providing common services to identify potential threats and vulnerabilities to organizational and customer assets, manage sensitive cryptographic materials, detect or discover potential security incidents involving those assets, and provide timely and high-fidelity response to such incidents."

There is obviously a lot more responsibilities there than in the previous example. Not only does it include the services mentioned in the previous example but also includes security intelligence and analysis, certificate and key management, security technology engineering, and security technology operations. This would require a significantly larger team with multiple subteams focused on individual sets of similar services, under common leadership. In many organizations, this has moved the SOC far beyond the traditional monitor and respond mission to incorporate much of the information security mission.

During the rest of this chapter, we consider a SOC with a very wide remit to illustrate designing a complex SOC team. In your own case, you might have a much more contained mission that might be limited to one or two of the subteams we develop in the sections that follow.

Focusing on Services

As discussed earlier in this book, every SOC should start with a clearly defined services strategy that describes desired outcomes, the role of the SOC within the larger information security program, and how the SOC interacts with other parts of the organization. The services strategy also typically describes, at a high level, each service that the SOC is expected to provide in the short to long term. Examples include the following:

- **Service components:** Representing individual parts of a service
- **Identified sources:** What or who provides input or artifacts consumed by the service
- **Inputs/artifacts:** The specific data consumed by the service as provided by the sources
- **Outputs:** Data or information generated by the performance of the service
- **Consumers:** Groups, stakeholders, or other services that will consume the output generated by the service

Each short service description also includes expected benefits, information on typical service-level parameters that you can use for service metrics, and who will perform the service from within the SOC team.

For example, here is a sample service description for a security monitoring service, typically one of the core services provided by any SOC.

Security Monitoring Service Example

Service description: On a continuous basis, analysts are expected to observe cybersecurity events generated by consoles associated with key monitoring tools such as a SIEM based on use cases and correlation rules. Where security events have not been integrated into the SIEM, analysts monitor native management systems for security infrastructure deployed within the enterprise. Analysts also monitor incident reports made using other intake mechanisms, such as e-mail or a ticketing system. Analysts are expected to investigate such alerts performing triage, manage escalation, and provide assistance during remediation.

Benefits: Minimize disruption of IT services and reduce the impact of system compromise due to the ability to identify and escalate potential incidents in a short timeframe with high fidelity.

Service Components:

- Security event monitoring
- Alert/ticket handling
- Incident triage
- Incident escalation
- Knowledge capture
- Monitoring systems content feedback

Figure 8-1 illustrates sources, inputs, components, outputs, and consumers associated with this service.

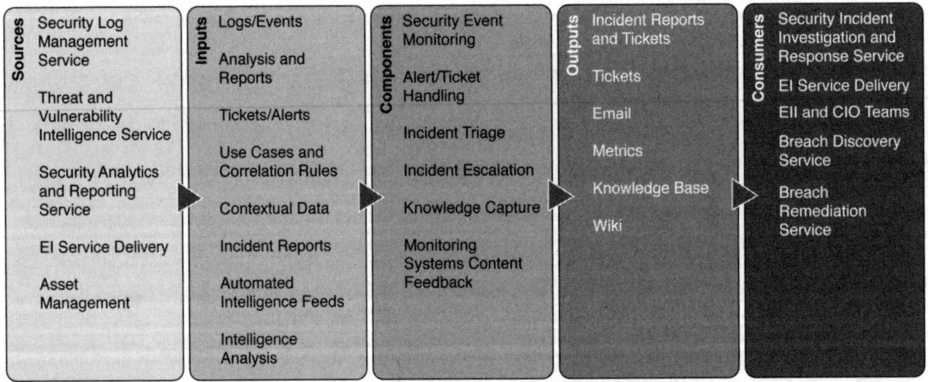

Figure 8-1 *Security Monitoring Service*

Let's look at how the services from this example can be used to guide the development of a SOC team. We will start with the basic service parameters.

- **Service-level parameters:** Service coverage, response time, escalation fidelity

At this level of detail, a few things might be useful to the person responsible for designing the SOC team. First, the components hint at the typical activities that the individuals delivering the service will need to perform. Second, sources and inputs help identify key dependencies. Third, outputs and consumers show what outputs or deliverables the service will be expected to generate and for whom. Finally, some idea of what types of service levels is also provided.

This is a good start but does not provide a sufficient level of detail for identifying the skills required from the SOC team. We should also look to the service design for more information. In particular, we'll be interested in understanding the following:

- **Service coverage:** Will the service be provided on a continuous, 24x7 basis, or will it be provided only during set business hours? Will on-call resources be available? Will coverage be provided by outsourcing or managed service providers? How will backlog or unusual burst capacity be addressed?
- **Financial constraints:** Does the service need to be delivered within known levels of budget?
- **Accountability and responsibility:** Who will be accountable for the service, and who will be responsible for delivering it?
- **Service levels:** What service levels are the service expected to maintain? Are these tiered service levels with different levels of expected service as it matures, or is it a single service level? Is it aggressive?
- **Expected load:** Based on how the service is provided today, is there an expected workload that the service will need to handle? Will there be the opportunity to reevaluate load after some defined "burn-in" period after the new services goes live?
- **Similar services:** Are there other services that share similar parameters that can or should be bundled together under common accountability/responsibility?

All of these parameters will prove helpful to determine the size and makeup of the SOC team, but it is also handy to help understand the individual roles that might make up a SOC team. For example, consider the following real-world example of a very comprehensive SOC intended to provide a very wide range of services in addition to the security monitoring service. Examples of services this example SOC would be responsible for include the following:

- **Security services management (SSM):** SSM provides services that help ensure that the SOC services are effective and continue to exhibit improvement. SSM typically acts as primary liaison for integration of services between the SOC and other parts of the organization, in addition to third parties. They are also responsible for cross-service management practices, including alignment to enterprise IT service management practices, compliance and audit support, processes, procedures, and staffing and training. SSM typically focuses on overall stability, cost performance, and optimization of services across the SOC services catalogue.

- **Security services engineering (SSE):** This service provides low-level design consulting and engineering in support of information security tools and projects within the SOC. SSE develops and validates structural enhancements to platforms and specialist tooling employed by the SOC based on strategic and operational requirements. It also prepares and validates major platform updates and releases in the aforementioned systems and contributes to major changes in existing systems.
- **Security services operations (SSO):** Whereas SSE focuses on new technologies and major releases, SSO focuses on providing for the stable and reliable operation of security technology solutions deployed to support the SOC's mission and aligned with the ongoing requirements of SOC services. It manages and maintains security tools deployed to provide SOC services. It performs and supervises changes to SOC infrastructure using the organization enterprise change management processes.
- **Security incident investigation and response service (SIIR):** Typically paired closely with the security monitoring service, the goal of this service is to ensure a consistent and effective approach to the management of information security incidents. It is responsible for the investigation into reported security incidents and managing appropriate response. Once the incident has been validated and classified, the service will also manage escalation to the appropriate teams and provide assistance throughout remediation.
- **Security log management service (SLMS):** Also typically aligned closely with the security monitoring service, the goal of this service is to collect, normalize, parse, and store security-relevant log data from network, security, and host systems and to provide access to these logs for consumption by various monitoring and reporting tools. This includes log information that may need to be extracted from source systems (for example, Windows event logs) and log information that is received from source systems. This service must also evaluate new log or event sources as required by service consumers for inclusion within the service, and be prepared to deliver such log sources in a number of different ways. Such consumer requirements will also be fundamental to short-, medium- and long-term capacity planning.
- **Vulnerability discovery service (VDS):** Whereas vulnerability management is an enterprise service provided outside of the SOC, this service focuses on vulnerability scanning as a service. It identifies potential vulnerabilities in the IT environment resulting from poor system configuration, hardware or software flaws, or operational deficiencies through automated scanning tools. Threat actors may exploit such vulnerabilities to compromise the confidentiality, integrity, and availability of the organization's data. This service is not focused on the detection of such exploits

provided by the security monitoring service or detailed vulnerability analysis, which will be provided by the threat and vulnerability intelligence services.

- **Threat and vulnerability intelligence service (TVIS):** The purpose of this service is to provide current and trustworthy intelligence gathered from relevant threat and vulnerabilities sources, both internal and external. This includes the selection and provisioning of automated threat and vulnerability intelligence feeds, but the service will include analysis of these sources and provide threat modeling to determine relevance and fidelity. The team will also work with different SOC services in supporting design for security content in SOC platforms such as new use cases based on emerging threats to update their SIEM and other threat management tools.
- **Security analytics and reporting service:** This service collates information from the other SOC services and provides common analytics, reporting, infographics, and data visualizations. Results from analysis are also fed back into other services to identify previously undetected breaches as part of anomaly detection practices and for continuous service improvement.
- **Breach discovery service:** This service identifies evidence of current or past breaches in targeted IT assets through retrospective analysis, enterprise digital forensics, and anomaly detection typically against samples of the organization's key systems. This service works to limit false positives and escalates potential incidents to be further investigated under the security incident investigation and response (SIIR) service. This is considered a supplementary service to core SOC services. It focuses in-depth examinations of IT assets through agent or agentless means to identify potentially compromised assets.

As you would suspect, this particular organization would need a large team with multiple roles, split into multiple teams and subteams. For a SOC with a narrower range of services, the team would obviously be more limited. You might have noticed that these services can also be divided in different ways. In some organizations, security monitoring and security incident investigation and response are rolled together. Likewise, you may see vulnerability discovery as just an element of threat and vulnerability intelligence. There is no one right or wrong answer, and it can be subject to some intense debate regarding which is the right way to manage these services. In general, it is best to approach these as services with potentially different inputs, outputs, consumers, and service levels and divide them accordingly.

Determining the Required SOC Roles

There are a wide variety of roles within a SOC. We have outlined many of the types of roles that we have seen within traditional and extended SOC teams. Many may be familiar, whereas others may not be. In your organization, many of these roles may fall within other teams outside of the SOC, and the SOC may leverage these shared resources rather than fulfill them within the team. Again, role assignment comes down to the services and the service levels that the SOC will be providing.

Leadership Roles

Within the SOC, there are usually a number of leadership roles. It is usually led by a SOC manager or director responsible for the overall leadership of the SOC. Managers or team leads provide the leadership of teams within the SOC, normally aligned with common sets of services. For example, security monitoring and incident response teams may be lead by a common director with individual team and shift leads providing day-to-day management for monitoring and response.

Analyst Roles

Analysts are usually the heart of any SOC, and may provide a variety of services within the SOC. Responsibilities can include security event monitoring, incident report investigation, incident handling, threat intelligence, vulnerability intelligence, and reporting. In most SOCs, these are organized in levels or tiers, with more junior tiers of analysts providing initial analysis or triage and more senior tiers providing escalation and more advanced capabilities, such as forensics and malware analysis.

Engineering Roles

Systems engineering may be performed outside of the SOC, but some SOCs are responsible for their own systems engineering given the relatively specialized nature of the platforms involved. Security engineers are usually responsible for the testing, staging, and deploying new technology platforms or major releases/updates to those platforms. They tend to be more project focused than other roles within the SOC and tend to develop deep skills in particular technology platforms. Internal engineers are often supplemented by vendor or contractor engineers who are engaged on a temporary basis for specific projects.

Operations Roles

Whereas SOC engineers tend to focus on new projects, SOC operators spend their time maintaining and operating the currently deployed SOC platforms. Unlike SOC engineers, SOC operators focus on the maintaining the availability and stability of the existing platforms, and typically provide coverage to match expected service levels within the SOC. Operators may be supplemented by vendor or contractor engineers, although this tends to be less common. In the case of managed or outsourced services, however, this role may be fulfilled by the service provider rather than by internal resources.

Other Support Roles

Most SOC have a large number of other support roles, many common to any complex IT-focused organization. These include the following:

- Business operations and finance
- Project managers

- Business continuity planning / disaster-recovery (BCP/DR) coordination and support
- Compliance and audit support
- Incident and problem managers
- Process/procedure developers
- Training specialists
- Communications specialists
- Vendor and contract management

Working with HR

Having high-level descriptions of roles within the SOC is rarely sufficient for developing a team. To recruit and develop your SOC staff, it is important to engage the help of the human resources (HR) department. There are a number of key ways that HR is involved in the design of the SOC organization: job role reviews, market analysis, and assisting with the design of the organizational structure. Let's look deeper at these HR tasks.

Job Role Analysis

For every role within the SOC, there typically must be a matching job description that both accurately describes the job role and adheres to internal standards for such descriptions. A formal or informal job role review is often used to evaluate proposed job descriptions, make amendments, and match job roles to appropriate pay grades/levels across the organization. In most organization with formal grades or levels, these determine not only what level of responsibility may be expected of the role but also how they are compensated.

It is particularly important for the documented job roles to reflect a common industry understanding of the role and an appropriate range of salary expected in your local job market. Because the role will be used to recruit, it must be clear to an outside candidate. It must also reflect what desirable candidates can expect to be paid.

Such job roles are also often used to outline career progression, and in some more traditional organizations these can have very strict divisions. For any SOC's success, it is important to try to avoid any progression model that inhibits individual growth and lateral movement within the organization.

Market Analysis

This is another area that is usually provided by HR. They typically use the documented job roles to perform a detailed analysis of the local labor market. This usually includes an evaluation of the job role itself in comparison with similar roles in industry peers and an assessment of the full compensation package that is comparable.

Organizational Structure

In addition to influencing jobs and roles, HR often has a big impact on how the SOC team is organized. In most medium-size to large organizations, HR often enforces a series of standards that are intended to ensure that all teams are organized along common principles. For example, the organization may have a policy that requires a flatter organizational structure with a few managers or team leads. Such managers or team leads may need to have a minimum or maximum number of individuals who may be allowed to report to them. They might also be required to be structured according to common service metrics that are used to evaluate their performance and compensation.

In the example of the complex SOC mentioned earlier, this could be represented in an organizational structure that looks like Figure 8-2.

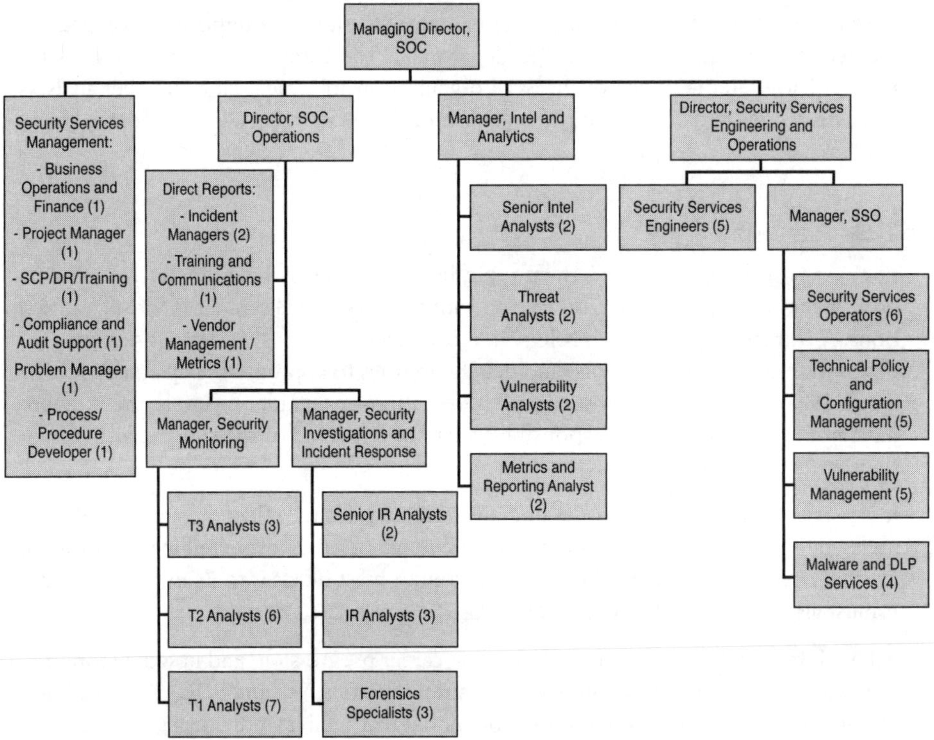

Figure 8-2 *A Sample SOC Organization Structure*

This example takes into account not only the roles as defined but also requirements for the numbers of direct reports that have to report to each manager or director as per the organization's HR standards.

Calculating Team Numbers

Once you have a clear idea of how you want to organize the SOC team, it can be much less clear how many analysts, engineers, or operators you may need within the SOC. For some functions where workload can be calculated using known parameters, this might be relatively straightforward; in other areas, though, it might need to be a bit of an educated guess.

Let's consider a fairly straightforward example where you are trying to calculate the number of resources that will provide first-line security event monitoring and triage based primarily on a number of collated and alerted events within a SIEM that have to be examined and assessed by an analyst within certain amount of time to meet expected service levels. Removing budget as a factor for this example, you need to know the following:

- **Hours of service:** It can make a big difference if the service is being offered during business hours in a particular location or if it needs to be provided continuously, 24 hours a day, and 7 days a week. Even if the service is only provided during business hours, what about alerted events that may occur after hours? How will they be addressed?
- **Average collated events per interval:** On average, how many alerted events will the analysts need to examine and assess within a particular interval (for example, every half hour during the hours of service). This gives a rough idea of total load, but keep in mind that this is an average: Actual event loads might by many *times* more or less depending on an individual point in time.
- **Individual staff availability parameters:** How many days on average can each analyst work? How many hours or minutes in a day are they actually available to monitor events? These sorts of parameters are often both ideal and very, very regional.
- **Average event handling time:** How long does it take for the analyst to handle an event in his or her queue? Again, this is only an average: Simple alerts might be easy to handle, whereas more complex ones may take much longer.
- **Acceptable queuing time:** How long can something sit in the analyst's queue before he or she has to do something with the event or have it drop out into the backlog?
- **Expected service levels:** Will the service need to address alerts within expected time frames 90 percent of the time? 95 percent? 99 percent?
- **Acceptable backlog:** Even under ideal conditions, some events will not be handled and fall into the background, resulting in an annual backlog. How big is that backlog allowed to be?
- **Acceptable staff ratios:** How many staff members will be required to be working at any point during the hours of service? Can the SOC work with less, and what is a mandated minimum?

- **Legal working hours:** How long individual staff members are allowed to work in a given period can vary widely from location to location. This might not only be constrained by local legislation but also agreements with unions or contractual terms.
- **Personal time off, administrative activities, and sick days:** How many days per year is each analyst provided for public and personal holidays, for the performance of administrative tasks, or for paid sick days? These will also affect your calculations.

Assuming you know these parameters, it might not be too difficult to calculate the number of required SOC team members. Keep in mind that this should be considered a guide that will still provide only a best guess for the right-size team. Reality has a way of surprising even the best-staffed SOC. Time will tell whether your SOC is close to being properly staffed.

There are lots of less-straightforward examples. It can, for example, be much more difficult to decide how many forensics specialists or malware analysts you may need given that demand for these skills is often sporadic. Or how many security engineers or operators may be required to build and maintain infrastructure that has not yet been deployed. In these cases, it is often best to look to industry peers in your region for some insight. It is also not such a bad idea to keep in contact with them, as discussed in Chapter 11, "Reacting to Events and Incidents."

There are other ways to calculate capacity numbers if you have other existing operations teams internally. For example, if you are in an organization that provides existing 24x7 network operations, you may be able to take advantage of similar shift scheduling and well-worn rules of thumb used by those who manage such teams. For example, we recently worked with an organization where we were calculating the numbers of resources needed to provide a basic 24x7 service with relatively low volumes. A typical rule of thumb is that you require around six people to provide any service 24x7. However, a quick chat with the network operations center lead revealed that local labor regulations pushed this up to nine. A big difference!

In either case, ensure that you have the opportunity to baseline team numbers on a regular basis. This should be more often in the early days of the SOC after going live, after major service improvements or platform changes, and based on long-term trends. Although a few months of work effort data may prove useful for some estimates, you will not really know whether you got it right until you hit your first real large-scale incident.

Deciding on Your Resourcing Strategy

Now that you have calculated the size and structure of the SOC team, you have the difficult task of deciding how to resource it. Should you use internal staff recruited from other parts of the organization? Should you recruit your own staff from the market? Should you engage an outsourcer or managed service provider? How about contractors or service bureaus? How you answer these questions may affect not only how your SOC works but also what service levels you can provide in the short to long term, in addition to whether your SOC may be more or less sustainable.

Building Your Own: The Art of Recruiting SOC Personnel

Assuming that you are going to build at least some of your SOC team using internal resources, you are going to need to recruit them. How and where you recruit your SOC staff will have direct impacts on the success of your SOC, particularly where higher staff retention is an important goal.

Retention is a particularly bad problem for most SOCs. Even world-leading SOCs who pay well and offer considerable benefits and career potential have a problem keeping their people. There are simply too many jobs for too few candidates, and it is very easy for most young SOC analysts, engineers, or operators to find work elsewhere for better pay or less stress. The grass, as they say, is always greener on the other side of the fence.

We have found that many inexperienced SOC leads tend to make the same mistakes that lead to low retention rates, particularly among SOC analysts. We discuss retention issues and strategies again in Chapter 12, "Maintain, Review, and Improve," but it is worth noting here that where and how you recruit is often to blame for poor retention.

Many new SOCs tend to recruit junior analysts, engineers, and operators from recent graduates with fresh security knowledge with the idea that they will be able to develop their skills, provide certification training and support, and leverage their growing institutional knowledge for the long term. We are sorry to say that this is simply not the case. Regarding SOC managers we have worked with, retention among such employees tends to be very low. In one case, they lost almost every junior analyst within 6 months of joining the organization. Why? Look at it from the analyst's point of view: Once you have skills and knowledge, why would you stay?

More successful SOCs tend to recruit differently, and it tends to show with better retention rates. Rather than recruiting from recent graduate communities, some SOCs recruit from other internal teams, particularly existing operations centers such as systems or network operations, help/service desks, and other support teams. Although they may not have much security knowledge, they have often stayed within the organization in similar roles, have considerably deep knowledge in related areas, and probably most importantly have considerable experience dealing with difficult and upset people. Even then, it is often better to recruit passionate individuals who work well together than it is to recruit for skills. If skills are an issue, you can always supplement temporarily or permanently with contractors, outsourcers, or managed service providers, as discussed in the section that follows.

That is not to say that we would not recruit from recent graduates, but it would be risky to rely on them to stay if there are other opportunities are out there for them.

Working with Contractors and Service Bureaus

In some cases, it might be preferable to engage appropriately skilled contractors or service bureaus that tend to provide multiple contracted resources under a common master service agreement.

Contractors and service bureaus often come with a number of advantages and disadvantages. Contractors can be engaged to provide a specific set of skills and experiences that may be lacking or where the organization specifically chooses not to invest internal staff development. They also can be used to provide temporary capacity for a fixed or flexible period of time. They may be able to provide on-demand burst capacity during major incidents where quickly engaged, skilled resources are highly valuable (for example, where specific niche skills are required).

As with internal staff, it is most important that you engage contractors who are a good fit with the rest of the SOC team. Although you might not have a long-term commitment to them, even a short-term contractor can be highly disruptive to the smooth and effective working of a high-pressure SOC.

Working with Outsourcing and Managed Service Providers

For many cyber SOCs (particularly new ones), the number and variety of resources required to staff the team may simply be too much. The organization may look to external outsourcing or managed service providers to compensate for insufficient internal investment in high-capacity functions, to fulfill roles with very high skills requirements, specialist backgrounds, or to provide highly aggressive service levels for particular services.

In general, such services to a SOC tend to focus on low-end, high-capacity functions and high-end, low-capacity functions. On the one hand, some organizations use outsourcing to provide first- or second-tier security monitoring, leaving the provider with the task of delivering 24x7 monitoring and initial triage with high volumes of events and aggressive service levels. On the other hand, some organizations work with service providers that are only provided occasionally or may require skills that can simply not be built internally. For example, it is common for many organizations to engage firms to provide on-demand malware analysis or advanced forensic analysis, including court- or government-recognized investigators where evidence collection is the requirement.

What is less common is for services that require considerable knowledge of the organization's assets, network, systems, and applications outside of discovery services, usually part of a network audit or assessment. It is also less common for service providers to provide front-line interfaces when employees or customers want to engage the SOC.

Although it might be somewhat arbitrary, we tend to separate outsourcers from managed service providers according to how deep into the service stack they are providing. Outsourcers typically rely on the organization's own infrastructure (and capital investment in that infrastructure) to provide their services. They provide skilled resources to replace or augment internal resources, using the organization's own tools and technologies as they have been deployed. In this way, contractors providing staff augmentation may be considered a type of outsourcing. Managed service providers, however, tend to provide not only resources but also the infrastructure used to provide the service. An example is acquiring a SIEM and engaging an outsourcer to provide analyst resources to monitor it, whereas a managed service provider would tend to provide their own SIEM (and related supporting infrastructure) as part of their service.

In both cases, a good vendor relationship and a good contract are key. You want to work with vendors with a good track record and a good relationship with the organization. The contract should accurately reflect your expectations and clearly outline the rewards and penalties if they should or should not be met.

Your organization's procurement management processes will also be very valuable because they can help to ensure that you are engaging with the right organization after some due diligence has been performed. This will typically include an examination of the vendor's financial health, insurance, standard terms and conditions, and the results of external audits and certifications (such as SSIE16 audits or Payment Card Industry Data Security Standard [PCI DSS] certifications). Although it might seem obvious, such due diligence should also include the vendor's information and physical security posture.

It should also be clear whether you have the expectation of transitioning a service provided by an outsourcer or managed service provider into the internal team at some point in the future and how that transition will work. Most providers will work closely with you to ensure a smooth handover, but it is also useful to note that such transitions are rarely seamless and there will usually need to be period of time when relaxed service levels may need to be in place.

Another thing to keep in mind is the effect that using such providers may have on your ability to develop and retain your own internal resources. If you choose to engage a provider for low-end, high-capacity services, you may lose a valuable recruiting ground for more senior analysts, engineers, or operators. If you choose to engage a provider for high-end, low-capacity services, you may lose some ability to retain highly skilled internal resources who want to develop into those areas. Informing internal resources of expectations for transitioning resources to internal roles could inspire for job growth meaning job retention if communicated properly.

Working with Processes and Procedures

So, you have designed your SOC team and started to build your SOC. You have managed to recruit a good blend of experienced and junior staff, and have even brought on a few contractors and service providers to help out. One of the things you need is a good set of processes and procedures to help control how your SOC services will be delivered. As we teased earlier, you'll see, however, that there are limits to what good processes and procedures can do for a well-functioning SOC, and there are even reasons to believe that good processes and procedures can even damage the SOC.

But the first thing you'll need to do is clearly distinguish between processes and procedures.

Processes Versus Procedures

The words *process* and *procedure* are so often spoken together in this industry that they often come across as one word rather than two (*processesandprocedures*). There seems to be little to distinguish between them: Both refer to a series of actions that are directed to some specific goal, performed in a specific way. In fact, there are some differences between them, and those differences can be very important for a SOC.

Within a SOC, *processes* are used to describe a set of proscribed actions that are taken to perform a particular set of activities under a service. These actions are usually shared between multiple different parties that must cooperate together to accomplish a common goal. The results of these actions are then fed back into the process, typically to guide improvement. Processes are usually used to guide the output of shared decision making. For example, most SOCs will have security incident management processes that describe how SOC analysts and other technical teams work together to determine whether an incident has occurred, what to do about it, and how do improve on the result. When it comes to process, you can talk about *maturity*: It is possible to get better at aligning to the process and improving upon it.

In contrast, *procedures* describe a specific step-by-step way that an individual performing an activity must perform that activity. They are intended to provide the approved way to do something in specific. For example, a typical SOC procedure describes how to open a case within the case management system. Unlike processes, SOC procedures are not cooperative, nor is there a forced feedback loop included; there is no "improvement" for a procedure. In other words, you either do the procedure correctly or you do not. We rarely talk about maturity when we talk about procedures.

Both are intended to guide or constrain how activities are performed. Processes tend to offer multiple options, but those options are still relatively limited. Procedures tend to offer no options. They can be blended: Processes can include multiple procedures, but not the other way around.

In general, processes and procedures are used when you need consistency and repeatability. In most organizations, SOC processes and procedures do not stand alone. Particularly in the case of processes, they must often integrate with (or be superseded by) enterprise service management processes that are shared across all IT functions. This includes some important processes that are fundamental to every SOC.

Working with Enterprise Service Management Processes

If processes are shared between multiple parties, enterprise service management processes represent processes that are shared across the enterprise IT organization to ensure that there is a consistent way that certain activities are performed throughout the organization. Most of these are either directly or indirectly based on management processes thoroughly documented within IT Infrastructure Library (ITIL) and baked into every service management platform on the planet. Although not all ITIL processes may be relevant to a SOC, a large number are.

Event Management

Basically, anything that can be observed and recorded can be considered an event. Such recordings typically take the form of computer logs that record salient information about what occurred around the event, but can also include a wide variety of machine exhaust (changes to configuration files, time stamps within the file system, and so on) that also indicate that something happened.

Event management is focused on monitoring events that occur throughout the infrastructure. That includes both events that indicate normal, expected conditions and exceptions that may require escalation. The process focuses on collecting and analyzing event information to identify potential exceptions that could compromise services.

The SOC is usually a big consumer and participant in this process. Focused on security-related events, the SOC often drives what types of security-related events are collected, filters such events for things of interest, and typically has some input into how such event data is stored and for how long. The SOC also consumes both raw and normalized event data, looking for potential exceptions worth investigating.

Where a SOC is engaged in anomaly detection, this falls squarely under event management. Chapter 11 touches on event management in more detail.

Incident Management

An incident can be described as an adverse event. At its base, every SOC is in the business of detecting and responding to security-related incidents with the goal of finding them as quickly as possible and helping the organization deal with them. The SOC typically works within the more general incident management process used in the enterprise, leveraging its common tools and functions. It also works within that process to coordinate with other teams that may be required to help investigate or remediate any given security incident.

Problem Management

Typically, part of the investigation into an incident is the search for root cause, the ultimate reason why the incident happened or what conditions were in place to allow it to be more extensive or damaging. In some cases, such root-cause analysis can point to underlying defects that may allow such incidents to recur. Problem management is focused on addressing such defects. As part of their investigations, SOC analysts often help discover such defects.

Vulnerability Management

Vulnerabilities represent weaknesses in a system that may be targeted and exploited by a given threat. SOCs may not drive enterprise security vulnerability management practices, but they often use vulnerability data, correlated with active threats in the environment, and help determine whether a given threat may be successful. As such, they often provide valuable intelligence to help prioritize the remediation of vulnerabilities within the enterprise. It is also typically correlated with the current state of patches and updates applied across the technology estate to ascertain levels of risk.

Other IT Management Processes

Depending on whether the SOC is responsible for its own engineering and operations, other enterprise IT management processes may also be relevant. *Change management* is relevant to ensuring that any changes to SOC systems are properly documented, tested, approved, and executed. *Configuration management* is relevant to maintaining the settings and content within those systems and ensuring they are properly documented. *Release management* is relevant when any large-scale systems or applications roll out or upgrades are being performed within the SOC.

The Positives and Perils of Process

People do not just document processes for the fun of it. They do it because they are expected to adhere to them, or either risk having the activity fail or at least not work as intended. When they do not work, they are not expected to operate outside of the process, but work within it to improve it. To this end, entire industries have been created related to developing, maintaining, and improving processes in any sizable organization.

As discussed earlier, there are number of process improvement models based on maturity. Most of these are based on a simple idea: Things work better when we follow a defined process and are committed to improving on it. Originally designed to guide improvements in software (that is, improve the quality of code through better process), it is an idea that has been compelling for a wide range of activities.

Within a SOC, defined processes and their related procedures can be found all over the place, particularly where the SOC interfaces with other teams or the sources and consumers of SOC services. For example, it is handy to have a defined process to guide security incident management where you are trying to coordinate a large number of actors, from executives to normal end users, from SOC analysts to engineers, from incident response specialists to technical teams remediating breached systems. The same goes for vulnerability management processes where the SOC may provide valuable information concerning vulnerabilities under active threat but where remediation such as patching the vulnerability lies with other teams.

It is possible, however, to overdo it on process and procedure development. Just because you *can* document a process or procedure does not mean that you *should*. In general, processes and procedures are best suited to particular types of scenarios where we know all the necessary information intended to guide decision making through a process or perform the discrete steps in a procedure. For example, once a system generates an event (usually in the form of a log with known structure, syntax, and content), it is great to have a process describing how it will be managed. Similarly, after we know that an incident has occurred and know most if not all of the relevant information needed to handle it in one way or another, it is great to have a process for managing that. It is also awesome to have a procedure telling the junior analyst what to do when the SIEM sends a specific alert indicating that a critical system is under attack.

Processes and procedures are much less useful in situations commonly encountered in a SOC where we do not know much information or must behave in creative ways to deal with unorthodox attacks. Imagine processes and procedures intended to constrain how to investigate potential anomalies in the environment or tracking the less-well-modeled attacks used by an advanced threat source to evade detection by the SIEM. They just would not work.

Even worse, inappropriate processes and procedures often negatively impact the SOC's ability to perform its core services or remain a viable concern. On the one hand, they can negatively impact some service levels. On the other hand, they can impact the SOC team members themselves in unexpectedly negative ways.

To the first point, consider the core security monitoring service. As discussed earlier, it is usually driven to a number of service levels that are very sensitive to processes and procedures: average response time, average escalation fidelity, queue backlog, and procedure conformance. Let's look at each one of them for a moment.

When it comes to average response time, it might seem intuitive that a documented procedure for handling events in a consistent way would have a positive impact on average response time. After all, it would ensure that every event was responded to in exactly the same way. In reality, a procedure would tend to ensure that every event was performed in *at least* a certain amount of time; there would be no way to short-circuit the procedure to deal with some less-complex events faster so that you can spend more time on more complex ones. This also has an impact on the ability for the SOC to keep the queue backlog within acceptable levels.

For average escalation fidelity, the goal is to measure and typically reward analysts for being correct when they choose to escalate or choose not to escalate an event that comes into their queue. Although they tend to be well meaning and helpful for junior analysts, processes or procedures intended to guide their investigation into an event will work well only if the event is simple and represents a clear cut incident or a clear-cut false positive. They will typically be blind to unanticipated or complex events where some creativity or skill may be better suited.

Finally, it is obvious that if you want to measure their conformance to documented processes and procedures, every process or procedure you document will make it more likely that they will not be able to conform.

Apart from missing service levels (which can certainly be upsetting), inappropriate processes and procedures can have a direct impact on the SOC team members as individual contributors to the SOC's mission in some unexpected ways. In other areas of IT, well-documented processes and procedures have legitimately been used to streamline how IT services are delivered and decrease the reliance on individual heroes. Although this might work in some fields, in a SOC we tend to encourage the development of such heroes. So, as long as they are effective and help the SOC serve its mission, it can be beneficial to grant SOC staff a high degree of autonomy. In the long run, this cannot only ensure we identify strong SOC performers but retain them as happy members of the team.

Best practice is to focus process and procedure development in your SOC only on areas either with direct service-level impact, where consistency is a strong requirement, or where integration with enterprise processes is critical. Avoid unnecessary processes and procedures that impact service levels or that compromise the autonomy and creativity of the SOC team. We look at some examples next.

Examples of SOC Processes and Procedures

Let's look at SOC processes and procedures that tend to have either a positive impact on service levels, promote consistency, or help ensure alignment with enterprise management processes. Not all of these will be suitable for your own SOC, depending on what SOC services you may offer or where you might want to leave some things undefined to allow for greater flexibility.

In some organizations, you might end up with dozens of relevant and desirable processes and procedures suitable for your SOC. To make it a little easier to determine which ones may be appropriate, we have grouped them according to service and have tried to indicate what they would typically cover and what benefit they would have. Keep in mind that you may already have some of these processes or procedures in place even before you have built your SOC. In that case, you should be looking to adopt or enhance existing processes and procedures.

Security Service Management

Processes and procedures under security service management tend to address common cross-service requirements to perform certain activities in a consistent, repeatable way. Many of these may be processes within the organization's overall information security management system (ISMS). Relevant processes and procedures in the SOC domain can include some or all of the following:

- **Enterprise management processes:** The processes previously discussed.
- **Continuous service improvement process:** A process to review previous service-level attainment along with key performance indicators and key risk indicators to determine where improvements can be made. It also includes the process to review such findings, prioritize improvement initiatives, manage improvement, and provide feedback to management related to the results.
- **New process/procedure development process:** A process to initiate the needs analysis and development of new processes and procedures typically involving management, participants (actors) in the proposed process/procedure, and key stakeholders/consumers affected by new processes or procedures.
- **Metrics and reporting process and procedures:** A set of process and related procedures to capture chosen service metrics and provide regularly scheduled and ad hoc reporting based on those metrics.
- **Records retention, archive, and disposal process and procedures:** As SOCs generate a wide range of records, there must be a clear process and related procedures to ensure that records are retained, archived, and disposed according to documented policies and standards.
- **Service intake management process and procedures:** There should be a common process to manage how SOC services are engaged by consumers within the organization and related procedures describing how such intake will be managed on a day-to-day basis. This usually includes separate procedures for each type of intake.

For example, a service request ticket management procedure, service request call management procedure, service request e-mail management procedure, and a service request portal management procedure.

- **Audit and compliance support process and procedures:** SOCs often receive requests from internal or external audit or the security governance function to provide support (usually in the form of data and records) to support audit and compliance activities. This would also include procedures for how to provide commonly requested information when requested.
- **Enterprise IT service management integration process:** This process typically helps govern how SOC-specific management processes will be integrated with or superseded by existing, new, or updated enterprise IT service management processes. It includes the review and feedback to those processes on behalf of the SOC team.
- **Business continuity planning/disaster-recovering planning (BCP/DRP) support management process and procedures:** As a business function, the SOC must fully participate in enterprise BCP/DRP activities. The process covers how such participation will be managed with specific procedures documented related to service recovery/restoration, training development, and execution and test/exercise development and execution.
- **Vendor management process and procedures:** Even a relatively small SOC will need to manage multiple vendors, partners, and suppliers. This process governs overall vendor management, and specific procedures are in place to govern how engagement, escalation, and reviews are performed with each vendor.
- **Training management process and procedures:** SOCs must develop and provide training for their own teams and key consumers of SOC services. The process governs training activities as a whole with specific procedures in place to request and track training activities.
- **Financial and operations reporting process and procedures:** The SOC must be able to provide sound, consistent, and trustworthy financial and operations reporting to executive sponsors and key stakeholders. The process governs overall financial and operations management of the SOC with specific procedures in place to ensure consistency.

Security Service Engineering

Processes and procedures under security service engineering address how new or upgraded SOC systems are deployed and transitioned into production. In contrast with security service operations discussed next, this tends to focus on large-scale changes to the environment as project-based work, typically involving significant capital investment. As with security service management, many of these processes and procedures may already be in place as part of the ISMS. Relevant processes and procedures can include some or all of the following:

- **System lifecycle (SLC) process and procedures:** Where the SOC is responsible for managing the lifecycle of their own platforms, there will need to be a process and related procedures in place to manage the full lifecycle, including requirements analysis, high-level design, low-level design, development/build, testing, staging, deployment, and retirement/replacement/disposal.

- **Major change/release management processes and procedures:** Usually closely integrated with enterprise IT service management processes, there will typically need to be specific change and release process and related procedures for SOC-specific platforms engineered by the SOC team.
- **Platform configuration/implementation procedures:** Typically provided by product vendors or by the developers, SOC engineering will require procedures to ensure that any platforms are configured and implemented consistently.
- **Event source onboarding and change management process:** Although this might be considered a specific type of major change, there is often a separate process governing how new or updated event sources are brought into existing SOC platforms, particularly SIEMs and data analysis platforms. This covers the analysis, modeling, and onboarding of such event sources to help ensure that they do not compromise the current operation of the environment.

Security Service Operations

Processes and procedures under security service operations address approved methods to maintain SOC systems and content. This can include some or all of the following:

- **Systems monitoring process:** This process covers how SOC platforms are monitored, particularly for potential issues that may affect their ability to support SOC services and meet expected service levels.
- **License monitoring process:** This process addresses how vendor/supplier licenses will be monitored and reviewed over all SOC platforms.
- **Platform maintenance process and procedures:** When the SOC is responsible for maintaining some or all of their own systems, this process and related procedures governs how day-to-day platform maintenance will be performed including minor upgrades and patching, maintenance procedures, and related checklists.
- **Platform and platform content configuration and change management processes:** There will also need to be processes in place to manage configuration and change within SOC platforms, following enterprise change and configuration management processes. Within security services operations, this is normally limited to maintaining current state and making minor changes.
- **Platform testing process and procedures:** This process and related procedures describes how SOC platforms are tested, particularly as part of the transition of a new or updated service into production.
- **Platform content maintenance process and procedures:** This process and related procedures addresses how new or updated platform content such as SIEM correlation rules, use cases, alerts, filters, and monitors will be implemented into production.

Security Monitoring

Processes and procedures under security monitoring address how commonly occurring events and incident reports should be examined, assessed, and escalated if necessary. This can include some or all of the following:

- **Security event monitoring and escalation process and procedures:** This process, and related procedures, manages how security events will be monitored, investigated, and escalated. Procedures will tend to be platform specific and highly detailed, particularly when used for junior SOC analysts.
- **Common alerts triage and escalation procedures:** For commonly occurring alerts, it may prove useful to have specific procedures for each type of alert to streamline how they are examined, triaged, and escalated appropriately. These also often cover commonly occurred false positives.
- **Case management process and procedures:** When a potential incident has been identified, related information is usually put into the case management system as a case and escalated appropriately. This process governs how such cases are created, updated or closed with specific procedures covering how this will be accomplished within the specific case/investigation management platform used by the SOC. Related ticketing procedures are covered under in the security services management discussion earlier.
- **Third-party alert process and procedures:** In many cases, some security monitoring may be provided by third parties, particularly if they have been engaged to provide either outsourced or managed service. This process manages such alerting and how they will be handled with specific procedures for each supplier.
- **Knowledgebase and wiki management processes and procedures:** These processes and procedures manage how content is created, updated, retired, or replaced within the SOC's knowledgebase and wiki systems.
- **Monitoring system content feedback process:** This process governs how feedback on existing content (particularly alert settings) as currently configured within SOC monitoring platforms is provided and managed.

Security Incident Investigation and Response

Processes and procedures for security incident investigation and response address how to perform investigations and handle incidents in highly consistent and rigorously defined ways where appropriate. This can include some or all of the following:

- **Security incident management processes and procedures:** Typically working within enterprise incident management process, this process manages security specific incidents from triage through investigation, containment, and recovery. Specific procedures may be in place to constrain particular types of incidents, particularly major, catastrophic incidents requiring direct executive control.

- **Case management process and procedures:** As covered under security monitoring, when a potential incident has been identified, related information is usually put into the case management system as a case and escalated appropriately. This process governs how such cases are created, updated, or closed, with specific procedures covering how this will be accomplished within the specific case/investigation management platform used by the SOC. Related ticketing procedures are covered under the "Security Service Management" section.
- **Investigation procedures:** Although there is often a fair bit of creativity involved with incident investigation, there might be specific procedures in place to ensure that certain investigations are performed consistently. This is particularly important for digital forensics process and procedures.
- **Malware analysis process and procedures:** There are usually separate process and procedures in place to investigate potential malware, often because both internal and external analysis will be performed. This covers how malware samples are collected, analyzed, stored, reported, and disposed.
- **Platform content feedback process and procedures:** As with other services, appropriate incident investigation and response is dependent on well-configured and comprehensive platform content across SOC systems and systems consumed by the SOC such as platform, application, and network security platforms. This process and related procedures manage how such feedback is provided and reviewed and what actions are taken.

Security Log Management

Processes and procedures for security log management are focused on how to manage the entire log management lifecycle consistently and according to enterprise-wide policies and procedures. Although this might be provided through a common log management solution, it is also common for the SOC to be responsible for security log management specifically. This can include some or all of the following:

- **Log source analysis and onboarding process:** This process manages how new or updated log sources are analyzed, assessed, and on boarded. It typically also evaluates available sources against consumer specific requirements.
- **Log collection procedures:** These procedures cover how specific log sources will be collected or received from native systems, including whether raw and/or normalized logs will be collected.
- **Log storage procedures:** These procedures cover how logs will be stored, including online, near-line, and offline storage. There tends to be separate procedures for each storage platform because there can be wide differences from one platform to the next.
- **Log normalization procedure:** This procedure covers how collected logs may be normalized/parsed into a standardized format or structure.

- **Log query/extraction procedure:** This procedure addresses how logs can be queried or extracted from the log management platform, either for streaming (real-time) analytics or historical (bulk) analysis.
- **Log disposal/archive procedure:** This procedure describes how logs will be disposed of or archived according to documented retention policies and standards.

Security Vulnerability Management

Processes and procedures for security vulnerability management are focused on how to manage security vulnerabilities on in-scope assets monitored by the SOC. Although the SOC may not be responsible for the full end-to-end process (for example, they are rarely responsible for vulnerability remediation except on their own platforms), they often provide automated vulnerability intelligence feeds and vulnerability scanning/discovery services. This can include some or all of the following process and procedures:

- **Security vulnerability scanning and reporting process and procedures:** This process, and related procedures, covers how scheduled and ad hoc vulnerability scanning will be performed and results reported to service consumers. Some level of analysis may be provided here, but in-depth analysis is usually provided via the security (threat and vulnerability) intelligence services described later.
- **Automated vulnerability intelligence feed process and procedures:** The process manages which and how vulnerability intelligence feeds will be evaluated, onboarded, provided, and assessed. Procedures specific to each feed are used to describe how the contents of each feed will be provided for consumption.
- **Security vulnerability remediation tracking process:** The process tracks the current state of remediation efforts after security vulnerabilities have been reported. This also typically covers refreshed or updated notifications or escalations when remediation has not been performed within an allotted period of time as dictated by vulnerability management policy.

Security Intelligence

Processes and procedures for security intelligence, including threat and vulnerability intelligence provided by human intelligence analysts, are focused on how to provide human-readable intelligence based on current threats and vulnerabilities within the environment and on external intelligence relevant to the organization. This can include some or all of the following:

- **Threat identification process:** This process describes how threats will be identified and evaluated in a consistent way, leveraging internal and external sources of threat, including industry groups, threat intelligence providers, and other sources.

- **Vulnerability identification process:** This process describes how relevant vulnerabilities will be identified and evaluated in a consistent way, leveraging internal and external sources of threat, including industry groups, vendors, suppliers, developers, and other sources.
- **Threat and vulnerability modeling process and procedures:** This process and related procedures manage how the likelihood, relevancy, and severity of threats and vulnerabilities are evaluated based on the organization's asset inventory and the criticality of each asset.
- **Briefing and notification process and procedures:** This process manages how briefings and notifications are provided regarding security intelligence. Procedures typically cover how briefing requests are made and handled, how notifications are provided depending on the communication method used, and what common templates may be used.

Security Analytics and Reporting

Processes and procedures for security analytics and reporting cover how raw security and SOC services data/outputs will be analyzed and reported. This includes both scheduled and ad hoc reporting for a wide variety of potential consumers. This can include some or all of the following:

- **Data gathering process and procedures:** This process and related procedure manages what data is gathered and how it is gathered for analytics and reporting purposes based on consumer requirements. Procedures tend to be specific for each data source depending on how such data is collected or received.
- **Report request procedure:** This procedure covers how requests for ad hoc analysis and reports are requested and handled.
- **Report formatting and delivery procedures:** This procedure addresses how individual reports will be formatted and delivered based on individual consumer requirements.
- **Analysis/query management process and procedures:** This process manages how new analysis or queries will be designed, tested, executed, and scheduled within the environment. Individual procedures will cover how such analysis will occur on specific platforms or against specific data sets.
- **Big data modeling and mining procedures:** These procedures describe how long-term historical and trending data will be used for analysis, specific to the individual platform and consumer requirements.

Breach Discovery and Remediation

Processes and procedures for breach discovery and remediation cover how potentially compromised assets will be examined and potential breaches reported. It also covers manual or automated remediation activities that may be taken to mitigate specific breach conditions. This tends to be a highly advanced set of services that may only be found in some SOCs. This can include some or all of the following:

- **Breach discovery process and procedures:** This process and related procedures cover how breach discovery is performed against organization assets, typically by in-depth examination for known indicators of compromise (IOCs) or for anomalies that indicate that the asset may have been compromised. Procedures tend to be specific to individual assets being examined.
- **Breach notification process and procedures:** This process and related procedures cover how consumers of the service will be notified of potential or confirmed breaches. Procedures tend to be specific down to the individual type of asset and preferred mode of communication.
- **Breach investigation and incident support process and procedures:** This process and related procedures try to ensure that investigations into potential breaches and how that information is used to support incident investigation and response is provided in a consistent way.
- **Breach scenario modeling and remediation design process:** This process is used to model common breach scenarios to determine how they may best be detected and when detected what options or preauthorized actions may be used to address them. Resulting models are used to design appropriate remediation activities that may be performed manually or through automation.
- **Breach remediation testing process and procedures:** This process focuses on testing potential remediation options to determine their effectiveness and their potential impact on the asset and the organization. It also covers how testing results are collected, evaluated, and presented to key stakeholders. Specific procedures cover how testing will be performed on particular types of assets or within particular environments.
- **Breach remediation execution procedures:** These procedures cover how approved or preapproved breach mediation activities will be performed.

This is obviously not an all-inclusive list of the SOC processes and procedures you may have in your environment. You will see how some of these processes and procedures may guide event and incident management within a SOC in Chapter 11, and how such processes and procedures may be evaluated or improved in Chapter 12.

Summary

This chapter covered how to develop a staffing model to recruit and retain a SOC team. The chapter started by discussing different resourcing strategies for recruiting, ranging from what to look for when identifying potential candidates to how to leverage an outsourcing or managed service providers. The chapter then covered when it is smart to use processes and procedures, so that you do not negatively impact the SOC team's performance. The chapter concluded by providing a bunch of examples of SOC processes and procedures that can be copied and adjusted to meet your organization needs.

Next, we look at the technologies used by a SOC.

Chapter 9

The Technology

"Technology is the campfire around which we tell our stories."—Laurie Anderson

Now that you know about the people and processes, it is time to review the technology used by security operations center (SOC) teams around the world. This chapter focuses on what SOC architects should consider as they evaluate different technologies. The chapter covers best practice considerations for designing high-level categories such as network, security, systems, collaboration, and storage. The chapter then goes deeper into design considerations for products found in most SOC environments. The chapter wraps up with SOC architectures that bring together all the technologies covered.

Before evaluating technologies, let's first review the different SOC environments.

In-House Versus Virtual SOC

Chapter 4, "SOC Strategy," introduced the concept of in-house and virtual SOCs. An in-house SOC assumes that the technology, processes, and people capabilities are developed and provided within a facility that hosts the SOC team and services, regardless of the facility location, size, and features. The advantage of this approach is the familiarity with the SOC environment inherent in using local staff and technology. A virtual SOC outsources some or all of the SOC services to an external provider. This helps speed up the creation of the SOC and offers additional capabilities that might not be available locally. Table 9-1 lists the advantages of both approaches.

In some situations, a company might use variations of an in-house and virtual SOC in a hybrid format. One hybrid use case is to monitor the internal network with an in-house SOC while using a virtual SOC to scale to remote sites. Another use case is to first use a virtual SOC to stand up SOC services and then slowly migrate to a new in-house SOC as it becomes operational.

Table 9-1 *In-House Versus Virtual SOC*

Advantages to an In-House SOC	Advantages to a Virtual SOC
Local and dedicated staff.	Less capital expenses because technology is outsourced.
Familiar with the local environment.	More data from difference customers.
Logging can be stored locally.	Typically, less expensive than in-house.
Can have ownership of technology.	Unbiased, being outside of company politics.
More likely to notice correlations between internal groups.	Usually more flexible and scalable.
Global companies can keep data in region.	On-staff experts.
	Service level agreement (SLA) and outsourced documentation.

Each SOC model will impact the technologies that will be used during daily operation. An in-house SOC has a higher cost based on the responsibility to acquire and maintain all products. Outsourcing SOC services also means outsourcing some tools. However, even a completely virtual SOC environment will have some local technology that should be designed and managed appropriately. This chapter covers all common technology topics found within mature SOC environments, focusing on the development of an in-house SOC. For virtual SOC environments, some topics might not apply to your organization if the technology covered is outsourced. Those topics can be considered reference points to understand what is required to move the outsourced technology in-house and how to verify that the service provider is properly using the technology.

Let's start by reviewing broader technology topics. We start with high-level design concepts for network, security, systems, storage, and collaboration categories. We follow the general technology recommendations with an overview of common technologies found within mature SOCs. First up, let's look at network design considerations.

Network

The foundation of any SOC is the network on which it operates. The design details and area of responsibility will differ for each environment, but some general concepts are common across most networks. The network the SOC protects is considered the *inside*, and everything that is not part of the organization's network is considered *outside*. As simple as this sounds, it is critical to define what the inside network is so that monitoring tools can recognize when an unknown or outside IP address appears on the inside network. Typically, the inside network is broken up into different segments that are assigned different levels of trust. The most common segmentation is having three zones, where the outside has no trust, demilitarize zone (DMZ) has some trust, and inside is completely trusted. The idea behind this basic architecture is to place systems that require connectivity to both the inside and outside such as web servers on the DMZ, giving them some trust but the same level as systems inside the network. Figure 9-1 shows this basic architecture. Note that this is a basic trust model. Most likely, there will be different layers of inside trust to protect from different variations of insider threats.

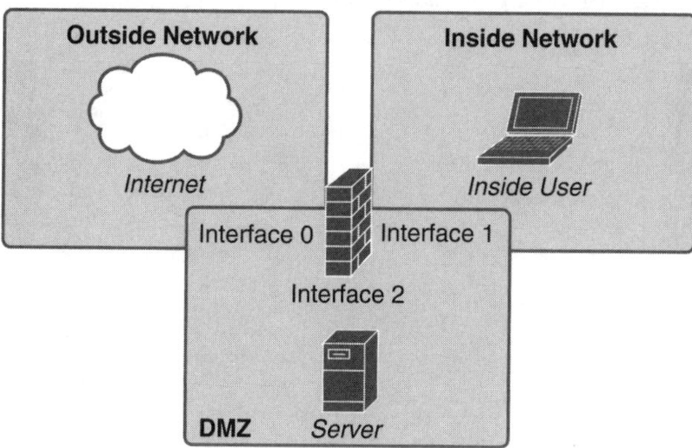

Figure 9-1 *Basic Network Architecture*

Best practice is to have a more granular layer of trust by further segmenting the inside network into different security zones, such as separating the data center from the common inside network traffic. It is also important to implement traffic controls within internal security zones using various forms of virtual LANs (VLAN), access control lists (ACL), and security group tags (SGT). Controls can be built in to network segmentation or can be something that is applied after access has been permitted into a network segment.

Segmentation

The most effective but expensive form of network segmentation is physically separating network equipment. A more cost-effective approach to maximize a hardware investment is to logically separate capabilities or segment traffic within the same hardware. Logical segmentation can be virtualizing two or more appliance capabilities within a physical hardware solution, such as using separate firewall contexts that function as independent systems while sharing the same hardware. The networks within a firewall context can be carved into different virtual LANs, meaning separating network traffic into logically segmented networks that can't communicate with each other unless provided permission to do so. That same VLAN traffic can be further segmented by using ACLs, which can limit specific ports or protocols between VLANs. For example, printers on the 192.168.3.0/24 network could have an ACL limiting their traffic to certain ports, while users on the same VLAN are able to access more resources.

These can be even further segmented by using a newer form of segmentation that goes down to the packet level called security group tags. SGTs use the device and user credentials acquired during the authentication process to classify packets by security groups as they enter the network. The packet classification is maintained by tagging packets on the network so that security policies can be enforced as the packets travel the network.

Most organizations use different combinations of segmentation. Figure 9-2 shows the six layers of segmentation from the least to most granular option.

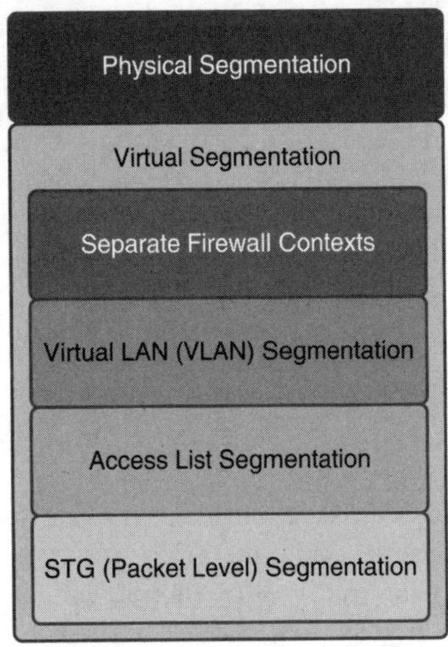

Figure 9-2 *Six Layers of Segmentation*

Enforcing segmentation can be accomplished using a few different approaches. Physical segmentation requires acquiring hardware dedicated to a specific network. This might be a requirement for high availability, regulation such as separating classified information on its own network, or a general best practice to protect mission-critical data such as the SOC management network. This approach provides reliable segmentation, but it is also the highest-cost option.

VLANs are a less-expensive approach to network segmentation when configured properly. VLANs isolate networks and can limit specific protocols to certain segments. VLANs also offer additional benefits beyond physical segmentation by being flexible to user mobility. For example, a VLAN can be shared throughout the network so that users accessing different networks will have their assigned VLAN regardless of physical location. This includes extending segmentation to other types of technology such as a virtual private network (VPN) and wireless if VLANs are supported. However, VLANs can also be designed to be private, preventing sharing and access to a VLAN segment if data isolation is a requirement.

Using VLANs could introduce risk to securing data. The first risk is that if something happens to the hardware, all networks regardless of importance may be impacted. This risk includes errors caused by administrators implementing a configuration mistake or an attacker exploiting vulnerabilities in the hardware, software, or configuration that permits access to all networks. An example of this type of attack is a VLAN hopping attack, where the attacker imitates a trunking switch by speaking the tagging and trunking protocol used to maintain the VLAN, thus making multiple VLANs accessible to the attacker. Another example is a MAC address flooding attack, where the CAM tables are filled up so that the switch becomes a hub. Security measures can be put in place, such as enabling **switchport nonegotiate** on Cisco switches to prevent automatic trunk negotiation or not using VLAN 1; however, these are some of the many possible risks when sharing sensitive data on the same wire as standard traffic. Best practice when using VLANs for segmentation is to include more granular segmentation within VLANs to protect when VLAN leakage occurs.

ACLs are one approach for segmentation within VLANs. ACLs allow the administrator to be more granular with controls, such as having employees and administrators on the same VLAN but limiting specific services for employees. ACLs can also include various forms of alerting to help administrators better understand and be aware when certain actions are seen within a VLAN. An example of combining ACLs and VLANs is the use case to filter traffic based on the direction of the traffic itself. Two routers can be connected on the same VLAN segment as hosts, and an ACL can be configured on a secondary VLAN so that only traffic generated by hosts is filtered while traffic between the routers is not impacted. A more sophisticated example is leveraging a network access control technology that places two user groups on the same VLAN but dynamically pushes a ACL to limit specific ports and protocols for one of the user groups. When that user leaves the network, the ACL is automatically removed. We use this second example to show the value of automating these tasks, because manually managing ACLs can be a cumbersome task for larger networks and can include a lot of overhead.

SGTs are becoming popular for solving the problems associated with network and security management administrative tasks. For example, if a doctor needs to launch a new server, she may need to contact a data center administrator to stand up the server, a network administrator to provision the proper IP information, and a security administrator to punch holes in the firewall for specific services. Administrators may not have the skill set or knowledge to understand how their changes may impact other parts of the process, meaning that changing a firewall rule could potentially negatively impact data center services if changes are not properly coordinated. SGTs can solve this by having tagging enabled so that systems are aware of the tag name versus understanding the network the packets are riding along. So, the doctor could request a server, which is placed on the healthcare secure network tag. With SGTs, the network and firewall understands which packets should and should not be permitted between the user and this healthcare server, thus reducing the steps to provision this service.

Network segmentation can be implemented in many fashions. Some companies may use VLANs as a way to determine which floor the switch port is located on, such as VLAN 201 for the second floor east wing and VLAN 202 for the second floor west wing. Companies may limit a specific user group using a combination of VLANs and ACLs, such as limiting guests with an ACL to only Internet services via port 80 and 443. Figure 9-3 shows one possible network diagram that is enforced after segmentation has been developed. Each segment has a specific level of security permissions associated that can be linked to an authentication system to ensure that only the proper users and devices have access. The Voice over IP (VoIP) phones are segmented off on their own voice VLAN or use ACLs to limit the phones to only required services. The data center segmentation could have additional segmentation between data center clusters (known as *east-west traffic*) or leverage SGTs to control which packets are permitted to specific servers.

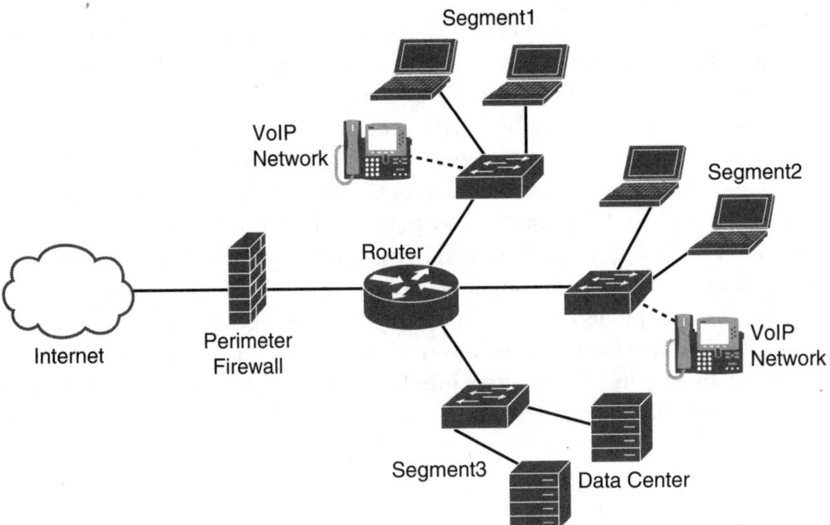

Figure 9-3 *Mature Network Segmentation Example*

Some SOC environments might not be responsible for the entire network, meaning that parts of the inside network should not be designated as outside but instead should be segmented off as an internal nontrusted domain. An example is a SOC responsible only for a data center within an organization, while the perimeter is monitored by an in-house SOC or outsourced to another service provider. This example uses a different type of network diagram, but leverages similar segmentation principles for segmenting and controlling services within the data center environment. Figure 9-4 is an example of a data center-focused SOC.

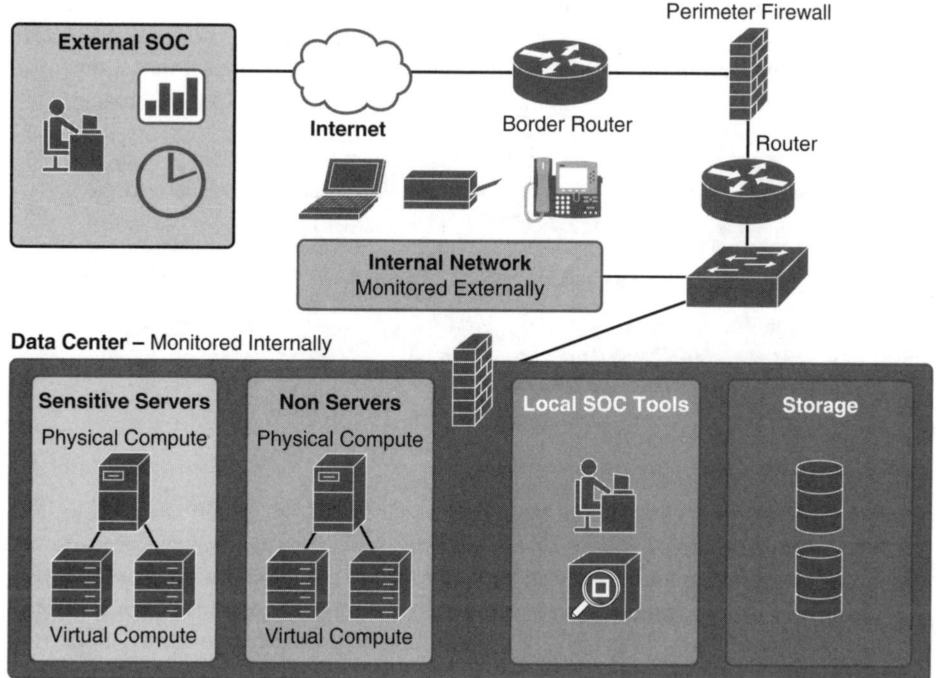

Figure 9-4 *Data Center-Focused SOC*

VPN

There might be design requirements to connect two or more separate network segments or remote users in a secure manner. An example is an organization with multiple branch offices located all over the world that need to share internal resources. This can be accomplished by connecting locations using site-to-site VPN or provisioning host-based VPN to remote systems. The fundamental concept behind site-to-site VPN is establishing an encrypted tunnel between two or more locations and having network reachability extend across the tunnels. This permits employees at one location to act as if they are inside a remote location without having to make any changes to how they are using the network. Cisco offers many variations of site-to-site VPN technology, such as GET-VPN, Dynamic Multipoint VPN (DMVPN), generic routing encapsulation (GRE)-based VPN, Easy VPN, and standard IPsec.

Host-based VPN is extending a secure tunnel between a specific device and the internal network, giving the user the same experience as if that device is locally plugged in to the inside network. The most common forms of this technology are either using a client that is installed on the host or provisioning a tunnel using web browser-based services. Client-based VPN technology from Cisco offers many features such as automatically connecting when the device uses a noninternal IP address, multifactor authentication, endpoint assessment for policy requirements such as having antivirus installed, and so on.

Figure 9-5 shows an active AnyConnect agent circled and a version screen representing AnyConnect 4.0.0048. When this device's network connectivity is lost, the AnyConnect lock image will cycle until a new network connection is shown. If that connection is not the internal network, Cisco AnyConnect automatically reconnects the VPN tunnel.

Figure 9-5 *Cisco AnyConnect Client*

Clientless VPN[1] works by using an Internet browser to access a specific website, which assesses the device and provisions access to hosted services depending on the vendor and enabled features. Cisco Secure Sockets Layer (SSL) can provision a customized web portal that contains or *sandboxes* activity within the portal. Access to specific services, such as remote desktop, e-mail, and so on, can be enabled and controlled within the portal environment. When the web page is closed or the session is terminated, the web browser's cache can be cleaned to remove traces of the session from the local system. This is ideal for provisioning trusted services to a nontrusted device such as a guest computer at a hotel. Figure 9-6 shows a very basic Cisco SSL web portal. The look and feel is customizable with regard to logos, colors, available services, and so on.

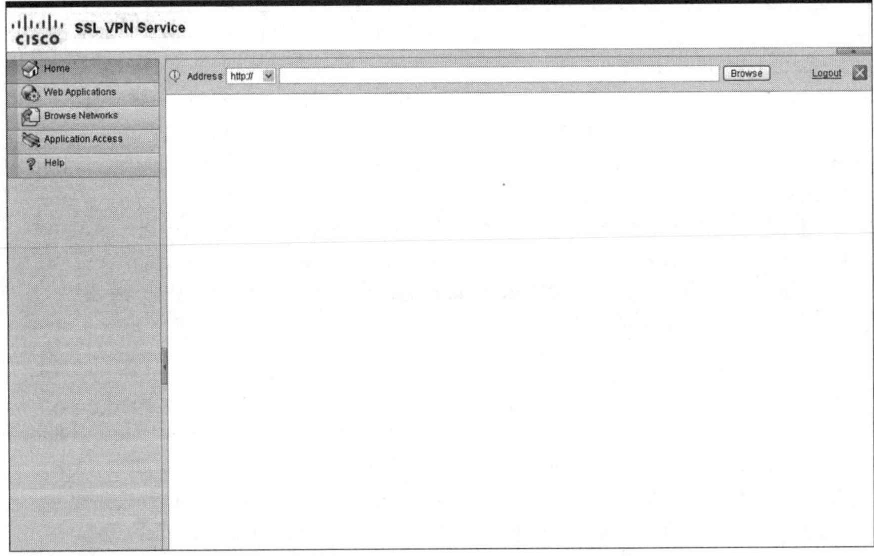

Figure 9-6 *Basic Cisco SSL Portal*

Deciding when to use a client and clientless VPN can depend on a few factors. Client-based VPN provides the host direct access to the resources, which may be a requirement for employees who need to upload and download data quickly. The risk of this approach is that any malicious traffic can also travel across the VPN and directly access the resources. This requires trust in the host system; best practice is to include different types of security controls that ensure that the system is safe before provisioning access. Examples of security controls are Cisco dynamic access policies (DAP) that check for the latest updates, that antivirus is running, and so on; endpoint zero-day detection agents verifying that malware is not present; and segmenting off VPN access to required resources only. Typically, client-based VPN is offered to employees who access the network often.

Clientless VPN can provision resources to less-secure systems because the entire session is hosted in a controlled sandbox. The level of security enforced depends on what is provisioned in the sandbox, meaning that administrators can grant access to configuring systems by using a Remote Desktop Protocol (RDP) agent, provision access to resources, and so on. This is usually ideal for contractors or employees who require access to resources from an unsecure system. Clientless sandboxes are not 100 percent safe, meaning that attacks such as key loggers and screen-capture attacks could obtain sensitive data that is sent to the sandbox from the host system. See the manufacturer's design guide for information about the risks associated with the VPN approach that you are considering using to protect your users.

High Availability

One important network design consideration that all SOC architects will face is when to provide high availability for different network components. Providing high availability means developing a plan for when a system outage occurs. The most common solution is to acquire a second separate system that mirrors traffic from the primary system, such as purchasing two firewalls that are the same model running the same version of code. High availability can also be components within a solution, such as having multiple power supplies in each firewall in the event of a power failure. Some organizations purchase extra equipment or components and store them as replacements in case of a system failure. If an organization uses this approach, it is important to back up configurations often so that new replacement equipment can quickly be enabled in the event of a failure. Another option for high availability is an alternative route, meaning that if traffic is unable to access one system, it is redirected a different way until the primary route is reestablished.

It is important to implement the appropriate failover process when considering high availability. The best option is automatic failover, where a heartbeat timer between the primary and backup systems experiences a delay beyond a specific setting. It is also good to have the failover system capable of automatically determining when the primary system is back up and automatically passing back primary rights. Be careful to verify automation capabilities, because some vendors offer high availability but failover is achieved only by using manual efforts. It is also important to understand how licensing impacts acquiring a failover solution. Some vendors charge to license both primary and any backup systems, whereas other vendors may only charge for the hardware and have all systems share the primary license. Cost will most likely be the biggest determining factor for including high availability, so best practice is to calculate the risk of losing the system against implementing different high-availability options.

Support Contracts

Another option for providing support in the event of a failure is to purchase a support contract. Most vendors offer different levels of support, typically based on the time to provide a resolution for the identified problem. An example is requiring an engineer to remotely troubleshoot a problem or mailing out a replacement appliance. Common offerings are next business day (NBD), 8 hours, 1 hour, and so on, where the cost is higher for faster support. Support may be separate for supporting hardware failures and receiving software support, so make sure to verify that you have the proper support based on the product you are protecting. You might find that there are discounts for bundling support contracts together and purchasing multiple years upfront from a single vendor.

To summarize general network design recommendations, basic concepts that the SOC architect should consider include the following:

- Break networks into security zones and assign a level of trust for each zone.
- Build segmentation within a security zone based on controlling the minimal ports and protocols required for users and systems to function.
- Unify all tools monitoring the network with the same understanding of the different security zones and associated trust. A major value of this approach is tracking when unauthorized IP addresses appear on the inside network.
- Connect remotely separate networks and users in a secure manner using VPN technology. Automatically enforce VPN when devices are connecting to external networks.
- Compare the cost of losing data against different segmentation options to determine the best investment. For example, extremely critical systems should have dedicated networks.
- Consider high availability if a network outage would impact the business. Validate that you have the right level of high availability through separate hardware, components, or network routes.
- Make sure to verify support and upgrade contracts if the business requires.

Regardless of the network design, security must be scoped into the architecture. Best practice is to include security in the beginning of the network design versus as something added at a later time. Doing so saves the organization time and money and helps avoid any negative impact caused by a breach after the SOC is operational but possibly not secured. Let’s look at some high-level network security concepts.

Security

Security is a fundamental requirement for all SOC environments. There are many ways to build in security to a network environment, and it should be a continuous process. One popular saying within Cisco Systems that describes this concept is this: *Security is a journey, not a destination.*

We covered segmentation using networking concepts, but segmentation can also be provisioned through security tools in conjunction with VLANs, ACLs, and SGTs. Some security technologies that can provide segmentation and traffic controls are firewalls, content filters, and network access control solutions. The most traditional approach is using physical or logical firewalls between major network segments. Logical firewalls are when a physical firewall is virtually carved into separate firewall instances that are completely separate systems to manage yet operate on the same physical hardware. Figure 9-7 shows an example of placing a single firewall on a network perimeter and using a multicontext firewall configuration to host three virtual firewalls to secure the administration, red, and blue network. This environment could have a super administrator account that has access to all three virtual firewalls, while administrators for each network could have access to only their specific virtual firewall.

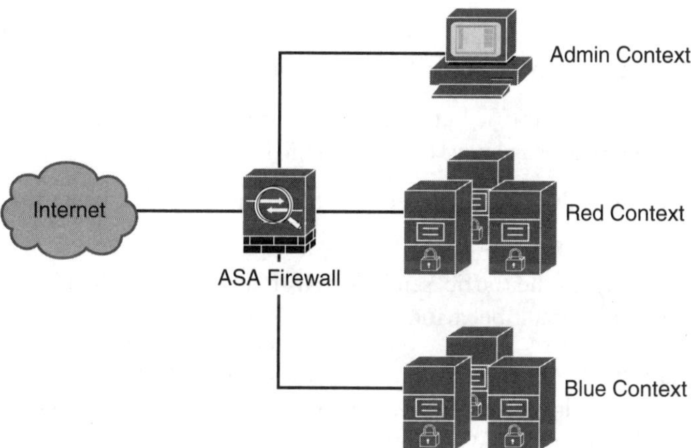

Figure 9-7 *Firewall Diagram*

Network Access Control

Controlling access to network segments is critical for maintaining the value of segmentation. Enforcing access control could include the types of network sources available (wireless, LAN, VPN), how users are authorized to resources, and the posture of devices based on corporate policy. Traditional access control is enforced using a combination of physical security and network access security features available on network switches. Physical security can be enforced using technology such as enabling special locks that require PIN codes or key cards to gain access to a specific security zone.

Additional security measures can be bundled together such as using a mantrap to stop people from following authorized users who know the PIN code into a controlled area, also known as *tailgating*.

Network access control is important for controlling who and what can connect to a network after they are physically granted access. The traditional method to control network access is by using port security features found on access layer switches. Many Cisco switches offer port security features (such as one named, appropriately enough, Port Security,[2] which retains an authorized MAC address and disables the port if a new system attempts to access the port). Let's look at an example of using port security.

The following steps show how to enable port security on Cisco switches using sticky MAC:

Step 1. The switch port must be set to Layer 2. Use the command **switchport** to confirm this.

Step 2. Enable port security using the **switchport port-security** command.

Step 3. If you need to increase the number of MAC addresses permitted on the interface, use the command **switchport port-security maximum** *number*, where *number* is the maximum number of stored MAC addresses. The default is to store one MAC address.

Step 4. You can specify the action to take when a violation occurs by using the command **switch port-security violation** {**protect** | **restrict** | **shutdown**}.

- **a. Protect** discards the traffic but keeps the port up and does not send a Simple Network Management Protocol (SNMP) message.
- **b. Restrict** discards the traffic and sends an SNMP message but keeps the port up.
- **c. Shutdown** discards the traffic, sends an SNMP message, and disables the port. This is the default behavior.

Step 5. You can specify the MAC address value using the command **switchport port-security mac-address** *mac_address*. You can use this command multiple times to add multiple MAC addresses.

Step 6. You can avoid manually adding MAC addresses by using the command **switchport port-security mac-address sticky.** This command tells the switch to learn the first MAC address that connects to the port.

There are many disadvantages to the port security approach. Disadvantages include having to manually enable any ports that go down due to a violation, being vulnerable to MAC spoofing attacks, and the high level of resources required to manage port security on multiple switch ports. A more effective approach to port security is to automate the process using a network access control (NAC) technology. Automated access control technologies vary in how they provide enforcement, but the basic features generally include automatically determining who and what is attempting to access the network and only provisioning specific access based on predefined policies. An example of this technology is Cisco Identity Services Engine (ISE), which is covered later in this chapter. Enabling Cisco ISE requires 802.1X to be enabled on access points within the network where network access control is needed (that is, where different users will be accessing the network). A good example is network ports in a conference room; a bad example is the network port for a server in a restricted part of the network, because different devices should never touch that network port. Most modern network devices support 802.1X, such as switches and wireless access points. You can find a complete list of which networking devices support Cisco ISE by referencing the latest version of Cisco ISE at http://www.cisco.com/go/ISE and searching for 802.1X support documentation.

Authentication

NAC, in addition to many other security technologies, uses authentication factors to validate people and systems. The most common factors used for authentication are one or more of something you know, something you have, and something you are. Many regulations are adapting a minimal of two-factor authentication requirements, but organizations that require higher levels of security may have multiple factors depending on the sensitivity of the data in the network segment.

Examples of something from each category type are as follows:

- **Something you know:** Password, username, answer a security question
- **Something you have:** One-time password token, personal identity verification (PIV) card, common access card (CAC)
- **Something you are:** Voice print, retinal scan, fingerprint scan

When considering authentication factors, a best practice is to have a centralized repository of all users, such as Active Directory (AD), which other systems can use to verify assigned privilege levels. An example is creating an employee and administrator user group where anybody with administration privileges is placed in the administrator user group, giving more rights than for employees in certain security segments or systems. Outside of granting access, one of the most important values of a centralized repository of users is being able to quickly reduce or remove privileges from people or systems that no longer require a specific level of access. The most common requirement for this is the ability to remove access rights to someone who is no longer employed by the organization.

Another important function for a centralized authentication system is accountability. Many network and security solutions can pull in user data from a centralized repository and tie it to how they use network resources. For example, an application layer firewall could show that user Sarah Tae from the human resources department was using the Internet rather than just showing her IP address of 192.168.45.15 in the firewall management interface. Accountability can extend to administrative rights and accountability such as permitting Damon Buffum permission to log in to a router and record all configuration changes he makes while in the system. This can prove useful if there is a network problem and the system administrator needs to identify who implemented the undesirable configuration changes. An example is identifying that Damon misconfigured the default gateway of a branch office while making changes during a nonapproved point in time (that is, not during an authorized maintenance window) taking down the location for 30 minutes.

On-Network Security

After putting network segmentation and access control technologies into place, the next security consideration is how to monitor and protect people and devices on each network segment. You can accomplish this by using various forms of signature and behavior technologies (covered later in this chapter), such as intrusion prevention systems (IPS), breach detection, and network behavioral analysis. Best practice is to ensure that detection is network-wide, layered, and viewing all types of traffic. This includes considering throughput requirements at each detection point so that security does not impact network performance beyond tolerable thresholds.

The most common placement of an on-network monitoring solution is to enable features within the network gateway firewall or to place a solution directly behind the gateway firewall. Common security features enabled at this point of the network are IPS, content filtering, application controls, antimalware scanning, and certain forms of data-loss prevention. An example of a security appliance that provides these features is the Cisco FirePOWER offering, which can run within the Adaptive Security Appliance (ASA) series firewall appliance or as a dedicated appliance that sits behind a gateway firewall. On-network security appliances can tap into other parts of the network, such as within the data center or across the network depending on where network detection is designed.

On-network monitoring should not be limited to a network gateway or random taps inside the network. Network telemetry can be harvested from common network devices to monitor for unusual behavior between security checkpoints such as IPS appliances. NetFlow can be enabled on most common network devices and sent to a tool that can digest and analyze it for security events. It is important to be aware that all NetFlow collection tools are not created equally, as covered in the discussion about NetFlow later in this chapter. Packet-capturing technology can also be placed on specific parts of the network to collect and analyze traffic for threats. Both NetFlow and packet-capturing technologies can identify threats based on behavior, but there might be additional investments in storage and network upgrades to properly implement the technology.

Security is bound to fail, and it is important to have security measures in place to detect when a breach has occurred. Breach-detection technology performs evaluation methods that target identifying when an organization has been compromised, such as quarantining suspicious applications in a sandbox to monitor their behavior, monitoring for unusual behavior, port scanning, file manipulation, or identifying communications with known external threats. Breach-detection products are usually architected like other on-network security technologies that need to be able to see traffic to perform analytics. Best practice is to have breach detection on both the network and all endpoint systems for complete visibility. Examples of this technology include FireEye, Cisco Advanced Malware Detection (AMP), and Bit9.

One challenge for many on-network detection technologies is extending visibility to the solution. These technologies can only examine what they can analyze, meaning that traffic that is not reachable or hidden by encryption cannot be evaluated. If a network is properly segmented, this could mean either a requirement for access points or "taps" for the monitoring technology to view into each segment or acquiring dedicated units for each network segment, which can become expensive. In addition, Network Access Translation (NAT) can confuse monitoring technology by concealing the identity of devices hidden behind the NAT point. For example, 20 devices could all be seen inside a network as one IP address if the monitoring tool has visibility of only inside traffic. Some options to overcome NAT concealment is to integrate an access control technology to stitch together what devices are authenticating behind the NAT with what traffic is seen by a monitoring tool or to place taps for the monitoring tool in front of the NAT point.

Encryption

Encryption can be challenging for monitoring tools that do not have access to the unencrypted data. For example, traffic hidden within a VPN is encrypted and cannot be analyzed by a monitoring tool. This is a good thing because it prevents a malicious user from performing a man-in-the-middle attack on users attempting to access trusted resources over an untrusted network. Encryption can also work against a security administrator when a malicious user uses encryption to hide an attack and later encrypt communication to and from the inside network after breaching the network. There are ways to control which ports and protocols are available (to block unauthorized VPN connects), such as capabilities within firewalls and enabling network trend-monitoring tools so that they are tuned to alarm when unauthorized VPN tunnels are identified on the network. Newer VPN technologies require only common network services, such as port 80 and 443, making it extremely difficult to detect and prevent unauthorized VPN tunnels. This is why breach-detection technologies are important, as covered later in this chapter.

Another form of encryption that a SOC architect must consider is web traffic encryption, also known as Secure Sockets Layer/Transport Layer Security (SSL/TLS). The challenge is that many websites, such as social media sources, encrypt traffic from the user to the website, bypassing network security tools. Decrypting SSL can be accomplished with some tools, but those devices must be certified as a trusted authority and have the processing power to handle the traffic load that must be decrypted. Without a trusted certificate, endpoints treat the decryption point as a man-in-the-middle attack and terminate the communication. Examples of SSL decryption options from Cisco include the SSL appliances, running SSL decryption on a FirePOWER security appliance, decrypting on a Web Security Appliance (WSA), and decryption using Cisco Cloud Web Security. Be mindful that at the time of this writing, all vendors in the industry experience a heavy performance hit when enabling SSL decryption when attempting to view live traffic entering and leaving the network. A best practice to reduce the impact is to selectively decrypt traffic with a high risk for attack using traffic categories such as social media and search engines versus decrypting everything.

Regarding the performance impact of handling encryption, it is important to identify when decryption is not needed, in addition to not processing encrypted traffic through a monitoring tool. A common mistake found in the configuration of on-network monitoring technology is monitoring traffic that is not required or irrelevant to what the tool is used for. An example is running all traffic through an application layer firewall with IPS capabilities, including large data backups that kill the performance of the firewall during the backup cycle. Best practice is to trust or whitelist the data backup traffic unless some unusual requirement states that you must process data backups. Another example is how administrators of IPS appliances can dramatically improve performance by not processing encrypted traffic that the IPS cannot understand. One way to accomplish this on Cisco devices is to use the following **access list** commands to drop encrypted traffic and permit everything else:

```
access list 1 deny https any any // drops all encrypted SSL traffic
access list 1 permit any any // monitors everything else
```

To summarize architecting security into a SOC, the following are common topics a SOC architect must consider:

- How is access controlled to the buildings and network?
- How is access controlled between network segments within the network?
- Where will user accounts be stored?
- How many factors of authentication will be used to grant access to different network segments?
- What policies are enforced and services granted to different user accounts?
- What types of on-network security monitoring and protection should be enabled?
- Are there any gaps for on-network visibility, and how many layers of capabilities exist at each network detection point?
- Are there ways to bypass monitoring such as encryption or VPN?
- What is used for detecting network breaches?
- Are you meeting all requirements for regulations and corporate policies?
- How will all security technologies be managed and monitored?

Details on many of the security products mentioned in this section are covered later in this chapter. Now let's look at considerations for architecting systems that will run on the SOC network.

Systems

A SOC will be monitoring traffic from many sources, including systems used by employees of the organization and data center servers. Depending on the size of the organization, securing systems may be the responsibility of desktop support or data center administration or could fall under the SOC. When the SOC is not responsible for maintaining the security posture of host systems and servers, there should be collaboration between the responsible team and event log collection to SOC monitoring systems so that the SOC understands how those systems impact the overall security posture of the organization. Collaboration between teams could mean providing updates on recent threats for vulnerability management purposes, aligning technical goals of all teams to business objectives, and integration of SOC and system support security tools.

When the SOC is responsible for provision security for endpoint systems used by hosts, there should a common set of security measures put in place to harden all systems. The first recommendation is to standardize on a hardware and operating system if possible. This will simplify acquiring technology because it can be purchased in bulk, automate hardening procedures because all systems can run a unified system build, and shorten the training cycle for ongoing support. A unified operating system and hardware might not always be possible as technologies such as bring your own device (BYOD) increase in popularity. When multiple device types are required to be supported, best practices include automating the onboarding process and enforcing a standardized policy regardless of the device type. This could include certain levels of operating system updates within a 30-day period, having specific types of products installed such as the same antivirus package, scanning for threats upon connecting to the network, and so on. If the user network is flat, meaning that BYOD and standardized systems are running on the same network, it is recommended to leverage NAC to implement segmentation between device types and quarantine devices that fall outside the standard endpoint build. For example, users bringing personal devices such as tablets are limited to Internet and specific services, whereas corporate-issued laptops are allowed access to additional services. Best practice is to have different level of access for administrators, employees, contractors, and guests, following the structure covered earlier in this chapter.

Operating Systems

When selecting an operating system, stick with a widely used business version if possible. Sometimes, choosing a common operating is unavoidable, though, such as in development environments. In those cases, you should provision a separate network if those customized systems are limited in number because they will most likely introduce a different type of risk than the standard operating system build. Operating systems such as Windows and OS X include many security features that should be enabled, such as firewalls, antivirus, antimalware, and so on. Best practice is to provision a centralized management platform that will simplify enforcing policy and provide one source for the SOC to collect logs from. An example for Windows is Windows Server Update Services (WSUS). If multiple variations of operating systems are used on the network, it is recommended to at least standardize on enabling native security features and leveraging a third-party security product that is supported across multiple platforms. Vendors that offer host-based security products include McAfee, Symantec, and Sophos. Vendors such as these may include overlapping security features with what is offered by the native operating system, such as the firewall feature, but the native firewall can be disabled to standardize the host system configuration across the network.

Hardening Endpoints

To reduce the risk services being exploited by an attacker, most operating systems let you disable certain services if you determine them unnecessary. You should follow a formal guide to harden host systems, such as NIST 800-70, NSA Security Configuration Guide,[3] CIS Security Benchmarks for Windows,[4] and Mac,[5] or direct guidance from the vendor.

Some common recommendations for hardening a host operating system are as follows:

- **Disable all unnecessary services:** This might be difficult to do when dealing with multiple types of systems. Best practice is to follow recommendations from the vendor or industry standards such the ones previously recommended. Windows services that you can probably disable include offline files, network access protection (NAP) agent, Windows parent controls, smart card removal policy, Windows Media Center schedule services, fax, Windows file and printer sharing, HomeGroup Listener, HomeGroup Provider, and tablet PC input service.
- **Remove unnecessary executable and Registry entries:** An attacker could abuse old executable and Registries that have been disabled but not removed.
- **Apply appropriate restrictive permissions to files, services, endpoints, and Registry entries:** Attackers could take advantage of systems with more privileges than they are supposed to have. A classic example is permitting systems to run the CMD.EXE as LocalSystem, which gives an attacker a back door to the system.
- **Automatically patch systems:** As stated in Chapter 1, 99.9 percent of vulnerabilities exploited had patches available for more than a year. Automation can help improve reaction time to exposure of vulnerabilities within your environment.
- **Use strong passphrases versus passwords:** Passwords are becoming too long to remember or too short to prevent being broken with today's computing power. A better approach is to use a passphrase made up multiple words or a password that equates to a long passphrase. An example of a passphrase is "I look forward to my next vacation in Jamaica." An example of making a long password out of a passphrase is the first letter of each word in the previous sentence plus four digits and a special character. This results in IlftmnviJ1357!. Either of these password policies should be easy enough to remember and difficult to crack by password-cracking technology. Regardless of the strategy used, make sure to set all passwords to expire at some point, such as in 90 days.
- **Purchase and maintain business-grade antivirus:** Many common attacks can be prevented by having a good antivirus package installed and current.
- **Enforce screen lock timers and autoshutdown:** This reduces the exposure time when users walk away from their systems.
- **Use software restriction policies:** This prevents executables from running outside specific folders, such as \Program Files or \Windows.
- **Disable AutoRun and AutoPlay:** Make sure that users are aware of what is running, instead of permitting software to run on its own.

Endpoint Breach Detection

Security features found within most operating systems and many general host security products might not include the capability to detect advanced persistent threats (APT). Common security products rely heavily on signature detection with limited behavior features. These stop many attacks, but some advanced threats might not be known or are designed to bypass commercial security products. Best practice is to use technology that focuses on breach detection for endpoints to identify abnormal behavior such as modifying boot records or file polymorphism. Features for endpoint breach detection should include tactics to identify day-zeros and autoremediation, track modifications, verify files against external reputation sources, and export threats for further analysis. Most endpoint breach-detection products include a centralized manager that should be able to export logs to the SOC centralized data-collection tool. Figure 9-8 shows the Cisco AMP for endpoint dashboards showing the capture of six Trojans on a Mac laptop running McAfee antivirus and the Cisco AMP agent.

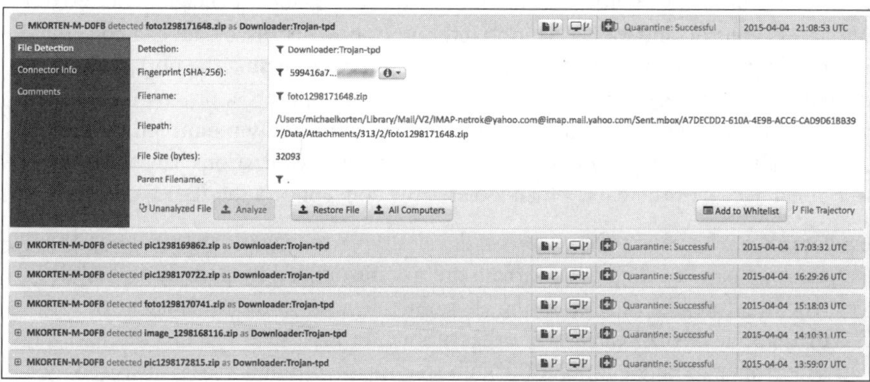

Figure 9-8 *Cisco AMP Removing Six Trojans*

Caution Breach detection does not replace the need for antivirus. The purpose of breach detection is to complement antivirus by focusing on threats that are missed. Not having antivirus exposes your systems to hundreds of breaches that might not be detected by a breach-detection technology. The reason for this is most breach-detection technologies do not rely on signatures and are not designed to stop *unknown threats*. Signature based-detection tools such as antivirus target *known threats*, meaning they act as the first layer of breach detection stopping the majority of threats that will attempt to impact host systems. Consider signature-based security and breach detection as two separate categories of threat detection with little overlap in capabilities that have the same end goal of preventing host systems from being compromised.

Mobile Devices

Mobile devices, such as phones and tablets, introduce additional challenges for security. Reasons include operating systems such as iOS limit what can be installed and accessed, user concerns when personal devices are monitored by the organization, and the mobile nature of this device category. Mobile devices include native security features that should be enabled, and like host systems, third-party products are available that can also assist with standardizing security policies; these are known as mobile device management (MDM) products. Best practice is to use an MDM solution to manage any mobile device that is in contact with company data that should not be made public. Common MDM capabilities include enforcing that the VPN is enabled, verifying certain applications are or not installed, putting security policies in place such as a password and specific lock timeout, locating devices, and selective wiping. MDM products include a centralized management system that you should configure to export data to the SOC's centralized data-collection tool.

Alternatives for using an MDM to secure mobile devices include leveraging sandboxed portals, access control, and VPNs. Sandboxed portals host sensitive data in a controlled environment, limiting the threat of compromised systems accessing the portal. The advantages of this approach are that users do not have to opt into a program and install software on their mobile devices and that the portal can be easily monitored by the SOC. This might work for some environments, but many organizations have users who request direct access to the data, which violates the concept of a sandbox.

Access control can be used to limit certain devices types to specific data sources, thus protecting other parts of the network from the risk introduced by permitting mobile devices. The disadvantage of segmenting all mobile devices on the same network with NAC is that mobile devices can attack other mobile devices. VPN can be used to always force traffic from a mobile endpoint through an encrypted tunnel that is analyzed by enterprise security products and to only provision internal sources. The advantage of this approach is that the organization's security policies are enforced as traffic enters and leaves the company, but this is challenging to scale for large companies and bypassed if the mobile device turns off the VPN or uses cellular services.

Servers

Securing data center servers is similar to hardening host systems. The major differences for servers are the types of services that will be used, the operating system versions, possible use of virtual networking, and functions such as daily backups and storage will also need to be enforced securely. Many servers have multiple users and administrators accessing these systems, so access control should be used to enforce role-based access using only secure login procedures and tracking of all changes to the system. Internet access for servers should be limited to updates and required services. When working with files on a network server, it is important to encrypt login information so that it is not passed in clear text. Additional regulatory requirements may need to be met if certain types of data are present, such as Payment Card Industry Data Security Standard (PCI DSS) 2.0 for any server handling financial data. Beyond these and a few other items, the same practices for system patching, antivirus, breach detection, and so on should be enforced on data center servers.

To summarize architecting security for endpoints and network servers, the following are common factors a SOC architect should consider:

- What hardware and operating systems will be used?
- How will system patch management be centrally enforced?
- What services and protocols can be disabled to harden systems?
- What host-based antivirus, IPS, and antimalware package makes sense for the organization?
- Is there an endpoint breach-detection strategy?
- What tools are used for daily operations and can event data be exported?
- Are mobile devices permitted, and how are they secured?
- What support contacts are required to protect the organization's investment in systems?

Now that we covered network servers, let's look at how to secure the storage systems that network servers and other devices depend on.

Storage

SOC services have a heavy focus on data analytics to detect and prevent threats. This involves collecting and storing massive amounts of data in an electronic format that contains information about the business, personal information (about employees, clients, and associates), and other general information. There are also regulations that require a minimum of 1 year of archived records in the event evidence is needed for a forensic investigation. These and other operational requirements demand a need for storage that protects data during the entire storage lifecycle.

The first step to secure data from the SOC is to determine what should be stored and its value to the organization. Based on that value, the SOC can request a specific tier of protection for systems that will be storing the SOC data, along with the level of associated security. An example of a four-tier offering for an in-house or cloud storage provider is as follows:

- **Tier 1 (99.671 percent availability):** Data center provisions single uplink and server with no redundancy.
- **Tier 2 (99.741 percent availability):** Data center provisions some redundant capacity components for storage systems.

- **Tier 3 (99.982 percent availability):** Tier 1 + 2 level provisioned with redundant power and multiple uplinks.
- **Tier 4 (99.995 percent availability):** Entire storage system, power, chillers, storage, and components are all designed for fault tolerance.

The higher the tier requested, the higher the cost for the SOC to store the data. Best practice is to follow the formulas provided in Chapter 6, "Security Event Generation and Collection," to calculate business requirements, identify all mandated storage requirements, and qualify what data sources should be backed up to avoid storing unnecessary data or overprotecting nonessential data. Many SOC tools will not have enough local storage and will require external storage, but that does not mean everything must be backed up using a Tier 4 storage plan unless a regulation mandates such data archiving. Benefits of tuning down storage requirements include SOC storage cost savings, less network bandwidth required (because of shorter backup cycles), and less responsibility if some systems that are not necessary are removed from the archiving plan.

The SOC architect might have to make many decisions that balance the security and availability of storage systems to administrators and other users. It is recommended to enforce the concept of least privilege so that only the necessary services and user access are permitted. You can do this by using network segmentation and security concepts previously covered to protect servers and endpoints. One additional important security concept for storage systems is enforcing data-loss protection.

Data-Loss Protection

One common requirement for some industry regulations and organization policies is protecting certain data from falling into the wrong hands by using data-loss protecting (DLP) technology. Data loss can be verified at two points in time. The first is *data in motion*, which is the concept of checking data as it moves from one system to another. An example is placing a data-in-motion motion checkpoint in front of an e-mail server so that you can verify that e-mails entering and leaving the network do not contain sensitive data.

Data-in-motion solutions must be configured to look for specific things deemed sensitive, and DLP checks should have detailed algorithms that validate that the data is truly sensitive, to avoid overloading the administration with false positives. A common DLP check used by many U.S. organizations is to look for Social Security numbers, meaning a number that is formatted as xxx-xx-xxxx. It is possible that non-Social Security numbers could follow the same format, such as 111-11-1111. So, to avoid alarming for random numbers in an xxx-xx-xxxx format, a strong DLP solution would also be aware of the numbering formula used by the U.S. government to generate Social Security numbers. Typically, DLP solutions for data in motion include subscription feeds that update popular categories for DLP checks, such as Social Security numbers, bank account numbers, phone numbers, credit card numbers, and so on. Data-in-motion DLP solutions can also be configured to look for preassigned sensitive data, but that requires a data-at-rest component to be installed on the system creating the data and assigned sensitivity. We cover this concept shortly.

The second point of verification when data can be checked is *data at rest* (sometimes referred to as data in use), which controls who and what has access to data while it is on a system. This also includes the ability to expire access to that data, and hence the term data at rest. There are two types of data-at-rest solutions. The first type works by installing some form of agent on servers where data is created to catalog the different types of data. Once data is cataloged, it can be broken into sensitivity levels. Data of certain sensitivity can be encrypted anytime it is accessed or moved so that only authorized parties will be able to unencrypt the files. For example, if user Irene Muniz pulls some files from a sensitive system and stores them on her personal computer, those files will be encrypted, and only people configured with the rights to open those files will be able to access the data. Irene can use an endpoint client or web portal to authenticate against the file to validate that she has rights to access the data. Irene will be verified every time she opens the file, and if the owner of the data decides to revoke access rights, the next time Irene attempts to open the file, she will be presented with a deny screen.

Another type of data-at-rest technology is disk encryption. This technology works by installing a software package that encrypts part of or the entire computer hard drive and authenticates access to the data. The difference between server DLP at rest and this approach is that data does not have to be classified because specific folders or the entire endpoint hard drive is encrypted regardless of the type of data present.

When planning to design and install a DLP solution, first determine the type of DLP technology you will use and where it will be placed on the network. There are four places to consider placing DLP technologies:

- **Network:** This can be a physical or virtual appliance that monitors traffic as it crosses the network. Network DLP is a data-in-motion technology that can use a combination of predefined data categories, regex checks, or sensitivity classification determined by a server DLP as it catalogs data within the organization. Network DLP solutions can quarantine sensitive data or be set up to monitor only depending on how it is configured and the available capabilities.
- **Server:** Server DLP requires software installed on all servers so that data can be categorized and classified. Access rights can be assigned to different classification levels so that only authorized users and devices can access the data while it is on the server or if it leaves the server. Typically, this data categorization and classification is accomplished by using clients that run on servers and report back to a centralized management system. Some server DLP products can also install agents on endpoints to expand what data is categorized and classified; however, this is not a common practice.
- **Endpoint:** There are two types of endpoint encryption offerings. The first is a software package that encrypts some or all content of the endpoint. The other endpoint DLP option is a client that is used to auto-authenticate the endpoint to data that is classified by a server DLP solution. Without the agent, a web portal is usually available to manually enter credentials to verify that access rights are available to the data.

- **E-mail:** DLP for e-mail works by quarantining e-mail temporarily to verify that it does not contain sensitive content. Checks are based on predefined categories and can also use sensitivity classification determined by a server DLP solution that has categorized the organization's data. E-mail DLP solutions can perform various actions on e-mail that contains sensitive information. Actions include removing the sensitive content and sending the e-mail, sending the e-mail back to the user with instructions about why the e-mail was not permitted to leave the network, sending the e-mail to other parties, such as management or HR, encrypting the e-mail to protect the data if encryption is available, or sending the e-mail while generating an event to a logging system. Figure 9-9 shows an example of DLP actions configured on Cisco Email Security Appliance (ESA).

> **Note** There are data-loss vectors to consider outside of what DLP technology can cover. Examples include physical access to systems, printers, scanners, photography, and so on.

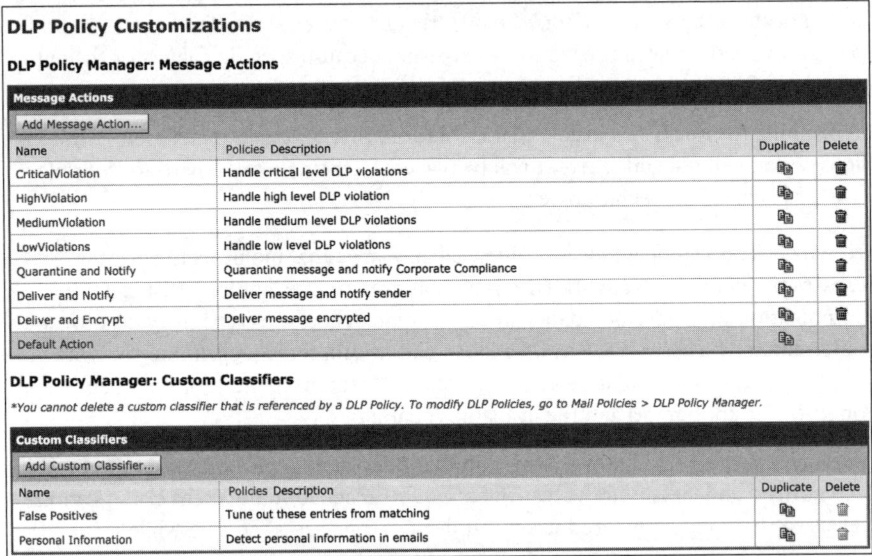

Figure 9-9 *DLP Action Example in Cisco ESA*

A data-in-motion DLP can be a feature enabled on an existing network security solution or can be a dedicated physical or virtual hardware placed on the network where data can be monitored. Common points to place network DLP appliances are at the end of the network behind the gateway firewall, at the gateway of the data center, or on parts of the network that contain sensitive information that the organization wants to monitor. Similar to an IPS/IDS, a data-in-motion DLP must be placed inline to prevent unauthorized data; otherwise, it will only be able to monitor and alert when sensitive data is identified. Some application layer firewalls and web content filters include DLP options that can monitor data that crosses the appliance. Other security solutions redirect traffic through a dedicated DLP appliance. For example, Cisco Web Security Appliance (WSA) can send traffic to an external DLP appliance. Figure 9-10 shows the configuration page for this.

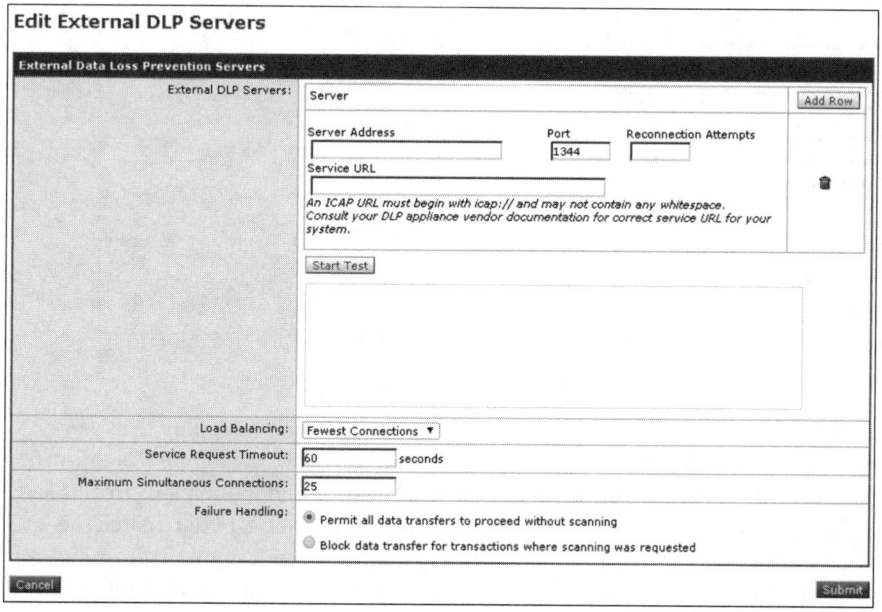

Figure 9-10 *WSA DLP Forward Configuration Page*

Deploying DLP on servers typically requires a centralized manager to be installed that will control software agents. Software agents are deployed on systems so that they can continuously monitor changes and classify data. DLP audits stop once data is classified, but protecting data requires a process to encrypt the data that is deemed sensitive. Authentication of encrypted data is usually integrated with a centralized user repository so that roles can be assigned to user groups. This simplifies the process of granting and denying access to data categories. For example, a policy is configured that enforces "all files deemed sensitive are accessible by employees in Active Directory only." Most DLP vendors recommend limiting the lifetime of the data, meaning having an expiration date automatically set to lock down access after the data has been off the server a certain amount of time. Authentication is usually enforced with an endpoint client or via web access when a system lets users manually authenticate to the file to validate their identity.

E-mail DLP solutions must be installed inline to block e-mail, but a copy of the e-mail can be sent if monitoring and alerting are the only required features. E-mail DLP is usually installed as a dedicated appliance or as a feature of an e-mail security appliance that also provides antispam, antivirus, and so on. For example, the Cisco ESA includes DLP in motion as an optional license. Many DLP checks are available, grouped under different categories. Figure 9-11 shows options under the regulatory category, along with other main categories.

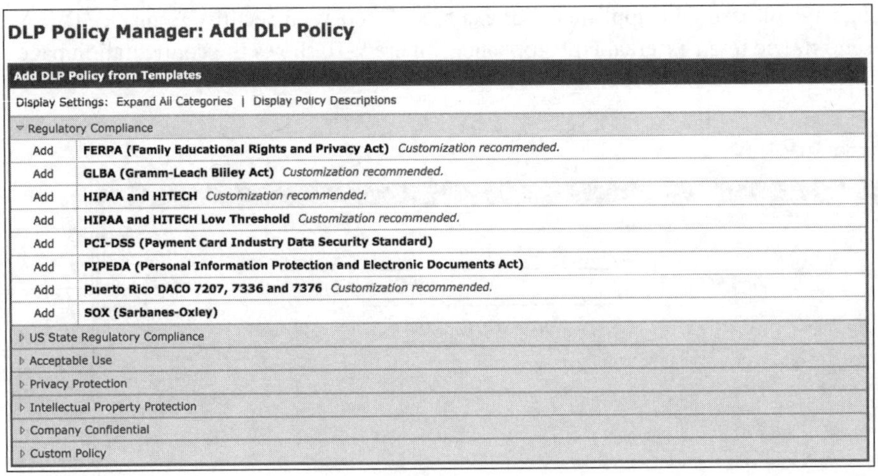

DLP Policy Manager: Add DLP Policy

Add DLP Policy from Templates

Display Settings: Expand All Categories | Display Policy Descriptions

▿ Regulatory Compliance

Add	**FERPA (Family Educational Rights and Privacy Act)** *Customization recommended.*
Add	**GLBA (Gramm-Leach Bliley Act)** *Customization recommended.*
Add	**HIPAA and HITECH** *Customization recommended.*
Add	**HIPAA and HITECH Low Threshold** *Customization recommended.*
Add	**PCI-DSS (Payment Card Industry Data Security Standard)**
Add	**PIPEDA (Personal Information Protection and Electronic Documents Act)**
Add	**Puerto Rico DACO 7207, 7336 and 7376** *Customization recommended.*
Add	**SOX (Sarbanes-Oxley)**

▹ US State Regulatory Compliance

▹ Acceptable Use

▹ Privacy Protection

▹ Intellectual Property Protection

▹ Company Confidential

▹ Custom Policy

Figure 9-11 *Regulatory DLP Checks in ESA*

In general, data-in-motion DLP will be less expensive and easier to deploy than data-at-rest DLP. The most common ways data enters and leaves the organization is through e-mail and via the web, so many organizations start with data-in-motion investments and later add data at rest as requirements determine the need. Make sure to research the entire cost of the project before committing to a full-blown DLP solution. Most end-to-end DLP strategies will be very labor intensive and require a large part of the SOC budget to maintain.

Cloud Storage

Many organizations use cloud storage as a way to outsource costs for hardware, maintenance, elasticity, and so on. Moving storage to the cloud provides many benefits, but also introduces some risk as well. It is critical that the SOC architect validate the service provider to ensure proper processes are used to secure data and that the level of support meets business requirements.

The first thing a SOC architect should do when reviewing a cloud storage provider is to identify the degree of redundancy that is implemented for all systems containing company data. Details should include whether automatic failover is used for disks, servers, and failover to other locations. If a failure occurs and your organization needs the backed-up data, there should be a guaranteed expected time to restore data. The SOC architect should verify whether the service provider offers versioning of stored data or whether the cloud storage service is only storing the most current version of files and data objects. It is also important to know how long the cloud storage service will store data and whether that timeframe can be extended with a future contract.

Another consideration when reviewing cloud storage services is how easy it is to access and monitor the data being stored. Most cloud storage service includes some type of management console; you want this to be available from any location in case of an emergency. Make sure to verify that their storage systems can accept all formats of the data your organization will be sending and that the reporting options meet your needs.

The last and more important consideration is the pricing structure. Some cloud storage providers may charge for every file access, in addition to per-gigabyte upload and download charges. This model is great for an organization moving large blocks of data, but it is costly for an organization that requires many database lookups and updates. Make sure that all costs and services are crystal clear in the service contract.

When choosing a storage source for SOC data, do not put all your eggs in one basket. If the organization plans to leverage in-house storage, make sure that redundancy extends beyond a single local data center if possible. If the SOC decides to use a cloud storage provider, make sure to spread out the backup between two providers or use a hybrid approach where critical data is also backed up using in-house services.

Now let's look at design recommendations for SOC collaboration technology.

Collaboration

A successful SOC collaborates with many different groups. This includes internal SOC members, human resources, desktop support, external vendors, members from leadership, and so on. Collaboration should be designed for daily operations and for pandemic scenarios that include everything from the phones and conference systems to file-sharing systems.

Most collaboration tools should already exist within the organization. Examples are e-mail, internal websites, conference products, and mailing lists that you can use for specific SOC purposes. These tools might need to be customized for the SOC, such as creating a dedicated e-mail alias that the organization can use to alert the SOC of any questionable activity seen while using the organization's resources. Additional hardware may be required to segment SOC systems, such as creating a separate phone system with its own network.

Documents will probably need to be shared between different groups using some form of repository. Options include professional applications such as Microsoft SharePoint, cloud storage options such as Dropbox, or creating an open source wiki-like page. Factors that should help determine the right document repository for your organization include the need for an approval process to post documents, integration with a centralized authentication system, integration with other collaboration tools such as desktop calendars, ease of use, and security options to protect the data.

Voice over IP (VoIP) and video are popular network-based collaboration technologies that can be leveraged by the SOC in a secure manner. For example, most modern collaboration systems offer end-to-end encryption to ensure that conversations are protected. Hardening VoIP and video is essentially following the same practices as securing network traffic and hardening servers because most VoIP services run on commercial server operating systems. Best practices for securing the VoIP and video systems include the following:

- Maintain patch management for the VoIP/video applications and all services on the server.
- Run only applications required for delivering VoIP and video.
- Use strong authentication and authorization strategies for administration access.
- Audit administrative sessions associated with VoIP and video maintenance.
- Ensure host-based firewall, antivirus, and so on are installed on all VoIP and video servers.

All collaboration technologies should have event logs sent to the SOC and tuned for security-related events. This should include login records, device failures, security product status checks, and so on. One final consideration is customizing different collaboration tools to assist during a pandemic event.

Collaboration for Pandemic Events

In some situations, the SOC will need to quickly react to an event but first require authorized people to make critical decisions. Many business-level conferencing and collaboration packages offer features for contacting members using e-mail, the web, or direct dialing people into an emergency conference bridge. Steps can follow a specific route, meaning that the first attempt is a call, followed by text, and then e-mail, depending on the user's preference. Pandemic settings should be available to prioritize calls, meaning that the system can interrupt an existing call or videoconference if a high-priority call is seen.

Some conferencing solutions offer location services that identify the MAC or IP address of the mobile device and determine its general location. Different contact methods can be used based on location, meaning that the mobile device can be used first if it is tracked outside the office network. A key feature is that the pandemic collaboration setup can accommodate different types of devices and methods to bridge people in, because most likely people will be out of the office and using various types of mobile phones to call in when an emergency occurs.

The Cisco Emergency Responder is an example of a collaboration architecture made up of voice, video, and web collaboration products and is customizable for incident response situations. This solution is also designed to accommodate the need to autodial emergency 9-1-1 responders and determine the correct location of the person requiring assistance. This can be a problem when using a VoIP system that shows a different physical location for the call than where the phone is actually located, meaning that the emergency response team could show up at the wrong location if the system cannot track the true location of the user.

Cisco Emergency Responder may be tuned to meet a pandemic situation by contacting internal emergency resources rather than external 9-1-1 unless that is required for the situation. You can learn more about Cisco collaboration technologies at Cisco.com or work with your solution provider to learn how you can customize your existing collaboration technologies to meet your pandemic needs.

Technologies to Consider During SOC Design

Up to this point in this chapter, we have covered concepts that are important for a SOC architect to consider during the design phase of building a SOC. This section looks deeper into specific technologies and shows how they should be placed in the SOC design. Let's start by looking at designing firewall technology.

Firewalls

Firewalls were introduced in Chapter 6 as a system designed to prevent unauthorized access to or from a private network. Many variations of firewalls are available on the market, ranging from a simple stateful firewall to feature-rich appliances that can perform IPS, content filtering, application control, and so on. The basic use case for a firewall is implementing segmentation and controlling access between segments. The method used by a firewall to segment a network can differ depending on what mode the firewall is configured to operate in and the type of segmentation used (based on the six-layer segmentation model covered earlier in this chapter).

Firewall Modes

Most modern firewalls offer the following operational modes:

- **Routed mode:** This is usually the default mode of a firewall. Routed mode uses two or more interfaces to separate Layer 3 domains. For example, a routed mode firewall segments off an inside, outside, and DMZ network and route traffic between these segments. Figure 9-12 is an example of a basic routed mode firewall separating an inside and outside network segment.

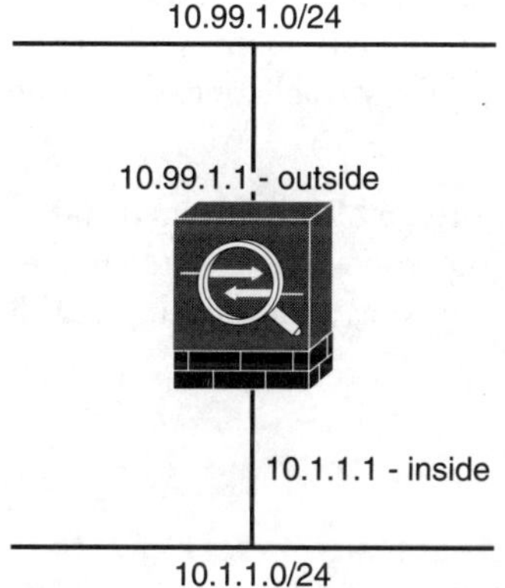

Figure 9-12 *Routed Mode Firewall Example*

- **Transparent mode:** This mode provides Layer 2 bridging of networks, also known as a "bump in the wire." Only Address Resolution Protocol (ARP) packets pass without an explicit access control list (ACL). The same subnet exists on all interfaces in the bridge group, and different VLANs exist on both sides of the bridge. Advantages of transparent firewalls include that most environments do not need to be modified to deploy the firewall, the firewall does not need routing protocols, many protocols can establish adjacencies through the firewall, multicast streams can traverse the firewall, and non-IP traffic can be allowed. Figure 9-13 shows a simple transparent mode design.

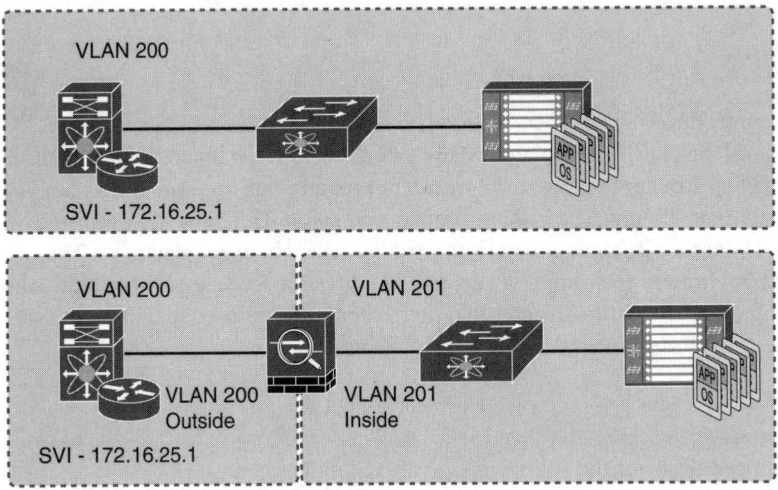

Figure 9-13 *Basic Firewall Transparent Mode Example*

- **Multicontext:** Multicontext mode carves a physical firewall into virtual firewalls that can be routed mode or transparent mode. Each firewall context is an independent device with its own security policy, interfaces, and administrators. It is important to be aware that some features may not be available when enabling multicontext mode. For example, Cisco ASAs do not support remote-access VPN and dynamic routing protocols while multicontext mode is enabled. Figure 9-14 shows an example of creating three virtual context firewalls on one physical firewall.

- **Mixed mode:** Mix mode uses multicontext mode to offer a blend of routed and transparent firewalls. For example, a SOC could use one context as a routed mode firewall for the network perimeter and use another context as a transparent firewall monitoring traffic inside the data center.

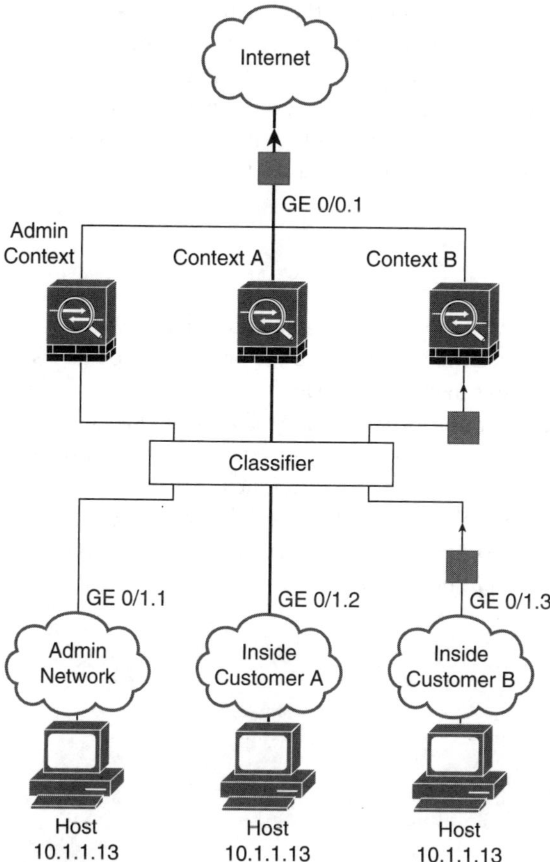

Figure 9-14 *Multicontext Mode Example*

Most firewall architectures use a routed mode firewall, but the SOC architect may choose to use a multicontext mode firewall for a few reasons. First, multicontext mode firewalls support active/active failover; however, you should avoid using this approach if it consumes more than half of the available bandwidth when using this feature. Second, you can save money by provisioning multiple firewalls using the same hardware. This is ideal for a SOC providing firewall services to multiple customers or provisioning firewalls to different teams with their own security policies.

There might be disadvantages when enabling multicontext mode depending on the vendor. For example, Cisco ASAs do not support VPN, quality of service (QoS), multicast routing, and dynamic routing protocols when multicontext mode is enabled. In addition, regulations, sensitivity of data, or performance requirements might prohibit the use of multicontext mode.

SOC architects may consider a transparent firewall when they want to place a firewall on a network without making changes to the existing IP addressing structure or impacting existing routing protocols. This is ideal for inserting a firewall into an existing data center or when monitoring network segments that the SOC cannot make changes to. A transparent firewall could also be placed on a Switched Port Analyzer (SPAN) port for monitoring a specific network segment, which is common when testing a security product during a proof-of-value exercise.

Firewall Clustering

Throughput requirements might exceed a vendor's single appliance capability. Some vendors such as Cisco offer firewall clustering to aggregate firewall bandwidth to increase performance capabilities. Clustering also can provide dynamic N+1 stateful redundancy, meaning that if a hardware failure occurs, other systems in the cluster can maintain operation at a lower performance until the system that is down is returned to a functioning state. Clustering works by electing a master among the cluster members for configuration synchronization only. A cluster control link is used to speak between the clustered systems. Some Cisco products that support clustering are the ASA 5580 and 5585 appliances. Figure 9-15 shows the basic concept behind clustering.

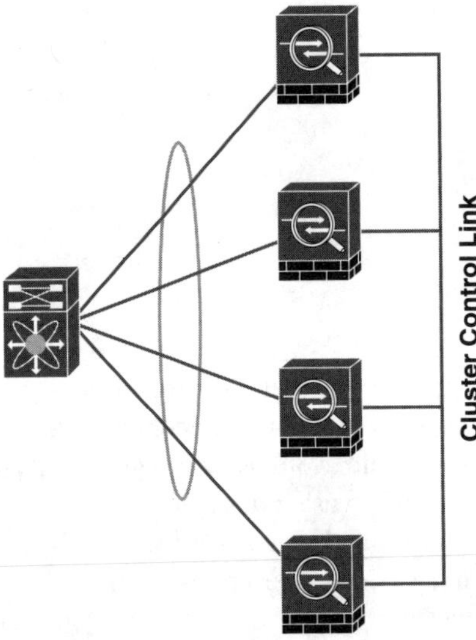

Figure 9-15 *Clustering Firewall Diagram*

Firewall High Availability

Most firewall designs include some form of high availability. This is extremely important when the firewall is a central point of failure, such as the perimeter gateway.

High availability can be physical using two or more appliances that have synchronized configurations or virtual depending on the vendor's capabilities. Typically, failover includes monitoring of the active or primary firewall using a heartbeat counter. When a delay beyond the configured threshold is seen by a secondary firewall, a failover occurs.

For Cisco ASA firewalls, the requirement for high availability is having two identical ASAs connected through a dedicated failover link and, optionally, a state link. The ASA supports two failover modes: active/active failover and active/standby failover. Active/standby has one ASA act as an active unit, while the standby unit does not actively pass traffic. When a failover occurs, the active unit fails over to a standby unit. Active/standby supports single-context and multicontext mode configurations. Active/active failover enables both ASAs to pass network traffic. This can be enabled only when an ASA is configured in multicontext mode by dividing the security contexts on the ASA into two failover groups. A failover group is a logical group of one or more security contexts. When a failover occurs, it happens at the failover group level.

Firewall Architecture

Most SOC environments acquire a firewall for the network perimeter. A network perimeter firewall is used to segment off different network zones, such as the outside, DMZ, and internal resources. Trust levels are assigned between network zones, and policies are put in place to control what resources are available in each zone. Network Address Translation (NAT) and Port Address Translation (PAT) are used to conceal network scopes and consolidate IP addresses. Figure 9-16 shows a generic network perimeter design.

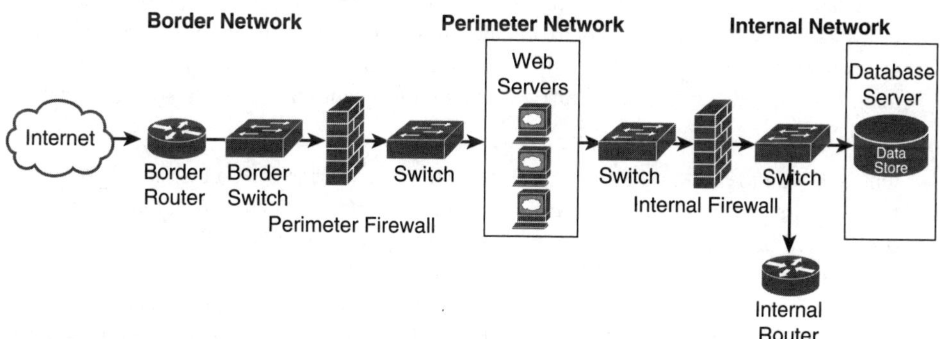

Figure 9-16 *Basic Network Architecture*

If you were going to configure Figure 9-15 on a Cisco ASAx series appliance, you would need to create a perimeter, internal, and border network. The basic setup of the outside or "border"-facing interface would need a name, security level, and IP address, as shown in the next configuration:

```
interface GigabitEthernet 0/0
description Border Interface
```

```
nameif OUTSIDE
security-level 0
ip address X.X.X.X 255.255.255.0
```

Two other interfaces are set up to represent the internal interface with a trust of 100 and perimeter interface with a trust of 50. Other services such as PAT could be added later to meet the business requirements for this part of the network.

Another common use for a firewall is protecting the data center. Data center firewalls have a similar purpose as perimeter firewalls; however, the traffic loads tend to be different, and sometimes they are virtualized. Most perimeter firewall traffic is entering and leaving the network, but data centers tend to see the majority of the traffic internally, also known as *east-west traffic*. Data center firewall requirements tend to be less tolerant with regard to packet loss and require higher performance rates than other firewalls.

The SOC architect will probably consider two types of data center firewalls. The first is a data center perimeter firewall covering traffic entering and leaving the data center, known as *north-south traffic*. Feature requirements tend to be similar to what is needed for a perimeter firewall, but Internet-bound features such as content filtering may not be needed because those capabilities tend to be covered by a perimeter security solution. In addition, performance may be higher than a perimeter firewall because no Internet service provider (ISP) throughput limitation impacts the sizing of perimeter firewalls and many servers can deliver large traffic loads.

The second firewall type that may be included in a data center architecture is a transparent firewall designed to segment off services within the data center. As stated earlier, transparent firewalls do not require changes in IP, and many protocols can establish adjacencies, making it easy to place within an established data center. A common requirement for segmenting east-west traffic is for a multitenant environment, where virtual services need to be logically segmented.

One important feature that a SOC architect should consider when choosing different types of firewalls is a centralized management platform. The centralized management tool should be able to push out and enforce configuration changes, back up configurations, unify software images, centralize alarming, and be able to export alerts to an external data-collection tool. Role-based access should be available, and a desirable feature is the ability to have nonauthorized configurations be placed on hold until approved by the proper authority. Cisco Security Manager (CSM) includes these and other features.

Figure 9-17 shows an example of implementing multiple firewalls across a network for perimeter and data center security. A centralized manager is placed on a separate management network and configured to export events to the SIEM managed by the SOC.

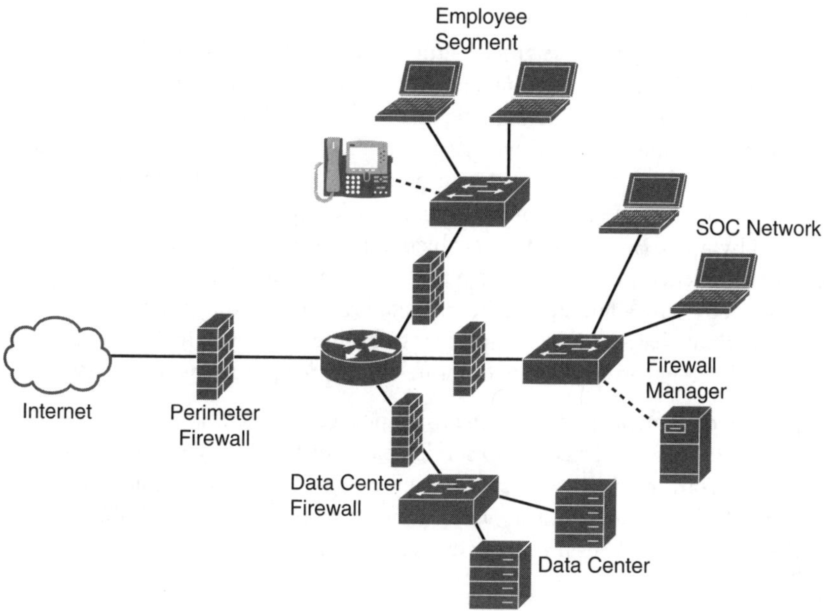

Figure 9-17 *Mature Firewall Deployment Example*

Host system and servers will also have virtual firewall options that should be enabled. Best practice is to use a third-party security application that includes firewall features and is supported on multiple platforms. This will help standardize firewall configurations for all cooperate-issued assets and centralize event logging. We covered this concept under system recommendations.

Now that we have reviewed firewall designs, let's look at considerations for deploying routers and switches.

Routers and Switches

Networks are made up of routers and switches. The SOC architect may be required to design the network infrastructure or involved with the design and able to request network devices that include certain features. Many routers and switches available today offer capabilities that extend beyond common networking requirements, such as security and collaboration features. The most common feature request for routers and switches from a SOC will be for event logs from a centralized network management tool. Individual device logging can also be enabled; however, it can be extremely tedious to manage and is not common practice.

Securing Network Devices

Network devices can offer many security features that can benefit the SOC. When hardening a network device, it is recommended to consider management traffic, traffic processed by the network device, and traffic that is forwarded. To secure management access, it is highly recommended to leverage a centralized authentication, authorization, and accounting (AAA) tool such as the AAA framework. AAA provides authentication of management sessions and can also limit users to specific commands and can log all commands entered by users. Even with AAA enabled, it is also important to enable local system passwords with encryption as a backup for when AAA fails. These local passwords should be known by only a limited number of high-level administrators and should be changed on a periodic basis. It is also important to enable local login locks after a specific number of failed login attempts, to stop brute-force attempts against local passwords.

There might be requirements to protect against exposing configurations on devices that are physically stolen. Cisco offers the **no service password-recovery** function, which prevents the password-recovery process from unlocking a device that the administrator does not know the local password for. Devices can be reset to factory default, but all configurations will be lost, thus protecting the organization's network data.

When accessing the management platform of network devices, use secure protocols whenever possible. For example, use Secure Shell (SSH) rather than Telnet so that both authentication data and management data are encrypted. When transferring files such as software images, use Security Copy Protocol (SCP) rather than File Transfer Protocol (FTP). Make sure timeouts are enabled so that an open session within a network device will close after a period of inactivity. The command for Cisco devices is **exec-timeout** *<minutes>* [*seconds*]. It is also recommended to enable keepalives for TCP sessions, which ensures that the device on the remote end of a connection is still accessible while half-open connects are removed. The commands to enable keepalives are **service tcp-keepalives-in** and **service tcp-keepalives-out**. A loopback interface should be used for management access rather than an interface that may go down.

Hardening Network Devices

It is recommended to disable unused services. The following is a basic list of services that should be disabled unless used for a specific purpose. Note that some of these configurations are enabled by default, so they will not be listed when viewing the default system configuration.

- **TCP and UDP small services:** Use the commands **no service tcp-small-servers** and **no service udp-small-servers.**
- **Finger service:** Use the command **no ip finger.**
- **Disable Bootstrap Protocol (BOOTP):** Use the **no ip bootp server** global command.
- **DHCP services can be disabled if DHCP relay services are not required:** Issue the **no service dhcp** global command.

- **Disable Maintenance Operation Protocol (MOP):** Use the command **no mop enabled** on the interface.
- **Disable Domain Name System (DNS) resolution services:** Use the command **no ip domain-lookup** from the global configuration.
- **Disable Packet Assembler/Disassembler (PAD) service, which is used for X.25 networkers:** Use the **no service pad** command.
- **Disable HTTP and HTTPS server:** Use the **no ip http server** and no **ip http secure-server** commands.
- **If Cisco IOS devices are not retrieving configurations from the network during startup, disable the service config:** Use the global command **no service config.**
- **Disable Cisco Discovery Protocol (CDP) and Link Layer Discovery Protocol (LLDP) on all ports connected to untrusted networks:** Use the command **no cdp enable.**

Manufacturers such as Cisco offer many security features that can be enabled to protect network devices. IP Source Guard works to minimize spoofing for networks that are under direct administrative control by performing switch port, MAC address, and source address verification. Unicast Reverse Path Forwarding (Unicast RPF) provides source network verification and can reduce the number of spoofed attacks from networks that are not under direct administrative control. Dynamic Address Resolution Protocol (ARP) Inspection (DAI) mitigates attack vectors that use ARP poisoning on local segments. It is recommended to request documentation for all vendor network devices and review the available security features. Most likely, there will be similar features as the ones covered in this chapter.

Port security can be used to validate MAC addresses at the access layer; however, best practice is to automate this process using a network access control (NAC) technology such as Cisco Identity Services Engine (ISE). Disadvantages of port security include the following: Port security is difficult to maintain, requires heavy manual efforts such as manually enabling any port that is disabled, is limited in what it can evaluate a device for, and can be bypassed with a MAC spoofing attack. Let's look at how to design a NAC solution.

Network Access Control

NAC is used fundamentally to control who and what is accessing specific parts of the network. More advanced NAC offerings include automation of the NAC process and additional features such as device profiling and posture. NAC technology may be features available on access devices or a product that interacts with network devices such as an appliance that uses Simple Network Management Protocol (SNMP) to issue commands to network switches.

Most modern NAC technology offers the following features:

- Automated access control for LAN, VPN, and wireless
- Guest access that includes options for
  - Self-registration
  - Creation of temporary accounts for lobby ambassadors
  - E-mail, print, or SMS guest passwords
  - Customized guest portal for business branding purposes
- Device profiling that can determine what a device is based on various types of traffic seen on the network. An example is identifying that a device is an Apple iPad based on radius and Dynamic Host Configuration Protocol (DHCP) information captured by the NAC technology.
- Posture assessment of devices, including options for
  - Checking system updates
  - Checking antivirus solutions are running and current
  - Verifying the existence of certificates
  - Verifying the existence of any file type
  - Checking whether an application or process is installed and running
- Remediation options if a device does not meet network policy, such as updating software
- Limit or deny access to devices based on policy compliance or administrative actions

NAC should be leveraged across the entire network and consider all user and device types. If an endpoint or network device is not supported, there should be alternative options to include those devices in the NAC deployment. An example is using MAC address whitelisting or automated device profiling to secure systems without advanced operating systems that require network access such as door card readers or IP-enabled refrigerators. The end result of a NAC deployment should segment off different user and devices based on the minimal services required to perform job duties. This level of segmentation should be gradually achieved rather than enforced when the system is first deployed.

Deploying NAC

Deploying NAC solutions should follow a crawl, walk, and run strategy, in which the first step is deploying in a monitoring-only mode if that capability is available. Cisco ISE can be deployed in monitor-only (a.k.a. permit all) state that can show whether devices would potentially fail (so that troubleshooting can be performed before access control is enabled). If monitor-only mode is not available in your NAC technology of choice, it is recommended to enable a very small subset, such as a few access ports, to test functionality before adding the rest of the network.

Profiling should be enabled during the monitor session to identify the number and different types of assets found on the network. Organizations might think that they know what is on the network, but they might be surprised to find out that somebody has been sneaking a PlayStation on the network during lunch. (We had this happen during a deployment.) Profiling is also an important step for identifying devices that might not support the method the access control technology uses, meaning that they may have to be added to a whitelist (a MAC address table as a alternative to 802.1X as an example ISE customers will deal with). One value of profiling with Cisco ISE is that devices are continuously profiled while on the network to detect MAC address spoofing attacks. Profiling can also detect rogue network devices such as hubs and unauthorized wireless access points.

The walk phase of a NAC deployment should enable access control in a very limited fashion regardless of the goals for the final deployment. The most common walk deployment is to verify whether users are employees based on a simple check, such as if users are part of a specific Active Directory group. All other users (meaning anybody without an Active Directory account) are given limited access. Figure 9-18 shows this basic configuration on Cisco ISE 1.4.

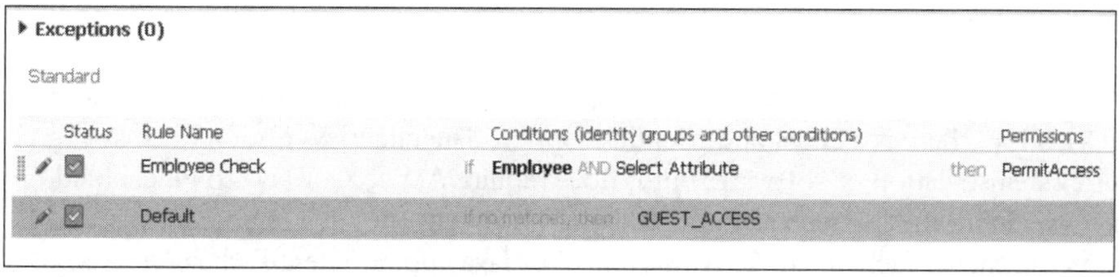

▸ Exceptions (0)

Standard

Status	Rule Name	Conditions (identity groups and other conditions)	Permissions
☑	Employee Check	if **Employee** AND Select Attribute then	PermitAccess
☑	Default	If no matches, then GUEST_ACCESS	

Figure 9-18 *Basic ISE Configuration*

This simple configuration should be run for at least a week or more to provide ample time for all users who normally access the network to experience the new access control technology. After the normal population has gone through the NAC technology without problems, the final part of the walk phase can start by adding segmentation policies. For example, mobile devices may end up on the same network as employees, but the data center is blocked using an access list because administrators should not access those services from a mobile device. Specific device profiles can also be created, such as a policy for VoIP phones limiting traffic to specific protocols. Segmentation profiles should be tested and slowly added to avoid introducing too many changes. (Introducing too many changes could make it difficult to determine the cause of any possible errors.)

Once network segmentation is established, the run phase can kick off by implementing advanced policies such as enforcing posture. It is recommended to start with a simple posture policy using monitor mode if available, such as verifying whether a specific antivirus vendor is installed and running. This will allow the administrators to test whether the enforcement technology is installed and working on endpoints before expanding on the posture checklist. Once the simple posture check is used for a period of time, NAC administrators can start tailoring posture checks to IT goals. Best practice is to introduce new posture checks in a monitor mode and gradually enable enforcement to avoid disturbing the user population. Here is a list of some popular posture checks used by NAC customers:

- Check for a specific version of Windows updates and antivirus based on what is used by the desktop support team.
- Check all guests and contractors for any form of antivirus, and check that all updates are installed within a 30-day update timeframe.
- Identify a hidden certificate on laptops and desktops to validate they are corporate-issued hardware.
- Verify certain applications are installed and running. If missing, autoprovision the applications.
- Verify that the host firewall is enabled.

NAC Posture

Most NAC vendors will use a client or some form of scanning script to validate posture. For Cisco ISE, there is a client and clientless option. The clientless option does not require the installation of software, but it does require ActiveX or Java to be enabled. When executed, the ISE web agent installs the web agent files in a temporary directory on the client machine via ActiveX control or Java applet. The ISE clientless assessment runs a scan of the system and shows whether the host has passed or failed posture checks. The clientless assessment does not offer autoremediation, meaning that the end user must manually remediate any identified failures in posture. If the device passes the assessment process, that device is granted access to the network. The clientless option is designed for guests and contractors who do not want software installed on their system and periodically access the network.

The ISE client is a lightweight application that simplifies the posture-assessment process. The client quickly provides Cisco ISE the current posture of an asset and can either autoremediate or let the end user manually remediate any failed checks based on how the ISE posture check is configured. An example is having ISE autolaunch a Windows update session if a device is found to not have run a Windows update within a 30-day timeframe. The client can be deployed upon connection to the network or distributed as an installed application. For organizations using Cisco AnyConnect 4.0 for VPN, the ISE agent component is now built in to that VPN agent, removing the need for any additional software. The ISE agent is recommended for employees who will access the network regularly and required for automatically authorizing users based on system credentials known as single sign-on.

Architecting NAC

Architecting a NAC solution typically requires physical or virtual hardware to run the product, licenses to enable desired features, software to install on endpoints depending on how the solution functions, a understanding of your existing network infrastructure, and an idea of the number of devices that will be supported. Next, we walk through designing a Cisco ISE architecture. Most NAC vendors should have similar steps to design a NAC solution. Be prepared to answer the following questions the day you start evaluating NAC solutions. Usually a ballpark number is sufficient for many of these questions:

- Are you looking to only protect the LAN, VPN, and wireless or a combination of these?
- What is the timetable for completing the purchase and deployment of the NAC project?
- How many users are on the network? What parts of the network are they on during what time?
- How many devices are on the network?
- What are the expected endpoints to secure, including operating systems?
- What policies do you want to enforce for trusted devices?
- How would you like to segment off the network with the NAC technology?
- What are the model and code version of LAN, VPN, and wireless technology?
- Are there any regulations or compliance mandates that you are required to meet?

Cisco ISE can be run on a physical or virtual appliance, and functions can be centralized on one piece of hardware or distributed between different appliances. There are two different physical appliances, the 3415 and 3595, which support 5000 and 10,000 devices as a standalone appliance. Functions such as the administration, monitoring and policy service can be separated so that the ISE solution can scale to larger numbers. Table 9-2 shows how to select Cisco ISE hardware. Note that virtual hardware can be used in the same way as a 3415 and 3495 appliance as long as the virtual server's specifications are identical.

Table 9-2 *Selecting Cisco ISE Hardware*

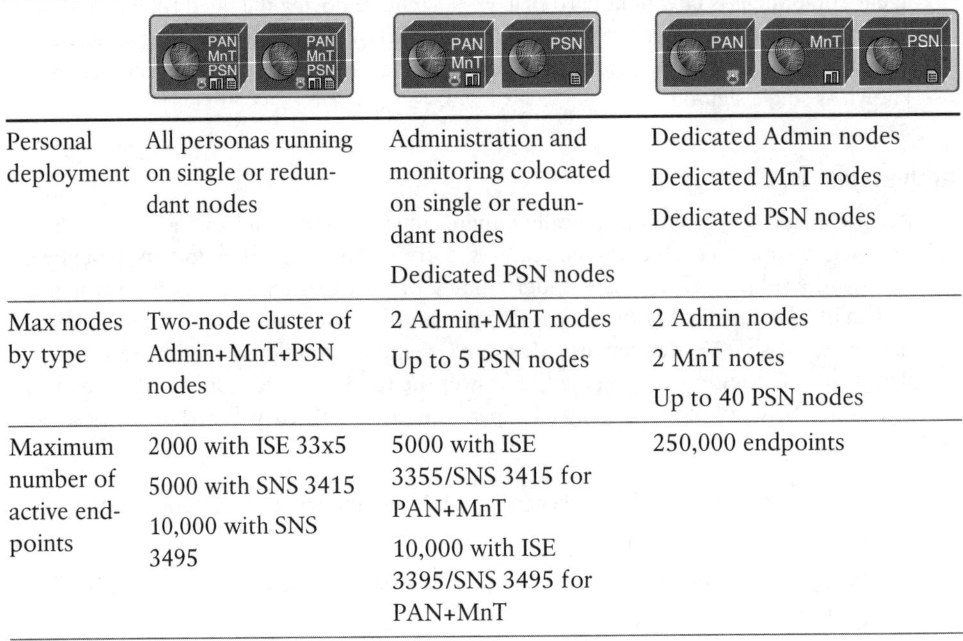

Personal deployment	All personas running on single or redundant nodes	Administration and monitoring colocated on single or redundant nodes Dedicated PSN nodes	Dedicated Admin nodes Dedicated MnT nodes Dedicated PSN nodes
Max nodes by type	Two-node cluster of Admin+MnT+PSN nodes	2 Admin+MnT nodes Up to 5 PSN nodes	2 Admin nodes 2 MnT notes Up to 40 PSN nodes
Maximum number of active endpoints	2000 with ISE 33x5 5000 with SNS 3415 10,000 with SNS 3495	5000 with ISE 3355/SNS 3415 for PAN+MnT 10,000 with ISE 3395/SNS 3495 for PAN+MnT	250,000 endpoints

Once hardware is selected, the next step is to select the proper licensing. ISE has three license options for a fully functional solution, and a mobility-only license for a wireless-only deployment. The licenses are based on concurrent devices, meaning that a license is consumed when a device is on the network and released when the device disconnects. Table 9-3 shows the license options for a full ISE deployment, and the last row shows the wireless-only option.

Table 9-3 *ISE and Wireless-Only License Options*

ISE License Packages	Perpetual/ Subscription (Terms Available)	ISE Functionality Covered	Notes
Base	Perpetual	Basic network access Guest management Link encryption (MACSec) TrustSec ISE application Programming interfaces	

Table 9-3 *continued*

ISE License Packages	Perpetual/ Subscription (Terms Available)	ISE Functionality Covered	Notes
Plus	Subscription (1, 3, or 5 years)	Bring your own device (BYOD) with built-in certificate authority services Profiling and feed services Endpoint protection service (EPS) Cisco pxGrid	Does not include Base services; a Base license is required to install the Plus license.
Apex	Subscription (1, 3, or 5 years)	Third-party mobile device management (MDM) Posture compliance	Does not include Base services; a Base license is required to install the Apex license. Note: When you use Cisco AnyConnect as the unified posture agent across wired, wireless, and VPN deployments, you need Cisco AnyConnect Apex user licenses in addition to Cisco ISE Apex licenses.
Mobility	Subscription (1, 3, or 5 years)	Combination of Base, Plus, and Apex for wireless and VPN endpoints	Cannot coexist on a Cisco Administration node with Base, Plus, or Apex licenses.

Licenses can be mixed depending on requirements. For example, a company with 500 employees may plan for 1000 or 1500 devices (because many people carry more than one IP-enabled device). That same company may have other devices to consider, such as VoIP phones and printers, which can increase the overall device count to 2000 to 3000 devices. In this case, the total device count that would consume a Base license is 3000 licenses, and users who need to be evaluated against the ISE policy may require 1000 to 1500 Apex. Note that if this were a wireless-only deployment, the license would just be the number of total devices because the Mobility license includes all level of licenses for wireless only. If a customer wants to move from a wireless-only to full ISE deployment, a conversion license must be acquired. Also note that Base licenses are a one-time purchase, whereas all other licenses are a subscription available for

1, 3, or 5 years. Plus and Apex licenses are stacked on top of Base licenses, meaning that you must have at least one Base license with any Plus or Apex. Our advice is this: Because Base is cheap, plan to use two to three times your user count plus all other devices and 20 percent growth to figure out your total number for Base. Align requirements for Plus and Apex to properly size those numbers. In this example, the licenses purchased would be 3000 Base licenses and 1500 Apex licenses.

After the hardware and licenses have been selected, the final step is to develop a design for the deployment. There are two common approaches to deploying ISE. The first is to use a centralized deployment where all ISE services are running on the same appliance. A second appliance can be used for high availability, replicating configurations between both appliances. All network devices (wireless, LAN, and VPN) report back to the primary ISE node for access control information. This includes devices spread across a site-to-site VPN, meaning that authentication data must be able to access the ISE solution from any location. For a centralized deployment, best practice is to place the ISE systems close to the existing authentication system because user authentication will most likely already be set up to be sent to that area when they connect to the network. If your organization has multiple authentication forests, meaning that multiple locations have their own authentication system, ISE can support multiple authentication domains. However, it might make sense to have a local ISE appliances depending on the size of the branch location, bandwidth between the primary and branch office, and available budget. Figure 9-19 shows a high-level overview of this design.

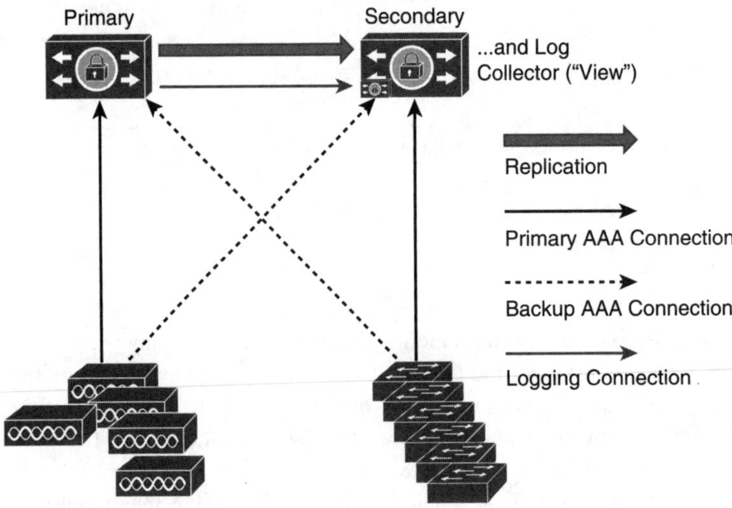

Figure 9-19 *Centralized ISE Deployment*

The other common ISE deployment is distributing functions across different ISE appliances. The administration and monitoring functions are separate from the policy server (PSN) because network devices communicate directly with a PSN. This is ideal for scaling beyond the capabilities of a centralized deployment, accommodating for large branch offices that use local authentication and increased high availability. This deployment can scale even larger if the monitoring and administration functions are separated to allow up to 500,000 devices. Figure 9-20 shows a common distributed ISE deployment separating the PSN functionality for three different locations while the administration and monitoring is run from the same ISE appliance.

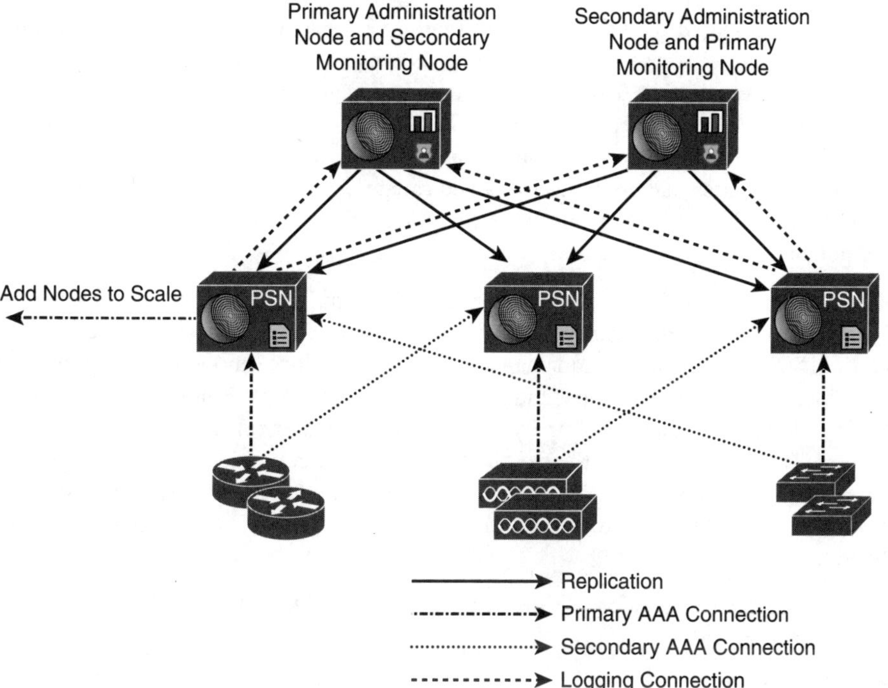

Figure 9-20 *Distributed ISE Deployment*

Regardless of the manufacturer, a NAC solution installation requires a lot of upfront services. Once the NAC solution is put in place, adding more control points is usually simple because the security policies are already in place. For 802.1X-based NAC solutions like Cisco ISE, it is recommended to develop device templates containing the required 802.1X code needed to enable network devices. Using templates will reduce the chance of misconfiguring the required configuration and speed up the deployment of the ISE solution. Best practice is to use a centralized network management utility for this purpose. We also highly recommend using a contractor to assist with a NAC deployment if budget permits.

NAC is important for controlling who and what accesses the network, but it has a limited view of what devices are doing after they are granted access to the network. Next, we look at security technology that provides on-network protection.

Web Proxies

Once users are granted access to the network, most likely they will attempt to interact with the Internet using network browsers and e-mail. Permitting access to the Internet introduces a lot of risk to the organization, and therefore protection must be put in place to prevent a breach from occurring. The first layer of protection for web defenses is enabling filtering of potentially high-risk or inappropriate web sources. Content filtering is usually provided through a web proxy or application layer firewall that has a continuously updated feed of the current Internet environment. That feed can include categorizing websites based on their content or applying a reputation score based on associated risks and other data (such as threat intelligence about what other customers are seeing when they access that web source). Categories that organizations tend to block include adult material, gambling, hacking, and hate. Note that tuning may be needed for websites that are part of blocked category but deemed safe. A common example is blocking gambling but permitting lottery websites that showcase local lottery numbers.

Most web proxies have security features that evaluate traffic for threats. You learned about the IronPort Web Security Appliance (WSA) in Chapter 6, which offers content filtering, reputation security, scanning for threats with multiple antivirus engines, outbreak filters, day-zero protection, and a Layer 4 botnet monitor. Features are licensed for a specific term, such as 1, 3, or 5 years. The goal is to layer protection so that if one engine fails to detect a threat, the next layer of security can provide a different type analysis and hopefully prevent the attack. WSA also includes Cisco Advanced Malware Protection (AMP) breach detection as an additional license. We cover AMP later in this chapter.

Let's look deeper at reputation security because it is a valuable first layer of web protection.

Reputation Security

Reputation security is becoming a critical feature for proxy services. Many attacks are launched from Internet-based sources that are provisioned purely for malicious intentions. These malicious sources can be identified and blocked before permitting users access to those sources, thus stopping an attack before it can occur. For example, if a website claims to be for banking, most likely most organizations will permit this traffic through a content filter. If a banking website is found to have been on the Internet for only a few hours and is hosted from a shared service provider in a foreign country, however, it is most likely not a bank and should be blocked. Another example is that a website is a bank, but it has recently been breached and is being used as a launch pad for deploying ransomware. Vendors seeing multiple attacks from a single source could identify this threat if the proper data correlation is put in place, protecting future users from accessing the recent high-risk banking website. The benefit of stopping threats at this point of the attack is that the connection is dropped before traffic is introduced, saving process resources on the vendor's product that you can use to evaluate other possible risks and prevent the attack from occurring before it can be launched. This is key because your security defenses may not have the technology to block the attack if it is launched against your users. Reputation security blocks the attack before it can launch.

Note Reputation security is not 100 percent effective, but it is a great first layer of security defense. Detecting reputation for a legitimate but compromised site can be difficult unless there is a dramatic change in traffic seen from that source.

You can test the concept of reputation security by going to http://www.ihaveabadreputation.com. This website is rated as a malicious site, but it will not harm your system. The purpose is to see whether your existing web security defenses include reputation security capabilities. If they do not, the concept is that this website could have potentially launched an attack against the user accessing it. You will see a red ghost and warning message if this happens, as shown in Figure 9-21.

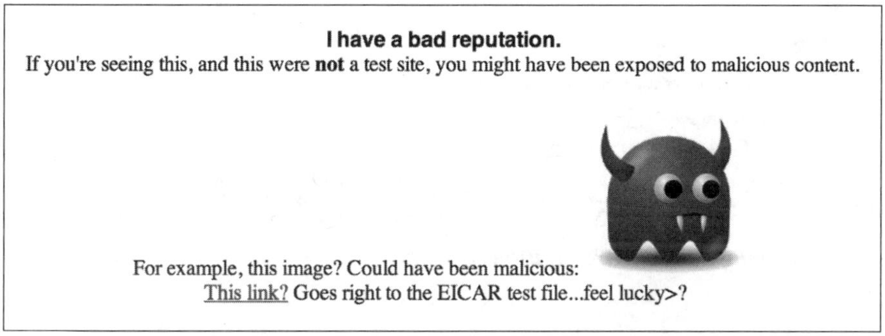

I have a bad reputation.
If you're seeing this, and this were **not** a test site, you might have been exposed to malicious content.

For example, this image? Could have been malicious:
This link? Goes right to the EICAR test file...feel lucky>?

Figure 9-21 *Example of ihaveabadreputation.com Without Reputation Security*

If you have reputation security enabled, it should block this website. Figure 9-22 shows Cisco WSA blocking the ihaveabadreputation.com website base on a –9.5 reputation (along with other details on why this website was blocked). Cisco shares reputation security through most of the available security products that have web capabilities, meaning that a different product may have a different-looking warning message when blocking this website, but the back-end technology is based on the same security research.

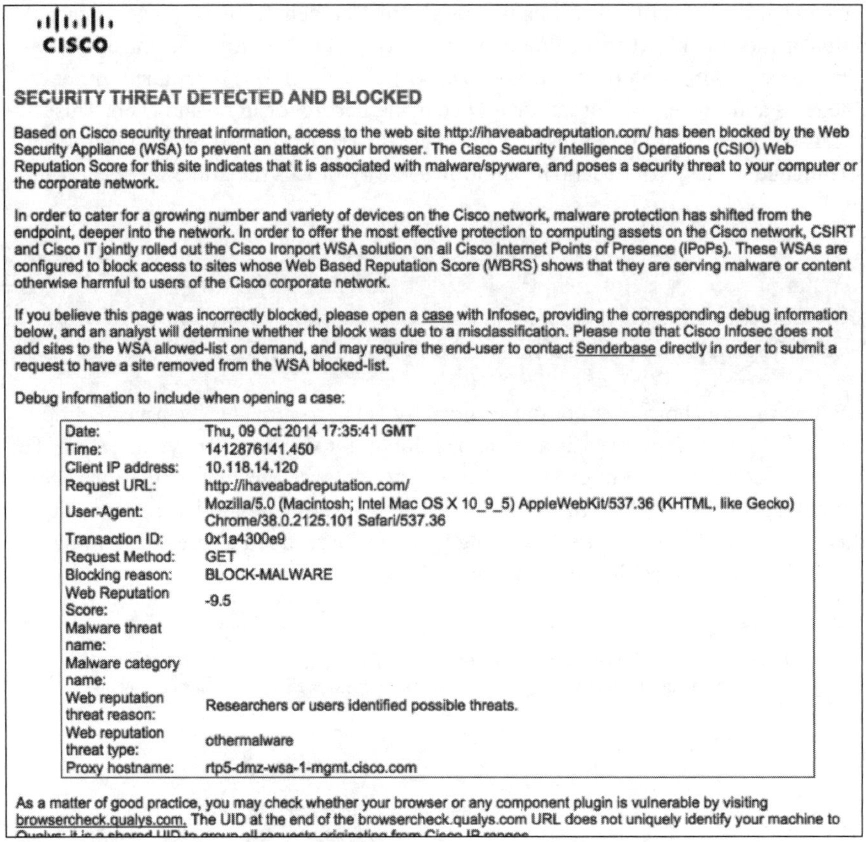

cisco

SECURITY THREAT DETECTED AND BLOCKED

Based on Cisco security threat information, access to the web site http://ihaveabadreputation.com/ has been blocked by the Web Security Appliance (WSA) to prevent an attack on your browser. The Cisco Security Intelligence Operations (CSIO) Web Reputation Score for this site indicates that it is associated with malware/spyware, and poses a security threat to your computer or the corporate network.

In order to cater for a growing number and variety of devices on the Cisco network, malware protection has shifted from the endpoint, deeper into the network. In order to offer the most effective protection to computing assets on the Cisco network, CSIRT and Cisco IT jointly rolled out the Cisco Ironport WSA solution on all Cisco Internet Points of Presence (IPoPs). These WSAs are configured to block access to sites whose Web Based Reputation Score (WBRS) shows that they are serving malware or content otherwise harmful to users of the Cisco corporate network.

If you believe this page was incorrectly blocked, please open a case with Infosec, providing the corresponding debug information below, and an analyst will determine whether the block was due to a misclassification. Please note that Cisco Infosec does not add sites to the WSA allowed-list on demand, and may require the end-user to contact Senderbase directly in order to submit a request to have a site removed from the WSA blocked-list.

Debug information to include when opening a case:

Date:	Thu, 09 Oct 2014 17:35:41 GMT
Time:	1412876141.450
Client IP address:	10.118.14.120
Request URL:	http://ihaveabadreputation.com/
User-Agent:	Mozilla/5.0 (Macintosh; Intel Mac OS X 10_9_5) AppleWebKit/537.36 (KHTML, like Gecko) Chrome/38.0.2125.101 Safari/537.36
Transaction ID:	0x1a4300e9
Request Method:	GET
Blocking reason:	BLOCK-MALWARE
Web Reputation Score:	-9.5
Malware threat name:	
Malware category name:	
Web reputation threat reason:	Researchers or users identified possible threats.
Web reputation threat type:	othermalware
Proxy hostname:	rtp5-dmz-wsa-1-mgmt.cisco.com

As a matter of good practice, you may check whether your browser or any component plugin is vulnerable by visiting browsercheck.qualys.com. The UID at the end of the browsercheck.qualys.com URL does not uniquely identify your machine to

Figure 9-22 *Blocking ihaveabadreputation.com*

Proxy Architecture

When architecting a web proxy, you need to decide how traffic should be directed through the proxy. The most common approach is to redirect traffic that enters a gateway firewall through the proxy using Web Cache Communication Protocol (WCCP). This forces all user traffic through the proxy without having to modify the endpoints. This can be configured to include remote users who have traffic passed through the firewall over a VPN tunnel, meaning that traffic would terminate on the DMZ network, hit the perimeter firewall, and route to the proxy like all other internal traffic that enters and leaves the network. Figure 9-23 shows the traffic from a Cisco ASAx series firewall configured to redirect traffic to Cisco WSA using WCCP.

A less-popular approach is to configure endpoint browsers to route traffic to the proxy to access the Internet. This approach, also known as an explicit proxy, can be enabled using a desktop management tool that only desktop administrators can disable or a setting that end users can add to their Internet browser settings. The problem with this approach is that end users could use other browsers or disable the proxy inside the browser settings unless controls are put into place to only permit traffic to the Internet using the approved explicit proxy.

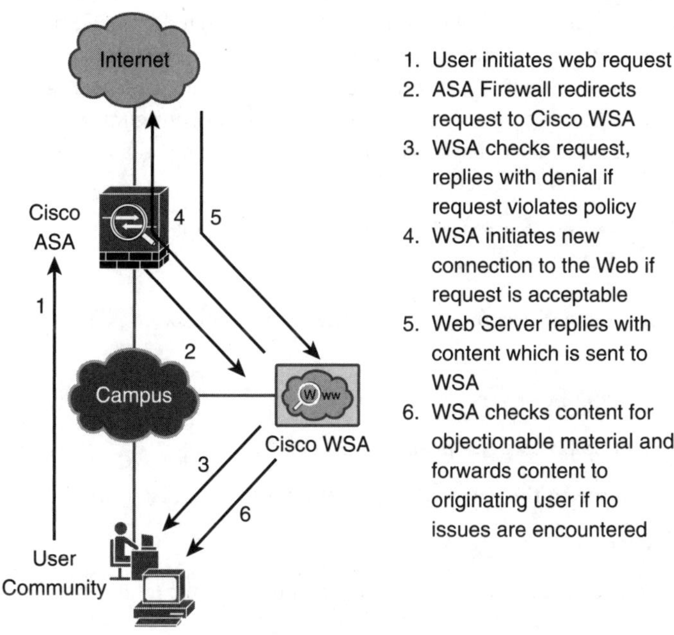

Figure 9-23 *Logical Traffic Flow Between Firewall and WSA*

It is important to be aware that a web proxy can only view Internet-bound traffic such as HTTP, HTTPS, and FTP. Nonstandard Internet ports will not be evaluated by this technology. One workaround is to lock down other ports using a firewall or consider solutions that are application aware, such as an application layer firewall to work with the proxy to protect all ports and protocols.

Many administrators leverage authentication to the web proxy to control which web servers are permitted to the user using the proxy. This is not NAC because the systems accessing the proxy are permitted network resources regardless of how they auth enticate to the proxy, but controls can be put in place to prevent or limit Internet-bound traffic.

For example, all user groups except administrators and HR are denied any website classified as pornography. Authentication is also used to monitor usernames rather than IP addresses, making it easier to track people in the proxy reporting tools.

Most web proxy security features are enabled using the appliance's management graphical user interface (GUI), which is connected to a management port. However, some other features may require additional network resources. For example, WSA offers a Layer 4 botnet scanner that requires a separate SPAN port that it can monitor for botnet phone-home communication. Some vendor web proxies may separate security features with different hardware platforms or offer a centralized manager when deploying multiple proxies. Multiple Cisco WSA systems can be managed by an M-Series management platform. A best practice is to work with the vendor of choice to identify all hardware required to centrally manage your web proxy deployment so that all configuration and reporting is unified. Also make sure that the management platform is capable of exporting logs to the SOC centralized collection solution.

Here is a summary of the questions that you should answer before deploying a web proxy:

- What types of websites (categories) does your organization want to block and monitor?
- Are there file types, protocols, or other requirements that must be controlled?
- Do you need to support SSL/TLS decryption for HTTPS traffic?
- Should the proxy be routed to the gateway or a configuration on host systems?
- Will you use a physical or virtual appliance?
- Will you need a centralized manager when deploying and managing multiple proxies?
- What additional security features do you need (antivirus, outbreak controls, data-loss detection, day-zero protection, on-network threat scanning, and so on)?
- Can an existing tool or consolidated offering meet the web proxy requirements?
- Do you want to integrate authentication and enforce user login to access the Internet?
- Do you need high availability, and should the proxy fail open or closed?
- Are there compliance requirements or regulations that must be met that align with this project?

Web proxies are a good first layer for protecting users while they are on the network accessing the Internet. If traffic connects through the proxy, the next layer of security should be some form of intrusion detection system (IDS) or intrusion prevention system (IPS).

Intrusion Detection/Prevention

Detecting threats is usually accomplished using a signature- or behavior-based security solution. Chapter 6 introduced the concept of IDS and IPS. In summary, IDS solutions can monitor for threats, and an IPS can monitor and take action against attacks. An IPS must be deployed inline; otherwise, the system will be viewing a copy of traffic and therefore can only be an IDS. Threats are detected, depending on the vendor's features, using a blend of threat signatures, abnormal behavior detection, and threat intelligence feeds. Signature and abnormal behavior detection can be defined as the following:

- **Signature-based detection:** A signature is a known attack pattern, meaning a threat that has been seen before and documented. Signature-based detection compares traffic, files, or behavior against a known list of attack signatures. If the matching signature is not enabled for an attack or the attack is unknown, that attack will bypass a signature-based security solution. Typically, signatures are published and shared between different parties to improve the overall industry's ability to block a known attack.
- **Statistical anomaly-based detection:** Statistical detection, also known as behavior-based detection, looks for abnormal behavior from network trends. Examples include alarming when spikes in bandwidth are seen, unusual ports are being used, shifting traffic patterns at unusual hours, and so on. Statistical detection is not always accurate and requires proper tuning to avoid either being bombarded with false alarms or not being sensitive enough to detect events of interest.

IDS IPS Architecture

You have a few options for deploying an IDS: placing the sensor off of a SPAN port, placing an IDS tap on a network segment, putting the appliance inline with traffic, or a combination of these options. For an IPS or IDS to monitor for security events, it must be able to see the traffic. Visibility requirements vary between solutions, so at a minimum, the IPS/IDS must have network reachability to a system to include it in its analytics. Figure 9-24 shows some diagrams that display common types of IPS and IDS deployments.

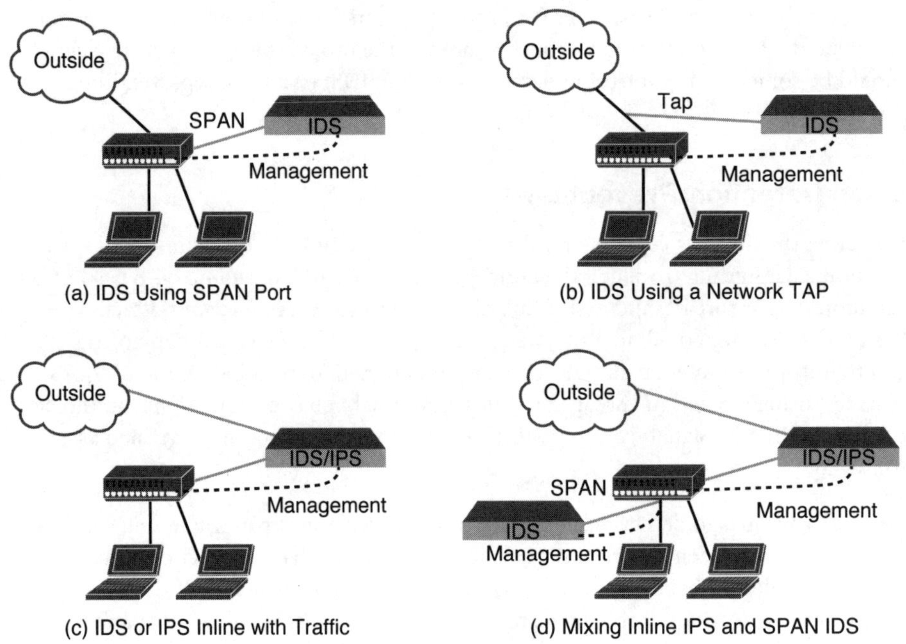

Figure 9-24 *Common IDS/IPS Deployment Types*

Evaluating IDS IPS Technology

When evaluating an IDS or IPS for your SOC architecture, consider the following factors:

- **What you are trying to protect with the IDS/IPS:** The simple answer would be everything on the network. However, as stated earlier, an IPS can only evaluate what it can see. In most cases, you will be considering a security checkpoint behind or integrated with your perimeter gateway, inside or behind your data center perimeter, and inside any sensitive network segment, including protecting the core network. An example may be the requirement for five monitoring taps that will sit at the gateway, data center, inside the guest network, inside the internal network, and inside a development network.
- **Determine your performance requirements:** This will impact the size of IDS/IPS the vendor will position for your SOC. IDS/IPS in general are based on throughput numbers, but many factors can take away from the promised performance. For example, an IPS may be able to perform at a very high rate doing a specific function, but as other features are enabled, more signatures are used, and large amounts of traffic hit it, it might slow down under expected throughput numbers. There are ways to improve performance, such as tuning the IDS/IPS to only examine necessary traffic, as covered earlier in this chapter. The proper balance of enabling features and tuning should bring your performance to the vendor's promised rate. Our recommendation is this: For perimeter IPS deployments, consider your ISP speed and add future growth to your number. For internal network throughput,

consider the wire speed and types of traffic that will be inspected. Include in your sizing exercise room for extra events due to an attack, because that is when you will most likely experience the highest performance impact.

- **How hands-on will you be?** There are two types of IPS markets catering to two types of customers. The first customer is buying an IPS to secure the network, but they are not planning to spend time on a daily basis looking through logs, tracking down attacks, tuning the system, and so on. Their goal is to have the IPS automatically update and run so that they can set it and forget it unless it identifies a substantial attack they should investigate. The solution for this is an *IPS light* offering that has few settings and limited tuning options. An example of this type of IDS/IDS is Cisco's Meraki MX series firewall, which includes an IPS light feature. Events can be exported to the SOC, but the threat data is limited because IPS light offerings tend to have a subset of the signatures and capabilities found in an enterprise IPS offerings.

The other IPS market is for most SOC environments. The requirements are to be feature rich and a tool that will be accessed often to investigate different events. This requires an enterprise-level IPS that stores more signatures than can be enabled, has options for viewing data at a high level all the way down to the packet level, and capable of scaling to large performance numbers with all features enabled. Enterprise IPS offerings require more work to install and maintain, but in return provide much more valuable data than a light IPS.

IPS light features are ideal for enabling within an existing security product to gain additional visibility or are okay for small remote offices. If budget permits, a SOC architect should always consider an enterprise IPS whenever designing security for a SOC network.

- **What form factor?** Do you need a dedicated appliance, or can this be a function within another security offering? If it is protecting the data center, can a virtualized appliance meet the needs? Note that your performance requirements may impact the available form factors. Typically, dedicated IPS hardware can outperform integrated IPS offerings.

- **What are your management and reporting requirements?** What type of management interface is ideal for your team? Each vendor will have a different approach to what is available to tune and view from the management interface. Things to consider are how well the data is presented, how easy is it to drill into the data, what actions are available on captured events, reporting options, role-based access control options, and tuning and data-export options. This question also relates back to how hands on your team will be with the solution. A feature-rich management product might not make sense for an environment that does not plan to access the management interface often.

- **Support and coverage:** What type of installation and ongoing support do you need for your solution? Some SOCs may not have staff capable of deploying the technology and so might need services from the vendor or a solution provider to perform the installation work. Another important factor is the ongoing support for hardware and software. Do you need separate support contracts, and what type of support does it give you? Do you need configuration help or just support when something is not working?

Tuning IDS/IPS

An IDS/IPS, by default, can be useful, but it must be tuned to see its full potential. Most default deployments include downloading a general list of signatures and enabling basic logging that will alert administrators when events are triggered. It is recommended to first let the default configuration run for at least 24 hours and monitor what events are triggered. Most enterprise IPS solutions offer actions that can be taken on events, such as blacklisting (blocking the source) or whitelisting (permitting and not alarming on any future events from the source). Figure 9-25 shows blacklist and whitelist options for an IP seen by Cisco FirePOWER.

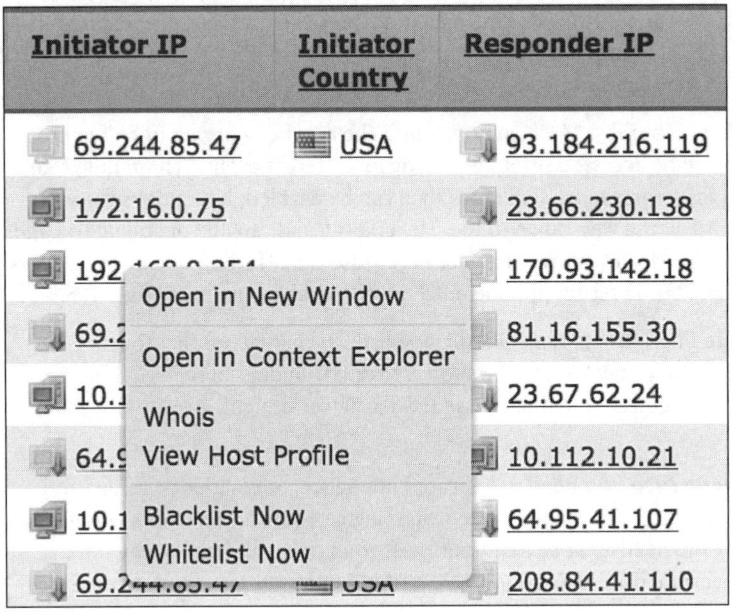

Figure 9-25 *Blacklist Whitelist Example*

The next steps for tuning the IPS is to view the rules that are enabled and verify whether protection is enabled for all devices and applications seen on your network and what is potentially not on your network. Turning off unnecessary signatures will improve performance, but it should be done after running the IPS for a good length of time and verifying that logs are not being generated for those signatures. Most vendor default signature categories include the majority of common threats; however, that does not mean they will enable everything needed to protect your environment. It is recommended to view what categories of signatures are enabled and search other categories that are not enabled for devices that exist within your network. Once new signatures are found that are not enabled, make sure to enable those in monitor-only mode and verify that they are being properly triggered before considering elevating those signatures with a block capability.

Be aware that most enterprise IPS offerings have more signatures than the vendor will recommend to enable, meaning that enabling everything could dramatically negatively impact performance of the security solution. Most vendors will probably suggest enabling a single signature category to verify whether your organization needs those signatures enabled and turning off what is not needed before moving to another signature category. A more effective approach is to obtain an asset list and work with the vendor or trusted consultant to verify that the proper signatures are enabled versus an enable-and-tune approach.

Some IPS offerings include the ability to use local vulnerability scanning or import vulnerability scans from other products such as Tenable's Nessus vulnerability scanner. This data is used to identify vulnerabilities within the organization that the IPS should enable protection for. Vulnerabilities are anything from a buffer overflow vulnerability on a server to a host having an out-of-date software package. Figure 9-26 shows a Cisco FirePOWER's built-in vulnerability scanner identifying multiple vulnerabilities on various types of systems. This data is used to improve the IDS/IPS capabilities by helping the system tune the signatures to defend against all identified vulnerabilities.

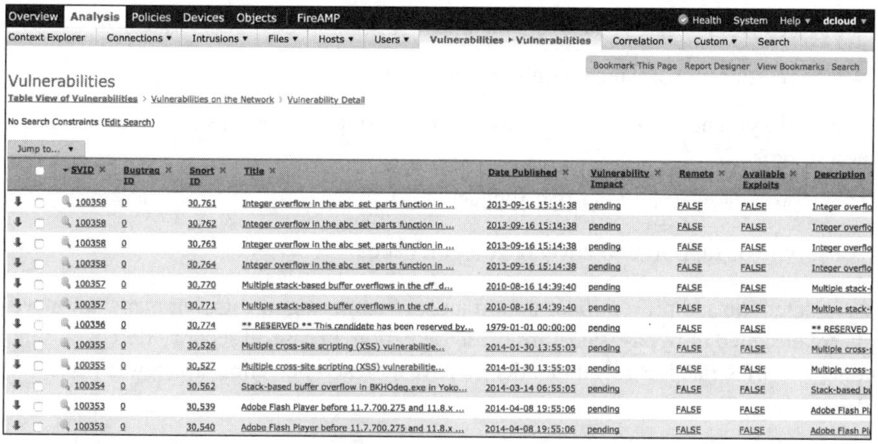

SVID	Bugtraq ID	Snort ID	Title	Date Published	Vulnerability Impact	Remote	Available Exploits	Description
100358	0	30,761	Integer overflow in the abc_set_parts function in ...	2013-09-16 15:14:38	pending	FALSE	FALSE	Integer overflo
100358	0	30,762	Integer overflow in the abc_set_parts function in ...	2013-09-16 15:14:38	pending	FALSE	FALSE	Integer overflo
100358	0	30,763	Integer overflow in the abc_set_parts function in ...	2013-09-16 15:14:38	pending	FALSE	FALSE	Integer overflo
100358	0	30,764	Integer overflow in the abc_set_parts function in ...	2013-09-16 15:14:38	pending	FALSE	FALSE	Integer overflo
100357	0	30,770	Multiple stack-based buffer overflows in the cff_d...	2010-08-16 14:39:40	pending	FALSE	FALSE	Multiple stack-
100357	0	30,771	Multiple stack-based buffer overflows in the cff_d...	2010-08-16 14:39:40	pending	FALSE	FALSE	Multiple stack-
100356	0	30,774	** RESERVED ** This candidate has been reserved by...	1979-01-01 00:00:00	pending	FALSE	FALSE	** RESERVED
100355	0	30,526	Multiple cross-site scripting (XSS) vulnerabilitie...	2014-01-30 13:55:03	pending	FALSE	FALSE	Multiple cross-
100355	0	30,527	Multiple cross-site scripting (XSS) vulnerabilitie...	2014-01-30 13:55:03	pending	FALSE	FALSE	Multiple cross-
100354	0	30,562	Stack-based buffer overflow in BKHOdeq.exe in Yoko...	2014-03-14 06:55:05	pending	FALSE	FALSE	Stack-based bu
100353	0	30,539	Adobe Flash Player before 11.7.700.275 and 11.8.x ...	2014-04-08 19:55:06	pending	FALSE	FALSE	Adobe Flash Pl
100353	0	30,540	Adobe Flash Player before 11.7.700.275 and 11.8.x ...	2014-04-08 19:55:06	pending	FALSE	FALSE	Adobe Flash Pl

Figure 9-26 *Cisco FirePOWER Vulnerability Scanner*

Tuning can be a very labor-intensive process; however, it is important to continuously do it to improve the capabilities of the IDS/IPS. One value Cisco FirePOWER offers is the ability to automate many of the tuning recommendations covered in this chapter using FireSIGHT recommendations. This feature self-tunes based on what is seen by a built-in vulnerability scanner and application-visibility function. FireSIGHT will autodisable or recommend to disable any signature that is enabled for assets not found on the network and will auto-enable or recommend to enable any signature that is not enabled for an identified risk or asset that does not have protection. Figure 9-27 shows a few rules found within FirePOWER that are configured to drop events; however, FireSIGHT recommendations suggest to fully enable these rules by showing a green arrow next to the rule. By clicking the radar circle icon above these rules, you gain the ability to enable all recommendations if the administrator determines this is the best course of action.

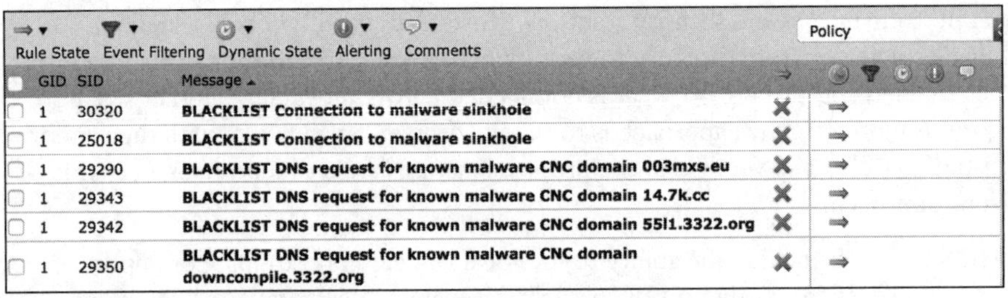

Rule State | Event Filtering | Dynamic State | Alerting | Comments | Policy

GID	SID	Message
1	30320	BLACKLIST Connection to malware sinkhole
1	25018	BLACKLIST Connection to malware sinkhole
1	29290	BLACKLIST DNS request for known malware CNC domain 003mxs.eu
1	29343	BLACKLIST DNS request for known malware CNC domain 14.7k.cc
1	29342	BLACKLIST DNS request for known malware CNC domain 55l1.3322.org
1	29350	BLACKLIST DNS request for known malware CNC domain downcompile.3322.org

Figure 9-27 *FireSIGHT Recommendations Example*

Here is a summary of the questions you should answer before deploying an IDS or IPS solution:

- What type of traffic do you want to inspect?
- Do you need to decrypt SSL traffic?
- Is this a capability that you can enable on an existing or consolidated tool?
- What are your performance requirements?
- Where do you need detection points (the network perimeter, inside the data center, and so on)?
- How feature rich should the IDS/IPS be?
- What type of support and coverage do you need?

Intrusion detection and prevention is important for identifying threats, but many advanced threats are designed to bypass signature-based detection. In case all security defenses, including your IPS, fail, it is recommended to have a breach-detection strategy in place.

Breach Detection

This chapter has covered many security technologies that all help reduce the risk of being compromised. Even with all these technologies enabled, you are still at risk of being breached. Breach detection was introduced in Chapter 6 as a tool designed to monitor for threats that have bypassed all your security checkpoints. Breach detection is not designed to replace antivirus or IDS/IPS, because those technologies are targeting known attacks using different techniques than what breach detection uses to identify unknown threats.

Breach-detection technologies tend to include one or more of the following techniques:

- Malware identification using signatures/behavior analysis
- Network traffic analysis of content, network flows, and other trends
- Using sandboxes that can mimic real internal devices
- Browser emulation
- Reputation security and threat intelligence

Let's look at some examples of breach-detection techniques and how they are designed within a SOC environment.

Honeypots

Security tools can use different approaches to provide breach-detection solutions. One classic method is to use a honeypot. The concept is to place on the network a computer, piece of data, or network segment that appears to be part of the real network, but is isolated/monitored, as a trap. When attackers breach a network, the ideal situation is that they access the honeypot believing it is something of value but alert the real network of the intrusion. The key to the success of a honeypot is the bait used to lure in malicious parties.

There are many variations of the honeypot concept; however, they can be broken down into two deployment methods:

- The first is a network honeypot that is designed to be part of the network defense strategy, meaning it is used to identify threats that have bypassed other security products.
- The second type of honeypot is designed for monitoring, meaning that an attacker places a system on an open network that people connect to and that is monitored, similar to a man-in-the-middle attack.

An example of a monitor honeypot (also known as a rogue access point) is placing a free wireless network access point in a public area with the hope that somebody will use it to access sensitive data, such as logging in to e-mail. When a victim connects to the wireless access point, all traffic is monitored and stored by the attacker.

There are other variations of honeypot techniques, such as honey clients and interactive honeypots, but the general principle is the same for all types of honeypots.

If the SOC architect considers using honeypots, the deployment strategy will depend on the type of honeypot. File honeypots can be given an interesting name, such as Passwords or Credit_Records, and placed on sensitive systems. This might seem silly, but remember that attackers need a lot of time and effort to locate and access sensitive systems. The hope is that the attacker will believe he has reached his goal and not be as cautious about what he is going to take, or that the attacker is using an automated tool that will take any file located in the breached computer. Network-based honeypots could either be one or more vulnerable systems placed on different network segments or a fake network segment that is made vulnerable yet appears to be secured and important. All honeypots should be monitored by a centralized system that is tuned to avoid false positives.

Honeypots can be a decent breach-detection strategy if used properly, but there are many reasons why an attacker could possibly not trigger a honeypot (for example, the bait was not good enough, the attacker was targeting other systems, the coverage area of a honeypot is limited, or false negatives).

Sandboxes

Another form of breach detection is using a sandbox to examine suspicious data. A sandbox by itself is an isolated computing environment that you can use to test things without impacting the surrounding networks. Security companies have combined sandbox technology with threat analytics to create tools that can test traffic in a sandbox and monitor behavior for malicious intent. If the malware executes in the sandbox environment, alarms are triggered, and all associated traffic is flagged to determine whether there has been a breach (and future communications are stopped with the source that sent the malicious traffic).

The most common forms of sandbox-based breach-detection products are appliances that are placed in similar locations as IDS/IPS appliances (gateway, data center, attached to sensitive networkers) or a cloud service that remotely tests traffic sent from a local system. When considering a sandbox for breach detection, it is important to determine whether it will only monitor for threats or if there are enforcement features included. Alarming capabilities are absolutely critical, as are the details of the attack, including tracking anything that could potentially already be inside the network. Another important feature is the ability to prevent the attack from happening again through the use of developing new attack signatures or behavior detection on existing security products. This can prove even more valuable if these new detection capabilities are shared with other customers as a threat intelligence to improve the effectiveness of the sandbox detection capabilities for the product's user community.

Sandbox breach detection can be very effective, but it does have some weaknesses. When the technology was first introduced, sandbox breach detection caught the majority of malware that crossed its path. Hackers realized that their malware was getting blocked and purchased popular sandbox detection technologies for reverse engineering and research purposes. Many versions of malware seen today have sandbox detection capabilities, such as examining processes to see whether they are in a virtual environment before running, delaying execution longer than most sandboxes will examine data, only launching on specific systems versus launching on the first vulnerable system found, and so on. Sandboxes are also a point-in-time technology, meaning that if traffic is let through, it is on the network regardless of whether the sandbox later flags it as being malicious. This is trouble if a file spreads or changes after the sandbox lets it through and later identifies it as malicious, because administrators would have to figure out all actions taken by the malware on their own that followed the sandbox permitting the file. Figure 9-28 shows how malware could potentially bypass sandbox detection.

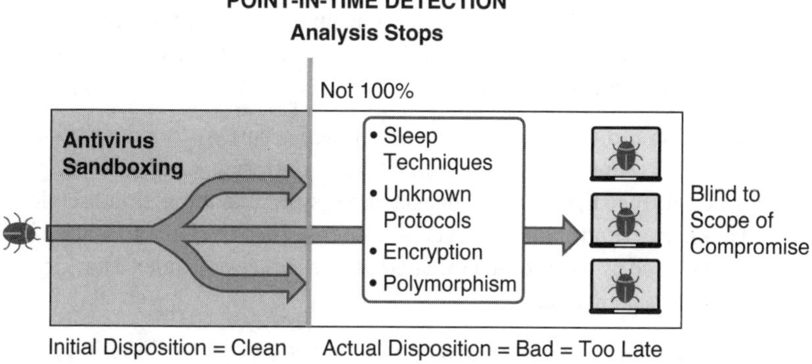

Figure 9-28 *Bypassing Sandbox Detection*

Combining network sandboxing with other security technologies can mitigate weaknesses in network sandbox detection tools. An example is how Cisco Advanced Malware Protection (AMP) stores records using a hash of all files evaluated by AMP. If a threat is identified, AMP leverages application firewall visibility to go back in time and track how the file was introduced to the network (and track anybody who is associated with the breach). This is known as *retrospective security* (see Figure 9-29).

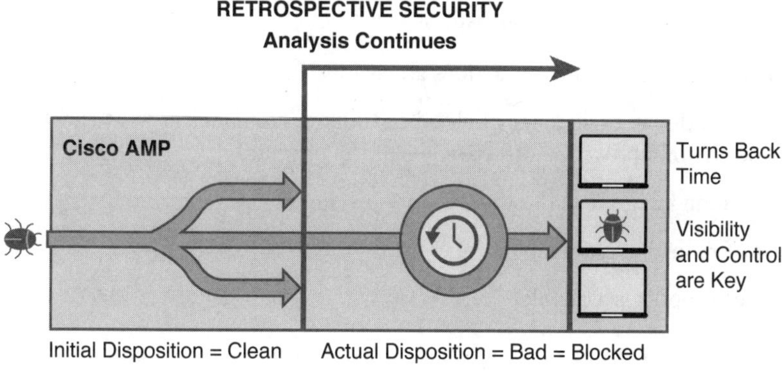

Figure 9-29 *Retrospective Security Concept Diagram*

Another way to fill the gaps in sandbox technology is to monitor endpoints to track behavior of traffic that has passed the network sandbox. Let's look at endpoint breach-detection capabilities.

Endpoint Breach Detection

A common breach-detection tactic is to install an application on endpoints that monitors all system processes and files to determine unusual behavior associated with unknown malware. Endpoint monitoring can also include features like application whitelisting that help improve security controls. The key is that the endpoint client has the intelligence to determine independently that there is a threat and be able to respond regardless of the endpoint state. Many attacks attempt to modify privileged level areas of the system, including the system's boot process.

Endpoint breach detection can come as part of a host-based security product suite or operate as an independent client depending on the vendor's offering. Configuration profiles are usually pushed to the clients from a management system that is a cloud service or physical/virtual appliance. Endpoint clients could send up files or characteristics of files in a thinner format such as hash to be evaluated against other customer data, cloud-based analytics, and threat intelligence.

Key questions to consider when evaluating endpoint breach-detection technologies include the following:

- What is the required space and process cycles to run the agent on an endpoint?
- What endpoint types are supported, and to what degree of support?
- How are the endpoints managed?
- How is the solution priced out?
- What capabilities beyond what exist within the current detection technologies and standard antivirus does the solution provide?
- What remediation and alerting is available?
- How far back are files and process actions archived?
- Do any external threat intelligence or cloud capabilities complement what checks are done locally to improve the effectiveness of the product?
- Does the solution integrate with other security products?
- What type of reporting is available?
- What level of support is available?

Endpoint breach detection is great for understanding the environment for endpoints; however, it is blind to traffic outside the endpoint. Many endpoint breach-detection vendors include integration with network offerings that together provide a network-wide monitoring solution. An example is Cisco AMP for Network and Endpoint combined to provide monitoring files as they cross the network and what they do once they access a endpoint. If a threat is found, the network manager can push out an alert to all endpoints to clean all files associated with the newly identified threat. AMP for Endpoint could also identify a threat and alert AMP for Network to identify any other system, including those without the AMP agent, vulnerable to the threat and to add preventive measures to block future access to the newly identified threat. Figure 9-30 shows the AMP for Network identifying multiple endpoints that have been identified with the infection. Note that the Clean button would trigger any system with the AMP for Endpoint agent to automatically remove this file.

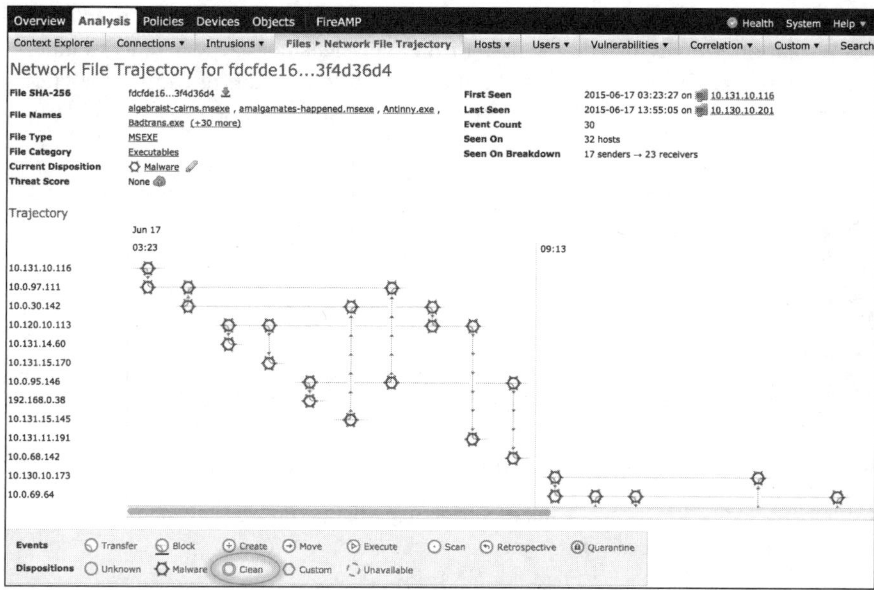

Figure 9-30 *AMP for Network Identifying Threats on Endpoints*

Clicking the first user 10.131.10.116 in Figure 9-30 shows the details of the file conspicuously-postpone.msexe; it was downloaded from 10.0.97.11 at 3:23:37 on 6/17/2015 using a web browser, as shown in Figure 9-31.

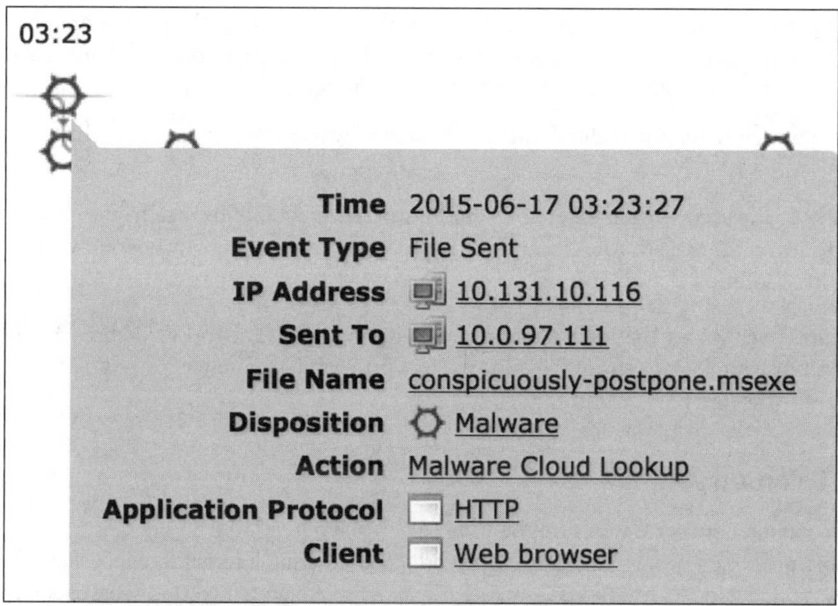

Figure 9-31 *AMP for Network Identifying Threats on Endpoints*

Figure 9-32 shows details of a malicious file that was quarantined by the Cisco AMP for Endpoint solution. Details include the hash of the file, filename, size, where it attempted to install, and so on. The file is requested to be pulled to the cloud for further analytics and for other actions, such as blocking, restoring, whitelisting, and so on.

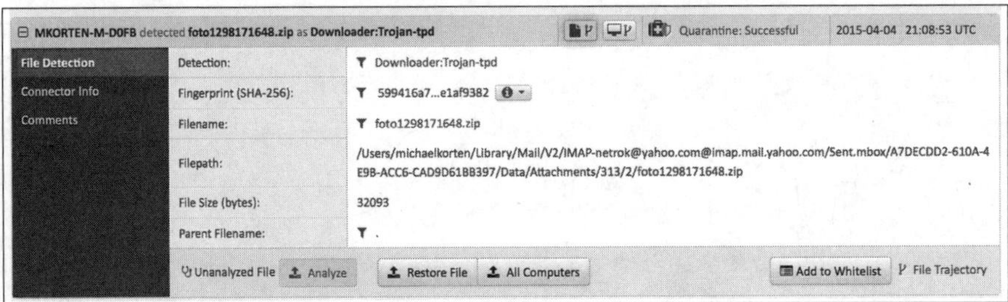

Figure 9-32 *Cisco AMP for Endpoint Example*

Let's summarize some key points when determining what is the best breach-detection technology for your organization:

- Breach detection can be network or endpoint based. Identify all supported network and endpoint devices that are needed to support your organization.
- Tune all breach-detection products to avoid false positives and true negatives.
- Verify whether you need to monitor only or both monitor and enforcement for stopping breaches.
- Best practice is to include retrospective security to identify how the breach first entered the network, instead of just alarming to the first system found and not knowing how to track whether other systems are infected.
- Some breach-detection technologies are limited in where they can monitor for threats.
- Marketing-leading breach-detection solutions offer threat intelligence from other customers and research to expand the knowledge of possible threats beyond what the local solution is aware of.

One security technology that offers significant value, including network-wide breach detection is using telemetry from the existing network, wireless, and virtualized network equipment for security analytics.

Network Telemetry

Data in common network devices can be used for breach detection if this data is harvested and processed properly. Chapter 6 introduced detecting internal threats using NetFlow, and included a brief overview of Lancope's StealthWatch NetFlow-based solution. The basic concept for using network telemetry for security is enabling NetFlow to turn existing network devices such as routers, switches, access points, and virtual switches (in addition to security products) all into one large sensor grid. This sensor grid can be used for network analysis and for monitoring for various types of security events.

NetFlow security products collect flows over a period of time and build a baseline of what is considered normal behavior. The more trend data is captured, the easier it becomes to detect anomalies from normal behavior. For example, if Jeff Wells sends data to a popular cloud storage website (Dropbox, Box, or so on) during normal business, that may seem fine to a NetFlow security product. However, an alarm will probably go off if Jeff Wells is identified sending over 600 MB of data to an unknown cloud storage mailbox located in another country at 3 a.m. for the first time in 2 years of monitoring the network. Figure 9-33 shows an example of flagging a user who is sending a large amount of data out of an unusual port (via port 25) for the first time using a StealthWatch Peer Versus Port diagram. The data loss being flagged is circled in this figure.

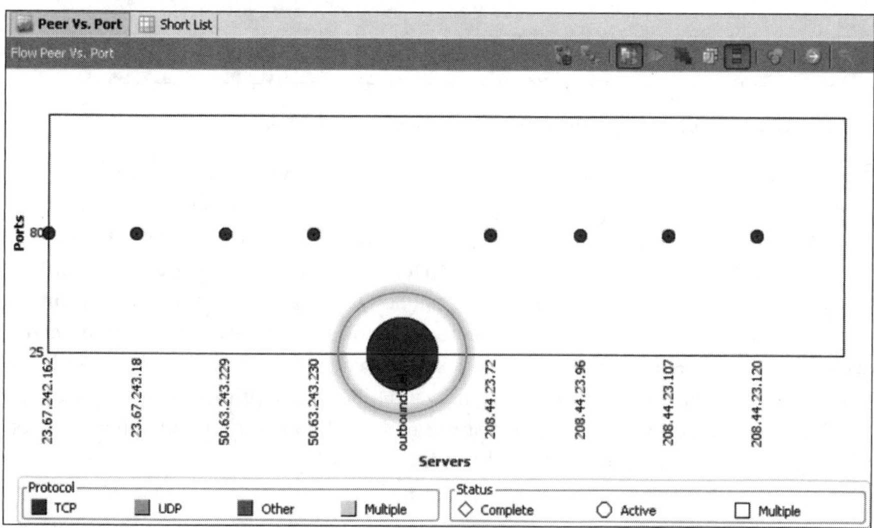

Figure 9-33 *StealthWatch Showing Data Loss*

Not all detection triggers in NetFlow security products depend on storing network trends. Looking back at the previous example where Jeff Well sent 600 MB of data to an unknown cloud storage mailbox, a rule is configured to alarm when any file more than 500 MB leaves the network. This would trigger an alarm when Jeff Wells sends this file transfer, regardless of how much trend data was seen. Tools like StealthWatch can combine the trend concerns of the time and locations of the file transfer (3 a.m. file transfer and international file transfer would both add concern) with the trigger of exceeding the 500-MB check to provide a higher alarm to administrators than if one of the single events were triggered. Figure 9-34 shows StealthWatch presents multiple events with a concern index (CI) of over 1000, representing a combination of multiple high-level alarms. We circled one CI value that is more than 1700, meaning that this system has set off a number of high-level alarms, making this a very clear malicious event.

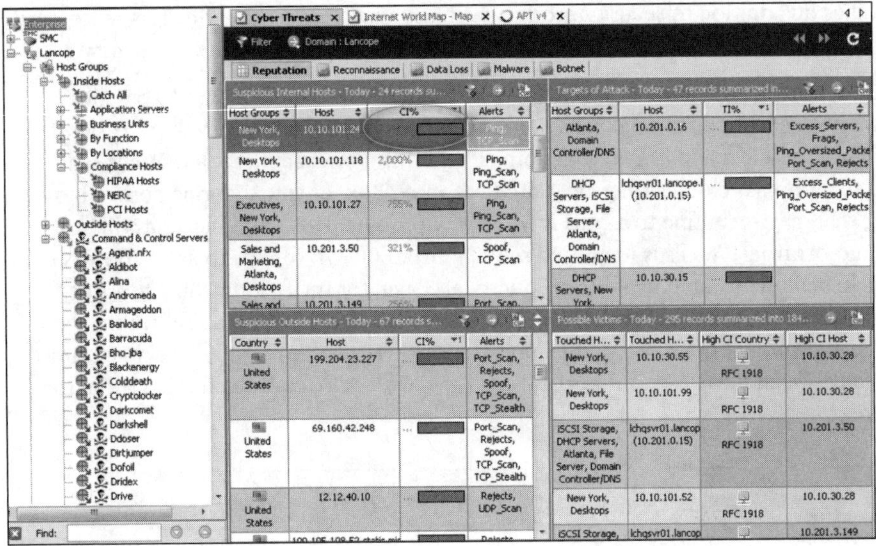

Figure 9-34 *StealthWatch Showing Very High Concern Alarms*

Note that security-based NetFlow tools have different capabilities than network performance-focused NetFlow tools. Both types of NetFlow tools usually can provide basic network trend data; however, security tools include checks for indications of compromise, such as port scanning, unusual file transfers, protocols associated with distributed denial-of-service (DDoS) attacks, and so on. So, it is important to select the right NetFlow tool for your organization. If breach-detection features are desired, you need a NetFlow tool that includes those capabilities. For basic bandwidth monitoring and troubleshooting, viewing network talkers, and validating traffic prioritization policies, a general NetFlow collector or integrated feature with a SIEM or other collecting product may meet your requirements and probably be less expensive.

Enabling NetFlow

SOC architects planning to deploy NetFlow should first consider what it takes to enable NetFlow. Most modern network devices support NetFlow, but it is important to make sure to verify whether and what version of NetFlow is supported by each device that will be part of the deployment. If performance is a concern, enabling NetFlow usually provides a minimal increase in CPU usage. For example, a fully loaded Cisco Integrated Services Router (ISR) sees around 15 percent or less CPU uptick resulting from NetFlow enablement. This can vary depending on the type of NetFlow used and number of events seen.

There are nine versions of NetFlow; however, you will most likely use NetFlow 5 or 9 on your devices. Table 9-4 shows the different NetFlow releases. Notice how many versions were created but never publicly used.

Table 9-4 *Different Versions of NetFlow*

Version	Status
1	Similar to v5, but without sequence numbers or Border Gateway Protocol (BGP) info
2	Never released
3	Never released
4	Never released
5	Fixed format, most common version found in production
6	Never released
7	Similar to v5 but without TCP flags, specific to Cat5k and Cat6k
8	Aggregated formats, never gained wide usage in the enterprise
9	"Next-gen" flow format found in most modern NetFlow exporters; supports IPv6, Multiprotocol Label Switching (MPLS), multicast, many others
IPFIX	Similar to v9, but standardized with variable-length fields

NetFlow works by hosts generating network flows of information that use particular services and applications. NetFlow collectors gather metadata and build a flow record based on different fields, such as source and destination IP address, source and destination port number, Layer 3 protocol type, type of service byte, and so on. If one field is different, a new flow is created in the flow cache. This can quickly add up to a lot of records when dealing with the more advanced versions of flow such as NetFlow 9, which has more than 160 fields. Figure 9-35 shows an example of flow records found in NetFlow 9.

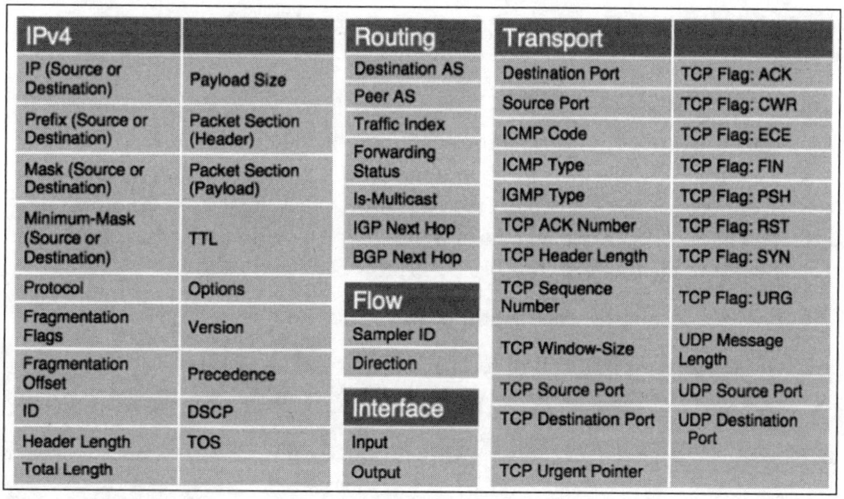

IPv4	
IP (Source or Destination)	Payload Size
Prefix (Source or Destination)	Packet Section (Header)
Mask (Source or Destination)	Packet Section (Payload)
Minimum-Mask (Source or Destination)	TTL
Protocol	Options
Fragmentation Flags	Version
Fragmentation Offset	Precedence
ID	DSCP
Header Length	TOS
Total Length	

Routing
Destination AS
Peer AS
Traffic Index
Forwarding Status
Is-Multicast
IGP Next Hop
BGP Next Hop

Flow
Sampler ID
Direction

Interface
Input
Output

Transport	
Destination Port	TCP Flag: ACK
Source Port	TCP Flag: CWR
ICMP Code	TCP Flag: ECE
ICMP Type	TCP Flag: FIN
IGMP Type	TCP Flag: PSH
TCP ACK Number	TCP Flag: RST
TCP Header Length	TCP Flag: SYN
TCP Sequence Number	TCP Flag: URG
TCP Window-Size	UDP Message Length
TCP Source Port	UDP Source Port
TCP Destination Port	UDP Destination Port
TCP Urgent Pointer	

Figure 9-35 *Fields Found in a NetFlow 9 Flow Record*

If you are using network telemetry for security, it is not recommended to use sFlow. sFlow uses sampling such as one out of every *N* packets. When sFlow is used, the recommendation is a sample rate of 1/128 packets. Regardless of the sample rate, sFlow performs poorly in low-bandwidth environments or when full flow details are required, such as for compliance. For these and other reasons, use NetFlow, also known as unsampled flow, whenever possible.

Flows typically cross numerous hops between clients and servers. Think of flows as one-way communication between each device; so, a simple conversation between a user and web server is represented by a bunch of flows as traffic crosses the network, translates through the gateway router, and later returns back to the host. Flows are also subject to asymmetric routing, which can cause problems for flow collection.

A great feature that flow tools like StealthWatch offer to address these collection problems is the capability to provide deduplication and stitching of flow records. All flows are put together into a logical conversation for accurate traffic accounting, meaning that the previous example would consolidate all flow records to one line showing the user communicated to a web server. This is important for large networks with multiple ingress/egress points so that flows are counted only once. Without deduplication, flow traffic rates would be misstated, and false positives would occur due to the duplicate flows received by the collector.

NetFlow cannot identify user attributes or application layer data in its raw form. NetFlow solution providers typically offer integration with data stores, such as pulling host information from Active Directory, and link that data to the associated-host IP traffic. StealthWatch can provide this with the StealthWatch Identity appliance or provide even more context, which includes the device type (iPad, iPhone, and so on) when integrated with Cisco Identity Services Engine (ISE). Identifying applications with NetFlow requires the use of Cisco Network-Based Application Recognition (NBAR) using IOS 15+ or a tool that can add the application data to the flow record, such as the StealthWatch NetFlow Sensor.

Architecting Network Telemetry Solutions

NetFlow vendors will probably size solutions based on the number of flows consumed. Calculating estimated NetFlow bandwidth requires some guesswork unless a NetFlow collector is used to gather a real sample. Free NetFlow collectors that are used for this purpose are available from vendors like SolarWinds. For estimation purposes, you can use the following formula to generate a basic NetFlow bandwidth number:

Assume 50 flows per second for each 10 Mbps of traffic.

Note Lancope offers a free NetFlow bandwidth calculator at https://www.lancope.com/bandwidth-calculator.

Developing a bill of materials (BOM) required to deploy a flow telemetry solution will depend on the vendor of choice. We introduced the components for StealthWatch in Chapter 6, and will use this as an example for creating a network telemetry solution BOM.

The different StealthWatch products are as follows:

- **StealthWatch Management Console (SMC):** The centralized manager used to view all data collected by the StealthWatch solution.
- **StealthWatch FlowCollector:** A FlowCollector is used to harvest NetFlow from devices that are capable of producing any form of NetFlow, Jflow, sFlow, IPFIX, and so on. You must configure network devices to export flow toward the collector.
- **StealthWatch FlowSensor:** Some devices or environments do not support flow. A FlowSensor converts raw data into NetFlow so that it can be sent to a collector for analysis.
- **StealthWatch Identity:** This appliance is used to add user data from a centralized data repository to StealthWatch so that usernames are seen attached to events rather than just IP addresses.
- **UDP Director:** The UDP Director receives flow from multiple devices and forwards it to one or many destinations. This means only the UDP Director needs to be configured when new NetFlow collecting tools are added to the network, which also increases the number of destinations to which the SOC can send flow data.
- **SLIC Threat Feed:** SLIC is a threat feed that monitors communication to known command-and-control servers, also known as CnCs.

Note All StealthWatch products except the StealthWatch Identity appliance can be physical or virtual appliances. The StealthWatch Identity appliance is available as a physical appliance only.

To develop a StealthWatch solution, you will at a minimum need an SMC and one or more collectors to consume NetFlow. Different collector model sizes are available, such as the FC1000, FC2000, FC4000, and FC5000, depending on the number of flows per second required. To gain network-wide visibility, you can use physical and virtual FlowSensors where NetFlow is not available. An example is a MAC mini hosting multiple virtual servers, where a virtual FlowSensor could convert raw data seen inside the MAC mini to NetFlow for a StealthWatch solution. If the SOC administrators only want to enable NetFlow one time on all network devices, a UDP Director can be used to update where flow is sent as new SOC tools are purchased or existing networking tool IP information is changed. One final addition is a subscription to the SLIC Threat Feed to enhance StealthWatch's ability to detect CnC communication within the network.

Here is a summary of key points used to determine the best network telemetry technology for your organization:

- Identify whether you will be using only flow telemetry for network analytics or both network and security analysis.
- Validate what equipment is capable of producing flow. Verify that equipment is not oversubscribed, because enabling NetFlow will add a small performance hit.
- For security purposes, use unsampled flow whenever using network telemetry.
- Flow-based security products tend to show value after a minimum of a week of flow data is collected, but some triggers do not depend on time.
- To properly size a flow telemetry solution, make sure that you have an idea of the flows per second you will be experiencing on your network.
- Identify requirements for the flow solution, because there are many use cases. The most popular are a need for breach detection, identifying malware, detecting potential data loss, viewing top bandwidth usage, top talkers on the network, and so on.

Detection technologies are great for identifying threats, but more advanced tools may be required for network forensic purposes to investigate breaches or other events.

Network Forensics

In some situations, the SOC might need to investigate an event. Forensics is the practice of investigating evidence and establishing facts of interest that link to the incident. Many organizations do the initial steps of an investigation; however, if the event is deemed to be a major breach, legal authorities who have the proper training and technology for a digital investigation are usually brought in. We recommend identifying contacts within different legal departments (local police, FBI, and so on) before experiencing an event so that the SOC can quickly react when an event occurs.

If the SOC plans to perform a digital forensics investigation, they should follow specific guidelines to avoid corrupting evidence. For example, the investigator should never turn off any systems that are considered to hold evidence. The power-off cycle could remove critical evidence or corrupt event logs. It is highly recommended to only authorize individuals who have been properly trained in digital forensics to be involved with an investigation or contract specialized resources for any real investigations.

In general, you want to follow three rules when performing digital forensics:

- **Rule 1:** Never work with original data. Always create one or more copies and do all investigation work with a copy of the data. Make sure to document the entire copy process and use a method that includes the ability to validate the original data and copies. Tampering with the original data could corrupt the evidence, and it will most likely not be able to be used in most legal trails. An example of tampering that could corrupt data is making a change that adjusts the time stamp in the system logs. From an investigation viewpoint, there would be no way to distinguish this change from an amateur analyst mistake or hacker trying to cover his tracks.

- **Rule 2:** Examine anything that can be stored. Evidence can be found on various types of gadgets, such as digital cameras, video game consoles, tablets, mobile phones, or other random digital devices. Anything with storage should be part of a forensics investigation.
- **Rule 3:** Document the entire investigation. This includes all steps and evidenced used to reach a conclusion so that it can be presented in a court of law. An independent investigation must be able to follow the same steps used in your documentation to draw the same conclusion; otherwise, your investigation is deemed inconclusive. It is also important to include a timeline of events when specifics occurred and how they occurred. Timing may impact your results and explain any differences between what you found and future independent investigations.

Digital Forensics Tools

You can use various tools for digital forensics. The first tool to consider is a digital forensics framework that can assist with documenting the entire investigation. Tools such as the Digital Forensics Framework,[6] Open Computer Forensics Architecture,[7] and Autopsy[8] are used for this purpose. Other tools that should be considered are disk- and data-capture tools; file, e-mail, Internet, mobile device, and other analysis tools; duplication tools; and storage. There are specialized certifications such as the EC-Council Computer Hacking Forensic Investigator certification that cover what tools and training should be used to properly perform a digital forensics investigation.

Most likely, a SOC will provide capture data to a digital investigator rather than lead the investigation. One common tool used to provide evidence is a packet-capture technology. Packet-capture solutions sit on a specific part of the network and capture some or all packets that cross the wire. Packets are organized and can be searched for points of interest depending on the vendor's offering. An example of a popular open source packet-capture tool is Wireshark,[9] which can run as an independent application or within a security product. Different network devices can point traffic through Wireshark, or Wireshark can be placed on a network tap. Figure 9-36 shows the packet-capture wizard available in the ASAx Adaptive Security Device Manager (ASDM) management platform that is designed to assist with sending traffic to a packet-capture technology such as Wireshark.

More advanced packet-capture technology such as RSA NetWitness[10] include various investigation and alert tools to help identify and react to threats recognized by the packet-capture technology. The benefits of the more advanced offerings is automation in analyzing data, less expert-level knowledge required to understand what is found, and additional capabilities such as mapping data history and various reporting features.

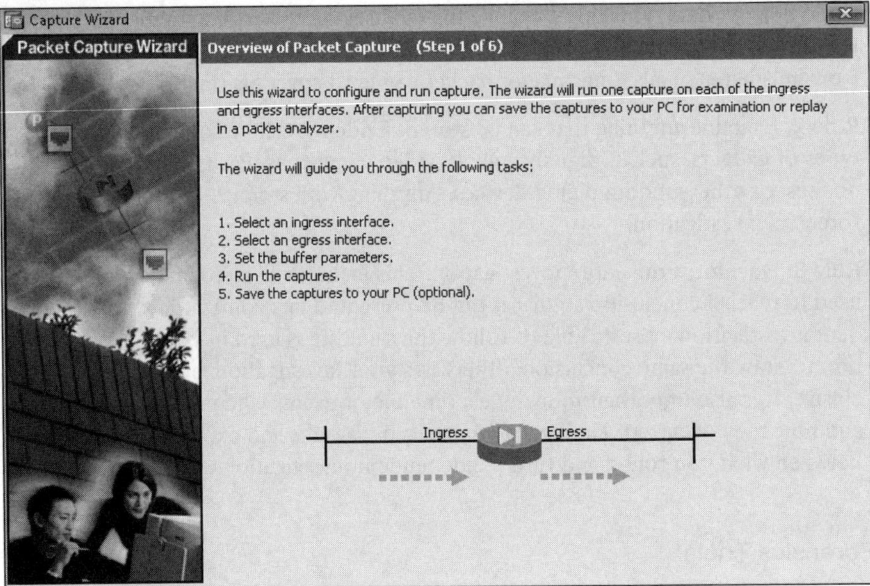

Figure 9-36 *Packet-Capture Wizard in ASDM*

Packet-capture technologies can be valuable for a digital investigation but also very expensive to purchase and properly maintain. The highest cost for designing a solution is usually the required storage because capturing packets can require massive amounts of data depending on what is captured and how long it is stored. Some vendors may also charge for licenses based on the amount of data captured (which can increase as the organization grows). Many packet-capture tools also need an analyst who understands the data, which may require additional training or recruiting for that skill set. Best practice is to consider all aspects of purchasing and maintaining a packet-capture technology for a specific time period when budgeting for a packet-capture solution.

Other tools that a SOC may use for digital evidence are collected event logs, data found in different security solutions, endpoint data, network telemetry logs, access control logs, and so on. Most investigators require documentation specifying when the data was captured, all parties with access to the data, what systems were used to capture the data, and so on. Make sure to contact an authorized digital investigator before exporting any potential evidence of a digital crime.

Now that we have covered the SOC technologies, we will now put all the technologies covered into a network design.

Final SOC Architecture

We have covered many different technologies and design concepts in this chapter. Each topic addressed a specific use case. Now we need to bring these concepts together to see how the technology would look in a mature SOC architecture. Let's start by considering Figure 9-37, which shows a SOC leveraging most of the concepts, devices, and technologies covered in this chapter. Every network will differ, but this example provides a general representation of security technologies usually placed within an organization.

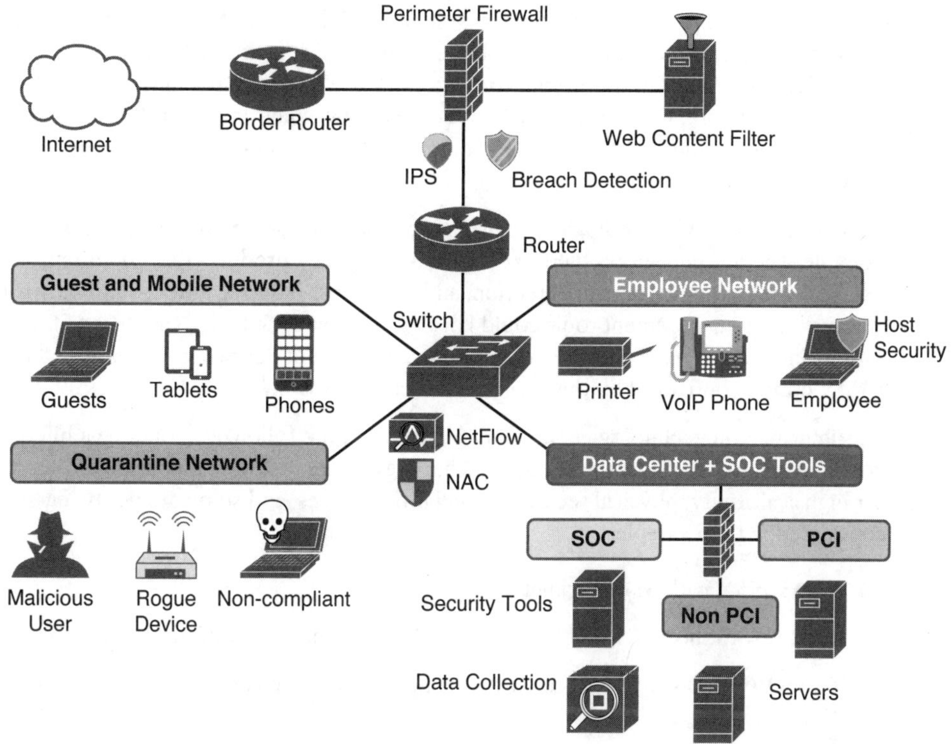

Figure 9-37 *Example of a Mature SOC Architecture*

The first technology we cover from Figure 9-37 is the gateway security solution. We will then work our way to the internal networks. This company is using a security appliance that is acting as a firewall (stateful and application layer), IPS, and breach-detection solution similar to the Cisco FirePOWER offering with IPS and AMP licensed. A dedicated proxy is performing web content filtering by having traffic redirected using WCCP to the proxy from the gateway firewall as traffic enters and leaves the network. The web proxy is a product from Cisco (WSA), BlueCoat, Websense, and so on.

The internal network is segmented into four networks using a combination of VLANs and ACLs. Authorized devices and company-issued computers are placed on the Employee network. All guests and personal devices, such as tablets and phones, are placed on the Guest network. Cisco ISE is used for network access control to enforce these policies. If a device does not meet NAC policies, such as having the latest updates, or has a form of antivirus installed, it is placed on the Quarantine network. In addition, any unauthorized wireless access points or hubs identified by Cisco ISE are quarantined.

The entire network is monitored using NetFlow-enabled equipment that is monitored by the SOC. The NetFlow tool is integrated with ISE and acts as a post-access control solution with the ability to quarantine anything deemed a high risk by other network security tools.

The data center is segmented with a dedicated firewall separating PCI and non-PCI systems. The SOC has its own network that hosts its Splunk SIEM, and various security tools used to monitor the network and hosts. If any tool identifies a high-level threat on the network, they can use Splunk to trigger Cisco ISE to send the device to the Quarantine network. Other tools, such as their NetFlow solution, StealthWatch, can send high-concern devices to the Quarantine network by leveraging Cisco ISE as the network enforcer.

Many other security technologies are present but not represented in this network example. The diagram shows there are host-based security products that could represent antivirus, endpoint breach detection, and other host-based security solutions. Most likely, desktop management tools could have events sent to Splunk to assist the SOC with maintaining security compliance. Remote access is not addressed, but is available as a VPN option configured on the perimeter Cisco ASAx firewall.

To summarize the technologies shown in Figure 9-37, the following would be a bill of potential materials for just the security technology. Note that design considerations for high availability, physical security, installation services, and so on are not being considered in this example.

- **ASA5555X with SSD:** Perimeter firewall
- **FirePOWER license for IPS and AMP:** IPS and breach detection
- **Cisco WSA S380:** Web security proxy licensed for McAfee antivirus and outbreak filtering
- **Cisco ISE VM server:** NAC manager
- **Cisco ISE based and Apex licenses for 500 users:** ISE user licensing
- **Lancope StealthWatch SMC:** NetFlow manager
- **Lancope StealthWatch Collector:** NetFlow collector
- **Lancope StealthWatch Sensor:** Data to NetFlow converter placed in data center
- **Splunk:** SIEM for data collection

Now let's change gears and look at how a possible virtual SOC is designed. Figure 9-38 shows an example of a virtual SOC environment, where Cisco is providing the virtual SOC services to a customer. Network devices at the customer location are set up to send event logs and other data to systems that are monitored by the external SOC. Because Cisco is providing the virtual SOC services, all SOC tools are hosted from a Cisco data center. Communication between the customer site, Cisco SOC, and Cisco data center hosting various tools is sent over encrypted web-based channels. There is a portal available for the customer to access the data monitored by the virtual SOC team, along with a ticketing system to identify what events are being addressed.

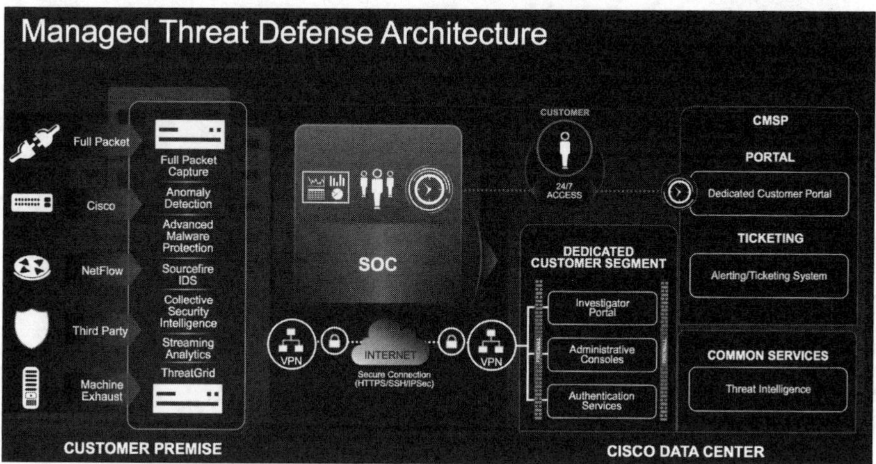

Figure 9-38 *Virtual SOC Environment Example*

Virtual SOC pricing can be based on many factors, such as the number of devices being monitored, the type of SOC services requested, the operation of support, location of the customer offices, and so on. A hybrid SOC could look like a blend of Figures 9-37 and 9-38, where some technology is owned and managed by the SOC and other pieces could send traffic to the Cisco data center to be monitored by the virtual SOC team. Both examples are very high level, but they represent common ways that SOC environments use the technologies covered in this chapter.

Summary

This chapter focused on the technology involved with most modern SOC environments. We kicked things off by going over design considerations for SOC network, security, collaboration, and storage technologies. The chapter then reviewed a handful of security product categories that are found in most SOC architectures, such as firewalls, intrusion prevention, breach detection, and network telemetry. This chapter concluded with an example of an in-network and virtual SOC architecture that featured many technologies covered in this chapter.

The next chapter covers how a SOC should prepare to go to a live operational phase.

References

1. http://www.cisco.com/c/en/us/td/docs/security/asa/asa81/config/guide/config/webvpn.html
2. https://supportforums.cisco.com/document/26331/how-configure-port-security-cisco-catalyst-switches-run-cisco-ios-system-software
3. https://www.nsa.gov/ia/mitigation_guidance/security_configuration_guides/operating_systems.shtml
4. http://benchmarks.cisecurity.org/downloads/browse/index.cfm?category=benchmarks.os.windows
5. http://benchmarks.cisecurity.org/en-us/?route=downloads.browse.category.benchmarks.os.unix.osx
6. http://www.digital-forensic.org/
7. http://sourceforge.net/projects/ocfa/
8. http://www.sleuthkit.org
9. https://www.wireshark.org
10. http://www.emc.com/security/security-analytics/security-analytics.htm

Chapter 10

Preparing to Operate

"The best preparation for good work tomorrow is to do good work today."—Elbert Hubbard

This chapter provides an overview of the typical steps you need to complete to make your SOC fully operational. This means developing a clear transition or transformation plan for the SOC and ensuring that all the major pieces you need to be effective are in place. It also means managing executive expectations, usually to previously agreed-upon timelines with their own pressures. So, preparing a SOC to operate comes down to managing a shifting target, all with the help of executive sponsors. This chapter describes how to structure this transition stage and how to prepare your team to take on the heavy load associated with a new operational SOC.

Key Challenges

You must address a number of key challenges to successfully transition a new SOC to the point where it becomes an effective way to detect and address cybersecurity incidents within the environment. This includes challenges right across the spectrum, from people to processes to technology. Let's start by looking at these challenges.

People Challenges

Challenges with people start at the very top: the executives who have sponsored the development of the SOC. Requesting to build a SOC often originates out of a serious cybersecurity incident, when passions and the desire to throw money at the issue are at their hottest. In the heat of the moment, executives keen to address the risk may be willing to invest heavily even though that investment can be huge, both in upfront capital investment and ongoing operational costs. In the beginning, a sponsoring executive such as the CISO may feel that the SOC is an initiative that receives broad support, not only from his or her own superiors (for example, the board, the CFO, the CEO) but also from his or her own peers within the organization.

By the time you have designed an appropriate SOC based on their initial requirements, a lot of time may have passed. Priorities may have changed. A previously unlimited budget may suddenly be more restricted or reallocated to other initiatives. What seemed like a big priority may suddenly take second (or lower) place to more pressing business needs. Broad support may now be much more narrow. The costs may simply be too high for the executive to provide the same level of support you might have been expecting.

The smart SOC leader should be prepared for a bit of a rebaselining as the SOC gets closer to moving into a real functioning capability within the organization. Interdepartmental friction will certainly increase, and you will need to have a lot of support to transition the SOC to an operational state. Working closely with your sponsoring executive is key to showing that the investment in the cyber SOC continues to be sound, while also helping to ensure that inevitable compromises don't affect the success of the SOC.

Past such executive concerns, you also need to concern yourself with your new SOC team. Even if you have managed to recruit a solid SOC team, that team is going to be fragile when you first deploy the SOC and they begin to feel the weight of high expectations. The team may be inexperienced or incomplete. They may have a lot of experience within the organization but do not yet have a lot of experience working with each other, particularly under crisis conditions. There might also be third-party contractors and suppliers playing key roles in the SOC team, and smooth operations between internal and external team members may take some time to sort out.

Process Challenges

Inexperienced SOC leaders tend to believe that solid, mature processes and procedures will solve many people problems. After all, consultants and their own peers have likely told them that a well-defined, thorough process is a cure for inexperience or a lack of skill. Unfortunately, that is rarely the case; processes and procedures come with challenges of their own.

As discussed previously in Chapter 8, "People and Processes," processes and procedures have limited effectiveness in a SOC environment. Processes often describe the ideal ways that multiple parties (both inside the SOC team and with other teams outside of the SOC) will interact to make decisions and get things done. They almost always look good on paper, but often negatively impact how a SOC performs its core mission: detecting and responding quickly to potential security incidents. This becomes particularly obvious when multiple parties must be engaged to make key decisions. Procedures can also look good, but can be so constraining (or limited under a very narrow range of conditions) that SOC analysts cannot perform their jobs effectively. In particularly constrained environments, this tends to have an almost immediate impact on SOC team morale and retention. Speaking from personal experience, almost all cyber SOCs start with an overabundance of processes and procedures.

Technology Challenges

As described in Chapter 9, "The Technology," the typical cyber SOC requires a substantial technology investment to be even modestly effective, and it is extremely unlikely that you will be able to deploy all your desired technology estate before you need to go live. As you are transitioning the SOC into production, you will typically find challenges associated with longer-than-expected deployment timelines for key technologies, important event or enrichment data may be delayed or missing, integration between key systems may not be working, or funds for that new intelligence feed may have just dried up. The smart SOC leader needs to carefully manage expectations (including, as well, those of their sponsors, team members, and service consumers). A lot of that will come down to constantly monitoring the deployment of the technology estate and jumping on challenges as quickly as they appear.

Managing Challenges Through a Well-Managed Transition

Although it might seem obvious, the deployment of the SOC is a *project* with many moving parts and a lot of associated risks like the challenges previously mentioned. In the most complex SOC deployments, it may even take the form of multiple overlapping or concurrent projects that will have to be managed under a common program. Whether your SOC deployment is being managed as a single project or as multiple projects under a single program, it will need strong, consistent management. It will also need a strong and capable *project/program manager*.

The SOC lead is not typically also that project/program manager (the PM), but provides day-to-day leadership for that individual on behalf of the executive sponsor. The PM may not even have previous experience with security projects, but should have a strong track record delivering complex projects involving multiple partners, suppliers, and services. What they will provide is the structure and management of the effort, from managing the individual resources involved in the deployment to the costs associated with them. They will manage issues and risks. They will work with the SOC lead to develop an appropriate project/program plan, and track attainment to milestones within that plan so that expected SOC services are deployed on time and on budget.

As such, that transition plan will be dependent on resources and time available to transition SOC services into projection by some agreed-upon date (often called go-live). Outside of the usual Gantt charts loved by PMs around the world, a service transition document is often used to capture what must be accomplished and the checks that will be performed during transition into normal operations at go-live. It also documents dependencies and prerequisites that must be in place before each check, in addition to risks and related mitigation strategies, including potential impacts to the existing services, staff, and end users of the service. During transition, it is also valuable to maintain a risks and issues register to manage any issues that may occur that threaten a successful transition and into ongoing operations.

In general, the service transition is successful if SOC services are deemed fit to perform their intended function and can be supported by the SOC team. Things that might not be working but are not critical to SOC services are tracked but not seen as major roadblocks. If, for example, as a result of this transition being carried out, a service defect is discovered that does not severely impact the operation of the service, the investigation and rectification of this defect will continue to be managed under normal operations during the period after go-live.

Elements of an Effective Service Transition Plan

Over the years, we have seen many service transition plans used to guide SOC deployment, and most of them share some common success factors:

1. **Success criteria are explicit and clear.** A simple point-form list of success criteria should be negotiated with the sponsors as part of design and form the basis for managing expectations and execution.
2. **Resourcing is very detailed and very structured.** Resources may refer to people, time, or money. It should be very clear how and when each resource is expected throughout the project or program.
3. **Requirements for skills, technologies, deliverables, and content are clear and achievable.** Your team has to be sufficiently skilled by go-live to do the work. Required technologies, deliverables, and content have to be in place, but that means focusing on what those requirements really are.
4. **Simple checks can be performed to verify that something has been completed successfully.** A simple checklist should be developed that clearly outlines how the results of each activity, task, or milestone will be evaluated.

We discuss each one of these in the remaining sections of this chapter. Let's start with the success criteria.

Determining Success Criteria and Managing to Success

Designing a SOC is relatively straightforward, but deploying one tends to be anything but. After all, the SOC design discussed earlier may represent not only elements that can be deployed within the short-term but also long-term strategic investments that may not happen for years. One of the most important things to keep in mind is that a strong SOC will typically take a long time to develop, while even the most forward-thinking executive sponsor will be looking for quick wins and short-term gains in capability. Therefore, you must base your success criteria on your sponsors' and consumers' most immediate priorities without losing track of long-term evolution. It can be a difficult balance to achieve and can be frustrating for the new or inexperienced SOC lead. There are, however, a number of possible ways to approach this.

When deploying a new SOC, stick with simple, achievable goals within the timeframe allotted. It would be great for you to be able to deploy that new industry-leading big data platform to provide anomaly detection, but if you cannot deploy it within the time you have, it is obviously not a priority. Instead, focus on ways to show rapid improvement. Success will usually make your sponsors look good, and give you the support you need for that costly big data platform you are hoping for.

It is also best if you align your own success criteria closely with your sponsors' criteria for success. What do they really want to accomplish and by when? You may, for example, want to deploy a SOC capability that leads your industry peers, but your sponsors may only be interested in getting their auditors off their backs at the lowest price point. You may be personally unhappy with their criteria, but remember that making them successful will make it more likely that they'll support you as you wish to grow beyond their initial expectations.

Where possible, you need to manage expectations for success, with your sponsors, the consumers of your service, and your own team. There are two keys ways to manage to success:

- Deploying your SOC to deliver services within expected service levels
- Deploying your SOC to address high-priority use cases

Deploying Against Attainable Service Levels

When designing SOC services in earlier chapters, there was a clear distinction between metrics, service levels, key performance indicators, and key risk indicators. When deploying a SOC, your focus should be clearly on initial service levels while validating that expected metrics could indeed be measured. The key word is *initial* because the service levels you will likely be able to provide in the early days of the SOC will be quite different from what you may be able to provide as the SOC develops. You may even require a "burn-in" period for a number of months to determine what service levels you can even commit to! Regardless, attaining service levels is a key way that your sponsors and consumers can validate that you are providing the services you have agreed to deploy.

Every service must have clearly defined service levels that can be measured and tracked quantitatively over time. They determine whether that particular service is successful at a particular point in time or within the latest reporting period. They are intended to reflect the priorities and requirements of the SOC's sponsors and key service consumers. Service levels also drive investment in automation and operational capacity. They can even have an impact on who will provide the service. Service level attainment is usually captured on a monthly basis and included within normal operational reporting. It is monitored closely, particularly during the first 3 months after the service goes live and baselined according to actual performance.

For example, let's consider some common types of service levels that most SOC monitoring services have to fulfill from the first day after go-live: response time, escalation fidelity, queue backlog, and procedure adherence:

- **Average incident response time** refers to the average amount of time that a SOC analyst takes to complete security event analysis of a security event, perform incident identification/classification, decide whether the incident requires escalation or remediation, and escalate based on defined parameters. It is not uncommon for a new monitoring service to be able to attain a fairly aggressive response time service level (for example, less than 15 or 30 minutes from the moment it enters their queue), even with junior analysts. Without the fidelity service level described next, however, analysts tend to escalate anything that comes close to the service level.
- **Average escalation fidelity**, sometimes also referred to as *response fidelity*, measures whether escalation activities taken by the monitoring analyst were appropriate. This usually reflects a number of factors. Based on root cause analysis after the incident, a lower-than-expected level of fidelity may indicate (a) gaps in individual analyst skill/knowledge and thus requiring additional experience or training, (b) prevalence of false positives within automated systems and thus requiring tuning, or (c) inappropriate or imprecise procedures and thus requiring update. In general, this service level is used to temper the response time service level by encouraging analysts to be sure that they are escalating actual incidents, but it is also common for new analysts to be wrong a large percentage of the time at go-live, although they tend to improve quickly.
- **Event and ticket queue backlog** refers to the phenomenon that even well-staffed SOCs do not always address every event or ticket that crosses their screens. Events not addressed by a SOC analyst typically accumulate over time. Often (but not always) these are informational or low-severity events that have been deprioritized by more severe incidents. A larger-than-expected backlog typically indicates either the need for higher staff capacity or more automation. It is not uncommon for annual backlogs of between 4 percent to 7 percent annually.
- **Incident management procedure conformance** is a service level often used to track conformance to specific documented procedures. First-generation procedures, however, tend to be imprecise or incorrect and can be a factor in nonconformance. Ideally, however, the service level should quickly ramp up to 100 percent.

As you have likely noticed with each of these service levels, there is often an initial target with the opportunity to set clearly defined improvement over time. This may be suitable for organizations building SOCs using internal resources with relatively little previous SOC experience; however, if aggressive service levels are more desirable, this will either require more aggressive recruiting of highly experienced resources from the market or the use of outsourcing or managed service providers willing to sign up for the service levels (and associated penalties).

Focusing on Defined Use Cases

There is a lot of discussion across the security industry what constitutes a "use case," but at its most general, a use case describes how individuals (often called *actors*) will act and react under specific scenarios. In a SOC environment, such actors include not only human actors such as the individual roles and team members within the SOC, threat actors, service consumers, and service provider personnel but also automated system actors such as security information and event management [SIEM], case management systems, ticketing systems, and other infrastructure. Scenarios usually cover a wide range of possible situations, covering both simple and more complex cybersecurity incidents that may be experienced by the organization.

When it comes to use cases used to guide SOC deployment, the focus is on developing SOC services to quickly and reliably address scenarios that the organization has or can be expected to experience. Such use cases address understood areas of risk based on some known parameters. Naturally, this can run into hundreds of potential scenarios covering a wide range of threats and threat actors, in addition to critical or noncritical information assets they may be targeting. It can even include scenarios that are focused on noncompliance or events that may be simply interesting from a regulatory perspective. Even relatively inexperienced SOC analysts could likely think of dozens of possible scenarios they may encounter on a daily basis.

The sky is quite literally the limit, but so is the cost and effort associated with addressing every use case you could think of. Every use case comes at a cost, particularly if you are hoping for any sort of automated detection or response. For example, your SIEM may be used to automatically detect and respond to a wide variety of potential events, but it has to be able to collect, parse, collate, and interpret events from a potentially wide range of sources. Even collecting information for the sake of the SIEM's rules may have costs: You might need to augment or replace existing infrastructure, turn on costly performance-impacting debug modes, or enrich standard event data using expensive intelligence feeds to make them useful. You may require asset information and detailed network modeling that may simply be unavailable in the short term. On the SIEM side, you might even need to deploy more SIEM infrastructure to accommodate new event streams that were not included within the original capacity plan. Even when these costs are manageable, there may be considerable costs associated with increasing internal SOC team capacity or increasing the capacity being offered by your chosen third-party provider.

In short, use cases are investments, and like all investments, they require you to make some hard decisions.

When documenting potential use cases, you need to capture a fairly substantial amount of information:

- **Use case ID:** Given the large number of potential use cases, you will certainly need a consistent way of naming and numbering them. At a minimum, they should also indicate scope.

- **Scope:** In some cases, your SOC services may be serving a smaller or larger scope within the organization, and an individual use case may be limited to a single part of that environment. For example, perhaps the scope of the use case is limited to enterprise IT, or the cloud environment, or your customer-facing applications. Scope should capture the intended range of the use case.
- **Use case category and subcategory:** Use cases can cover a wide range of potential scenarios. Although some categorization might seem arbitrary, it is most useful if you can categorize them based on how the analyst would be expected to respond to them. For example, they would respond very differently to an abuse of privileges alarm versus malware infection or a policy violation. Such categories are also useful when implementing use cases within SIEMs where they can be grouped and associated with specific procedures.
- **Use case objective:** What is the use case intended to achieve?
- **Use case logical flow:** What exactly is the use case trying to capture? What events are being used to trigger the use case? In other words, what sequence of events is the analyst or the SIEM looking for out of the data available to them?
- **Correlation rules and data analysis:** What existing or required correlation rules are needed in the SIEM or other analysis systems to automate detection of the use case?
- **Data-collection points:** Where will event and other data be collected from to determine whether the use case is occurring? Is there a specific source on each point where that data can be found (system log, security log, application log, flat file, and so on)?
- **Damage potential:** What is the potential damage that can be associated with this sort of use case given the scope?
- **Implementation and ongoing operational effort:** How difficult will it be to implement the use case or maintain it over time? Some use cases are relatively straightforward to implement because they can take advantage of out-of-the-box components and features, but other use cases may require individually developed and customized components to work properly. Some may also require significant ongoing effort to keep current.
- **Views and visualizations:** How will a triggered use case be viewed inside of monitoring systems? On dashboards? In regular or ad hoc reporting?
- **Compliance mapping:** Does the use case meet any particular regulatory or compliance standards requirements? For example, will it fulfill requirements for ISO/IEC 27001 or PCI-DSS or HIPAA?
- **Standard responses and escalations:** How should analysts respond to triggered use cases? Are there standardized escalation paths? What are they?

For the initial SOC deployment, it is often best to focus on a relatively small number of use cases negotiated with your sponsors and service consumers while being prepared to expand the number of use cases the SOC can support within its first year. Look at cybersecurity incidents that the organization has experienced over the past few years. Are there any commonly occurring scenarios? Look at recent audit findings. Are there any findings that could be addressed by being able to detect and respond to particular threats to particular assets more effectively? Look at your chosen SIEM. Are there any use cases that can be relatively easily deployed using easy-to-integrate event and data sources with off-the-shelf correlation rules within the SIEM? These should be your focus.

Here is a typical example of a relatively simple use case from one of our recent customers. As a result of a recent audit, all administrative access to critical systems was moved to a small set of authorized "jump servers," dedicated systems where admins could log in before moving on to other systems. The advantage of this setup was that admin activities could be recorded; however, the move was not a popular one, and the organization suspected that some direct admin access continued to occur. Management requested a use case that could be used to flag potential policy violations for further investigation.

Using this structure, this was the way the use case was documented:

- **Use case ID:** Critical Systems – Admin Access 1.
- **Scope:** Critical Systems.
- **Use case category and subcategory:** Policy Violations – Inappropriate Administrative Access.
- **Use case objective:** This use case is intended to generate an alert whenever administrative access is granted to a critical system without going through an appropriate jump server.
- **Use case logical flow:** Where administrative access is granted to a critical system, it should be checked to see whether this access is being granted from an authorized jump server. If not, an alert should be generated.
- **Correlation rules and data analysis:** Asset management feed to be used to capture the current set of critical systems. Correlation rule: Administrative access success events on all critical systems, correlated with administrative access success events on all jump servers. Where administrative access on critical systems is successful without a matching event on jump servers OR where IP address of host logging into critical system is NOT a jump server, generate a High Priority alert to the main channel.
- **Data-collection points:** CMDB (for asset criticality). Event logs and syslog associated with all critical systems. Event logs and system associated with jump servers.
- **Damage potential:** High due to risk associated with inappropriate administrative access.
- **Implementation and ongoing operational effort:** Simple. No additional advanced parsers or customization required.

- **Views and visualizations:** Alerted as High Priority within main channel and Compliance channel. Relevant alerts to be reported via ad hoc and regular compliance reporting.
- **Compliance mapping:** Administrative Access Policy.
- **Standard responses and escalations:** Alerts to be investigated by analysts to determine if direct administrative access has occurred or if this is a false positive. In the case that this appears to be inappropriate behavior by an authorized admin, alert admin's direct supervisor or manager.

Every use case should be reflected in the SOC's run book that describes at a high level what should be done to investigate and manage particular use cases. This can be particularly helpful when certain use cases occur infrequently. Remember that the SIEM will only tell you when you might want to investigate something, not how!

Managing Project Resources Effectively

As already established, resourcing for the SOC deployment/transition is a complex combination of people, time, and money.

Looking back at the SOC organization described in Chapter 8, it should be clear that proper resourcing of the SOC is critical. However, resourcing *within the project/program* is a little different from SOC resourcing: Project/program resources are not typically long-term staff or even operational staff provided by an outsourcing or managed service provider. Instead, these are often short-term, task-oriented individuals who are only engaged for a specific period of time to perform some defined task and then transition the results into steady-state operations. They may be internal staff used for a temporarily task to assist the SOC deployment or engaged through external partners.

A common risk is relying on the future SOC operational staff to provide project-based effort under the SOC deployment. While many SOCs have been deployed using internal resources that will eventually deliver SOC services, this can be much riskier when those resources are relatively inexperienced or where expected deployment timelines are particularly aggressive. In such cases, it can be useful to get additional resources from external providers, particularly if those providers are expected to provide ongoing service after go-live. For example, in the sample organization discussed in Chapter 8, forensic investigations were highlighted as a common function that is often provided by an on-demand service provider. In that case, you really want to use resources from your chosen provider to work with you during SOC deployment to ensure that any people, processes, or technology is in place for them to provide the expected level of service.

Whether internal or external resources are being used, it is critical that you have clearly defined expectations in the form of documented milestones to guide deployment. These should be communicated to the members of the deployment team at the beginning of the project and continuously referred to during the project itself. It never hurts to remind everyone what his or her priorities are and how closely he or she is meeting expectations.

At the same time, many SOC deployments may be unsuccessful because of unrealistic expectations or because of unforeseen delays. Although it would be great if every SOC project/program adhered to its original plan, it is more likely that some adjustment along the way will be required. A solid SOC lead should be able to negotiate such changes while also getting at least some of what the sponsors had originally desired within the expected timeframe and resources.

Marching to Clear and Attainable Requirements

Whether it is realistic or not, every SOC tends to be expected to be fully operational at go-live. In other words, when something bad happens, your new SOC team will be expected to not only detect when it happens quickly but also respond to it effectively. What do you need to accomplish that? The answers to that question will become your requirements for transition to normal operations.

The problem is that such requirements can be hard to define or can often seem a little overwhelming. To make it simpler, it is helpful to focus on a few key areas critical to the success of a new SOC deployment:

- **Staffing requirements:** Focused on staff capacity, initial training, and contacts/communications
- **Process requirements:** Focused on commonly used processes, procedures, and templates
- **Technology requirements:** Focused on technical solutions leveraged most frequently across SOC services

The sections that follow walk through each of these key areas. Chapter 11, "Reacting to Events and Incidents," describes examples of how people, processes, and technology will be expected to come together to investigate events and handle incidents. Chapter 12, "Maintain, Review, and Improve," examines ongoing evaluation and improvement. These sections should provide guidance for developing requirements for proper transition to operation.

Staffing Requirements for Go-Live

Chapter 8 discussed some typical organizational structures, team roles, and responsibilities and how you might determine appropriate capacity. As part of the transition to go-live, such roles and capacity requirements must be clearly defined, along with whatever the chosen resourcing strategy may be (in-house, outsourced, managed, or mixed). It must also be clear at what point expected service levels may need to be compromised if sufficient capacity cannot be provided by go-live. For example, if you will only be able to staff the SOC to provide business hours service, you can hardly continue to claim to provide 24x7 coverage without setting yourself up for failure.

It is also common to engage third-party contractors or other internal teams to provide temporary capacity when recruitment is incomplete or where ongoing burst capacity is desirable. In the first case, it is not uncommon to have been able to recruit some but not all of desired resources required for the SOC, either because the required numbers are high or because the local labor market is highly competitive, specific, or highly advanced skills are not available. In the second case, there may be situations where the baseline capacity you have built in to the SOC is simply not sufficient to handle the actual load. Rather than have the SOC fail, you should have appropriate mechanisms in place to top up your capacity as needed.

For your new SOC staff, ensure that they are adequately trained prior to go-live. New SOC staff with less or no experience within a SOC require significant training, not only covering general processes and procedures but also focused vendor-specific technology training so that they can use core systems like the SIEM and case management systems effectively. Keep in mind that even highly experienced staff with previous SOC experience require training. Nor should your providers be excluded, because at a minimum, they will require some training on how to work with the rest of the SOC or extended enterprise teams effectively. You may also be required to develop your own training materials or modify vendor-provided materials and deliver them within enterprise learning management platforms. These may even need to conform to enterprise learning standards within your organization.

Although it might seem obvious, how the SOC can be contacted or how the SOC will communicate needs to be very clear. Keeping in mind that the great majority of security incidents are reported by end users or consumers rather than by automated systems, there must be clear ways to engage the SOC. This could include enterprise portals, e-mail, instant messages, SMS, tickets, or phone calls to a hotline. We have seen many SOCs deployed without any clear way to engage the SOC team, even though this is the most obvious and public display that the SOC is in place and protecting the organization.

Process Requirements for Go-Live

As discussed in Chapter 8, you should only document the processes and procedures that you require, either because you need to do something consistently or because not having a documented process or procedure would negatively impact service levels. With that said, the number of potential processes and procedures could still run to the dozens.

For go-live, focus on developing processes and procedures you *need* on day one while expecting a lot of refinement and expansion in the first few months. At a minimum, the following processes should be documented:

- Event monitoring
- Incident triage
- Incident response
- Use case development and maintenance
- Correlation rule updates
- Ticket queue handling

On the procedure side, the most important procedures will be those used by junior SOC analysts to perform initial triage and investigation. This should include the following:

- Ticketing management system procedures
- Case management system procedures
- General investigation and escalation procedure
- Specific incident handling procedures (for example, malware investigation, brand protection, social engineering, unauthorized access, policy violation)

Reusable templates associated with each of these procedures will also typically be required prior to go-live so that they achieve a high degree of maturity early.

It is also a good idea to verify that supporting processes and procedures are in place. These are typically enterprise-wide processes and procedures developed outside of the SOC itself, but where the SOC will be expected to leverage them as part of their role in the enterprise. These could include the following:

- ITIL-based IT service management processes such as event, incident, problem, change, configuration and release management processes
- Other enterprise security and IT management processes such as security intelligence and analysis processes, policy violations handling, log management, or audit and compliance support processes

You also need to ensure that appropriate collaboration platforms are in place to manage documented processes and procedures, in addition to team-developed procedures to guide day-to-day activities such as reporting. This used to take the form of a single SOC handbook, but this is now commonly provided via online content management systems deployed as either knowledgebases or wikis. Knowledgebases are best used to provide management-approved content such as the SOC mission/charter, policies, standards, processes, procedures, and finalized management or operational reports. Wikis are best deployed to encourage team collaboration and learning and are typically used to capture reusable code, scripts, shortcuts, team-developed guidelines, and draft reports.

Ideally, you should also have both the knowledgebase and wiki platforms integrated with your SIEM and case management systems. This has a *big* impact on the amount of time it takes junior analysts to investigate and escalate commonly occurring SIEM events and incident reports.

Technology Requirements for Go-Live

Earlier chapters discussed a wide range of technologies that are typically deployed to support SOC services. In general, go-live preparations should focus on technology solutions that directly support core SOC services, directly impact the ability to provide services within expected service levels and can be deployed successfully within the agreed-upon timeframe.

As part of service design, you typically design a set of services from a technology-agnostic point of view and then use detailed service design to focus on technology requirements more carefully. A handful of key technologies are required to provide most core SOC services:

- Security log management
- Security information/event management (SIEM)
- Case management
- Enterprise ticketing
- Knowledgebase/wiki
- Telephony and collaboration

Keep in mind, however, that the specific SOC services you have agreed to provide by go-live may impact this list. For example, we have not mentioned forensic and malware analysis lab facilities here, but they certainly would be required if you were providing such services on day one!

You also need to verify that suitable physical facilities are in place or where suitable remote-access facilities are in place if remote working will be used. Although this does not necessarily need to include the fancy video wall systems, they certainly help to announce to your sponsors that you are ready to go.

Using Simple Checks to Verify That the SOC Is Ready

It is always a good idea to have a simple checklist that you can use to verify that all the required pieces are in place prior to go-live or to be able to clearly identify areas that may not be completed as expected. This is a valuable tool to engage with your sponsors and service consumers so that they clearly understand what they should or should not expect of the SOC services on day one and when they can expect the checklist to be complete.

The tables that follow provide a sample transition checklist for a SOC focused on providing security event monitoring and front-line security incident investigation and response where more advanced incident handling will be addressed by an existing CSIRT team. Each section outlines the individual checks that must be performed to confirm that all required people, processes/procedures, and technologies are in place before go-live. You can use a similar structure for almost any transition checklist regardless of the services in scope.

People Checks

People checks are useful when you are evaluating the readiness of the SOC analysts within your transitioned SOC. They will generally be specific to your own SOC; the following are provided as examples.

<table>
<tr><td>Check No.</td><td>PEOP.1</td><td>Rev:</td><td>1.0</td><td>Author:</td><td></td><td>Date:</td><td></td></tr>
<tr><td colspan="2">Check Category:</td><td colspan="2">People Readiness</td><td colspan="2">Required/Optional:</td><td colspan="2">Required</td></tr>
<tr><td colspan="2">Check Title:</td><td colspan="6">Level 1 Analysts Checks</td></tr>
<tr><td colspan="8"></td></tr>
<tr><td colspan="2">Check Purpose:</td><td colspan="6">To verify that sufficient Level 1 SOC analysts are in place to meet initial target service levels and that shift scheduling is in place through the first month after go-live.</td></tr>
<tr><td colspan="8"></td></tr>
<tr><td colspan="2">Check Setup:</td><td colspan="6">This check assumes that initial target service levels are known.</td></tr>
<tr><td colspan="8"></td></tr>
<tr><td colspan="2">Procedure:</td><td colspan="6">1. Check that recruitment and onboarding of new Level 1 SOC analysts is complete.
2. Verify that they have been assigned suitable workspace and equipment to perform SOC monitoring activities either within the SOC or remotely.
3. Verify that there is sufficient Level 1 analyst capacity to meet initial target service levels.
4. Check the shift scheduling for Level 1 analysts for the first month after go-live to ensure appropriate analyst coverage.
5. Verify availability of additional capacity if needed.</td></tr>
<tr><td colspan="2"></td><td colspan="6"></td></tr>
<tr><td colspan="8">Checks:</td></tr>
<tr><td colspan="6">Verify recruitment and onboarding of Level 1 analysts.</td><td colspan="2">Complete ☐ Incomplete ☐</td></tr>
<tr><td colspan="6">All Level 1 analysts have suitable workspace and equipment.</td><td colspan="2">Complete ☐ Incomplete ☐</td></tr>
<tr><td colspan="6">Level 1 analyst capacity has been validated to meet SLs.</td><td colspan="2">Complete ☐ Incomplete ☐</td></tr>
<tr><td colspan="6">Shift scheduling for Level 1 analysts cover up to end of M1.</td><td colspan="2">Complete ☐ Incomplete ☐</td></tr>
<tr><td colspan="6">Calculate availability of additional Level 1 capacity.</td><td colspan="2">Complete ☐ Incomplete ☐</td></tr>
<tr><td colspan="8"></td></tr>
<tr><td colspan="2">Complete: (initial)</td><td colspan="6"></td></tr>
<tr><td colspan="2">Incomplete: (initial)</td><td colspan="6"></td></tr>
<tr><td colspan="2">Reason:</td><td colspan="6"></td></tr>
<tr><td colspan="2">Remarks:</td><td colspan="6"></td></tr>
</table>

Check No.	PEOP.2	Rev:	1.0	Author:		Date:	
Check Category:		People Readiness		Required/Optional:		Required	
Check Title:		Level 2 Analysts Checks					
Check Purpose:		To verify that sufficient Level 2 SOC analysts are in place to meet initial target service levels and that shift scheduling is in place through the first month after go-live.					
Check Setup:		This check assumes that initial target service levels are known. It also assumes that Level 1 analyst checks are also complete.					
Procedure:		1. *Check that recruitment and onboarding of permanent or temporary Level 2 SOC analysts is complete.* 2. *Verify that they have been assigned suitable workspace and equipment to perform SOC monitoring activities either within the SOC or remotely.* 3. *Verify that there is sufficient Level 2 analyst capacity to meet initial target service levels.* 4. *Check the shift scheduling for Level 2 analysts for the first month after go-live to ensure appropriate analyst coverage.* 5. *Verify availability of additional capacity to cover gaps in Level 1 analyst coverage.*					

Checks:	
Verify recruitment and onboarding of Level 2 analysts.	Complete ☐ Incomplete ☐
All Level 2 analysts have suitable workspace and equipment.	Complete ☐ Incomplete ☐
Level 2 analyst capacity has been validated to meet SLs.	Complete ☐ Incomplete ☐
Shift scheduling for Level 2 analysts cover up to end of M1.	Complete ☐ Incomplete ☐
Calculate availability of additional capacity to cover Level 1.	Complete ☐ Incomplete ☐

Complete: (initial)	
Incomplete: (initial)	
Reason:	
Remarks:	

Check No.	PEOP.3	Rev:	1.0	Author:		Date:	
Check Category:		People Readiness		**Required/Optional:**		Required	
Check Title:		Initial Training Check					
Check Purpose:		To verify that Level 1 and Level 2 SOC analysts have received initial training in core processes, procedures, and technologies.					
Check Setup:		This check assumes all Level 1 and Level 2 SOC analysts have been onboarded and are available to attend scheduled training sessions.					
Procedure:		*1. Complete preparation of Level 1/Level 2 training materials.* *2. Hold formal training sessions for Level 1 SOC analysts.* *3. Hold formal training sessions for Level 2 SOC analysts.* *4. (Optional) Upload recorded versions of training into wiki or secure shared location.* *5. (Optional) Post training materials on Belgacom Learning Management System.*					

Checks:	
Training materials have been completed and reviewed.	Complete ☐ Incomplete ☐
Level 1 analyst training sessions have been scheduled and held.	Complete ☐ Incomplete ☐
Level 2 analyst training sessions have been scheduled and held.	Complete ☐ Incomplete ☐
Recording sessions are available to Level 1 and Level 2 analysts.	Complete ☐ Incomplete ☐
Training materials are posted on Belgacom LMS.	Complete ☐ Incomplete ☐

Complete: (initial)	
Incomplete: (initial)	
Reason:	
Remarks:	

Check No.	PEOP.4	Rev:	1.0	Author:		Date:	
Check Category:		People Readiness		**Required/ Optional:**		Required	
Check Title:		Contacts and Communications Check					
Check Purpose:		To verify that all SOC contact information is up to date and that appropriate communication channels between Level 1 and Level 2 are set up.					
Check Setup:		This check assumes all Level 1 and Level 2 SOC analysts have standard Belgacom computing equipment and IP telephones with individual phone numbers.					
Procedure:		*1. Distribute and complete contact information matrix to Level 1, Level 2, and L3 (CSIRT).* *2. Verify that instant messaging clients are set up with appropriate favorites/groups.* *3. Verify that hotline to CSIRT hotline is added to Level 1 and Level 2 analyst's IP phone profiles.* *4. (Optional) Verify remote IP phone capability for remote Level 1 and Level 2 analysts.*					
Checks:							
Contact information for all Level 1 and Level 2 analysts.						Complete ☐ Incomplete ☐	
IM analyst groups set up for all analysts.						Complete ☐ Incomplete ☐	
CSIRT hotline added to IP phone profiles for SOC analysts.						Complete ☐ Incomplete ☐	
(Optional) Remote IP phone capability for SOC analysts.						Complete ☐ Incomplete ☐	
Complete: (initial)							
Incomplete: (initial)							
Reason:							
Remarks:							

Process Checks

Process checks are useful when you are evaluating the readiness of the required processes and procedures within your transitioned SOC. They will generally be specific to your own SOC; the following are provided as examples.

Check No.	PROC.1	Rev:	1.0	Author:		Date:	
Check Category:		Process Readiness		**Required/ Optional:**		Required	
Check Title:		SOC Process Checks					
Check Purpose:		To verify that core SOC processes are documented and in place.					
Check Setup:		This check assumes that service design has been completed and accepted.					
Procedure:		*1. Confirm that the following processes have been documented and reviewed: event monitoring, incident triage, incident response, use case development and maintenance, correlation rule updates, and ticket queue handling process.* *2. Verify that all Level 1 and Level 2 analysts have received training in each core SOC process.* *3. Verify that core SOC processes have been published on either the team wiki or within knowledgebase.*					
Checks:							
Core SOC processes are documented and reviewed.						Complete ☐ Incomplete ☐	
Level 1 and Level 2 analysts have received training on all core processes.						Complete ☐ Incomplete ☐	
Core SOC processes have been published on team wiki and/ or knowledgebase.						Complete ☐ Incomplete ☐	
Complete: (initial)							
Incomplete: (initial)							
Reason:							
Remarks:							

Check No.	PROC.2	Rev:	1.0	Author:		Date:	
Check Category:		Process Readiness		**Required/ Optional:**		Required	
Check Title:		SOC Procedures Checks					
Check Purpose:		To verify that core SOC procedures are documented and in place.					
Check Setup:		This check assumes that service design and SOC process development has been completed and accepted.					
Procedure:		1. *Confirm that the following procedures have been documented and reviewed: case/investigation ticketing procedure, service manager ticketing procedure, and incident escalation procedure.* 2. *Verify that all Level 1 and Level 2 analysts have received training in each core SOC procedure.* 3. *Verify that core SOC procedures have been published on either the team wiki or within SIEM knowledgebase.*					
Checks:							
Core SOC procedures are documented and reviewed.						Complete ☐ Incomplete ☐	
Level 1 and Level 2 analysts have received training on all core procedures.						Complete ☐ Incomplete ☐	
Core SOC procedures have been published on team wiki and/ or SIEM knowledgebase.						Complete ☐ Incomplete ☐	
Complete: (initial)							
Incomplete: (initial)							
Reason:							
Remarks:							

Check No.	PROC.3	Rev:	1.0	Author:		Date:	
Check Category:		Process Readiness		Required/Optional:		Required	
Check Title:		SOC Procedures Checks					
Check Purpose:		To verify that core SOC procedures are documented and in place.					
Check Setup:		This check assumes that service design and SOC process development has been completed and accepted.					
Procedure:		1. *Confirm that the following procedures have been documented and reviewed: case/investigation ticketing procedure, service manager ticketing procedure, and incident escalation procedure.* 2. *Verify that all Level 1 and Level 2 analysts have received training in each core SOC procedure.* 3. *Verify that core SOC procedures have been published on either the team wiki or within knowledgebase.*					
Checks:							
Core SOC procedures are documented and reviewed.						Complete ☐ Incomplete ☐	
Level 1 and Level 2 analysts have received training on all core procedures.						Complete ☐ Incomplete ☐	
Core SOC procedures have been published on team wiki and/ or knowledgebase.						Complete ☐ Incomplete ☐	
Complete: (initial)							
Incomplete: (initial)							
Reason:							
Remarks:							

Check No.	PROC.4	Rev:	1.0	Author:		Date:	
Check Category:		Process Readiness		**Required/Optional:**		Required	
Check Title:		Supporting Processes and Procedures Checks					
Check Purpose:		To verify that supporting processes and procedures required by the SOC are documented and in place, and that SOC analysts understand them at a high level.					
Check Setup:		This check assumes that service design and SOC process and SOC procedure development has been completed and accepted.					
Procedure:		*1. Confirm that the following supporting processes and procedures are in place: log source heartbeat management, policy violations handling, CSIRT incident management, root cause analysis, security intelligence and analysis, log source management, and ITIL management processes.* *2. Verify that Level 1 and Level 2 analysts have received high-level training on these supporting processes and procedures.* *3. Verify that links to supporting processes and procedures have been published on either the team wiki or within knowledgebase.*					
Checks:							
Document and reporting templates are documented and reviewed.						Complete ☐ Incomplete ☐	
Level 2 analysts have received training on the use of SOC document and reporting templates.						Complete ☐ Incomplete ☐	
SOC document and reporting templates have been published on team wiki and/or SIEM knowledgebase.						Complete ☐ Incomplete ☐	
Complete: (initial)							
Incomplete: (initial)							
Reason:							
Remarks:							

Technology Checks

Technology checks are useful when you are evaluating the readiness of the core technologies within your transitioned SOC. This will generally include a combination of SIEM or security analytics platform, case management, intelligence platforms, and other technologies. They will be specific to your own SOC; the following are provided as examples.

Check No.	**TECH.1**	**Rev:**	**1.0**	**Author:**		**Date:**	
Check Category:		Technology Readiness		**Required/Optional:**		Required	
Check Title:		SIEM Platform Checks					
Check Purpose:		To verify that the SIEM infrastructure has been configured to be used by SOC analysts.					
Check Setup:		This check assumes that existing SIEM instance will not be used by the SOC at go-live and that new SIEM production infrastructure is available for use at go-live.					
Procedure:		*1. Check that SOC analysts have been set up with appropriate access within the SIEM. This includes, at a minimum, (a) SIEM content writer set up with author permissions, (b) Level 1 SOC analysts set up as operators, and (c) Level 2 SOC analysts set up as analysts.* *2. Configure live channel for operators.* *3. Set up and validate notification groups, escalation levels, and destinations settings.* *4. Validate installed use cases and correlation rules.* *5. (Optional) Validate that knowledgebase includes SOC processes and procedures.* *6. (Optional) Validate that knowledgebase includes links to support processes and procedures.* *7. (Optional) Setup and configure custom reporting templates within the SIEM.*					

Checks:	
All SOC analysts have appropriate roles and permissions inside of the SIEM.	Complete ☐ Incomplete ☐
Live channel for operators is configured.	Complete ☐ Incomplete ☐
Notification groups, escalation levels, and destination settings are set up and validated.	Complete ☐ Incomplete ☐
Installed use cases and correlation rules are validated.	Complete ☐ Incomplete ☐
(Optional) SIEM knowledgebase includes SOC processes and procedures.	Complete ☐ Incomplete ☐
(Optional) SIEM knowledgebase includes links to support processes and procedures.	Complete ☐ Incomplete ☐
(Optional) Custom reporting templates have been set up and configured within SIEM.	Complete ☐ Incomplete ☐

Complete: (initial)	
Incomplete: (initial)	
Reason:	
Remarks:	

Check No.	TECH.2	Rev:	1.0	Author:		Date:	
Check Category:		Technology Readiness		**Required/Optional:**		Required	
Check Title:		Case/Investigation Management System Checks					
Check Purpose:		To verify that the case/investigation management system is appropriately set up for use by Level 2 SOC analysts and (optionally) Level 1 SOC analysts.					
Check Setup:		This check assumes that case/investigation management system will be installed and configured and is available for use at go-live.					
Procedure:		*1. Check that Level 2 SOC analysts have been set up with appropriate access within the case/investigation management system.* *2. (Optional) Check that Level 1 SOC analysts have been set up with appropriate access within the case/investigation management system.* *3. (Optional) Validate that team wiki includes man pages and instructions on how to use the case/investigation management system, including workflow.*					

Checks:	
All Level 2 SOC analysts have appropriate roles and permissions inside of the case/investigation management system.	Complete ☐ Incomplete ☐
(Optional) All Level 1 SOC analysts have appropriate roles and permissions inside of the case/investigation management system.	Complete ☐ Incomplete ☐
(Optional) Team wiki has been updated to include man pages and instructions on how to use the case/investigation management system.	Complete ☐ Incomplete ☐

Complete: (initial)	
Incomplete: (initial)	
Reason:	
Remarks:	

Check No.	TECH.3	Rev:	1.0	Author:		Date:	
Check Category:		Technology Readiness		**Required/Optional:**		Required	
Check Title:		Telephony and Communications Checks					
Check Purpose:		To verify that the telephony and communications systems are appropriately set up for use by Level 1 and Level 2 SOC analysts.					
Check Setup:		This check assumes that telephony, instant messaging, teleconference bridging, and video walls are in place.					
Procedure:		1. *Check that all Level 1 and Level 2 SOC analysts have been set up with individual telephony access, and after-hours/on-call personnel have been assigned corporate mobile phones.* 2. *Verify that group teleconference bridges are set up and in place for use during incident escalation.* 3. *Verify that instant messaging and desktop video conferencing is working between Level 1 and Level 2 facilities.* 4. *(Optional) Update team wiki and/or knowledgebase with instructions on how to use telephony, group teleconference bridges, instant messaging, and video conferencing.* 5. *(Optional) Verify that desktop and video conferencing integration with video wall in Level 2 facility is operational.*					

Checks:	
Level 1 and Level 2 analysts have been set up with individual telephony and (where required) mobile phones.	Complete ☐ Incomplete ☐
Group teleconference bridges are in place.	Complete ☐ Incomplete ☐
Instant messaging and desktop video conferencing has been tested and is working.	Complete ☐ Incomplete ☐
(Optional) Team wiki and/or knowledgebase have been updated with instructions on how to use telephony and communications systems.	Complete ☐ Incomplete ☐
(Optional) Desktop and video conferencing integration with video wall in Level 2 facility is operational.	Complete ☐ Incomplete ☐

Complete: (initial)	
Incomplete: (initial)	
Reason:	
Remarks:	

Check No.	TECH.4	Rev:	1.0	Author:		Date:	
Check Category:		Technology Readiness		Required/ Optional:		Required	
Check Title:		Service Ticketing Checks					
Check Purpose:		To verify that appropriate shared SOC/CSIRT ticket queues are in place.					
Check Setup:		This check assumes that the enterprise IT ticketing system is in place and operational.					
Procedure:		1. *Check that Level 2 SOC analysts have been set up with appropriate access within the enterprise IT ticketing system.* 2. *Check that a shared, closed queue called SEC-CSIRT has been set up within service manager and that access to this queue is available to all SOC Level 2 and CSIRT staff.* 3. *(Optional) Check that Level 2 SOC analysts have received basic service manager training or possess service manager experience at Belgacom.*					
Checks:							
All Level 2 SOC analysts have appropriate roles and permissions inside of the enterprise IT ticketing system.						Complete ☐ Incomplete ☐	
SEC-CSIRT ticket queue is set up within the enterprise IT ticketing system and Level 2 SOC analysts can access the queue.						Complete ☐ Incomplete ☐	
(Optional) Level 2 SOC analysts have received basic service manager training or have previous service manager experience at Belgacom.						Complete ☐ Incomplete ☐	
Complete: (initial)							
Incomplete: (initial)							
Reason:							
Remarks:							

Check No.	TECH.5	Rev:	1.0	Author:		Date:	
Check Category:		Technology Readiness		Required/Optional:		Required	
Check Title:		Wiki and Knowledgebase Checks					
Check Purpose:		To verify that the secure team wiki and SIEM knowledge platforms are set up and loaded with core SOC processes and procedures.					
Check Setup:		This check assumes that base wiki platform has been set up and configured on CSIRT servers.					
Procedure:		*1. Check that Level 1 and Level 2 SOC analysts have been set up with appropriate access within the wiki.* *2. Validate that core SOC processes and procedures have been uploaded into the wiki and (where appropriate) the SIEM knowledgebase.* *3. (Optional) Validate that links to supporting processes and procedures have been uploaded into the wiki and (where appropriate) the SIEM knowledgebase.*					
Checks:							
All Level 2 SOC analysts have appropriate roles and permissions inside of the wiki platform.						Complete ☐ Incomplete ☐	
Core SOC processes and procedures have been uploaded into the wiki/knowledgebase.						Complete ☐ Incomplete ☐	
(Optional) Links to supporting processes and procedures have been uploaded into the wiki/knowledgebase.						Complete ☐ Incomplete ☐	
Complete: (initial)							
Incomplete: (initial)							
Reason:							
Remarks:							

Summary

This chapter covered the common steps required to transition a SOC to a fully operational state. We started off by touching on challenges that will be faced before going live, along with recommendations to overcome such potential roadblocks. Next, the chapter covered developing a transition plan and managing expectations for short- and long-term service levels. After that, you learned about the importance of project management and building attainable requirements so that the new SOC can quickly show value to the organization. The chapter concluded with various checklist examples that you can use to verify the SOC is ready to go-live.

Now that you know how to go-live, the next chapter addresses how to react to events and incidents.

Chapter 11

Reacting to Events and Incidents

"It's not stress that kills us, it is our reaction to it."—Hans Selye

At their core, every SOC is in place to provide the capability to detect and investigate events, identify potential security incidents, and respond to such incidents as they occur. As discussed in previous chapters, whether the SOC can provide these services effectively depends on great people, good supporting process, and well-deployed and -managed technologies.

In this chapter, you learn how the people, processes, and technology parts of an effective SOC come together to react to events and incidents. The chapter examines what events are in the context of a SOC and the different ways we look at such events to determine whether they indicate a potential incident. The chapter also delves into how the SOC may help the organization respond to security incidents.

To help with understanding these concepts, the chapter presents a typical SOC organization such as the one described in Chapter 8, "People and Processes," but perhaps with a slightly narrower scope. In this fictional SOC, the SOC team reports to the CISO and offers services limited to providing front-line security monitoring, security incident investigation and response, and a little digital forensics. Other internal teams provide vulnerability management and various security functions. The IT organization provides enterprise IT service management practices, security services, and operation functions, although the SOC team has a lot of control over how their own systems and related content are configured and run.

To make things a little interesting, front-line 24x7 monitoring has been outsourced because the internal team is providing services only during business hours with on-call support. Both the internal and outsourced monitoring teams use the same systems, owned and deployed by the internal IT engineering team. Outside of this outsourcer, a specialist firm has been contracted to provide regular breach detection across most organizational assets. They also provide on-demand advanced forensics, malware analysis, and emergency response services during major incidents.

The chapter presents how a SOC would react to a typical incidental malware infection. Chapter 10, "Preparing to Operate," uses the same scenario to identify potential areas for improvement.

A Word About Events

Let's start by talking a little bit about *events*, because they might not be what you think they are.

As discussed earlier, events are really things we observe based on artifacts we have that you can use to indicate what may have happened in the recent (or in some cases, distant) past. For most new SOCs, this tends to mean focusing on the events that come in the form of logs generated by assets and security controls throughout the organization, or collated events that analyze multiple logs in the context of each other. As a result, SOC members spend a lot of time working on building and tuning security log management and security information and event management (SIEM) to help collect and interpret such logs in real time or over historical periods. Unfortunately, events in the form of automated logs or alerts generated by SIEMs represent the smaller portion of events relevant to security incidents in most organizations.

In 2014, the Economist Intelligence Unit issued a sponsored report looking into a large number of organizations that had recently experienced breaches. Although SIEMs and other automated systems often represent large investments for most organizations, only a third of global information security incidents were detected by SIEMs. The large majority of incidents were reported by employees or through routine checks.

What is important here is that the automated systems a SOC relies on to alert when something bad is happening work only some of the time. Human beings continue to be the best sources of event data, and in most SOC environments, the SOC will heavily rely on them to be able to detect events.

This is why we need to have a very inclusive definition for the word *event*. Yes, an event may include automated logs and other "machine exhaust" that may be generated by assets. But it also may include information provided via a phone call or e-mail from end users who just experienced something odd or clicked on something they should not have. Just focusing on the SIEM means that you will likely miss many security incidents or detect them much later than you should have.

Event Intake, Enrichment, Monitoring, and Handling

With such an inclusive definition in mind and our fictional SOC described, let's look at the various ways that we intake, enrich, monitor, and handle events within the SOC, starting with the SIEM. Keep in mind that an event can really be just about any observable artifact that indicates that something has happened.

When it comes to our chosen scenario (a malware infection), such events can come from a variety of sources. These include automated events generated by the targeted asset's subsystems such as system processes, applications, or the file system, by antimalware systems on that asset or on upstream platforms, through tickets created by the service desk or help desk, or through direct communications from the affected end user. We may even have the advantage of having enriched event data where additional information related to key pieces of information in the event is available.

Events in the SIEM

As discussed in earlier chapters, SIEMs work by collecting and collating event data (logs) from a wide variety of event sources, collating them together, and using a set of rules to automate the discovery of potential security incidents. It then prioritizes what it sees and alerts the SOC analyst for further analysis. In some cases, a SIEM may even take automated or scripted actions based on defined triggers, such as automatically generating tickets or creating incident reports within a case management system.

In some cases, the SIEM just acts as the middleman; analysis and alerting may be generated by some upstream system (for example, an intrusion prevention system [IPS]), and the SIEM is really just used to deliver the alert like any other event.

Events within traditional SIEMs are most typically normalized, and do not represent the original logged event. Normalization is the process of converting the native format and syntax of the event into something consistent within the system to make it easier to analyze. Some SIEMs, however, provide raw event data as well.

As discussed earlier, SIEMs are also primarily real-time analysis systems, meaning that they are primarily interested in performing analysis based on events that occurred in the recent past. Depending on how the SIEM is architected, the SIEM may analyze event data only from the past few days or past few months. Few analyze information going back further in time without having to re-import archived data.

SIEMs can also be limited to only accepting logs in particular formats, from particular vendor solutions or even specific versions of those solutions. This is mainly because every event source typically requires a parser that can interpret that particular set of events and extract meaningful data from it for analysis. Even if the SIEM can understand most event sources in the enterprise, most SIEMs will be tuned to look for specific use cases, and filter or ignore event data that it has not been told is relevant. This is done for a variety of reasons. It may be that the SIEM has been architected to handle only an average number of events per second (EPS) before it becomes overloaded or unstable. It may be that more event data is being collected than is actually shown to the SOC analyst, to keep them from being overloaded. SOC analysts are usually monitoring a specific channel that limits how many events they actually see on their screens any one time.

Many SIEMS also take advantage of freely available and commercial enrichment data sources that provide more information to the SOC analyst. For example, this could include IP reputation data that indicates whether a specific IP address captured in an event is associated with known malicious activity or from a suspect geographic location. Even internal data such as where a particular asset is physically installed may be used to enrich event data.

Events in the Security Log Management Solution

Often, the SOC has not only a SIEM but also a security log management solution either integrated with or separate from the SIEM itself. When available, such solutions tend to provide for the collection and delivery of event data to multiple systems, provide longer-term storage and retrieval options, and provide some reporting and analytics functions against the data that it stores.

Even when it is available, SOC analysts rarely monitor the security log management platform directly. Rather, this platform typically is used as an investigative tool, particularly when looking for potentially related events that either may not be included in the scope of the SIEM or are beyond the locally available event data in the SIEM.

Events in Their Original Habitats

In many cases, neither the SIEM nor the security log management platform contains all the event data that may be relevant. For example, event data may be available only through a reporting portal provided by a third party, a common situation when a managed service is being used by the organization. Think of examples like upstream denial-of-service (DoS) protections provided by your Internet service provider (ISP) or cloud provider, brand protection services, or even communications platforms like Twitter. In other cases, some systems may not share event data with the SOC platforms for a wide variety of reasons, from performance impacts to confidentiality requirements.

In these cases, the SOC analyst may require access to these event sources as needed or as requested, but will most likely rarely monitor them directly. A word of caution regarding this approach: Any manual effort to monitor such events will have a definite impact on monitoring and response service levels. It is recommended to avoid splitting event data between different groups and systems whenever possible to avoid visibility gaps.

Events Through Communications and Collaboration Platforms

If people report the majority of incidents (rather than automated systems), events coming through communications and collaboration will most likely be the most important event data. Such events can include just about any way that a human can tell the SOC that something has happened that may need to be investigated, including the following:

- E-mail
- Phone calls/messages
- Instant messages
- Service management tickets
- Intranet portal forms

Events through each of these intake mechanisms have to be assessed like any other event in the SOC. Where they might differ slightly is in determining who will perform that assessment and the method of response. It is less common for first-tier SOC analysts to monitor and address such events; more experienced analysts usually handle these. Unlike automated events in the SIEM, such events typically need to be responded to, if only to thank the individual for bringing it to the SOC's attention.

To help the analyst, it is important for all relevant information to be collected consistently to help ensure that complete and accurate information is being captured. This is certainly harder to do with e-mail notifications, but most other communications methods are open to the use of consistent templates. Although it is not appropriate to create a template for every imaginable situation, we recommend focusing on creating and maintaining templates for commonly recurring events such as phishing and malware reports.

Working with Events: The Malware Scenario

Let's go back to our scenario to see how SOC analysts would typically work with event sources across multiple platforms to assess potential incidents.

Sarah Connor is a second-line SOC analyst at Wereabank, a leading financial services firm, with a number of years of experience working in the SOC. As a member of a team of six second-line Level 2 SOC analysts working for the organization and someone with a lot of experience as a help desk analyst in her previous position, she typically handles incidents involving VIPs within the organization. Like her fellow SOC analysts, she tends to work during the day but also provides on-call support when it is her turn to carry the support phone.

In addition to the standard channel that is monitored by all Level 2 SOC analysts, Sarah has also created a separate channel to highlight events associated with some of her executive VIPs. The SIEM does not generally collect logs on end-user equipment, but it does collect logs from the network and network security devices, directories, servers, and a few critical business applications that the executives interact with on a regular basis. She can search up to 90 days of online data and have the engineering team load older data into a special environment if needed for additional investigations. She also has access to many but not all of the native systems that feed the SIEM.

On a particular Tuesday at around 9:45 p.m., a standard SIEM use case intended to capture unusual administrator activity was triggered and an alert was sent out. It indicated that an administrative account associated with Robert, a systems administrator, was attempting to log in to multiple systems he did not normally administrate. As he was attempting to log in to a number of key business-critical systems, this was flagged as high priority by the SIEM. Sarah, as the on-call L2 SOC analyst that night, received the e-mail in the shared mailbox to investigate.

She first logged in to the SIEM remotely to examine the alert and the other events associated with it. A quick examination of the alert seemed to indicate that this was not a false positive; she could see Robert's account logging in to multiple systems (contrary to policy). A quick query of the past 90 days showed that, although Robert appeared to have access to many of the systems he was currently accessing, he had never logged in to them before this incident.

Next, Sarah started to examine related events to see whether she could reconstruct what was going on. A quick examination of the logs in the SIEM showed that Robert had logged in to his computer at 8:29 p.m. It appeared to be a local login rather than through a remote connection. He opened Internet Explorer and also started Outlook. Once in his e-mail, he accessed a number of e-mails. Shortly afterward, Internet Explorer connected to the Internet and to a number of sites. The web proxy logs showed that Robert connected to a number of sites, but a quick examination did not indicate whether this activity was of interest.

Not certain what was happening given the information in the SIEM, Sarah called Robert directly. Robert was surprised by the call, and denied that he had accessed any systems to that point. While he was waiting for his maintenance window, Robert had just been catching up on e-mails, surfing the Internet, and preparing for his scheduled work.

He did say, however, that he was expecting someone from the help deck to call him about his ticket in the morning. When Sarah asked him about the ticket, Robert told her that he had received an e-mail asking him to update his HR profile. When Robert had attempted to log in to the website, it only showed a message that the server was down and to try again later. An hour later, at 9:30, he received a second e-mail indicating that the site was now up and that he could log in. However, when he tried to connect to the website, he could not connect properly. He logged a service ticket in the enterprise ticketing system to have someone look into it. Sarah asked him to forward a copy of the e-mail.

With a quick call to the corporate security office, Sarah was able to confirm that system administrator Robert arrived at the building parking at 8:12 p.m. and was in his office at 8:25 p.m. He had gone home earlier in the day and returned to execute an approved change during the normal maintenance window at midnight. He had scheduled access to the data center that night to perform the change.

Sarah also examined the e-mail and found that it was suspicious; it looked like an internal e-mail, but the link provided to the "HR system" appeared to point to the Internet rather than to an internal address. She also confirmed that Robert had indeed created a service ticket highlighting the issue he had experienced.

Relatively certain that this was not an obvious false positive, Sarah opened the case management system and created an incident report. She attached the events from the SIEM and screenshots of the other events she had found during her initial examination. Following the documented process, she escalated the report to the Level 3 Cybersecurity Incident Response Team (CSIRT). She then called the L3 on-call number to notify them of the escalation.

As you can see from this example, Sarah was able to investigate a wide variety of events from multiple systems, including logs supplied by native systems into the SIEM, alerts generated by the SIEM, native logs on the native platforms (such as logs in the ticketing system), and even physical access data via her colleagues in the corporate security team. Not all events will be typically integrated into a common platform, so she needed to pull potentially relevant events from a number of locations to include in her incident report.

Handling and Investigating the Incident Report

If an event is some indication that something has happened, an incident report is an indication that something bad has happened and worth further investigation. In the preceding example, Sarah created an incident report in the case management system to indicate that she believed that the events she had investigated constituted a potential incident. In other environments, such incident reports may even be created by the SIEM or other systems directly depending on what the case management system may support.

As discussed earlier in this book, case management systems (also known as investigation management systems) are used to coordinate the investigation of potential and confirmed incidents. As with every police procedural drama you may have seen, most cases start with a report that an incident may have occurred. Investigators can then use these incident reports to collect and analyze all the information about a case before deciding whether it is an incident. Then they may use the case/investigation management system to coordinate all actions taken to resolve a particular incident.

There are a number of open source and commercial case management tools available on the market, most sharing a set of common features. Most coordinate the end-to-end response, investigation, and reporting of security incidents. Most provide a secure web-based collaboration platform that allows for multiple parties to work together to investigate incident reports and manage incidents. Most provide the ability to report on individual incidents and provide trending data for longer-term analysis. Most provide some level of integration with other systems to streamline investigations and response, particularly integration with SIEMs, forensics platforms, and enterprise ticketing systems. Some also support compliance and security incidents, providing for anonymous incident reporting for ethics violations.

In some cases, the enterprise ticketing system itself may be used to manage such investigations. After all, this often represents the enterprise-wide IT service management platform, enabling common incident and problem management processes used across IT. Most SIEMs support direct integration with a variety of enterprise-class ticketing systems. In our experience, security is the main concern with reusing this system to support confidential investigations. The ticketing system may support closed queues and role-based access controls appropriate for a good case/investigation management platform, but these features may have not been set up or adequately configured. In other cases, open back-end reporting functions and APIs may unfortunately compromise the security of such investigations.

Case management tools do not, however, need to be expensive. Request Tracker for Incident Response (RTIR, available at https://www.bestpractical.com/rtir/) is an open source alternative that was developed to provide case management to the open source RT platform. It is used by many CSIRTs. Although it might require some customization particularly related to integration, it continues to be a robust alternative to commercial tools when cost is a factor.

In some cases, an investigation/case management platform may also be included within the SIEM itself or may also be provided by your outsourcing or managed services partner.

In any case, once an incident report is entered into the system, a suitable analyst is assigned to investigate it. In general, it is the analyst and not the system who decides whether an incident report constitutes an incident or a false positive.

Let's look at how this might work using our example.

Dan Kaminsky is a Level 3 CSIRT analyst who works for Wereabank, and happens to be the on-call resource on the night that Sarah reports the potential incident through the case management system. Dan is relatively new to the organization, but has a deep background in digital forensics and security incident response in a similar organization. This is, however, his first time working with Sarah.

On the night in question, once Sarah enters the incident report, the case management system sends off an e-mail to the shared CSIRT mailbox. As the one on call that night, Dan receives the e-mail concerning the new incident report. After he has logged in to the environment remotely, Dan is able to use the link to the case management system in the notification e-mail to quickly dive into the report.

Using the enterprise secure instant messaging system, Dan reaches out to Sarah to let her know that he has received the incident report and has begun his investigation. Using the same system, Dan and Sarah have a quick chat to discuss the outlines of the report so that Dan can get up to speed quickly. They agree that the incident report is not likely the result of a false positive, and they believe that it is a security incident. Further investigation, however, will be required. Using the contents of Sarah's incident report, Dan opens up a case.

Note the use of a secure instant messaging system in this example. In general, a SOC should be using a system that offers robust authentication and cryptographic features to not only ensure that Dan and Sarah know they are talking to each other but also so that others cannot inappropriately intercept and read their exchanges. For this reason, some SOCs deploy and manage their own secure messaging platforms. You learned about the deployment of secure collaboration in Chapter 9, "The Technology."

Creating and Managing Cases

Cases are different from incident reports: Someone usually has to decide that there is something worth investigating. Not every incident report is investigated; low-grade incident reports may never become a case under investigation. In some instances, a case may be made of a single, discrete set of events being investigated. Other cases may also include the investigation of multiple, interrelated sets of events.

In either case, even a simple and straightforward investigation might have a lot of moving parts with multiple avenues of enquiry being performed by multiple individuals across a number of different teams and disciplines. As a result, you typically need a repeatable methodology and templates available to ensure that each step in an investigation is captured consistently. Ensuring that you not only perform investigations consistently but can also report on them consistently is the core function of a case or investigation management system.

It is worth pointing out that we have not yet talked about incidents, just investigations, because not all cases become incidents. In general, an incident is a decision made by the investigator that a series of events with adverse consequences has indeed happened. In a large number of cases, the investigator may simply not come to that conclusion.

One obvious case is the situation where the events do not meet the threshold of an incident as it has been defined. For example, an incident may require that a certain amount of financial damage must have occurred, or the definition of an incident may be extremely narrow, limited to either a narrow range of conditions or a narrow range of assets.

Although it might seem otherwise, the less-clear case is a false positive. False positives may occur where the individual analyst or some automated system misinterpreted the available data and came to the wrong conclusion. For example, consider the situation where a SIEM may simply be configured incorrectly and it inappropriately triggers an alert. This might seem more obvious, but consider that such a false positive may actually be considered an incident in and of itself, requiring investigation into the root cause and addressing that problem to prevent it from recurring. It really depends on the definition of an incident and the analyst's application of that definition.

Let's head back to our example.

Using the open case, Dan begins to log what information has been collected to this point, adding notes to the event data and other information he has received from Sarah via the incident report.

When looking at the incident report, a number of things stand out for Dan. First, the e-mail itself is highly suspicious; there is no reason why an HR system would show as an external URL. Dan quickly surmises that this may a spear phishing attack directed at Robert and perhaps other administrators. Dan asks Sarah to continue to investigate similar events, starting with the e-mail. Using her access to the e-mail logs, can she determine when the e-mail arrived and where it came from? Can she see whether other, similar e-mails were also received by other administrators like Robert? Second, are they sure that the SIEM is reporting the true extent of the potential incident? Sarah is not confident that the SIEM is catching all possible events because she knows that many systems do not provide logs to the SIEM. She volunteers to investigate the e-mail logs: although they are not integrated with the SIEM, she does have access to them.

While Sarah investigates the e-mail angle, Dan starts to plan out the rest of his investigation. Consulting with the team's knowledge base, he knows that he has a number of directions he can explore, but because critical systems are involved they are somewhat limited by time. He is going to need some help.

Working as a Team

It is usually difficult for individual analysts to successfully respond to an incident on their own, even when that incident is relatively simple. The reason why is the analyst is operating under a large number of constraints. They might not have the right personal skills, either technical or interpersonal. They might not be able to deal with the stress. They might simply not have the time to do it themselves.

In most circumstances, the individual analyst must work well with a larger team, including other members of the SOC team and other parts of the organization and third parties. This is part of the reason why we recommend hiring for fit and not necessarily for skills: A well-working team requires individuals that fit, that support each other and have a similar set of values.

Another concern to be aware of is overloading a team. This usually manifests itself as poor coordination or poor communications, particularly with less-technical folks. To assist team members when this happens, it is recommended to engage one or more dedicated incident managers to coordinate response and a problem manager or two to coordinate remediation. These individuals typically work well under pressure and focus mainly on coordinating actions and on communicating status to executives and other key stakeholders.

Fatigue is also a big factor in any team. Reliance on one or two individuals for key skills might be fine most of the time, but a major incident may quickly burn out these individuals. One typical mistake that many SOC teams make is bringing in and using all their best resources right at the beginning of a major incident. Although it might sound like a good idea, in the longer run, it is dangerous to the health of the team. In the better organizations we have worked with, the incident manager coordinating the response to a major incident will ensure that key response resources are time-staggered.

You might need to consider the downstream effects when a major incident happens. Typically, other activities will be neglected. Backlogs will continue to grow. Things will not get done. In the case of a major incident, it is not a bad idea to have the ability to leverage burst capacity, either from another part of the organization or from a third party contracted to provide it. In general, this is most successful when engaging burst capacity for low-end simple tasks, but some organizations also use it to supplement high-end complex effort.

In our scenario, Dan is able to use a playbook provided on the team's knowledge base to begin to get the team in motion. Given that critical assets are involved, he knows that the first thing he will need to do is get the team's incident manager, Vicki Vale, up and running. Dan calls Vicki to brief her on what has currently been done and to provide her with a link to the current case after assigning Vicki to it.

While Vicki gets up to speed, Dan proceeds with his investigation. With Sarah working on the e-mail logs, Vicki starts to examine her options on the forensics side. The organization recently deployed an enterprise forensics solution on most critical assets, both to provide ad hoc investigations and also to actively scan for indicators of compromise (IOC). Although not all the critical systems flagged by the SIEM are covered, she does have the ability to scan for IOCs on a few of them.

Using the vulnerability scanning results incorporated into the SIEM, Dan also notices that some of the systems have not been scanned recently and that some recent scans show old patch levels. To be sure, he logs in to the vulnerability scanning system and initiates a new set of scans on both Robert's computer and the critical assets that may be involved.

When the scans are running, he shifts to looking at the potential for network forensics. Before he instructs Robert to disconnect his computer and deliver to the SOC for analysis, he wants to make sure that he is taking advantage of collecting any active network traffic coming from and going to his computer. Unfortunately, a quick examination of the packet-capture infrastructure available to the SOC shows that it may not be feasible. He is going to need to reach out to the network and server teams.

Working with Other Parts of the Organization

Many security incidents involve multiple different parties within the organization, such as the following:

- **Asset owners and custodians:** Because asset owners are directly impacted by any risk to their systems, they are almost always involved in any security incident. Asset custodians who care for such assets on a day-to-day basis will also be involved because they may be most familiar with the impact the incident may have on the asset. Assets here may include almost anything of value, from data through applications and infrastructure. Who may need to be involved will depend on the scope of the incident.
- **Risk management:** In enterprise risk management, security incidents typically fall under a category of risk called *operational risk,* and then usually under an area of risk called *hazard risk*. They will typically be involved to assess and advise whenever actual damage or *actualized risk* is being incurred.
- **Other security teams:** The SOC is certainly not the only security team who may be involved. Your organization may have multiple security teams, including teams focused on security governance, compliance, engineering, or operations. They will usually need to get involved, particularly if the SOC has limited access to some skills and technologies provided by other security teams.
- **Systems and database administrators:** Although these may be considered a type of custodian, these individuals will almost always need to be involved particularly when it comes to containment and remediation.
- **Network administrators:** The SOC team typically has somewhat limited knowledge of the network and how data actually flows through it. Apart from this expert knowledge, network administrators also have access to tools such as traffic analysis, raw packet capture, and other telemetry data that can prove useful during an incident. In many organizations, they also control key network security controls such as firewalls and proxies.
- **End-user support:** This team is usually focused on managing and maintaining end-user equipment. They will also typically control what applications can or may be installed on end-user equipment and may also manage endpoint security controls such as host-based antimalware, IDS/IPS, firewall, and data-loss prevention (DLP) software suites.

- **Help/service desk:** This team will provide the front-end coordination and communication with end users. They might be the first people to hear about an incident, and they are typically the first people collecting information about it as relayed by the end user or customer.
- **Communications:** Not to be mistaken for networks, this team is responsible for communicating both inside and outside of the organization, managing internal communication channels and also media relations. During an incident affecting a large portion of the organization or where you are dealing with a public incident, they are critical.
- **Legal:** Some incidents may have a legal angle, particularly where malicious activity has been found that may lead to criminal or civil proceedings in a court of law.
- **HR:** Some incidents may involve staff behaving with such malice, requiring HR support.
- **Audit:** Although they might seem a little odd on this list, auditors may be involved for a number of reasons. They may be involved simply to verify that documented processes and procedures are being followed. They might also be involved because an incident may touch on business and financial controls.

During incident response, you almost always work with other parts of the organization to assist with investigations or execute remediation. How formal you may need to be is really based on the organization. In some cases, it is just a phone call between two colleagues. In most cases, however, it is always a good idea that you discuss how you will engage ahead of time and not during a period of crisis. Keep in mind that there may be politics involved, so do not hesitate to discuss this with your sponsoring executive.

When the engagement process is defined, engagement tends to have a number of common features. First, that coordination is almost always performed via the enterprise incident management process rather than just the security incident management process controlled by the SOC. This means that enterprise incident managers are involved to manage the incident, while functional managers or even executives may lead the effort depending on the severity of the incident. Status reports and corporate communications will most likely be formalized and follow existing templates. Team engagement and coordination will be provided using the ticketing system. The key point is that the SOC does not control how a major incident is handled when a formal engagement process is properly defined.

In our scenario, the results of the scans that Dan initiated are not good. On the vulnerability side, at least half of the critical systems that Robert's account logged in to have vulnerabilities that are highly exploitable, particularly with administrative privileges like Robert's. Even systems that have been patched recently have a number of vulnerabilities that may be exploited, although requiring a higher level of skill. On the enterprise forensics side, a smaller number of the critical systems appear to have been breached via those vulnerabilities within the past couple of hours.

Following the process, Dan calls Vicki back, and recommends declaring a major incident. This will initiate a number of different actions that will ultimately bring most of the internal support teams online to help address the situation. Within 15 minutes, most of the on-call resources are online and engaged via a group conference call. While Vicki coordinates, Dan and Sarah explain what has happened and what is currently known. To Dan and Sarah, the most important thing to do will be to contain what is at this point an ongoing breach.

Unfortunately, there are no clear guidelines on how best to contain the breach. The asset owners are extremely reluctant to take their systems offline to repair them. These are, after all, critical systems for a reason: They are core retail and institutional banking systems that would have large financial impacts if they were taken offline. A number of different options are discussed, including restoring from backup, invoking business continuity plans, or continuing to run with the breached systems. After some discussion, they are convinced to move up and extend the scheduled maintenance window to allow for the affected systems to be restored. Luckily, the affected systems were all virtualized, which not only allows them to do this quickly but also allows them to save copies of the breached systems for further analysis.

At the same time, Robert's administrative account is disabled to prevent him from accessing and breaching more systems. Rather than just turn off his computer, Dan works with the network team to isolate the network traffic associated with his computer and capture as much raw network traffic as possible coming from and going to it. After a period of time, Robert is instructed to hibernate his computer and deliver it to the SOC for further analysis, because hibernation may allow for more analysis of the memory on his machine that might be lost if he just shuts it off.

While Dan waits for network capture and Robert's computer to be delivered, Dan engages a number of third parties that work with the SOC to provide particular SOC services.

Working with Third Parties

In most organizations, the internal SOC team delivers some but not all SOC services. This means the SOC relies on third parties to be available, consistent, and reliable as required for the remaining services. Best practice is for the SOC to clearly define scope, processes, and procedures prior to engaging third parties to ensure a better working relationship between the SOC and outside help.

In general, such third parties fall into three basic categories:

- **Contractors:** Contractors are typically engaged to perform a specific scope of work or perform particular functions for a set period of time. They often act like internal employees but are engaged either directly via contract or via a provider that may provide one or more contractors under a common set of terms and conditions.
- **Outsourcing providers:** Outsourcing providers will typically be engaged to provide a set of services based on your organization's technology estate, although they may bring in some supplemental technologies or process to support. Unlike contractors,

outsourcing providers are usually engaged to provide an entire end-to-end service with particular service levels as per the contract. How they provide that service is most often up to the provider, but because they are using your technology estate, the services are a little less standardized.

- **Managed service providers:** Managed service providers can be similar to outsourcers, but they typically provide the majority of the technology estate required to deliver the service as part of the cost. Like outsourcers, they are usually engaged to provide an entire end-to-end service with particular service levels as per the contract. How they provide that service is almost always up to the provider and may include leveraging a common set of tools and technologies provided from a provider location or via cloud-based services.

There is no one right way to leverage third parties, and it really depends on your organization's preferences. Whether you use contractors, outsourcers, or managed service providers, you need to manage them effectively. This means taking advantage of enterprise procurement, legal and vendor management practices, and also supplementing those practices with vendor management within the SOC itself.

Over the years, we have seen third parties engaged to provide a variety of services, including the following:

- **Front-line SOC monitoring:** In many cases, it may be simply too cost-prohibitive or difficult to provide the full coverage model you want for the security monitoring function. For example, you may be able to provide an internal team focused on business hours and on call, but cannot provide 24x7 security monitoring. Rather than focus the third party on second-line or third-line monitoring where deep institutional knowledge is a must, many organizations engage contractors or providers to provide front-line SOC monitoring. They require a consistent set of processes and procedures to ensure that it is effective and meeting required service levels.
- **Threat and vulnerability intelligence:** Most SOCs should maintain their own security intelligence services, but even skilled internal intelligence analysts may be limited by the relatively narrow range of intelligence sources available to them. It is common to engage third parties to provide automated threat and vulnerability intelligence feeds that are consumed by automated systems. In some situations, providers have also been known to provide onsite intelligence analysis to supplement the internal team while having access to the provider's wider resources.
- **Emergency response services:** Some third parties also provide emergency or critical response. For a flat rate for a contracted period of time, the provider will provide additional support in the case of a critical breach, usually within a specified timeframe and often with deep levels of expertise. This can prove handy for organizations with a limited ability to address breaches themselves or where engaging a third party may help contain a very public breach.
- **Advanced forensics services:** Advanced forensics can cover a lot of territory. Although many SOC teams have some digital forensics skills, a third party might

sometimes be required or preferred. This is particularly true for situations that occur infrequently, for which developing and retaining internal skills may be more difficult. Some common examples include advanced malware forensics, breach discovery services, or forensic evidence collection by a licensed or court-recognized forensics investigator.

- **Security engineering:** Because security engineering is often project based, third parties are often engaged to deliver complex platform deployments, migrations, or major upgrades.
- **Security operations:** In some cases, third parties may be engaged to provide day-to-day operational support for particular platforms, and to maintain those systems to particular service levels.
- **Burst capacity:** Some third parties also provide the ability to obtain a certain number of skilled resources in a fixed period of time to address sudden and unexpected bursts. While these individuals rarely have sufficient institutional knowledge, they typically provide required skill sets, experience, and certifications to assist with the unexpected load for a specific period of time.

In our example, Dan and his SOC lead have a number of third parties that they can engage to assist.

As mentioned earlier, front-line SOC monitoring is provided by a third party. Dan contacts the engagement manager from the provider and has them increase front-line capacity for a short period of time to deal with some of the inevitable backlog. With the potential that many of the second-line and third-line analysts will be engaged in the incident, many other potential incidents could be missed without some help. The provider also agrees to provide a couple of highly skilled SOC analysts that can supplement the second line.

Dan can also reach out to his threat and vulnerability intelligence providers and industry peers to determine whether similar attacks are being experienced elsewhere. A quick check reveals that this is indeed being experienced by multiple banks and financial institutions in the region, although details appear to vary. The intelligence provider suggests some additional IOCs to look for. A quick call to a couple of peers and Dan also has some IP addresses and e-mail addresses they have seen associated with similar attacks on their infrastructures.

Finally, Dan also has access to a firm that specializes in malware analysis. He forwards the original e-mail sent to Robert and samples of potentially malicious code from Robert's computer and the critical systems that were targeted. He also forwards the same to the organization's antimalware provider for analysis. Because the code has not triggered any responses from the antimalware systems, an update may be required. Sure enough, within a few hours, both the malware analysts and the antimalware vendor come back with news: The code samples from Robert's computer and the critical systems are identified as previously unknown variants on a popular Trojan used to allow remote access via a set of rotating command-and-control servers. The antimalware vendor provides an update to look for the malicious code.

Dan informs the incident team during the next status call. Sarah reports that similar e-mails were sent to all the systems administrators within the environment within the past 24 hours. Three of them also look like they read the e-mail, but it is not clear whether they clicked on the malicious link. A quick examination of the proxy logs seems to indicate that they did not; no suspicious connections appear to be heading to the Internet from their systems. This is confirmed when the antimalware update is applied and scans run through the enterprise estate. Two additional servers were found to be compromised and so were added to the list of systems to be restored.

Although all affected systems were quickly restored, the investigation and remediation activities continued for some time. Detailed analysis of each system was performed with the assistance of a third-party forensics firm providing additional support. They concluded that a limited amount of proprietary information was likely exfiltrated from the organization using Robert's access. Luckily, no personal data was likely disclosed. On the remediation front, changes to address the vulnerabilities that were exploited took some time to be made.

When all the analysis and remediation was complete, it was decided that the case could be closed.

Closing and Reporting on the Case

Just as you have specific incident, case, and investigation management processes, you also need specific processes and related procedures associated with closing a case. In particular, you need to ensure that all relevant information gathered is fully captured within the case before memories start to fade or people get distracted.

Closing a case can be a little complicated in practice. Unless it is fully resolved, it is often inappropriate to close it, even though there is usually pressure to do so from anxious executives. In some cases, an incident may be closed while the case remains open. For example, the immediate incident may have been resolved but the underlying problem or defect that could cause the incident to recur may still be unresolved. In some cases, such problems can continue for an extended period while resolution waits on the next major release or upgrade. It really depends on the situation.

There are a number of good reasons why it is a good idea not to close cases too quickly. Remember that a case can typically involve more than one incident or investigative line of enquiry. Although it might not be a high priority during a critical incident, performing deeper retrospective analysis into older event records may show that the incident has been going on for longer than initially identified or involving a wider range of victims. It may also be that some forensic examinations could take longer periods to perform. Until you are comfortable that the case is closed, do not close it.

Once an incident can be considered closed, you should also be fully prepared to report on it. Major incidents may be reported a number of different ways (from one-page executive summaries to detailed analyses running hundreds of pages) intended for a wide variety of consumers. Minor incidents might not get red carpet treatment, but they need to be rolled up into comprehensive management and executive reports showing short- to long-term trending.

One key area for reporting is identifying areas for improvement. There is always room for improvement, even when things go well. Every SOC must deal with varying levels of false positives and false negatives. Every incident may point to ways that things could be streamlined, augmented, or reengineered. It is important to identify commonly recurring areas where improvement would be most beneficial.

Summary

As you can see from the example in this chapter, security event monitoring and incident response is far from being an exact science. To be effective, it requires a combination of robust technologies, clear processes, and high skill. The incident was eventually managed, but Dan's final report identified a variety of areas for improvement.

The next chapter delves into some of those areas. Beyond just learning through incidents, the chapter also looks at some of the ways to assess existing SOC programs and drive continuous improvement efforts within the SOC.

Chapter 12

Maintain, Review, and Improve

"The day I'm not improving will be the day I hang up the racquet."—Venus Williams

Let's face it: Many new security operations centers (SOC) are not as good as they need to be. For the organization that may have just spent a small fortune setting up their SOC, it can be somewhat disheartening just how much the SOC will need to improve to justify that investment. It can be equally upsetting for the organization that has spent that fortune only to have the SOC function fail in its core mission, to lose key staff to competitors, or to spend good money on technical solutions that never seem to do the job they were built for.

On the contrary, your new SOC may be highly stable and prove even stronger under pressure than anticipated. This, however, is still just the beginning of the journey because there is always room for improvement. Security incidents can be discovered faster, mitigated faster. SOC staff can improve. Processes and procedures can improve. Technologies can improve.

Your new SOC may fall into either of these categories of success or somewhere between. The important fact is that all new SOC environments will be forced to evolve or will eventually fail. On the one hand, as organizational objectives and priorities change, a good SOC will look to ways that it can change to support shifting need. As you will see, this requires regular and frank communication with the organization's leadership. On the other hand, there will also be plenty of new and evolving threats to keep the SOC analysts and systems alert.

This chapter describes how to review and maintain your SOC and its services and how to bake in a continuous improvement program to guide its evolution. The chapter also covers how to evaluate your SOC for risk and for signs of its fragility. In this chapter, you also learn how to identify these factors and what can be done to remediate them.

Reviewing and Assessing the SOC

The SOC represents a sizable investment for most organization and probably the company's largest investment in information security. It typically represents a major capital investment because of the technological and physical infrastructure required to properly build a SOC. It also represents a long-term investment in operating funds, not just to maintain that infrastructure but also to staff it with highly capable security staff. It should be expected that your sponsoring executive or the board of directors will be very interested to know, at regular intervals, how successful that investment has been.

Reviewing your SOC is not that different from reviewing any critical and costly business function. While you may have standard review methodology in your organization, we have found that a five-step method works well to develop a report that will address updating leadership on the current state of the SOC:

Step 1. **Determine the review's scope.** This can certainly include all aspects of the SOC as part of a comprehensive review, but it is often more helpful to limit the scope to focus on particular areas.

Step 2. **Determine participants.** You will need to understand who will perform and participate in the review. This may depend on the scope.

Step 3. **Establish a clear methodology.** You will need a clear methodology to guide any review, along with expected outcomes and deliverables based on a predetermined template.

Step 4. **Determine frequency.** You will need to decide how frequently to perform such reviews. Some types of reviews may or should occur more often.

Step 5. **Prioritize results and action items.** Although it might seem obvious, any areas for improvement and related action items need to be prioritized, executed, and followed up.

The subsections that follow examine each step.

Determining Scope

There are two different approaches to scoping the review of the SOC services. First, you can choose a wide scope including all SOC and possibly also related functions with the goal of looking at the services holistically. Second, you can choose a narrow scope to dive deep into particular core services. In our experience, the former is ideal when you want to show the general progress of SOC development or when peer comparison is the goal. The latter is preferred when driving out specific gaps and priorities for improvement, particularly when rebaselining service levels, confirming regulatory or legislative alignment, assessing team performance, or when you may need substantial investment in a particular area.

Most organizations choose to do a more holistic capability-based assessment as a way to determine the best areas to focus on for improvement. Other organizations instead rely on even more general security assessments across the entire security function (for example, an ISO/IEC 27001 or 27002 assessment) or information security audits to provide a holistic view. Some prefer to focus exclusively on core services that directly impact the SOC's documented mission.

A number of key areas can be examined during a review. This can include the overall services that the SOC provides or detailed dives into personnel/staffing, processes, and procedures and technology investments. Let's examine each of these. In general, the scope of any review depends on your goals and the goals of your sponsors and how often you propose to perform them.

Examining the Services

When you want to provide a comprehensive, holistic review of a SOC, we have found that taking a services-oriented approach is often most useful, and it can be helpful to examine it using an ITIL-based approach. ITIL (formerly known as the Information Technology Infrastructure Library) describes a comprehensive set of IT management practices focusing on service strategy, service design, service transition, service operations, and continuous service improvement. With its strong focus on aligning IT services to business needs, ITIL provides a vendor- and organization-agnostic way to establish a baseline for expected services and provides an excellent framework for IT services management and continuous service improvement. It also has the added benefit of providing many of the core enterprise IT management processes such as incident and problem management that the SOC will typically need to align with.

In short, using an ITIL approach will typically help the SOC focus on clearly understanding what the organization and any other consumers of their services (such as customers) may expect of them and helps ensure that the SOC delivers to those expectations.

A services-based review typically focuses on five areas, aligned with the five major sections of ITIL, as discussed in the following subsections.

Service Strategy

As part of your regular review cycle, take a look at the current state of the overall service strategy. At a high level, a service strategy focuses on outlining the high-level target state and objectives for SOC services, typically over a long period. Some questions to ask about a service strategy are as follows:

- Is the current SOC services strategy documented or are there existing plans intended to guide SOC development for the next 1 to 3 years?
- Are all the current SOC services described, along with how they governed?
- Are the consumers of the SOC services known along with their expectations?
- Is the mission statement of the SOC or individual services documented and current? Does it align with service consumers' expectations?
- Is the SOC service strategy aligned with the rest of the security organization? How about the organization's business goals?

Service Design

Also as part of your regular review cycle, it is a good idea to look at the service design. Service design typically delves into each SOC service in detail. The following are suggested questions that should be addressed or explicitly documented within the current design:

- Is the current services design documented?
- How are other security services designs documented within the organization?
- Is there a current RACI/RASCI model covering current core and auxiliary SOC services?
- Who are the primary consumers of SOC services? Have you documented or updated their requirements recently?
- What services are currently consumed by the SOC to provide their services?
- What services provided by others are supported by the SOC services?
- What external services are used by the SOC (for example, forensic evidence collection, malware analysis, threat/vulnerability intelligence, brand protection platforms, antifraud providers)?
- What are the current service levels, KPIs, KRIs, and other metrics tracked as part of the service? Can previous attainment data be shared in summary form?
- How are SOC services reported? To whom? How often?
- Is the current physical architecture/infrastructure documented, including physical security controls and SOC layout?
- Is the current technical architecture/infrastructure documented?
- Does the service design align with the current service strategy?

Service Transition

Although typically less frequently examined than strategy or design, it is important to look at how new SOC services are transitioned into production or major changes are made to existing services. You also need to examine how aging SOC services may be retired or replaced. A more structured approach is usually helpful. Some questions to ask regarding service transition are as follows:

- How are new services transitioned into production?
- How are existing services evolved or migrated?
- How are existing services decommissioned?
- Is there a standardized project management office (PMO) with related processes in place to govern SOC transitions?

Service Operations

Service operations are focused on the day-to-day effectiveness of the SOC services. This should be evaluated often to identify potential gaps and critical areas for improvement. We typically ask a number of questions intended to find common weaknesses in SOC services, such as the following:

- Do you have current processes, procedures, baselines, standards, and guidelines related to SOC services?
- How are these communicated to the SOC community?
- How is related service operations documentation shared? This may include not only copies of formal documentation but also access to current knowledgebases, SOC team portals, wikis, and other platforms as needed.
- How is financial performance of the SOC tracked and reviewed?

Continuous Service Improvement

Under ITIL, all aspects of SOC services need to be driven according to a continuous improvement program, including the service strategy, design, transition, and operations practices highlighted earlier in this chapter. Reviews in this area are obviously not going to be useful until you have your SOC services fully in place, but once you do, it can be invaluable. A few good questions can help to determine whether there is a suitable program in place and whether the program is healthy:

- Does the SOC currently engage in any closed-loop continuous service improvement processes?
- How is such improvement targeted and tracked over time?
- Can you highlight concrete actions that were taken to address highlighted areas for improvement?
- How are improvements reviewed and funded?
- Have improvements proven to be cost-effective?

Personnel/Staffing

When evaluating personnel and staffing, typical individual performance reviews are highly recommended and should be directly aligned with HR-driven employee development programs. In addition, it is also a good idea to use regularly scheduled reviews to examine capacity, scheduling, recruitment, and retention more holistically. The questions outlined in Table 12-1 should not only allow you to ensure that your personnel and staffing plans are properly documented but also that they are also effective. As you can tell, there are a lot of areas to dive into; it might be wise to plan separate reviews related to personnel and staffing.

Table 12-1 *Personnel/Staffing Questions*

Personnel/Staffing Concern	Question
SOC Operations Capacity and Scheduling	Identify the current staffing model (24x7, 8x5, 8x5 with on-call rotation, and so on).
	Describe how SOC capacity management is performed.
	What is your current shift model?
	How is your staffing model described? How many personnel do you have and do they have primary functions assigned (that is, roles and responsibilities)?
Staffing Model and Tiered Levels (Number of SOC Staff and Primary Task)	Does the SOC employ a tiered model (for example, L1 analysts, L2 analysts, L3, CSIRT)?
	How are these tiers intended to interact? Are such interactions generally effective?
Staff Recruitment	How is SOC staff recruited?
	Are staff contractor, internal hires, or external providers?
	Is project-based staff recruited in similar ways?
	Are standard job descriptions developed outlining required, recommended, and preferred job skills?
	Does the SOC have any relationships with outside academies and universitics?
	Does the SOC have any relationships with industry peer groups?
	Does the SOC have any relationships with recruitment firms or service bureaus?
Staff Development and Retention	Is there a current SOC staff development and retention program in place?
	What are current retention rates per job function?
	Does the SOC leverage any job rotation, secondment, or mentoring programs?
Staff Training	What general or specialized training is available or required for SOC staff?
	What internal learning management systems, vendor on-demand, or other training options are available to SOC staff?
	What is the frequency of staff refresher training?

Table 12-1 *continued*

Personnel/Staffing Concern	Question
External Staff	How is external staff leveraged within the SOC services (if applicable)?
	Are standard contract templates in place governing external staff?
	How is external staff evaluated from a performance and effectiveness perspective?
Staff Performance	How is staff performance measured?
	What programs are in place to focus on staff performance improvement or attainment?
	Is there a documented incentive program in place?

Without reading too much into a single incident, you may see a number of interesting areas to dive into from a staffing and personnel perspective with our sample scenario from Chapter 11, "Reacting to Events and Incidents." The Wereabank SOC team used in that example is fairly hierarchical with different tiered levels of analysts filled by outsourced and internal staff. It is critical to review the health and effectiveness of this type of organization on a regular basis. We refer back to the Wereabank example SOC team later in this chapter.

Processes, Procedures, and Other Operational Documentation

Most SOCs have fairly extensive processes, procedures, and operational instructions documented in a variety of ways. In general, you want to examine the completeness, currency, and effectiveness of any of the following:

- Network and systems diagrams covering SOC services scope
- Security services documentation within SOC scope
- Case/investigation management processes and procedures
- Incident management process and procedures
- Performance metrics and reports (daily/weekly/monthly/quarterly)
- Ticket/incident report management processes
- Wiki/knowledgebase access
- Document templates
- Analyst training materials
- Enterprise IT service management processes (for example, incident, event, problem)
- Vulnerability management process (including threat modeling)
- SOC systems documented configurations/policies

The scenario from Chapter 11 highlighted a number of key processes and procedures governing event, incident, and case management that could be in scope for review. Also note in Chapter 3, "Assessing Security Operation Capabilities," that we evaluated some of these items during the initial assessment of components that would be used to build a SOC or existing SOC. As stated in Chapter 3, the assessment procedure is a continuous process designed to improve the overall capabilities of the SOC.

Technology

A functioning SOC relies on a substantial technology stack to be effective. The following questions are intended to cover the technologies currently either monitored by the SOC or typically used by the SOC to provide its services:

- List all tools/products used to identify security incidents or managed by the SOC.
- Please list any security event sources in use in the environment. Although this list is not comprehensive, examples include the following:
  - Firewalls
  - Routers
  - Switches
  - Network IDS/IPS
  - Host-based IDS/IPS
  - Content filters
  - Antivirus or antimalware systems
  - Web proxies/gateways
  - Enrichment data (for example, DNS, DHCP, IP reputation)
  - Digital forensics platforms
  - File integrity systems
  - Antifraud systems
  - Directories
  - Other AAA systems
  - Servers
  - End-user equipment
  - Mobile device management systems
- Looking at the list you've put together, are there any sources that are available but not being used today? Why? Are these sources accessible to SOC analysts through their native platforms?

- Do you have historical metrics illustrating current technical capacity and integration? For example, how many security events are detected in a period of time and responded to?
- What products/tools are currently in place (if any) used to correlate/display incident information (for example, security information and event management [SIEM] systems plus other data analysis/reporting tools, native management platforms accessible by the SOC)?
- Are there any big data platforms currently in place for either real-time (streaming) or historical analysis? How are they used today?
- What case or investigation management tools/platforms are currently used today? Are these tools integrated with other systems, such as the SIEM, enterprise service management ticketing systems, notification/alert platforms? How is confidential investigation information handled?
- Do you use any products/methods to centrally collect/store security-relevant logs?
- What are current retention policies for such data? Are you currently aligned with these policies?
- What is the actual capacity for short-, medium-, and long-term data storage? Does this meet currently known requirements and growth projections?
- Does this also include raw packet captures, NetFlow, and other telemetry?

Again, our scenario covered a lot of the typical SOC applications and infrastructure that might be subject to review, including the SIEM, case management, service management, and enterprise forensics. It might also include the many source systems ingested by SOC systems.

Scheduled and Ad Hoc Reviews

Reviews should be regularly scheduled to occur at key points during the year and your SOC strategy. General reviews should occur on an annual basis with specific, focused reviews happening a few times each year. Some specific functions like threat intelligence and other enrichment may need to be evaluated more often.

Timing of assessments will be important, particularly because they provide valuable input to regularly scheduled planning and budgetary cycles. If, for example, you typically submit updated plans and budgets in June, it is a good idea to complete annual reviews at least a couple of month's prior. This gives you time to consider your priorities based on findings and marshal your arguments to get money you will need to execute. Scheduling the review in July would be counterproductive because it would be almost a year before you could submit requests for the following year's budget, and by then, your findings and priorities would probably be out of date.

It might also be important to time reviews around important audit, business continuity, disaster recovery, regulatory, and compliance activities. The reason being these activities typically require substantial resources from the SOC, which would not let them devote their time to the core mission. Trying to execute a review at the same time as running other large projects would likely be disastrous.

Ad hoc reviews can occur without much prior scheduling or coordination and, therefore, they must have a focused scope or risk causing considerable disruption to the SOC. They are best suited for evaluating SOC performance in a particular area or as a follow-up activity after an exercise. Such exercises are discussed a little later in this chapter.

Internal Versus External Assessments

A number of different parties can assess the SOC, each providing their perspective on SOC services.

Internal Assessments

Internal reviews are focused on self-assessment. Although it might lack the perceived impartiality of external assessments, such internal reviews are vital to discussing and solving issues within the SOC in an open environment. Internal reviews can also be used to identify potential areas of friction between individuals within the SOC or friction between the SOC and other parts of the organization.

Results of such assessments are not typically shared widely and may only be seen by a few key individuals. In this way, any "dirty laundry" can be evaluated discretely and may give the SOC leadership the time and latitude to deal with the situation within the organization.

External Assessments

External assessments involve an external party to perform the assessment. It is quite common to engage external parties to help assess the SOC, and the reasons tend to be so broad that a separate book could be written about them. Perhaps the assessor brings a wealth of real-world experience and a way to communicate effectively. Perhaps there seems to be so many issues within the SOC that it is hard to focus on any of them. Perhaps the organization just has a tendency to listen to consultants in a way that they cannot listen to their own people. Unfortunately, in the absence of focused international standards, the best that external assessors can do is assess a SOC against rather nebulous "best practices." Although this term tends to be overused, best practices are really just *peer practices*: what people in similar organizations are doing today.

Such comparisons can prove useful for a number of reasons. If you are working in an industry where peers are notorious for not sharing, such external assessments performed by a relatively neutral third party can give the SOC some insight. For most organizations, a positive comparison to their peers is extremely important. It is also critical to note that due care and due diligence require that you at least match what your peers are doing.

If you do engage a third party to perform an assessment, try to get the most out of it. Choose third parties with a proven track record of assessing similar organizations. Ensure that you clearly understand the methodology they will use to assess you. Where they may use automated tools (to evaluate your current technologies for example), ensure that they can explain the results in a format you can benefit from. Review everything they produce and do not accept any of their results at face value.

Most of all, ensure that the assessment meets the needs of the various different audiences for its deliverables. A detailed, technical assessment might be very useful to security engineers and operators but far less useful to executive sponsors. Glossy presentations and visualizations will be handy to illustrate current state for the executive, but will be much less useful for SOC staff looking for practical, straightforward ways to improve. Usually, you want deliverables in a number of formats that cater to both technical and executive audiences.

Assessment Methodologies

As mentioned earlier, there are no international, vendor-neutral standards for SOCs, and just about every consulting firm will have their own take on how best to assess SOC services. Most consulting firms, however, do have some common features that allow them to execute their assessments consistently and easily compare their various customers.

Maturity Model Approaches

Most external assessments are based in part on the application of a capability maturity model. As discussed earlier in this book, such models look at each major function within the SOC. They then determine both how mature they are and how that level of maturity compares to peer organizations. It also provides an easy and intuitive way to chart out future development based on higher maturity. For example, consider the individual finding from a typical assessment outlined in Table 12-2.

Table 12-2 *Operations Example of the Use Of Metrics*

Area	Current	12 Months	24 Months	Justification
Operations: Security Metrics and Measurement	2	4	5	Developing and applying metrics is critical to the operation of any security program. Metrics are calculated using measurements that are collected during the SOC services operation. It is expected that a number of simple metrics will be developed in the first two years, followed by more sophisticated metrics in the third year.

In this example, the customer has defined security metrics, but these are not being used consistently. By the end of the first 12 months after the assessment, the customer not only wanted to capture and use metrics consistently (a maturity level of 3) but also wanted to quantitatively measure and review the effectiveness of the metrics (level 4). After 24 months, they wanted to institutionalize continuous improvement (level 5) for the various metrics and other measurements for the SOC services.

This type of approach has obvious advantages and some rather not-so-obvious disadvantages. On the one hand, it allows you to focus development on areas where higher levels of maturity may be desirable or to align that development with industry peers. On the other hand, it really does not know how to handle elements of the SOC that may be highly effective but will *never* be mature. For example, a talented, autonomous SOC analyst might be able to respond effectively to security incidents without using a consistent and documented approach. This does not make their approach wrong, but it certainly would not tally well under a maturity-based approach.

Services-Oriented Approaches

One alternative to evaluate a SOC from a services perspective is to focus less on whether the services exhibit signs of maturity and instead target whether the services are actually successful. This means examining the services for evidence that they are meeting expected service levels during the in-scope report period and the status of key performance indicators (KPI), which tends to look at longer-term trending. Finding any point of underperformance should become the focus for prioritized improvement, whereas identifying a higher than expected performance may indicate an opportunity to raise baselines.

For example, the security monitoring service is a typical core service of the SOC focused on security event monitoring and security event analysis by SOC analysts to determine whether a potential security incident should be investigated. Service levels associated with this service typically focus on a number of key areas:

- **Average incident response time:** The average amount of time that the analyst takes to complete security event analysis of a security event, perform incident identification/classification, decide whether the incident requires escalation or remediation, and escalate to more senior analysts or the appropriate incident response team based on defined parameters. Service levels here focus on how quickly analysts are expected to respond when something is flagged for their review.
- **Average escalation fidelity:** Sometimes also referred to as *response fidelity*, this value represents whether escalation activities taken by the monitoring analyst were appropriate. This usually reflects a number of factors. Based on root cause analysis after the incident, a lower-than-expected level of fidelity may indicate (a) gaps in individual analyst skill/knowledge and thus requiring additional experience or training, (b) prevalence of false positives within automated systems and thus requiring tuning, or (c) inappropriate or imprecise procedures and thus requiring update. This particular service level can vary widely because it is usually based on the median experience of the analyst team (that is, more junior analysts have lower fidelity

responses than more senior analysts) or when using a managed service provider where high fidelity is a contractual requirement.

- **Ticket queue backlog:** Events that are not addressed by a SOC analyst typically accumulate over time. Often (but not always) these are informational or low-severity events that have been deprioritized by more severe incidents. A larger-than-expected backlog typically indicates either the need for higher staff capacity or more automation. Service levels here focus on the amount of backlog in automated event monitoring systems (for example, the SIEM) and manual event monitoring systems (for example, e-mails to the SOC shared e-mail box, phone calls to the hot line). The SOC is generally expected to maintain an acceptable level of backlog.
- **Incident management procedure conformance:** Where specific procedures are documented, SOC analysts are expected to follow them. This is in contrast to processes that are intended to guide decision making but not constrain. First-generation procedures, however, tend to be imprecise or incorrect and can be a factor in non-conformance. Service levels here focus on acceptable levels of conformance.

These are not to be mistaken for metrics that are simply elements of the services that can be quantified and presented as part of operational, management, or executive reports. They are often useful to show trending for the amount of work being performed over time. For security monitoring, this typically includes metrics related to the following:

- Number of events through the SIEM during the reporting period
- Number of phone calls received by SOC during the reporting period for user support
- Number of incident reports created during the reporting period
- Number of tickets during the reporting period
- Number of false positives identified during the reporting period
- Number of escalations during the reporting period
- Number of systems reporting to the SIEM during the reporting period
- Tracking of critical, high, medium, and low events discovered during the reporting period

Performance and metrics, however, are only part of the picture because they provide little insight into the future sustainability of the SOC services. A SOC may, for example, be attaining current service levels, but there may be undiagnosed risks that could jeopardize the ability for those services to be maintained into the future. Typical key risk indicators (KRI) for security monitoring services might include the following:

- **Capacity:** Upcoming shift schedules would indicate insufficient capacity to maintain service levels.
- **Backlog:** Current event backlog within monitoring systems is more than 7 percent; response to incident reports via other intakes is consistently taking longer than 24 hours.

- **Monitoring systems' content:** Monitoring systems are exhibiting a high number of false positives; incident reports via other intake indicate that monitoring systems are not catching relevant events/alerts.
- **Knowledge capture:** Wiki is inactive; knowledgebase has not been updated recently.
- **Skill coverage:** Current staff skills are not adequate to support the service.
- **Morale:** Staff morale is considered to be low.

These typically represent danger signals that will need to be addressed before they can lead to serious issues within the SOC service.

Using a formal evaluation of services based on service levels, KPIs, and KRIs does not work for every business. For a less-formal or at least more fluid approach that helps generate discussion, a simpler questionnaire-based approach is sometimes preferable.

Post-Incident Reviews

Another key way to evaluate current SOC services is by performing frequent post-incident reviews. Such reviews focus on building the narrative of the incident from the beginning through the end, combining the experiences of everyone involved. Because memories are notoriously unreliable, it is always best to perform such reviews within the first 72 hours of an incident, but often you may need to wait for a suitable lull to be able to follow up and report on how the incident was handled.

In our experience, we have seen such reviews take multiple forms, from formal inquiries to informal chit-chats. In almost all use cases, there is a big chance that the user being interviewed will go off the rails and cause long-term damage either to individual analysts or the team as a whole.

Why? Because incidents are *emotional.*

Incident response is not a mechanical process like processes, procedures, and technology. Incident response is the result of that strange and very human combination of skill, intuition, and passionate inquiry. Major incidents in particular require a huge investment, often where the analysts' own lives take second place. Sometimes dealing with a major incident can stress out a responder and damage their pride. Many responders that deal with a major attack against their performance do not recover from what feels like a very personal attack. Those responders lose passion to be part of the team, which contradicts the work the SOC team lead has invested to encourage a positive collaborative environment.

For this reason, post-incident reviews should be performed very delicately. Here is some general advice:

- **Know your team.** How well do you know your analysts? Do you think you can tell when they are happy, sad, angry, frustrated, confident? As individuals, do they do well discussing things in groups, small teams, or one on one? Are they introverts? Are they extroverts? If you do not know, how can you expect to choose the most appropriate forum, structure, and approach for the review? Take the time to really get to know your team. Activities such as team outings that do not involve work can really help in this area.

- **Be very careful with blame.** Even when a response is completely successful, there is always something that could have gone better (something that could have been detected a little faster or responded to more effectively). It is rare to find everything was done perfectly. So, when you decide that something or someone is to blame, it is important to gently put it into perspective. Even assigning blame outside of the team is a little dangerous; it might help you to build team morale but usually at the cost of valuable external relationships with other teams, providers, and partners.
- **Encourage self-assessment.** Honest self-reflection is a rare skill, but one that you need to encourage in your responders. Before you dive into things with your own opinions and conclusions, let them assess their own performances first. Did they respond well? Are there areas they wish they could improve? In most cases, you will find that good analysts will come to similar conclusions on their performance if you give them a little time. However, if they are wildly off the mark, you need to know that too; self-delusion is not a luxury you can afford within the team.
- **Avoid bias and favoritism.** As leaders, it will be important for you not to bias your own responses in favor of the people you happen to like more than others. Bias is, of course, natural and very human, but you need to be aware that it can often create odd blind spots in your analysis. Where you feel most compromised by your own limitations, it might be best to bring in a more neutral third party to help out.
- **Ensure any recommendations are practical and achievable in the short term.** Post-incident reviews are not the time to focus on long-term strategic improvements to SOC services. Instead, focus on what improvements could be made over the coming days and weeks. Is there ways to improve existing process or procedures? Perhaps the wiki or knowledgebase needs an update to guide better response? Perhaps some rules or use cases can be better tuned? Focus on the influence of incidents within the bigger strategy outside of the post-incident review process.

Let's look at a typical post-incident review. As you may remember from the scenario in Chapter 11, our SOC analysts, Sarah and Dan, worked closely with a large team of internal and external resources to deal with what turned out to be a major security incident. After the closure of the incident, and the related case, Mark Farina, the service manager for the SOC, was asked to provide a post-incident report to the CISO, who would then be presenting the results to his own executives.

Mark had gotten engaged once a major incident had been declared, but had not been actively involved in dealing with the incident, instead leaving that to Sarah, Dan, and the other resources to run with it. This was consistent with Mark's management style, preferring to provide guidance and an escalation path rather than managing every incident himself. He prided himself on providing his analysts with a wide degree of autonomy. He had obviously worked with Sarah for many years, but this was his first opportunity to see how Dan handled a major incident.

Within a few days of the incident, Mark sat down with his analysts and each of the major players involved to talk about the incident. What did they think went well? What didn't?

Sarah and Dan pointed out a number of areas for improvement, including the following:

- **Integration issues:** Both Sarah and Vicki noted that the SIEM was not really the "single pane of glass" into the environment that they hoped for. Major event sources involved in the incident (particularly the e-mail systems and forensics systems) were not integrated. In addition, there was no integration between the SIEM, case management, and service management systems. Manual cut-and-paste operations made them slower.
- **SIEM correlation rule improvements:** Sarah also noted that although the SIEM flagged some anomalous behavior by Robert (the administrator), it did not actually catch the actual incident. This would seem to indicate that some improvements could be made on the correlation rules that the SIEM used to determine malicious activity. This may have helped the outsource Level 1 monitoring flag the malicious activity earlier.
- **Coverage issues:** They also noted that some systems were not covered by the enterprise forensics platform. If it had been deployed on Robert's end-user equipment, this may have allowed the attack to be discovered more quickly.
- **Patch currency issues:** They also noted that many systems were not current with patches.

On the positive side, the analysts noted how well things worked with the outsourcing provider (who provided burst capacity although they were hampered by the SIEM) and intelligence, malware analysis, and forensics provided by their third-party suppliers.

Mark also talked with the other participants with the other IT teams. Overall, the feedback from Vicki (the incident manager) and the other IT people involved in the handling of the incident was generally positive.

For his part, Mark noted that although the Level 2 analyst (Sarah) had sufficient information to open a case, it only happened once Vicki (the Level 3 analyst) was engaged. This seemed to point to a possible issue with the way the team had been structured. During a brief one-on-one with Sarah, she confirmed that she just did not feel confident declaring a case without Vicki's support, even though she had the deeper institutional knowledge. Mark made a note to examine this in the context of the general staffing/resourcing review later in the year.

When Mark presented his initial findings to the CISO, however, he received a nasty surprise: The affected business units had already called up the CISO and bent her ear about how the response had seem disorganized and inefficient. They blamed the CISO for what they saw as substantial failures to protect the organization's assets. Mark passionately jumped to the defense of his analysts, but the CISO calmly sat him down.

As the CISO explained, the problem was not with the analysts, but with the expectations that the business units had of the services the SOC provided. While the business expected the SOC to be able to protect and respond actively to mitigate breaches, the SOC was really only enabled to monitor and escalate. In short, there was a problem with the very strategy that the SOC was based on. This was going to require significant improvements to SOC if it was going to align to the business's expectations.

Maintaining and Improving the SOC

Reviewing and assessing the SOC on a regular basis and after key incidents will certainly help identify areas for improvement, whether it is to services, the SOC team or the SOC's technology investment. Part of the team lead's job will be to prioritize and drive action to address the most critical areas while staying within financial means.

At the same time, it is often better to not rely on such reviews and assessments too much. It may be better to focus on maintaining the SOC the company has invested in as a way of addressing potential problem areas before they come up in a formal review.

In any case, let's look at the various ways to maintain and improve a SOC's services, teams, and technologies.

Maintaining and Improving Services

As mentioned earlier, the management of a SOC should include a continuous service improvement program. ITIL provides a well-structured way to help ensure that all elements of the SOC services exhibit a targeted level of quality and financial effectiveness.

Although we will not go into ITIL continuous service practices in depth here, it may be helpful to understand its goals and basic method. At its heart, ITIL focuses on ensuring the all IT services exhibit the desired levels of quality even though there is always room for improvement. Although there are many quality management models available nowadays, ITIL was based on one of the oldest: the Plan-Do-Check-Act (PDCA) model first proposed by Demming in 1950 and implemented by many organizations since. Although less explicit within the current version of the standards, ISO/IEC 27001 clauses implemented this approach in the development and operations of information security management systems (ISMS).

Using a PDCA model, ITIL looks at IT service management to ensure that there are appropriate plans in place, that these plans are executed as intended, that the results are checked, and that any deficiencies are acted upon. It also works to continuously align IT services with evolving business needs and ensure that they are cost-effective. When successful, an ITIL continuous service improvement program helps to ensure that the business gets the most out of what it is paying for.

In general, ITIL uses metrics derived from the day-to-day operations of a service to determine whether it is meeting expectations. As part of service strategy and design, you should define what metrics, service levels, and KPIs you plan to measure. Service design must also determine how the data associated with such measurements will be captured, collated, stored, analyzed, and reported. These are then implemented as part of service transition and executed under service operations. The data is regularly analyzed to identify trends, spot gaps, and highlight potentials areas that may impact the organization. Results are presented to the organization's leadership, identifying areas for improvement and providing recommendations as to how they may be achieved. Finally, the selected actions are taken, and the continuous improvement process begins again.

The services delivered by a SOC are no exception. To be effective, SOC services have to be closely matched to the organization's needs and expectations. As business goals, objectives, and related expectations change, the SOC must be expected to continue to show business value worth the investment in SOC services. You also not only need to maintain current levels of service quality but also show improvement as your SOC grows and matures.

Assuming that you set up your SOC services according to basic ITIL principles, building in continuous improvement is relatively straightforward. Using the metrics and other measurements for each service (such as the service levels and KPIs discussed earlier in this chapter related to security monitoring services), you can quickly determine whether they meet the documented business needs. On a regular basis, you can present not only attainment to stated goals but also make recommendations as to how they may be improved. Such improvements then form the basis of short-term fixes and long-term investment.

It is important to note that this approach is inherently *quantitative*. It is based on measurements, so it is important to be able to quantify just about anything you want to include under service improvement. For example, the consumers of your services may express a certain level of approval for the current levels of service being provided, but these have to be turned to quantitative data to be useful. At the same time, it is obvious from this example that some data will tend to be less subjective or more consistent than others; opinions are not only subjective but also remarkably inconsistent.

It is perhaps for this reason that pure ITIL-based approaches are more confident when it comes to using process maturity as a key metric. After all, it is relatively straightforward to measure and track improvement. However, as discussed earlier in this book, process maturity is not a terribly good way to ensure the success of your SOC. Therefore, you need to temper a pure ITIL approach with a heavy focus on more qualitative elements, particularly your SOC team.

In this scenario, a mismatch clearly exists between the business unit's expectations and the ability for the SOC to deliver to those expectations. Although the CISO understood that some of their reaction was in the heat of the moment, she recognized that similar feedback would continue to occur if nothing was done.

Thankfully, she had a great working relationship with the business unit executives, and they were willing to engage in a couple of short conversations about their needs and expectations. This also gave her the opportunity to level-set those expectations a little outside of the heat of the incident. Rather than present options or defend the SOC's current services, she chose to listen and engage, promising to come back with a strategy that was better aligned to their business needs, along with some shorter-term measures to close on urgent issues.

She then moved up the regularly scheduled annual service strategy review that was normally held just before budgetary planning for the following year. Providing the feedback from the business units, Mark was then able to determine how services may need to be updated over time, and presented the options back to the CISO. Not all the business concerns could be addressed due to fiscal constraints, but many proposed changes were relatively minor and could be implemented quickly. The CISO, in turn, was able to present an updated strategy to the business. Although they were not completely happy with it, most agreed that it was a step in the right direction.

Meanwhile, Mark turned to some needed team improvements.

Maintain and Improving Your Team

When it comes to a SOC, the SOC team and the people within it represent one of the most significant and, in many organizations, longest-lasting investment. At the same time, they are remarkably resistant to quantitative measurement and improvement. Think of all the report cards you received as a child. Did they help you maintain or improve your skills?

In general, a SOC needs a highly integrated team that bridges a wide range of technical, professional, and personal skills. The SOC needs a solid team of analysts to monitor, triage, and investigate alerts, incident reports, and anomalies. The SOC needs intelligence analysts who can perform high-fidelity threat modeling, manage multiple human and automated intelligence feeds, and provide human-consumable intelligence that you can use across the enterprise. The SOC will also likely require its own technology specialists to deploy, manage, and maintain core SOC technologies. All of these required skill sets are probably difficult to obtain and even more difficult to retain in your local market.

If that is not enough, the SOC also needs those same team members to bring that magical combination of knowledge, experience, and passion.

You can see why maintaining and improving a world-class SOC team can be a difficult feat to accomplish. To be successful, the SOC needs solid leadership to run the team. However, what is even more important than leadership is a solid game plan to recruit and retain key personnel.

Improving Staff Recruitment

As discussed earlier, your plan has to include a way to continuously recruit new talent into the team. In general, you want to cast your nets far and wide, focusing not just on the individuals with the right certifications but also on those who fit within your team dynamic. That means keeping an eye out for talent. At the beginning, it is okay to focus heavier on skills, but once the SOC is running, you should be in a good position to provide formal and informal skills training, not just to inexperienced analysts fresh out of school but even to nonsecurity professionals with deep experience and institutional knowledge within the organization. Because you must always expect some level of attrition, it is never a bad idea to be looking out for new candidates even when you might not need one at that particular moment.

Keep in mind that a strong, world-class team will also attract recruits, decreasing the need for you to pursue them. We have worked with many excellent organizations over the years that were surprised about how quickly the word got around about their environment and about how much easier it was to recruit than they were expecting.

Do not be shy to discuss your recruitment strategy with your HR partners, external suppliers, and even your industry peers. When you are first starting out, it is extremely helpful to have a market analysis in your hands concerning the roles you need to fill within your market. Such analysis will usually provide you with a lot of valuable information related to appropriate job descriptions, salary ranges, and available benefits within your market. Regularly updated analysis continues to be useful as you compare yourself to other organizations competing for the same talent pool. Your HR partners will also typically help you structure your organization and redefine job roles appropriately as you expand your services.

Improving Team Training and Development

After you have recruited someone, you should expect to take a very personal, individual interest in his or her training and development. Although it is nice to look for self-starters, even the most focused and driven individual will require coaching and guidance to reach his or her potential within the team. While in most SOCs this responsibility lies with the SOC manager or shift leads, in larger teams it might be a good idea to have dedicated individuals focused on this particular role.

Skills and Learning Management

Even when they may share job roles with others, each individual possesses a different set of technical, professional, and personal skills. Each person will also typically learn in different ways. During their first month or so and then at least once a year after, sit down with each individual to discuss what skills and learning that person may want or need to improve over time. Depending on the type and format of learning they need, develop a clear plan for their development.

In general, people learn best through a personalized combination of visual, auditory, and kinesthetic learning (hands-on learning). In other words, not everyone learns best by reading a book (even this one). Some people learn best in a structured classroom environment with a large lecture component. Others only learn when actually doing something either in a lab or in a live environment.

For technical skills, your team members will likely need a combination of theory and hands-on experience with all core SOC technologies. That usually means both general skills across all or most of the technologies they will encounter each day as well as very deep specialized skills in specific technologies. There may even be vendor-neutral and vendor-specific certifications that are appropriate depending on their job role.

For professional skills, you can look at a number of available professional certifications and even higher education paths that may be suitable. These are often less focused on specific technical skills than on the general application of such skills in a wide variety of contexts. There are too many to list here, but this will typically be a combination of professional security certifications from $(ISC)^2$, ISACA, SANS, and others, in addition to advanced degrees such as Masters in Information Assurance or Information Security. Depending on their role, it might even be appropriate for individuals to pursue management certificates and degrees.

Although it is often neglected, you should also consider personal skills, particularly for front-line team members who may need to successfully interact with all sorts of people. Many security incidents are successfully managed simply because the front-line analyst knows what questions to ask of a nontechnical user or because the lead investigator knows how to work with demanding executives, technical staff, and customers.

Such skills and learning development is a huge investment for any SOC. Ensure that you allocate appropriate funds or take advantage of enterprise learning programs and learning management systems where available to ensure that your SOC members get the training and education they need.

The Role of Team Exercises

You might think that dealing with security incidents day in and out is exercise enough, but usually it is not. SOC work can be exciting, but the truth is that it still tends to be repetitive; the same types of incidents happen again and again. This means that your team may become very, very good at handling some incidents while not so good at handling others. It will also be true that the team will learn to lean on a fewer number of key individuals when such incidents happen, particularly those who were seen as successful based on past events. It might even be that the existing SOC technologies are so heavily tuned that different types of threats are simply missed.

There are a number of ways to broaden the team's experience and introduce less-orthodox threats to evaluate your readiness. The first is to leverage unannounced but authorized professional penetration testing. The second is to build or use a cyber range to conduct structured exercises.

Penetration testing, also sometimes referred to as *red-team testing*, has been traditionally used to test the effectiveness of security controls, but it is also highly effective at testing the effectiveness of SOCs. Real or simulated attacks are conducted within strictly approved parameters by an external party or an internal team acting as the red team to see how the blue team or the protectors respond. The goal is to see whether the SOC can detect the attack and whether they can respond to it effectively. Ideally, it should be used to not only test orthodox attacks that are relatively easy to model inside of SIEMs and other platforms but also unorthodox attacks that are less likely to show up other than an anomaly perhaps worth investigating. The goal, then, is to learn and to improve.

Cyber ranges are controlled environments that are set up to simulate real conditions but outside of the production environment. They typically combine a sample of typical target systems (such as network devices, servers, and end-user equipment), technical security controls used in production, and manual or automated attack traffic directed at those target systems. This type of setup has a number of advantages, most notably the ability to simulate a wide range of orthodox and unorthodox attacks within a controlled, contained environment. We talk a little more about how to set up such cyber ranges in the "Maintaining and Improving the SOC Technology Stack" section that follows.

Improving Team Retention

Just about every SOC team struggles with retention. One customer we have worked with once said that he lost most junior SOC analysts after only 6 months on the job. Some were lost to simple burnout, but most left to find new jobs in a highly competitive job market. As a result, more pressure was placed on the analysts who chose to stay, and overall morale suffered as a result.

Obviously, retaining skilled and experienced staff must be a priority; otherwise, you risk having the SOC collapse under its responsibilities. This requires a strong focus on career recognition and progression.

Career Recognition and Progression

It is true that everyone who works in a SOC needs a little appreciation. They will typically be expected to work long and erratic hours. They will be dealing with difficult situations that they can rarely share outside of the SOC, even with their own families and friends. They will be working with difficult people under high degrees of stress (or at the opposite end of the spectrum, with long stretches of boring tedium when nothing really seems to be happening). It can lead to a lot of general and specific discontent.

You need a clearly defined and supported program for career recognition as a way to compensate. Although this can mean cash or its equivalent, benefits, time-in-lieu, and countless other mechanisms, most SOC staff I have worked with have told me that even personal thanks from the leadership that they can share can sometimes do the trick. Keep in mind that most people will swallow disappointment, but if it happens often enough, they are more likely to leave or, perhaps more damaging, become a poisonous member of the team affecting everyone else around them.

You also need a clearly defined program for career progression and mobility. Most members of your team will get a little stale if they do the same job for too long or become less happy the longer they feel they are kept from advancing in their careers. Although it is considerably beyond the scope of this book to address all the possible ways to address this problem, there are some common themes to consider:

- **Manage your team for variety.** Most individuals appreciate a little variety. Do not continually assign the same tasks or situations to the same individuals. Avoid pigeon-holing individuals into small boxes with little opportunity to grow their skills and experience. At the same time, some individuals will appreciate the regularity of a consistent set of tasks. For those individuals, do not push it.
- **Manage your team for mobility.** Even when upward career mobility is not available or unadvised, consider various ways to keep them mobile laterally. This usually means using short-term job rotations into other job roles within the SOC, secondment to

other teams or even to other organizations, or lateral moves into other job roles far outside of the SOC. If, however, they find something they really like to do, that is good. If they prefer to go back to doing what they were doing before, though, that is also good. The key is to offer the opportunities and recognize where those individuals feel comfortable.

- **Help them evade a trap.** Careers come with all sorts of traps. There are traps that result when you are so good at one job that no one thinks you should move to a new one. There are traps when people take a job that they quickly regret. There are traps when people take a job that they believe they are suited for but no one else agrees. For a SOC team lead, it is likely that a good part of his or her job is helping people get out of the traps they find themselves in. In general, consider using the same combination of job rotation, secondment, and lateral moves within the organization.

In our scenario, Mark had already recognized that he had some issues with the hierarchical setup of the internal SOC team. While this provided some advantages, such as easier integration with their outsourcing provider, it also came with issues where Level 2 analysts did not feel that they had the right to manage most incidents on their own, regardless of their length of time with the bank. While he had been able to recruit some great talented analysts and the whole SOC team worked well together, he had a relatively high number of Level 2 analysts leave the organization for similar roles in other banks. During exit interviews, some had complained that they were not really able to see career progression. In a candid (and overdue) conversation with Sarah, she confirmed that she was not very happy but continued to stay because she felt comfortable working with her colleagues. As a relative newcomer, Dan could understand the frustration and recognized that Level 2 analysts often did the "grunt work" while more interesting assignments went to the smaller number of Level 3s.

Ben recognized that there was no easy fix, but also recognized that if he lost Sarah, significant and valuable institutional knowledge and relationships would be lost. She worked with her on a career plan and focused on her personal development. Across the whole SOC team, he started to use group exercises and job rotations as a way to provide variety and mobility. These efforts didn't fix everything, but they were positive steps and retention of Level 2 analysts improved.

That just left the technology issues.

Maintaining and Improving the SOC Technology Stack

As discussed earlier in this book, the SOC relies on a large number of core and supporting technologies. Each one of these technologies must be properly designed, engineered, and deployed (and maintained over time). There are also typically a number of key areas where each of these technologies must be improved to address wider service scope, optimizations highlighted through the execution of SOC services, or more aggressive service levels.

Every SOC is a little different, but there are some general areas of improvement common to most of them.

Improving Threat, Anomaly, and Breach-Detection Systems

This book has highlighted a large number of technologies focused on detecting active threats in the environment, highlighting anomalies that should be investigated and identifying indicators of compromise (IOCs) in compromised systems. In most organizations, this requires a combination of technologies tightly or loosely integrated together, including SIEMs, big data analysis systems, and digital forensics platforms.

Maintaining and improving such systems is the primary responsibility of the security systems engineering and operations teams within the SOC. In our experience, the amount of effort required is often underestimated. Keep in mind that these are often some of the most complex sets of tools in the whole enterprise and require specialist skills.

Monitoring and Regular Maintenance

Given the complexity of modern SIEMs, big data analysis systems, or enterprise forensics, it should come as no surprise that they need to be monitored and maintained.

In general, your technology provider will provide considerable information on how their platforms should be monitored for potential issues. For example, most SIEMs must be monitored for abnormal spikes or prolonged periods of higher-than-expected activity and unexpected or undesirable configuration changes. Also keep in mind that all their underlying technology platforms such as servers and databases must also be properly monitored and maintained.

Changes, Updates, Upgrades, and Migrations

Most systems require regular updates and less-frequent upgrades. Updates typically include minor fixes and updated content to your existing platforms, whereas upgrades require more extensive upgrades and possibly even migrations to new hardware/software.

In most organizations we have worked with, changes and updates are typically coordinated and executed through the organization's change management processes. These help ensure that all changes to IT systems are documented, reviewed, tested, approved, and executed as documented. They also ensure that appropriate back-out steps are in place in case that the change is unsuccessful. Even relatively minor changes that have the potential to affect the system should go through the change management process.

Such changes and updates should be model tested in a separate test environment before deployment into production. This is done to determine whether executing the change may result in some unexpected or undesirable result. Ideally, you should deploy your systems into multiple different environments to ensure that they are suitable before they are deployed. Usually the number and configuration of such environments will be based on your enterprise standards. In many organizations, you often find at least four different environments: development, where new changes and updates can be developed; acceptance testing (sometimes called technical or user acceptance testing), where new changes and updates can be tested; staging, where changes and updates can be prepared for deployment; and production, where the update or change is promoted into the live, operational environment.

Upgrades and migrations typically require a more extensive amount of effort because they usually entail replacing the current system with a new one. They are often considered to be separate projects in themselves because they often require additional resources and capital to execute. Because they are usually intended to replace the existing version of the system in production, upgrades are typically managed under enterprise release management processes. As with changes and updates, however, you should use multiple environments to model and test upgrades or migrations before they are executed. Keep in mind that you may have enterprise standards that require you to maintain your systems within a certain window of currency; in other words, you may only be allowed to run systems that are one or two major versions older than the most currently available version. It is important to follow your documented and approved migration practices because not upgrading in a timely manner may cause your system to miss new features or access to security patches critical to protecting the resource.

Tuning

Tuning can refer to a wide range of activities intended to focus your systems on particular data coming into the system to help focus automated or manual analysis on the data you have determined to be more important. In a SIEM, for example, this means focusing on particular events, types of events, or other information that is best suited to detecting attacks. Such tuning is usually driven by the changing requirements of your use cases and what data is available to you at a particular point in time.

When you get right down to it, tuning is probably one of the most controversial and contentious activities we have to perform. Essentially, tuning is deliberately telling the system to ignore particular types of data. Contrary to some of the vendor literature, none of this data is "noise": It is all *legitimate, valid data.* We are simply choosing not to pay attention to it, typically because we do not have a way to ingest it, combine it with other data, or simply because we do not have the performance available on the system. In our experience, tuning leads to blind spots where neither the system or the analysts who rely on it sees it. This is one area where we see the most promise with current- and next-generation big data security analytics platforms.

However, given that traditional SIEM platforms have not gone away, you are still likely going to need to do some tuning either based on new or changing use cases, results of investigations into anomalies found outside of the SIEM itself, or from feedback from incident response. Keep in mind that any tuning will affect performance and storage capacity.

Widening Scope, Depth, and Retrospection

Of course, if you have the performance and storage capacity to spare, you should always consider improving your existing platforms.

On a SIEM or big data security analytics platform, this could include widening the ability for your platforms to detect a wider range of potential incidents. This generally means bringing in more event sources from systems that have been excluded to that point. It can also mean going deeper into existing data sources by using more data within the event sources you are already using. Finally, you could also look at improving retrospective investigation through storage, archiving, retrieval, and analysis options that enable you to see further back in time. One example of expanding capabilities is adding access control so that the SOC is aware of the details of devices access the network rather than figuring it out while they are on the network. One example of going deeper with existing equipment is adding NetFlow visibility from existing network devices to gain a better understanding of events seen by such devices that already report basic events to a SIEM.

On an enterprise digital forensics platform, you could look at a number of similar improvements. More hosts could be assessed or new types of hosts such as mobile devices included. Scans and assessments could be run more often. Like a SIEM, the IOCs that the platform looks for may also be extended.

Improving Enrichment

Enrichment refers to automatically adding additional data or data fields into security alerts to speed up automated analysis and investigation. In most cases, this data could be looked up manually, but this would introduce additional steps that would slow down investigations and analysis. Your SIEM or big data analysis platform is likely already providing some enrichment out of the box. It is common, for example, for such systems to provide GeoIP lookups so that you can determine whether a particular IP address is associated with a particular country. This can be useful when looking for connections from unusual locations.

There are a large number of ways that alerts can be enriched, so it is always best to start with your own use cases. Are there particular situations where automated enrichment would help speed up either automated analysis or investigation by an analyst? Because any enrichment will typically require some development and integration, you only want to enrich where it has the most benefit.

There are a number of typical ways that alerts can be enriched. In addition to the GeoIP enrichment, you can also generally enrich alerts with the following:

- **Asset information:** Of all the possible ways to enrich security alerts in your SIEM or big data analytics platform, this is the big one, but also one of the hardest to do successfully. Ideally, current asset information via a configuration management database (CMDB) would allow the system or analyst to quickly determine the criticality of a particular host, who owns it, and who is responsible for it. It would also provide updated configuration information and even allow the analyst to understand the upstream and downstream dependencies of that particular host. Unfortunately, such ideal conditions rarely exist, but it is worth investigating whether such enrichment is available in your organization.

  An alternative to a CMDB is leveraging an automated profiling system that can determine device types based on their network footprint. Profiling may not have as much data as a CMDB, but combined with an access control technology can provide useful information such as usernames, device types, and posture status of devices. That data can be exported to a SIEM to enrich reports by changing IP addresses to user names and system types.

- **Threat intelligence:** Threat intelligence is intended to provide you with current, relevant information on the latest threats. When matched with the asset information and vulnerability intelligence discussed earlier in this chapter, it can be used to provide a risk-based analysis of threats you are seeing in the environment. This can then be used to help categorize and prioritize the alerts to help the analyst focus on more severe attacks. External threat intelligence will typically be provided in the form of a continuously updated feed that is used by the SIEM or big data system to correlate with other data. Where available, internal threat intelligence (for example, from antifraud and industry peer groups) should also be fed into the system in a similar way. Intelligence feeds may, however, be quite expensive, so it may be best to shop around and pilot a number of options before you settle on your chosen provider.
- **Vulnerability intelligence:** This type of intelligence focuses not only on known vulnerabilities relevant to your systems but also vulnerability management data that would indicate whether such vulnerabilities are actually present. This can be useful to a risk-based approach to security alerts when combined with asset information and threat intelligence.
- **Directory information:** This sort of information is very valuable particularly in Windows environments using Active Directory (AD). When fully populated and current, AD can provide a lot of valuable information to the analyst about the authenticated host or user that they are investigating.
- **Reputation feeds:** There are a fairly large number of services that may provide updated information on IPs, domains, or even access point names that are known to be exhibiting malicious behavior. This can be useful to help determine whether an alert is more or less credible, but in our experience, this type of feed typically results in a relatively high number of false positives and false negatives. Consider using it to help confirm the severity of an alert but do not take it at face value.
- **Other event sources:** Security event data can often be enriched using other event sources that may not be security specific, but provide value to security analytics and investigations. For example, network flow data may provide information on anomalous traffic to and from particular hosts or networks. Events from network authentication, Domain Name System (DNS), and Dynamic Host Configuration Protocol (DHCP) services might provide valuable information on who is logged in to a particular host and where they have attempted to connect. Using any of these sources is very dependent on use cases, so it is best to start there to determine whether they will provide value.

Improving Case and Investigation Management Systems

As discussed earlier in this book, case and investigation management systems are a key (if often overlooked) aspect of any well-functioning SOC. It is also true, however, that the out-of-the-box tool may not be as well suited to your own particular organization as you would like. There are a number of areas where improvement is likely to be found:

- **Access control:** Most platforms will support a variety of access control models, but you will likely need to adjust the access control system to best suit your particular

SOC. It really depends on the types of actors who will use the system, and how you configure the system to allow or disallow access to specific features or underlying data.

- **Workflow:** Most platforms also come with a basic workflow describing the path from incident report through investigation through incident declaration and handling. This will likely need to be optimized for your SOC so that any unnecessary friction in the process is minimized.
- **Integration:** Depending on what your case management system supports, you may be able to integrate with many of your other platforms, including SIEMs, digital forensics platforms, big data analysis tools, and enterprise ticketing systems. Where such integration has a positive service level impact, you should certainly consider it, keeping in mind that any custom integration is usually going to remain your own team's responsibility going forward.

To determine the best place to focus your efforts, review recent incidents to determine whether improvements to the case or investigation management system would have made a difference.

Improving Analytics and Reporting

As discussed earlier in this book, the average SOC generates a lot of data requiring analysis and reporting. Information about event sources, events, threats, vulnerabilities, attacks, incident reports, investigations, incidents... all of these become good fodder for the generation of operational, management, and executive reporting. It is also true, however, that such reporting is often unappealing or unclear to the target audience. It is also common for such reporting to take a large amount of manual effort to generate.

Although you will typically start with the native reporting available within your core SOC systems (like the SIEM, case management, or digital forensics platforms), you will likely find that they do not meet the need to communicate effectively. If your audience does not understand reporting, you can hardly expect them to continue to pour their support into the SOC. We have seen many SOCs over the years lose support from executives simply because the executives do not see the value. Great analysis and reporting would have closed the gap.

Although there are some specific security reporting platforms on the market that are better at providing relevant output, these can be sometimes be a substantial investment. You might need to look to existing enterprise business intelligence platforms or open source security visualization platforms to provide better trending/reporting, automation, and self-service.

Improving Technology Integration

Almost all your systems should be able to integrate with each other or at least generate log data for an external centralized event log system such as a SIEM. Most modern SIEMs, case management systems, enterprise forensics platforms, big data analytics, and ticketing systems can all be configured to talk to each other. In most cases, either out-of-the-box point-and-click integration will be available or well-documented application programming interfaces (API) will be available to ease the integration effort.

Although it might seem like a good idea to integrate everything, you should really only look at integrating where it makes the most impact. Focus particularly on integration that helps the analysts do things more efficiently or with higher fidelity. For example, let's use the classic example of integration between SIEMs and enterprise ticketing systems. This is usually used to allow for the analyst who has determined that an incident has occurred to quickly open a ticket to notify another team, typically to perform remediation activities. If the ticketing system is not considered very secure, however, this integration may unfortunately share highly confidential information from the SIEM that may be inappropriate. In this case, integration with the confidential case management system should be a higher priority.

Look at every integration opportunity on a case-by-case basis. Use your analysis of past incidents to guide where it would have had the most benefit. Also take into consideration whether any manual efforts are required to make the integration happen, risk of integration, and required maintenance. The last thing you want is data corrupted due to a bug with the integration of data between systems.

Improving Security Testing and Simulation Systems

For the advanced SOC, we typically recommend improving your ability to run tests and simulations reflecting real-world attack scenarios. This usually goes beyond just testing for orthodox attacks that can be simply automated and modeled, but also unorthodox attacks that reflect techniques used by so-called advanced persistent threats (APT). Certainly, this should be a big priority for organizations that are regularly subject to unorthodox attacks.

Such testing and simulation systems are often deployed in a production environment in the form of advanced malware analysis platforms, particularly sandboxing technologies. These systems typically take live samples of code, files, or network traffic and analyze them for evidence of malicious activity. Some also use cloud-based services to compare new samples to previously found malware.

In general, however, it is not advisable to run most attack scenarios against your live production environment but instead to provide a contained environment where such attacks can be simulated. As described in a previous section in this chapter, this will allow you to provided advanced training for your SOC team and to test the effectiveness of current security controls and incident response.

A *cyber range* represents the most extensive complete testing and simulation environment you could put together. In general, a cyber range is like a firing range in the physical world. It involves the creation and maintenance of a closed environment that closely replicates applications and infrastructure (including security infrastructure) deployed within the real enterprise environment. This environment can be used to simulate attacks typically using simulated or replicated network traffic and responses to those attacks within a controlled, safe environment. It is a substantial investment that includes elements of your organization's computing environment, attack generation, and security controls. This can include the following:

- **Enterprise infrastructure and applications:** A well-equipped cyber range includes wired, wireless, and remote-access networks, along with simulated or virtualized clients, servers, and applications. These should be representative of similar infrastructure and applications that are found in the enterprise.
- **Traffic and attack generation:** The cyber range must generate representative amounts of "normal" (nonmalicious) traffic and a wide range of attacks. These are usually automated to make them act in a highly predictable way. Such tools can generate a wide range of attacks, including day zero attacks, denial of service, data loss, malware, or attacks against specific infrastructure or applications.
- **Security infrastructure:** The cyber range also includes a representative sample of most (if not all) of the security controls within the organization. This may include network security controls such as firewalls or intrusion detection/prevention systems (IDS/IPS), data-loss protection (DLP), antimalware systems, network access control, secure gateways, SIEMs, and other security controls.

As you can tell, investing in a cyber range can be extremely pricey and time-consuming.

Although they are more limited, there are also some managed or hosted options that provide preconfigured cyber range facilities suitable for training and facilitated self-paced learning.

Improving Automated Remediation

For the truly advanced SOC with highly aggressive incident remediation service levels, you might want to look at automating some remediation activities. In simplest terms, this means scripting or automating specific actions that can be take by the analyst or system after an incident has been declared. Because these actions are typically preauthorized, this would allow remediation to be significantly faster than if they had to be performed manually.

Simpler forms of automated remediation have been around for many years. For example, setting your antimalware platforms to quarantine infected files by policy is a simple automated action. Even simple automation, however, can have unforeseen effects. For example, a quarantined file could be mission critical, and by making it unavailable may have big consequences. Clear policy and tuning are certainly required.

More complex automation options are becoming available all the time. In organizations with highly developed network access control (NAC) deployments, infected or breached systems could be isolated automatically, patching systems could be alerted, and isolation could continue until remediation is completed. For highly virtualized environments, we have started to see on-the-fly reconfiguration of virtual networking to layer in additional security controls as needed or to isolate breached systems while bringing up clean snapshots. The options are really only limited by imagination.

Unfortunately, describing automated remediation is a lot easier than actually accomplishing it. Take the time to review the options you have available and make sure that you have strong executive support and a lot of testing under your belt before you ever try to implement these features in production. Automated remediation could just as easily break something rather than save it.

In our scenario, Mark could point to a number of issues that could be fixed in the short term (improvements to correlation rules within the SIEM) and the longer term (integration issues and onboarding new event sources). The specific malware scenario also pointed to the long-term potential for automated remediation, but in the meanwhile, limited preauthorized scripts could be made available to SOC analysts to mitigate the risks associated with commonly occurring incidents. It would take a lot of careful planning and a lot of time, but it would be worth the investment to avoid manually dealing with future incidents.

To wrap up our example story, technology improvements were made, and the SOC was generally seen as more effective and efficient than it had been, particularly by the analysts who had to work with these systems everyday. Improvements required investment from executives that was justified by the need to properly align expected performance for future incidents. Adjustments were made to processes to give analysts like Sarah more authority to own steps of the incident response process. Tools were tuned to provide more clarity about identified events. A few new technologies were acquired to fill gaps in visibility. Most important, the SOC learned from the incident and used it to improve its ability to handle future attacks.

Conclusions

As we wrap up this book, it should be clear that building and operating a SOC is hard work, requiring a lot of the people, processes, and technology. Developing a SOC requires a clear and current set of services aligned with the organization's needs and expectations. Operating a SOC requires a diligent, enabled, and enthusiastic team from the CISO on down. SOC documentation requires good but not too much process. Maintaining a SOC requires both good technology choices and a strong focus on improving on that technology.

With all those requirements, it might be easy to see why so many SOCs fail to fulfill their initial promise. No SOC is perfect, but a healthy SOC is one that can evolve and change. Efforts to maintain, review, and improve your SOC are fundamental to its longer-term viability. Remember, running a SOC is a journey, not a destination.

Index

A

B

C

D

E

F

G

H

I

J

K

L

M

N

O

P

Q

R

S

U

V

W

Y

Z